The Asbury Theological Seminary Series in Wesleyan/Holiness Studies

This volume is published in collaboration with the Center for the Study of World Christian Revitalization Movements, a cooperative initiative of Asbury Theological Seminary faculty. Building on the work of the previous Wesleyan/Holiness Studies Center at the Seminary, the Center provides a focus for research in the Wesleyan Holiness and other related Christian renewal movements, including Pietism and Pentecostal movements, which have had a world impact. The research seeks to develop analytical models of these movements, including their biblical and theological assessment. Using an interdisciplinary approach, the Center bridges relevant discourses in several areas in order to gain insights for effective Christian mission globally. It recognizes the need for conducting research that combines insights from the history of evangelical renewal and revival movements with anthropological and religious studies literature on revitalization movements. It also networks with similar or related research and study centers around the world, in addition to sponsoring its own research projects.

In this volume we present the insightful life journey of Barry L. Callen, seasoned and prolific author, editor and theological educator in the Church of God (Anderson). Professor Callen here offers a candid and thought-ful disclosure of his personal, spiritual, and academic development over the past six decades, drawing from the ecumenical perspective of his church tradition, and interfaced with a robust commitment to a Wesleyan/Holiness soteriology. The latter focus is grounded in his formative studies at Asbury Seminary. His life and work offers a personal embodiment of salient features of the developing revitalization of world Christianity which continues its trajectory within the twenty-first century. For that reason, along with his personal embodiment of the trajectory of the Wesleyan/Holiness tradition, his study contributes significantly to the research of the Center and so honors this series in which it appears. Dr. Callen's volume *Heart of the Matter* appeared previously in this series.

J. Steven O'Malley
Editor, The Pietist and Wesleyan Studies Series in the Asbury Theological Seminary Studies in Christian Revitalization

Educator, scholar, faithful friend, true servant leader, these describe well Dr. Barry L. Callen. He has managed to capture and communicate the history and theology of our Church of God movement in his many superb books. *A Pilgrim's Progress* is an amazing and captivating work that tells the life story of a surrendered soul who, despite his personal challenges, has remained faithful to the cause of Christ. This autobiography is a great read!

Handel Smith, Executive Director, United States and Canada Strategy of Church of God Ministries

A Pilgrim's Progress

The Autobiography of
BARRY L. CALLEN

FOURTH EDITION

*The Asbury Theological Seminary Series in
World Christian Revitalization Movements in Pietist/Wesleyan Studies*

EMETH PRESS
www.emethpress.com

ANDERSON
UNIVERSITY
PRESS

A Pilgrim's Progress: The Autobiography of Barry L. Callen

Fourth Edition, Copyright © 2024 by Barry L. Callen
Printed in the United States of America on acid-free paper

Library of Congress Cataloging-in-Publication Data

Callen, Barry L.
    A pilgrim's progress : the autobiography of Barry L. Callen. -- Fourth Edition.
        pages cm. -- (The Asbury Theological Seminary series in world Christian revitalization movements in Pietist/Wesleyan studies ; No. 13)
    ISBN 978-1-60947-146-0 (alk. paper)
    1. Callen, Barry L. 2. Church of God (Anderson, Ind.)--Biography. 3. Anderson University (Anderson, Ind.)--Biography. I. Title.
    BX7027.Z8C346 2024
    289.9--dc23
    [B]

                                              2013000692

Commendations of this Book
Additional Statements on the Back Cover

The opportunity to see into the life of Barry Callen is a wonderful chance to see how God mightily uses a willing heart and a competent mind. His thoughtful work as a theologian, professor, and writer is an exemplary model of servant leadership. The impact of his life will benefit church leaders and students for generations to come. It is difficult to imagine any serious engagement with the study of church history, holiness, or church unity without his influence. His impact on the establishment of the Wesleyan Holiness Connection and Aldersgate Press has been considerable.

> **Kevin Mannoia**, former bishop of the Free Methodist
> Church and president of the National Association
> of Evangelicals, now at Azusa Pacific University,
> Azusa, and president of the Wesleyan/Holiness Connection

I am a big fan of Barry Callen, a loyal churchman and profound ecumenist. While I have known him primarily as a theologian, author, and editor, I have discovered that he writes novels as well!

> **Donald W. Dayton**, celebrated author, former Professor,
> Asbury Theological Seminary, Drew University, and
> Northern Baptist Theological Seminary

Many of us have been waiting for this autobiography. Here is an unusually gifted and dedicated man who has done it all—preaching, pastoring, teaching and leading a college and seminary, and writing forty books of Christian theology, history, spirituality, biography, and three novels. With untiring devotion and creativity, Barry has served his university, denomination, congregation, the Wesleyan Theological Society, and Horizon International (ministry to AIDS orphans in Africa). As founding editor of Anderson University Press, Barry has assisted others with their own significant writings.

In these pages, he covers the full scope of his personal journey, one that touches the stories of so many other people (see the Index!)

Gene W. Newberry, former Professor and Dean Emeritus
of Anderson University School of Theology

Barry L. Callen's long tenure of key leadership in the Wesleyan Theological Society and the Wesleyan Holiness Connection have been invaluable to the life of scholarship in the Wesleyan/Holiness/Pentecostal traditions of contemporary Christianity. He has fulfilled well the ecumenical vision of his church base, the Church of God movement (Anderson), by being open to the fuller truth and not obstructed in his relationships and appreciations by denominational borders. A truly "catholic" theologian, Callen has united helpfully the traditional ecclesiastical concerns of his Church of God tradition with a Wesleyan soteriology and an Anabaptist emphasis on discipleship. His personal journey has wisdom to share with today's emerging Christian communities.

William C. Kostlevy, American church historian and
longtime officer of the Wesleyan Theological Society,
Director, Brethren Historical Library and Archives

Passion, fueled by authenticity and integrity, is a value evident in any serious follower of Jesus Christ. Barry L. Callen's life and ministry are a testament to this value, demonstrated so aptly in his updated *A Pilgrim's Progress*. The reader will come away from this delightful personal and professional history full of gratitude for a life well-lived in the lengthening shadow of the Master. I know, for I have observed this pilgrim as a student, close friend, and ministerial colleague across more than forty years of journeying together.

Robert W. Pearson, President of Horizon International,
former General Director of Church of God Ministries,
Anderson, Indiana

Table of Contents

Dedication

I have valued personal relationships with Mendell L. Thompson, President/CEO/Treasurer, Kevin Mannoia, Vice Chair of the Board of Directors, and Fawn Imboden, Vice President and Chief Development Officer of America's Christian Credit Union, Glendora, California (ACCU). This outstanding Christian organization represents much of what I stand for personally. It has sturdy Christian commitment and networks and resources Christians across denominational lines. It puts hands and feet to the life-changing and culture-shaping teachings of Jesus, and maintains responsible stewardship plans that enable healthy management of personal and business finances and life planning.

The ACCU has been exceedingly generous in supporting the vital mission, ministry projects, and associated institutions that comprise the Wesleyan Holiness Connection (WHC), Kevin Mannoia president. This interdenominational movement of God is focused on freshly applying Christian holiness to the pressing issues of our time. I have been privileged to be involved with the WHC from its beginning. My book *The Holy River of God* documents the many WHC denominational participants, and this present work gives voice to some of its vital concerns as I have tried to live them--see especially Appendix C and D.

The WHC's web address, *holinessandunity.org*, highlights what the Church of God movement (Anderson), my own church family, has been seeking to be and do since 1880, emphasize Christian holiness as the dynamic that can unify believers and maximize their mission impact for Christ. My many years of WHC involvement have been as representative of the Church of God (CHOG), Ronald Duncan and Jim Lyon, General Directors. I am particularly privileged to be the elected Editor of Aldersgate Press (AP), publishing arm of the WHC, David Han publisher. This involvement is what brought me into contact with the ACCU and only enhanced my appreciation for a comparable ministry arm of the Church of God, Servant Solutions (SS) led by the outstanding Jeffrey Jenness.

My main ministry service has been educating new generations of the young, primarily through Anderson University (AU), John Pistole president, and assisting thousands of AIDS orphans in six African nations through Horizon International (HI), Robert Pearson president. This service has been enhanced greatly by my involvement with the WHC that has been supported so well by the ACCU and has so many connections with the Wesleyan Theological Society (WTS) that I served for more than twenty years as Editor of its Wesleyan Theological Journal (WTJ).

I have an alphabet of valued associations. ACCU, AP, AU, CHOG, HI, SS, WHC, WTS, and WTJ are much more than a maze of letters. They are on the front line of what God is doing in our time, and are key reasons for my having been able to serve Christ meaningfully across the years. With great appreciation for them all, I gladly dedicate this, my personal life story, to the beliefs, values, leaders, and causes these superb Christian ministries so ably represent.

But there is more. My remembering is only a backdrop for my anticipation of what lies ahead. Soon the curtain will fall and my time on life's stage will be done. That's where my grandchildren and great-grandchildren come in. As they spend their time on life's stage, with all its sound and fury, joys and sorrows, my hope and prayer are that they will do more than survive. May they become aware, as did I, that lurking among the shadows and speeches of despair are the marks of the divine and the beginnings of a better future.

So, I also dedicate this book to my grandchildren and great-grandchildren (see *Appendix G* for the grandchildren, with Finn and Ezra now added as the first of yet another coming generation). May the paths I've walked shed some light on the ways that will open before them. When trouble comes, and it probably will, I hope they will read at least my 2018 books *The Jagged Journey* and *God in the Shadows*. May they deal in faith with the hard questions and take seriously what St. Paul wrote long ago. "As you therefore have received Christ Jesus the Lord, continue to live your lives in him, rooted and built up in him and established in the faith, just as you were taught, abounding in thanksgiving" (Colossians 2:6-7).

Barry L. Callen
Anderson, Indiana
April, 2019

IN THE MEANTIME

In the beginning, reports Genesis 1, there was God in the sovereign act of creating. At the end, Revelation 22 pictures the alpha-and-omega God inviting all who wish to take the water of life as a gift. In the meantime, through the sanctifying and sustaining ministry of the Spirit, we have this promise: "the grace of the Lord Jesus will be with all the saints."

Barry L. Callen
God As Loving Grace (1996, p. 341)

Foreword

Ihave treasured the rich literature that exists about spiritual pilgrimage. All should take such a journey, and none need walk alone. David Elton Trueblood wrote in his 1974 autobiography, that "in however slight a fashion" he hoped to add to the literature of pilgrimage. The final words of his book are: "Both the price and the glory of our finitude are indicated by the fact that we do not arrive; we are always on the way" (pp. 161-162). I have never fully arrived, but I have sought to make the trip.

Note the final chapter of my 2011 book *Heart of the Matter* (rev. 2016). It's titled "Tramps for the Truth." In this life, we all journey, some making real progress by faith, but still without ever finally arriving. I have sought to follow the spiritual path seen in the biblical psalms, finding joy in the journey, gladly tramping on (see *Appendix H*).

Few may be interested in my life story as I depart and future generations come and go. Be that as it may. Since I'm leaving this book behind, at least I want it to be accurate and reasonably complete. As I say in chapter nine, "I am a pilgrim in progress and these pages are but an interim report."

.

On Writing an Autobiography

Remembering Without Reverencing Myself
Recalling Yesterday for the Sake of Tomorrow
Celebrating Paths Old and New

Here are my thoughts as I begin telling my personal story. All that
follows should be taken in the context of these thoughts.

I once heard a famous author make a disturbing statement. He said:
"Autobiography is the most common form of fiction!" This is
disturbing because there is some truth in such a sarcastic observation.
How easy it is to tell one's own story in a way that covers tracks and
creates a "reality" out of what actually was somewhat otherwise. With my
best efforts and the help of the Lord, I hope not to be guilty of this
common sin in the following pages.

Part of my protection from faulty and self-
serving memory is my keeping of critical
documents over the years and my practice later in
life of keeping a detailed daily diary. I can be precise
about many things because I have good records.
Furthermore, I have no goal of making myself
larger than reality.

Architecture provides a helpful metaphor for
the proper task of an autobiography. In the year

Barry L. Callen

2000 I became fascinated with a book by John Harris titled *No Voice from
the Hall: Early Memories of a Country House Snooper*. As an aspiring
architectural historian, between 1946 and 1960 Harris roamed around

England and found more than two hundred once magnificent country houses now deserted. They were exuding a sense of hopelessness and "in a surreal limbo awaiting their fate." Most had served well some emergency role in the 1940s when the whole country was mobilized to survive the devastating German bombing of the larger English cities. After playing their heroic roles, times and owners changed and structural decay advanced. Reports Harris: "I believe I sensed an affinity with those houses that stood awaiting their sentence. I saw myself as their Apostle" (p. 227).

Life is much that way. Little holds still for long. Institutions and ideas are in motion—sometimes toward oblivion—while proud buildings and bodies too quickly decay. One reason I write this autobiography, then, is to circle around what easily could be despair; instead, I choose to be an apostle for what seems to me to be truly worthy and enduring. What endures does not include my once strong body or modest accomplishments, but it likely does include some people I have known and beliefs I have held dear.

Let's move from architecture to archaeology. On a morning just before the new millennium was to dawn (December 20, 1999), I was on the way to my office at Anderson University when I heard this on the car radio: "Only when we saw our planet from space did we realize that we should not have called it Earth. We should have called it Ocean." About seventy percent of this planet is covered by water, much of it very deep, with virtually all of this vast liquid world yet unexplored by humans.

We have worked hard at "dirt archaeology." I have had the privilege of wandering around many ancient sites in the countries of the Middle East. But humans have only begun to develop the technology necessary to engage in the unspeakable adventure of "nautical archaeology." My fascination with submarines relates to this adventure. See my novel *In Deep Water* (2009) and my book on the Bible titled *Beneath the Surface* (2012). There's still so much to be discovered!

When a man begins to ponder the life he has lived, his thoughts are only modest probings beneath a vast surface of what was not conscious, is not fully remembered, and has not been adequately understood. Bits and pieces are brought to the surface and a story slowly takes shape. I hope that my memories and data collection, however fragmentary, turns into wisdom formation for others. Such is the arduous task of an autobiography. It is the architecture and the archaeology of a life looking back in search of its meaning.

As I remember in these pages, I will try to do a little better than Andy Rooney's whimsical confession. He says that he tried to make his memoir accurate by checking memory against facts. But when he often found that the apparent facts clashed with his memories, "I assume that the facts are wrong" (*My War,* p. 3). I want my memories to square with the facts.

Stanley Hauerwas, whose substantial scholarly work has influenced my own efforts, speaks often of "vision." People are said to see in distinctive ways. Their realities are influenced greatly by the contexts in which they live, by the stories that form the stories of their own lives. In one important sense, then, an autobiography is an attempt to retell the stories that have come to shape one's own existence.

For me, these shaping stories have included the stories of immigration, war, hunting, camp meetings, a pioneering church-reform movement, a university campus, the ministry of one woman (Lillie McCutcheon), the partnership of two others (Jeannette Flynn and Fawn Imboden), and the wonderful love of two others (my wives Arlene and Jan).

The story of Jesus has been allowed to reshape the final meaning of all the other stories and relationships. I have sought over the years to capture many of these stories in more than fifty books (see *Appendix F*), with the story of Jesus always taking the lead. Here I try to pull them all together to see if the accumulation tells its own tale of life's meaning and destiny.

In June, 1973, Paul Samuelson wrote an editorial in *Newsweek* magazine about the troubled presidency of Richard M. Nixon. The main question was: "What determines the policies a president follows?" Samuelson rejects the cynic's claim that politicians think of one thing only—how to get elected again. Instead, he argues that politicians are motivated by a major concern for how they eventually will appear in the history books. To state his viewpoint positively, people of wisdom have their eyes on the long-range implications of their present actions. Put negatively, they tend to be vain and selfish, caring as much about what people think as about the rightness of what they do.

Since I am running for no office, I assume that my prime motive for writing these pages is probing the long-range implications of a life still being lived and the important ideas now carefully being evaluated. I have never campaigned for any office; I merely want to advocate for what I think is true.

I am very aware of the comments of two of my special sisters in Christ. Lillie S. McCutcheon once said this about her decades of preaching: "I have always avoided talking about myself because there was so much to be said about Jesus" (in my book *She Came Preaching*, p. 311). Gloria Gaither said this about herself and her husband Bill in her book *Because He Lives*: "How pointless it would be to tell your birth dates and the human history of two people who merely discovered the wonderful life of Someone else" [Jesus] (p. 12).

My sisters leave me with some questions. Is the writing of an autobiography the ultimate act of arrogance that neglects focus on the Master, or can it be an appropriate caring about the future as informed by the past? Dare the assumption be made that one's own life story is worth the paper, ink, and computer time required for its publication? Would anyone care? Should they? Maybe, maybe not. These may not even be the right questions. Allow me to list some alternate questions that could be more appropriate.

Does life have meaning? Is personal identity impacted greatly by memory, by the stream of tradition within which an individual is located? If so, is that where the meaning comes from? What stories from yesterday have been my stories? What people and events form my defining roots? Does God express the divine will and share divine grace and wisdom within the web of complex forces and events that we humans come to know as our history? Is our history finally *His-Story*? If so, then one almost has an obligation to pay attention to the flow of things, to reconsider the road now traveled, to look back for the distinctive marks of God etched along our paths. Others may come along later and benefit from an awareness of how the road got there in the first place and how God once directed some people in ways that prepared the way for others—maybe even you!

Is the telling of one's own life story too much of an ego exercise? Not necessarily. It actually can be an act of faithfulness, of gratefulness, of concern that what has been can become a small building block in the construction of what yet will be. I want to remember without unfairly reverencing or prematurely devaluing. The discipline of writing captures the stream of experience that is constantly slipping away. To tell one's story is an adventure in stopping the slip and expressing one's indebtedness.

I treasure my autographed copy of David Elton Trueblood's exceptional 1974 autobiography titled *While It Is Day*. Elton was a beloved teacher of mine when I commuted to Earlham School of Religion in Richmond, Indiana, to study with him in the mid-1960s. He was an encourager of young ministers and scholars, and his own story is rich and inspiring. He says: "As we all walk essentially the same path, we stumble the less if our predecessors have left a few markers. It is the duty of each person who has profited from some guidance to leave a few markers of his own" (p. x).

Two of my favorite books (so different from each other!) employ imagery similar to Trueblood's "markers." They are Dag Hammarskjöld's *Markings* (1993) and Baxter Black's *Cactus Tracks & Cowboy Philosophy* (1997). Many have left markers for me; I hope to leave a few myself—just doing my duty!

Numerous well-known scholars from various Christian traditions have been so kind as to write positive endorsement statements that publishers could use in marketing my books over the years. For my 1999 volume *Radical Christianity*, Clark H. Pinnock, a Baptist from Canada, began his endorsement with a quote of William Faulkner: "The past is not dead—it is not even past." How true that is! What has been is the foundation for what now is. Even though most of us take pride in the new and have lived in times so different from just a generation or two ago, yesterday still lurks in the shadows of our todays. What was, in many ways, still is. Much more than we realize, we remain shaped by people and events that have gone before us. To forget is to sever a key link with identity and meaning. Because of God's grace over the years, to remember can be a cause for rejoicing!

Since I accept all of this as givens of life, I now have managed to overcome the natural shyness of writing about my own past. To dwell on oneself can be an act of arrogance; it also can be a choice to reflect gratitude and share gathered wisdom that wants to shape days that are yet to be. Especially is my shyness moderated when I realize that I cannot tell my story without recounting briefly the long parade of sinners and saints, mostly saints, who have gone before me and helped to make possible my story. See the section "Saints and Icons" in chapter twelve.

The biblical tradition rests heavily on the significance of memory. The very process of my writing disciplines me to remember, and thus increases my awareness of God's having been moving in my life all along. Such remembering sets me to rejoicing! My story is hardly "inspired" as is the biblical text. Even so, I am confident that God has been involved in my life and is pleased that the resulting story—my memories and testimony—is being told.

Life is nearing its end when a preoccupation with memories is greater than the pursuing of fresh dreams. I write this autobiography aware that I am living in a late stage of my lifespan. Even so, the purpose here is more than remembering. It is rejoicing in the memories in a way that fulfills the present and, I hope, sets the stage for the future—that of mine and others.

The actor Alan Alda's beloved dog died when he was a boy. A taxidermist transformed the remains into a museum piece, but with a strange expression on its face that no one recognized. As time went on, reports Alda in his 2006 autobiography *Never Have Your Dog Stuffed*, "my memory of the real Rhapsody was replaced by the image of him sitting lifeless on the blue velvet board with a hideous look on his face." What Alda learned was that "stuffing your dog is more than what happens when you take a dead body and turn it into a souvenir. It also happens when you hold on to any living moment longer than it wants you to." Memory can be "a kind of mental taxidermy, trying to hold on to the present after it's become the past" (p. 24).

The following pages certainly contain many memories. While I would grieve their loss, I don't want to preserve them with altered faces or merely keep them from being forgotten. If the Bible is our model, and it has been mine, then some things deserve to be remembered as necessary building blocks for tomorrow. Note *Appendix A* called "Providence or Politics?" where I reflect on Psalm 114 in an attempt to locate the biblical memories really worth recalling. To those sacred memories of long ago I now modestly add a few of my own.

I record here my central memories as a man and a "theologian," one who understands his ministry to be a pilgrim thinker working on behalf of a pilgrim people. My writing attempts to explain the life journey of one Christian pilgrim. There is a trail of divine grace that I have been privileged to walk. I trace my pilgrim's progress down that trail. The journeys of many other pilgrims have instructed me. Let me refer briefly to three of them—many more will appear later.

Malcolm Muggeridge titled his 2006 memoirs *Chronicles of Wasted Time.* This man has a fascinating story, but his book title disturbs me. I have wasted my share of time, but I hope that I also have redeemed even more. Muggeridge, a famous English journalist, a self-proclaimed "vendor of words," calls an illusion the claim that a camera does not lie. It certainly does, he insists, because it grabs only dislocated chunks of reality and "its sphere of operation is at life's surface." By contrast, words can get "somewhere near the inner significance" (p. 550). Well, I have sent millions of words into the stream of public life, words that I trust have carried some significance. I "send" even more words in these pages, along with pictures, trusting that they are not shallow, dislocated, misleading, a waste of your time and this paper or computer memory.

Now comes the second pilgrim who has instructed me. At the 2004 North American Convention of the Church of God, convened in Anderson, Indiana, an exceptional man crossed my path. Rear Admiral Barry C. Black was a guest preacher. His 2006 autobiography, *From the Hood to the Hill,* records his amazing journey from a tough inner-city upbringing to being the first African American to serve as U. S. Navy Chief of Chaplains and Chaplain of the U. S. Senate. He is a faithful pilgrim guided by God. He reported that along his life's journey he has prayed: "Disturb us, Lord, when we are too pleased with ourselves; when our dreams come true, because we have dreamed too little; when we have arrived safely, because we sailed too close to shore" (p. 219).

Time will tell if I have dreamed too little and arrived safely only because I have lacked enough faith to sail far from shore. I ask God to give me grace to believe deeply, risk boldly, remember rightly, and write clearly for the sake of others.

And why write now when I am approaching eighty years old and may have years remaining? That question brings me to pilgrim number three. David Elton Trueblood wrote his 1974 autobiography years before his death, calling it *While It Is Day*. I join him in deciding to write while I can, while my mind is clear, memories sharp, and heart able and anxious to share. I am still in process. This is an interim report of a pilgrim's progress.

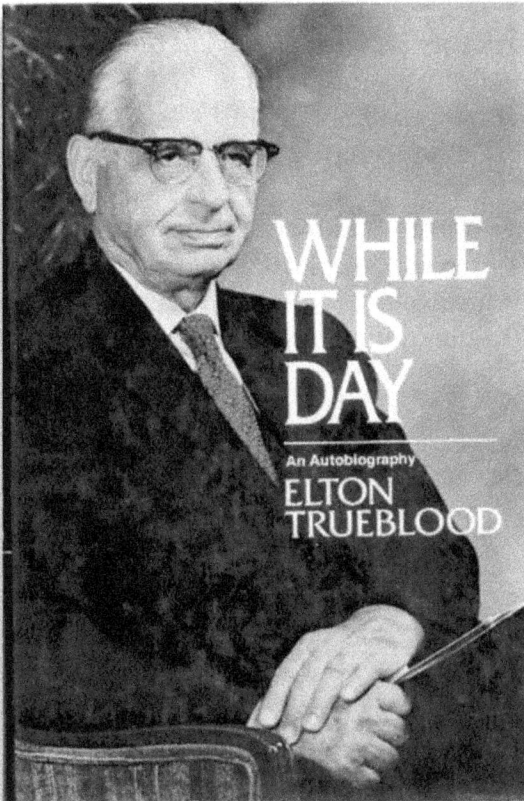

The 1974 autobiography of one of my revered teachers who remembered and wrote while his mind was clear and memories sharp. I have tried to follow his wise lead.

THE TEST OF TIME

Much in the past obviously will not stand the test of today. Even so, as C. S. Lewis said in 1949, "We need something to set against the present, to remind us that the basic assumptions have been quite different in different periods and that much which now seems certain is merely temporary fashion."

To forget is to lose identity and maybe destiny. To repeat thoughtlessly any past assumptions is to risk losing credibility in the eyes of a questioning world. Nothing is acceptable other than what seriously and simultaneously engages the hard questions of context, tradition, and transition.

Barry L. Callen
Seeking the Light (1998, p. 9)

Chapter I

Old World, New World

In search of a better life

It is only natural. Humans seek a better life. The search is a constantwarfare and natural disasters. Even the Genesis story of that ideal Garden of Eden is ruined by sinful actions that brought a tragedy still infecting the form of life we call "human." We are "fallen" travelers in search of a better place and way to be.

My wife Jan and I have participated in the "Genographic" study of the National Geographic Society. The overall purpose of this major research effort is to use the newest DNA technology to trace the migrations of humans across the ages. We were shown the dramatic impact of climate changes on where and why humans have moved and survived.

Jan and I each are reported to have ancient roots in eastern Africa among peoples who moved northward and eventually to Western Europe and the British Isles, on their way finally to North America. So says the DNA, the only "records" we now have. How ironic that, at the time Jan and I participated in this study, we were active in the great work of Horizon International, a ministry to AIDS orphans in eastern and southern Africa. We were "going home" after millennia of being away!

The human flow goes both ways. The ancients were stumbling forward toward a desired future; we moderns sometimes gaze backward in hope of finding our roots and the meaning they can give. Accordingly, Jan and I touched the "old world" in July, 2006. We had sailed into the lovely harbor of Plymouth, England, and sat anchored for the day. I looked from the balcony of our ninth-deck room on the cruise ship and tried to imagine the comparatively tiny Mayflower sailing from this very harbor long ago, a dangerous voyage in search of a new world. The tranquil setting of calm sea and rolling hills lying before us on that day made me wonder about the reasons for the desperation that had motivated that earlier voyage of relocation to a new world.

We sat comfortably aboard the Jewel of the Seas, a magnificent ship now returned from the new world with passengers interested in sights far away and times long ago. The next day, Jan and I were anchored in the large harbor of Cork, Ireland, from which British soldiers once sailed to fight their revolting colonies in North America, and from which prisoners were once shipped to bring European population to far-off Australia. For Jan and me, these were days of leisure that included reflection on days long past.

J. M. W. Turner (1775-1851) was the English landscape painter regarded as a Romantic preface to Impressionism. He insisted that what matters is not what you see, but *the way you see it*. For instance, Americans were long taught that Christopher Columbus "discovered" America. When my wife and I were in Iceland in 2012, we were reminded that it was the Vikings who had been on American shores long before Columbus, but they had abandoned the place because they saw dealing with the Indians as too much trouble to be worth the little gain.

By contrast, the later Europeans came and stayed in North America primarily because it was seen as a source of great new riches for their home countries. One recent American, tired of the European prejudice, said he hoped to win a lottery, build three little ships, fill them with Indians, and sail east to "discover" Italy!

For all of us, things are—at least for us—what we see them to be. As I look back on my own life and journeys, I pray for clear vision and not confused perspectives and displays of personal prejudice.

Moving West with the Conners

Knowing one's historic family roots seems necessary for gaining a sense of present identity. In a significant way, I am who, where, and how I am because of who, where, and how some others were before me. To remember is to be rooted, and thus wiser and more whole. The story of John and William Conner is helpful in my case.

The Conners moved from Pennsylvania to Ohio and then to Indiana, just like I did. They were pioneers who made their way through the troubled times of the nineteenth century, developing an appreciation for "native" Americans, in contrast to most others of the time. They served in public life and adjusted as the American frontier changed. They ended up in Indiana near where I have spent most of my adult life. Their legacy has been preserved in the living museum called Conner Prairie Farm near Indianapolis, and their dramatic story is told by Janet Hale in *The Conners of Conner Prairie* (1989).

In August of 2001, Arlene, my first wife, and I spent the day at Conner Prairie celebrating our thirty-eighth wedding anniversary. Then, on a lovely Saturday that October, my grandson Ian and his dad, our son Todd, spent a day at Conner Prairie for a Cub Scout event. They were taking their turn getting in touch with the world of the frontier and the everyday lives of both native Americans and the more recent European settlers.

Family roots for me lie deep in the tradition of European immigrants from the "old world" who sought a better life in the "new world" of America. My ancestors came from Germany, Holland, Scotland, and Ireland, all initially to Pennsylvania. They were rugged folk prepared to risk much for freedom and opportunity. They fled the old in frustration and pioneered the new with courage and hope. Their descendants survived economic depression and war. During World War II, several of them came to comprise my immediate childhood family. They were my heritage, roots, support system, and a large part of my identity. The more I have come to know about these people, now all gone from this world, the more I realize how they laid a good foundation for me and for those Callens now coming after me. As I remember, I rejoice.

The remembering begins in some faraway places. It's symbolized by a beloved American folk song that I learned to play on the guitar as a young teenager—one of the few musical achievements of my life. Dr. Brewster Higley had made his early living as a physician in Indiana. Then he staked a claim in Kansas in the 1860s. In 1872 he wrote the little song called "Home on the Range." It captured the romantic longing of millions who had immigrated to a newer world and now were moving west in the new world. Here are the simple words of longing for a fairer place:

> Oh, give me a home, Where the buffalo roam,
> And the deer and the antelope play,
> Where never is heard a discouraging word,
> And the sky is not clouded all day.

My ancestors were longing for a new home where discouragement could be minimized and homes made more secure.

Scottish Isle, German Farm, Dutch Castle

The Alans of the Isle of Bute, who sometimes appear in the records of Scotland as the Macallans or just the Callens, were permitted to wear the tartans of other clans, including Macdonald of Clan Ranald. Why? The Callens seem not to have established their own tartan, either because they were too few or too preoccupied with their popular and lucrative industry. When visiting the nearby Isle of Mull in 1999, my English guide teased me, a Christian minister, for having ancient relatives who were the best whiskey makers in all of the British Isles! Clans receiving the valued brew apparently were generous to my forebears. Whatever their product, I was proud to learn about of the Callens being the best at what they did.

However lucrative the island business once may have been, life was hard and soon intolerable. Some of the Callens eventually gave up their local farms and shops and the making of their popular product to join the flood of anxious humanity heading for a new life very far away to the west.

In corresponding with an engineer in Belgium in 2000 by the name of Paul Callens, I learned that he knew of no connection between the continental Callens (some of whom changed the name to "Collins" once in the United States) and those of Scotland, Ireland, and Wales. A pastor friend of mine in Indiana has an extensive history of the Callens who lived and died in Wales during the nineteenth century. It was other Callens, however, who forsook their homes in Scotland and Ireland and migrated far to the west. They became my personal roots in the new world.

Patrick Callen came to Pennsylvania by way of Ireland, thus the usual designation "Scotch-Irish." He arrived in the new world sometime before 1750 and died in 1825 in Armstrong County. My ancestry on the Callen side flows from Patrick through his son Hugh, Sr. (d. 1821), to his son Watson (d. 1876), to his son Alvin (d. 1929), to Alvin's son Charles (d. 1967), my paternal grandfather, and finally to my father Robert (1919-1974). My son Todd, knowing this family history, named his first son, my first grandchild, Ian Patrick. This name represents a stalwart and proud lineage rooted in Germanic (Grandma Callen), Dutch (Grandpa VanArsdale), and Scotch-Irish stock.

Hugh Callen, Sr., was born in Westmoreland County, Pennsylvania, on June 5, 1773. He had the reputation of being an honorable Scottish man, a Christian who now was also an American patriot. He was a soldier in the War of 1812 and later a U. S. pensioner for his services in that struggle. In 1812 he bought some 300 acres of good farmland in western Pennsylvania and settled down. In 1826 there was a survey of the Clarion

River that bordered the Callen property on one side. The intention was to build the Pennsylvania Canal through that immediate area. Mr. Callen immediately saw an opportunity and laid out the town of Callensburg by sectioning lots of his own land. He was hopeful that the coming canal would bring with it considerable commercial development. That development never came, but the lovely little town of Callensburg is still there today. A Presbyterian church was built on four acres donated by Hugh Callen at the time of the town's founding. The first sermon was preached there in 1825 and the last service was held on Easter, 1964. The town's history has been chronicled extensively by Arnold Kepple.

The town cemetery is where Hugh Callen, Sr., was buried in 1821. Other Callens are also resting there. One of Hugh's children was a son, Watson, born in Callensburg in 1816. One of Watson's children was Alvin, born in 1848, in Callensburg. Alvin spent much of 1864 as a private infantryman in the Union Army and was honorably discharged. He died and was buried in 1929 in Erie, Pennsylvania, where he had spent his last year as a widower in the Soldiers' and Sailors' Home. In the meantime, my grandfather Charles Callen was born in 1885, one of the ten children born to Alvin and his wife Sarah.

John H. Rupert was an evangelist of the young Church of God movement (Anderson) who had ministered in England and Germany in the 1890s. He held a revival meeting in Callensburg, Pennsylvania, in 1909. A small congregation of the Church of God soon began just opposite the old Presbyterian Church and town cemetery. From that congregation would emerge a superb leader of the Church of God movement, R. Eugene Sterner (he often walked into town for Sunday school from nearby Turniphole). Later in his life, Sterner retired in Anderson, Indiana, and became my friend, an elder Christian brother whom I loved and admired. Callensburg, however, would be the closest that the Callen family and the Church of God movement would come to each other until it happened again in the 1940s in the town of Newton

Falls in northeastern Ohio, about eighty miles to the west of Callensburg. Their coming together in Ohio would be very significant for me.

My paternal grandfather, Charles B. Callen, was born in Brockwayville, Pennsylvania, on August 10, 1885. He married Mary S. Rose on June 15, 1910. The marriage license says that Charles was a "painter" at the time, although Christian ministry would be his life's calling. Mary, my Grandma Callen, was a daughter of Christopher Rose (1849-1922) and Elizabeth Sophia Hoffsomer (1850-1933). Christopher and Sophia were childhood friends when both of their families lived in the town of Hitzrode, Kreis Eschwege, R. B. Cassel, Germany. Christopher's father was Jacob Rose (1812-1884) and his mother Dorothy (Felmenton) Rose (1818-1869). He was seven when his family immigrated to Pennsylvania. Over the years he would be a coal miner, storekeeper, and finally a plastering contractor and Christian lay leader. In the meantime, after nineteen days on a ship in 1871, his former friend Elizabeth Sophia Hoffsomer arrived in the Pittsburgh, Pennsylvania, area, with her immigrating family.

Christopher and Sophia became reacquainted upon her arrival in the new world and soon were married. They relocated to McKeesport, Pennsylvania, in 1884, where one of their children, Maria Sophia Rose, my paternal grandmother, was born in February, 1885. Christopher Rose died on March 13, 1922, with burial in Versailles Cemetery, in McKeesport. In later life, he was a committed Christian lay leader in the International Holiness Church. In a memorial, pastor Charles L. Slater reported: "We who knew him will never forget his shining face and wonderful testimony. The entire family was at his side to witness his death. His homegoing was wonderful. He saw Jesus and the angels, and spent most of his conscious minutes singing, praying, and exhorting. He has gone but will never be forgotten."

Four boys and two girls were born to my paternal grandparents, Charles Brunson and Mary (Rose) Callen. They were David Edger,

Glenford Ellis, William Charles, Robert Christopher, Edna Rose, and Violet Mae. Robert, later my father, was born on June 11, 1919, also in McKeesport, Pennsylvania. Receiving Christian baptism as an infant at the Avonmore Free Methodist Church on April 4, 1920, Dad ("Bert" to his friends) would get a "Seaman Passport" on October 12, 1943, make dangerous war voyages, accept adult Christian baptism in his bed in Lake Milton, Ohio, while nearing death from cancer in 1974, and do much living in his all-too-brief life of fifty-five years. But that's getting ahead of the story.

Grandpa, Charles B. Callen, was ordained a deacon in the Free Methodist Church in 1915 and an elder in 1917. Grandma, Mary Callen, was a preacher in her own right, holding an evangelist's license from the Free Methodist Church beginning at least in 1907. Together, they pastored faithfully from 1910 until 1952 when Grandpa's retirement came because of failing health. Grandpa's outstanding and very mobile ministry in the Pittsburgh Conference of the Free Methodist Church included pastorates as follows:

1910, Smithton; 1911, New Kensington; 1912-15, Glendale and White House; 1915, Cove Run; 1916-18, Fairchance; 1918, Mt. Pleasant and Bridgeport; 1919-21, Avonmore; 1921-24, Black Lick; 1924, McKeesport; 1925, Braddock; 1926-28, Belle Vernon; 1928-31, Natrona Heights and Pleasantville; 1931-34, East Liverpool, Oakland; 1934-1936, utler and Callery; 1936-40, New Brighton; 1940-43, Frankstown Avenue; 1946-50, Huntington, Orchard Grove; 1950, Blairsville; 1951, Farmington; with retirement in 1952. Grandpa Callen died on December 31, 1967.

Without doubt, as the published history of the Pittsburgh Conference of the Free Methodist Church admits: "The song 'Pack up the Old

Wooden Boxes' became a common refrain at each annual conference time. The reading of the appointments, which were a carefully guarded secret, was an especially anxious time for P.K.'s (preacher's kids) and hundreds of interested listeners. Years ago, frequent moves was the order of the day" (*History of the Pittsburgh Conference of the Free Methodist Church*, 1983, 29).

Often, this song of moving preachers was sung with very little joy. Each minister belonged to the conference and was assigned to a congregation annually—often without being consulted in advance. Ironically, Arlene Cooley, who one day would be my wife, had an uncle, Harry E. Cooley, who also had a distinguished ministry in the Pittsburgh Conference beginning in 1938. He pastored two congregations, Cove Run and Fairchance, that my grandfather Callen had pastored in earlier years. At the time of our meeting in college in 1959, however, Arlene and I were totally unaware of this and other church connections between our families.

As a little boy, I vividly recall being on the Free Methodist campgrounds in East Liverpool, Ohio, where my maternal grandfather, Charles VanArsdale, had a cottage next to Morrison Baker's in the big oval of quaint summer residences. Conference usually convened in early August, just after I and others of my family had been on the grounds for about ten days of camp meeting.

Talk at conference was of the pastoral "appointments" for the following year, with their public reading sometimes delayed and awaited with anxiety. When word went out that they were about to be read, everyone gathered at the tabernacle. It was not unusual, following the reading of a name and appointed place of ministry for the following year, that teenagers would run from the tabernacle either laughing or crying. In the latter case, their families had just learned that they must move to new locations within the following two weeks—even though their teenagers may have been about to begin a senior year in high school. This "appointment" practice was a holdover from the "itinerant" ministry typical of Methodism in pioneer America.

My father, Robert, had been abruptly moved like this more than once in his early years. It bred frustration and rebellion in him. He decided not to finish high school and became a drop-out from active Christian faith for most of his adult life. His reserve about things spiritual kept the home of my boyhood from being actively nurturing in Christian faith. There was perfunctory table prayer, but little else—except for the spiritual sensitivity of my mother and the positive influence of my maternal grandfather Charles VanArsdale. Some Christian faith remained in my dad, but any spiritual life was kept out of family sight, at least until his brother Bill got cancer in later life and reaffirmed faith prior to his death. Their brother, my uncle David, was a Free Methodist minister who died young, also of cancer. My father would find himself walking a similar road of health crisis in the 1970s. Before that, however, he would live as he saw fit, hard-working, self-absorbed, and aloof from any formal church life.

My grandfather Callen pastored in New Brighton, Pennsylvania, from 1936 to 1940. This was to be crucial for my future, even though I was not yet born. The VanArsdales were a prominent lay family in this Free Methodist congregation, with one of their daughters, Charlotte, soon to be my mother. Mom had been born on November 12, 1919, when her family was living on Oak Hill (1804 3rd Street, facing the New Brighton High School football field). She graduated from that high school in 1937. That year's edition of the school annual, the *Alarum*, carried the "will" and "prophecy" of its graduating seniors. Willed to my mother was "a pair of rollerless roller skates to make sure she maintains her equilibrium." The prophecy about her was that one day she would be found "satisfied with her work in Cleveland as an interior decorator."

Apparently Mom had experienced an awkward moment or two (thus safer skates) and had exhibited an artistic sense. I don't know where the reference to Cleveland came from. Mom actually would spend much of her adult life in northeast Ohio, although decorating few interiors except our modest little home in Craig Beach. After high school, Charlotte began working in the Collapsable Tube Company that made toothpaste containers. While the Callens lived in New Brighton with Charles as the Free Methodist pastor, their son Robert ("Bert") met, courted, and married Charlotte VanArsdale (June, 1940). I was born to them in New Brighton, Pennsylvania, on July 10, 1941.

The original city of Brighton, established in the 1830s, was situated in England on the estuary of the River Mersey. It commanded a spectacular view across Liverpool Bay and became proud of its heritage as an elegant Victorian seaside resort. The more recent New Brighton, location of my birth in the "new world," sits along the heavily industrialized Beaver River and railroad lines north of Pittsburgh, Pennsylvania. In was in 1946, when I was five years old, that the city of New Brighton continued its significance for me. My sister, mother, and I now were living with the VanArsdales in Newton Falls, Ohio—my grandfather had pulled the family westward into Ohio because of his shifting employment. The plant where he worked had burned and relocated to nearby Ohio. Dad was finishing his years at sea during World War II.

Back at the Free Methodist congregation in New Brighton, there was another meeting of eventual significance to me. It involved Lyle Flinner who came from a family in the area that was not church-going. He, however, had become a Christian in 1936 and an active area youth leader. He also returned from his own eventful time in the big war effort, missing the brutal D-Day assault on occupied France, and his likely death there, only because of an emergency hospitalization in England.

In 1946, at a youth gathering at the New Brighton Free Methodist Church, Lyle met Beatrice Jeffreys from Uniontown, Pennsylvania (an aunt of Arlene Cooley, later to be my wife). Bea had lost her husband when he piloted a bombing raid over Germany and was shot down on the return trip. Lyle and Bea married in 1947. He graduated in 1949 from the local Geneva College, then from Asbury Theological Seminary in 1952, pastored for the Church of the Nazarene in the Pittsburgh area, completed a doctorate in religious education at the University of Pittsburgh, and returned to the Geneva campus in 1958 as a full-time professor (with Bea functioning as a librarian). It was then that the Flinners entered my life as Arlene Cooley and I became freshmen on the Geneva College campus in 1959.

As I look back now, I see much similarity between my life and that of Lyle Flinner. Arlene and I would graduate from Geneva in 1963, and then I would do some pastoral work, complete advanced academic degrees, including one from Asbury Theological Seminary, and pursue an extended academic career in the service of the Church of God (Anderson). Lyle was the primary officiating minister when Arlene and I were married in the New Brighton Free Methodist Church on August 10, 1963 (my grandfather Callen's birthday). Lyle was assisted in the ceremony by my grandfather Callen, who had once pastored that congregation, and my own pastor at the time, Lillie S. McCutcheon of Newton Falls, Ohio. More about the college years and wedding will come later.

After retirement from full-time ministry in 1952, my Callen grandparents moved to Craig Beach, Ohio, on the western shore of Lake Milton, taking up residence in a little home just a few blocks from my family and amid scenes of my early growing-up years beginning at age five in 1946. I had hardly known my Callen grandparents until that time. Dad helped find secular employment for Grandpa—they had always lived in church properties, owned no home of their own, and had no social security income.

There was a little machine-shop nearby where Grandpa worked for a time—so did I as one way of making a few dollars for college. I remember stamping out little metal angles for screendoors—buckets full of them! It was hardly "my thing," but I managed. My Callen grandparents also worked together as custodians at the local school in Pricetown where I attended grades one through eight. My father was a member of the local school board at one time. I recall an extended vacation period, probably Christmas/New Years, when I helped my grandparents move chairs, desks, and tables and then scrub and wax the school floors, thousands of square feet of floors. It seemed wrong to me that elderly servants of the church had to do such labor-intensive work.

Charles and Mary Callen were very good, hardworking, and proud people who intended to earn their own way. My father was sensitive to their needs. Eventually, they moved back to Pennsylvania, living in a converted two-story garage, small but adequate for them. There were family and church roots around them there. Their two daughters lived in the area, my aunts Edna Canich and Violet Turner (we called her "Aunt Posie"). Grandma Callen was especially interested in Christian mission. For many years she was a leader of the Penny-A-Day program of the Pittsburgh Conference of the Free Methodist Church. At her death on November 12, 1978, some of her grandchildren brought their pennies instead of flowers. It was a fitting tribute to a faithful Christian woman who had the gospel of Christ in her heart and the mission of the church on her mind. She was a strong German-American lady whose life reflected Christ's.

I remember fondly a time when Grandma Callen had my son, Todd, on her lap. She was singing a little Christian song to him in German. I also remember the wonderful smell of fresh-baked bread that often filled her little home. It was a simple scene, but proud and precious.

I know less about the history of the VanArsdales. Grandpa VanArsadale was extraordinarily significant in my own young life, partly because he was always nearby. Sometimes one's presumed ancestors are really the result of more fanciful speculation than clear historical fact. For instance, I have encountered the "VanArsdale Myth" that reports the presumed European origin of this family as Jan VanArsdale, a knight of Holland. It is said that in 1211 he built the Castle Arsdale.

Assuming that this is true, even the chivalry of the proud and powerful could not keep the later descendants of this family from leaving for the "new world." In the family line of Jan, so one story reads, came a Symon Jansen VanArsdalen who emigrated in 1653 to New Amsterdam. Some with this surname did sail to Pennsylvania in 1768. By the 1800s there were several pockets of VanArsdales scattered around Pennsylvania, with the primary group residing in Bucks County near Philadelphia.

My maternal grandfather, Charles Gregory VanArsdale, was born to Abraham (1857-1930) and Fannie (Paulson) VanArsdale at Brush Creek, Beaver County, in western Pennsylvania, in March, 1883. Grandpa married Mayme Viola Main in June, 1906. She was born in February, 1882, in Dempseytown, Pa., the daughter of Theadore and Margaret (Mall) Main. All of the children of my VanArsdale grandparents were born in New Brighton, Pa., as I later would be in 1941. Three of them, the ones who survived childhood, would become significant in my life. Laverne (my "Uncle Van") was born in January, 1908. Evangeline (my "Auntie") was born in October, 1910, and Charlotte Marie—my mother— came along in November, 1919.

One of my prized possessions is a large and very old Bible passed on to me from my grandfather VanArsdale by way of my mother Charlotte at her death in 1979. Apparently, it had been in the VanArsdale family for about ten generations. It is a large-format King James Authorized version published in the English language in Amsterdam, Holland, in 1643! Grandpa loved the Bible, had memorized many passages, and saw this particular copy as a symbol of ancient truth with contemporary significance. The paper is now in very poor condition, but not the meaning on its many pages. I hope to pass it along when the time comes.

So, both branches of my lineage root in the "old world" and reflect the American dream of taking whatever risks were necessary to seek a new life in improved circumstances. These circumstances were mostly the worlds of the church, farming, coal, and steel in western Pennsylvania. By the early 1940s, the massive production capacity of the greater Pittsburgh area shifted to the production of war supplies. My father and his brother, my uncle Bill, would sail back to the old world, seeking to preserve the good life that their grandparents had once come to the new world to find. I arrived in this world as war was spreading almost everywhere.

A World Gone Mad

Conflict was already blazing in Europe in 1940. That year the Danish musical comedian Victor Borge (1909-2000) was blacklisted by the German Nazis and fled to the United States. He performed for the first time on Bing Crosby's radio show in 1941 just as I was beginning life. Many years later, I came to love his music and slapstick humor.

Also in 1940, the Ravenna Ordinance Plant, the "Arsenal," was established by the federal government on 24,000 acres just outside Newton Falls, Ohio, only a few miles from my boyhood home. During World War II, some 17,000 people were employed there in making small arms ammunition, artillery primers, and detonators. During America's involvement in this world conflict, my mother worked at the Arsenal, as did the father of my high school classmate Delores Ward (Stroup). The fathers of classmates Harry Crytzer and Larry Smith worked at the nearby Lordstown Army Depot. We were little kids in a world of conflict.

Most members of my high school class (Jackson-Milton, Ohio, class of 1959) were born in the shadows of America's final preparations for all-out world war. It was a time for some to be born and many others to die. Mercifully, I was too young to understand and be afraid. Just as the war was beginning, the famous Thomas Merton joined the monastic community of Gethsemani in rural Kentucky. The day would come that I would retreat often to Gethsemani in my own search for peace and spiritual depth.

The month of June, 2001, would prove to be a national milestone and a stimulus to my personal memory. My wife Arlene and I attended the first graduation of a grandchild. Ian had just turned six (I was about to turn sixty) and had completed his kindergarten year at St. Ambrose school in Anderson, Indiana. I had just overseen the release of the book *Ahead of His Times* by Douglas Welch, the biography of India missionary George P. Tasker and the first publication of the new Anderson University Press that I was leading as founding editor. I already was working on the coming publications of the autobiographies of two of my longtime colleagues and personal friends, Gustav Jeeninga and James Earl Massey. It also was the sixtieth anniversary of the "day that shall live in infamy," the surprise bombing of Pearl Harbor in 1941 by Imperial Japan. The American theaters filled with crowds watching the 2001 film *Pearl Harbor*. We as a nation were still trying to understand that horror of the 1940s. After six decades, Americans had new reasons to be afraid; this time I was old enough to understand and feel the fear.

The new film about the surprise attack that pulled the United States into the world conflict in 1941 is what stimulated my wondering about the past that lay just beyond reach of my memory. I wondered what my parents had been feeling and doing back then. They had married in Wellsburg, West Virginia, on June 4, 1940. A year later, my mother was eight months pregnant with me. Questions must have been many and anxiety levels high for them after one year of marriage. Europe was at war and the madness was spreading fast. It soon would touch almost everyone, including the Callens. On July 10, 1940, the Battle of Britain had begun with a wave of German bombers seeking to bring the United Kingdom—the "old world" of my roots to its knees. My family had left that world long ago, and now the United States hoped to stay isolated from the European conflict. It was not to be.

I was born one year later on July 10, 1941, in New Brighton, Pennsylvania (my sister Bonnie came along in January, 1943). On July 10, 1943, the Allies began the invasion of Axis-controlled Europe with landings on Sicily. In May, just weeks before this invasion, my father and some of his friends had become Merchant Marines, signing up in Pittsburgh as civilian seamen who would transport the materials of war. They knew they would be drafted soon and preferred working aboard a merchant ship to carrying a rifle on the ground in the Army. That was the very time when the German U-boats (submarines) were aggressively attacking merchant convoys in the Atlantic, resulting in the Merchant Marines suffering the highest casualty rate of any of the American military services (although they were not classed as official military personnel).

My father sailed into the horror detailed in Michael Gannon's 1998 book *Black May*, the epic story of the Allies suffering greatly and then finally gaining the upper hand on the menace of the deadly German U-boats. The dread and death were pictured by Hollywood in the 1943 film *Action in the North Atlantic*, an extended salute to the men of the Merchant Marines. Dad was spared death at sea and would make it home in 1946. In 2009 I would write a novel about submarine warfare in the 1940s, an intended tribute to my father. Titled *In Deep Water*, it captures the turbulent world that Dad had to endure.

The year 1941 saw much more than my birth and those of most members of my high school class. It also was a year of dramatic sporting records set. Baseball's Ted Williams hit .406, Joe DiMaggio put together his 56-game hitting streak, and a sensational thoroughbred colt named Whirlaway won the Triple Crown. The dreaded war began to affect millions of American homes directly. In July, the month of my birth, Andy Rooney joined a growing flood of young Americans reporting for active military duty. On December 7, 183 carrier-based fighters and bombers of the Japanese Navy carried out a surprise attack on the U. S. naval base at Pearl Harbor in the Hawaiian islands. Within minutes, 2,403 Americans were dead. So was America's isolationism.

The top ten bestselling non-fiction books in the U. S. in 1940 had included no "war books"; but 1941 would be very different. Led by William Shirer's *Berlin Diary*, there also were *The White Cliffs* by Alice Duer Miller, *Out of the Night* by Jan Valtin, and *Blood, Sweat and Tears* by Winston Churchill. The American public knew now that it was in a great struggle. I was only months old at the time and unaware of the global turmoil into which I had been born. But my parents certainly knew, and they had begun paying the high price.

The destruction that rained on America's Pacific Fleet that fateful December day in 1941 was great, but it proved to be a strategic Japanese blunder in the long run. The Fleet's three aircraft carriers were not there and escaped damage. Even more significant, Pearl Harbor quickly unified the American people into a crusading zeal that sustained them all the way to eventual military victory in both the European and Pacific theaters of war.

President Franklin D. Roosevelt called on Congress to declare war on Japan, saying that December 7 was "a date which will live in infamy." Three days later, Germany and Italy declared war on the United States. War was now a worldwide preoccupation. The early months of 1942 marked the low point of the conflict for the United States. That year the bestselling book of fiction was *The Song of Bernadette*, evidencing the strong appeal of a religious theme in a time of national stress. That same year, seven war books dominated the top-ten list of non-fiction bestsellers.

Many fathers of members of the Jackson-Milton, Ohio, high school class of 1959 (my class) saw action in the armed forces of the United States. Rarely was there an extended family that did not have someone in uniform. Robert, my father, was a carpenter who sailed as a Merchant Marine, carrying war supplies to destinations all over the globe. Ian

Worley, a good friend of mine in school and long after, spent time as a little boy with his family in rural Haiti assisting the U. S. government by growing a replacement supply of rubber. Japanese expansion had depleted the usual sources available to the Allies. Larry Smith's father was a pioneer in the development of radar for military purposes. While these fathers risked their lives in national service, their young children played at home as normally as possible, with little comprehension of the consuming conflict. From ages two to five, I lived with my mother and her parents, Charles and Mayme VanArsdale, and my sister Bonnie in the little northeastern Ohio town of Newton Falls. Our father was far away and in constant danger.

On my second birthday, July 10, 1943, the Allies landed troops in Italy, a real advance against the Axis powers. Gustav Jeeninga, my colleague and dear friend in later years, was then a prisoner of the Nazis in Berlin—see his autobiography *Doors to Life* that I was privileged to edit and publish through Anderson University Press in 2002. This social turmoil and sacrifice, shared by millions, led Aaron Copeland in 1942 to compose "Fanfare for the Common Man," his classic musical contribution to the big war effort that was being carried on the backs of common people.

I still have the "War Ration Book" carrying the names of Charlotte (my mother), Bonnie (my sister), and me. It is sobering just look at (see at the end of this chapter). My sister and I were fortunate. Dad did come home, impacted for life, but alive. Earl Hitt, a Marine and father of my second wife Jan, also got home alive, but with one eye gone. Many never came home at all. The sacrifices of one generation are rarely appreciated by another. It's hard to understand without having been there.

The big war had dominated American life for almost four years. Finally, on May 8, 1945, the welcome news was announced. The European war was officially won by the Allies. Many large German cities were little more than rubble from relentless bombing. Paris had been liberated. Hitler was dead by his own hand. A grateful world went wild with celebration on this joyous V-E Day.

Then, on August 6, it happened. The "it" was an American B-29 bomber unleashing an atomic bomb on Hiroshima, Japan. Another soon followed on Nagasaki. An estimated 220,000 Japanese died in these two bombings. Ironically, Captain Mitsuo Fuchida, Japanese commander of the Pearl Harbor attack, flew into the Hiroshima airport just after the American bombing there and was surprised to find himself facing "a procession of people who seemed to have come out of Hell." Those local residents who could still walk were burned, filled with radiation, and badly disoriented with extreme shock. The atomic age had begun.

My birth in July, 1941, had ushered me into a really troubled world! The first serious book I remember reading was the dramatic story of Jacob DeShazer. He was a member of the famed Doolittle Raiders who daringly bombed Japan in 1942 and then crashed and suffered forty months of cruel imprisonment in Japanese-occupied China. In that time of confinement, DeShazer read a Bible repeatedly, finally experienced forgiveness for his hate of the Japanese guards, and after the war returned to Japan as a loving Christian missionary. He became a friend of none other than Commander Mitsuo Fuchida, who had learned of DeShazer's amazing testimony and ministry and soon himself had become a Christian. Sometimes, he even joined DeShazer in witnessing to large Japanese crowds. This was a dramatic way to launch my reading career!

The Japanese emperor, shocked by the unprecedented destruction caused by this previously unknown atomic weapon, finally had enough of war. September 2, 1945, was V-J Day. Eleven Japanese leaders boarded the American battleship Missouri, anchored in Tokyo Bay, to sign the final surrender. My friend Ian Worley remembers hearing church bells ringing and seeing people in his little northeastern Ohio town riding on fire trucks and joyously yelling "the war is over!" While my family was equally glad, my father was also frustrated.

Instead of coming right home from his latest voyage in the Pacific theater of war, Dad saw his ship dump its cargo of war materials into Manila harbor and then be turned over to the Japanese for transporting home wounded Japanese soldiers. He would have to spend more time with the Allied occupation forces in Japan. His brother William Callen, my uncle Bill, spent some time in the devastated city of Hiroshima before he could come home. When he did, he brought with him a battered Japanese bugle. Chris Callen, one of his sons, would serve in Vietnam in the early 1970s and then, as a veteran, would inherit that old bugle. Into the twenty-first century, Chris occasionally played it at the funerals of American war veterans in central Ohio. War is full of agony, irony, and pride that last for generations.

Finally, the guns had fallen silent. It had been the deadliest conflict in human history. While the United States and the whole world would try to return to a more normal existence, little would ever be the same again. Peace had been bought at a great price. Democratic ideals presumably had prevailed. A new world would have to arise from all the rubble and death. The United States had gained world leadership. Could the exhilaration of victory be transformed into a better future that would feature peace, justice, and prosperity? My 1998 book *Seeking the Light* would detail this quest.

Prospects were uncertain at best. Already, Joseph Stalin had gained many concessions from Allied leaders that gave the Soviet Union control over vast land areas, and the chance to seek its own domination of the world's future. Now there would be a "Cold War," the stressful context of my elementary, high school, and college years.

Home to Build a New World

My father was discharged from the Merchant Marines on March 1, 1946, in Yokohama, Japan. Every American who served and survived had a dream of what they wanted to do when the war was finally over and home was safely reached. Some men claimed they would passionately kiss the first girl each saw. Others planned to sleep for a month, getting up only for home-cooked meals, or they might decide to blow their separation pay on the longest drinking binges of their lives. Many had seen too much of violence and death and didn't want to talk about the war with their families.

One German soldier, a prisoner of war for three years in Belgium and then Scotland, was Jürgen Moltmann. He had seen many Germans die in the camps because they had lost hope and grew ill in their despair. An American chaplain gave him a Bible that changed his life. By the 1960s he had become an accomplished Christian theologian pioneering the "Theology of Hope" school of thought that would impact my professional life from then on. The aftermaths of war are filled with ironies.

Moltmann agreed to come to the United States to be a guest speaker at the March, 2008, meeting of the Wesleyan Theological Society. I was pleased to finally have an opportunity to meet him personally. His works frequently appear in footnotes in my theology books. My 2008 conference assignment was to critique Moltmann's presentation—a little intimidating for me! On that occasion, I received an autographed copy of his new autobiography, *A Broad Place*, the moving account of a life shaped in the midst of war and then enlightened by hope in Jesus Christ. I gave him a signed copy of the first edition of my autobiography. Once enemies in war, we now were brothers in Christ.

I can only imagine how difficult it must have been for my father to be separated from a wife and two young children by the horror of war. His "Shore Leave Pass" for Alexandria City, Egypt, dated May 4, 1944, listed him as a 24-year-old carpenter employed by the "Seas Shipping Co., Inc." There are such documents for India, Australia, and elsewhere. Dad was awarded formal certifications by the War Shipping Administration for having served with the United States Merchant Marines in the Middle East, Atlantic, and Pacific war zones. I inherited a treasured photo of him taken in India in February, 1945.

The post-war dream of my father was to develop and operate a fishing camp on a beautiful lake (replacing the wild and dangerous oceans). There he would earn a living doing something he loved as an outdoor sportsman. Dad would work on this dream for the rest of his life, although it would be realized in only small ways. Peacetime can also be filled with its surprises and frustrations.

I have a series of letters my father sent to my mother from sea during 1945. They are always signed "Bert." They were addressed to her at 614 North Canal Street, Newton Falls, Ohio, where she, my sister, and I were living with my VanArsdale grandparents. Some of these letters are intensely personal, enough so that I almost felt it inappropriate for me to read them when I first found them in my garage after my mother's death in 1979. Dad's letter of August 10, 1945, was sent to Mom from somewhere on the Pacific Ocean where he reported his awareness of the atomic bomb, the pending surrender of Japan, and hopefully his soon return to the United States "and our new home in the west." Other letters made clear what this hope of a new western home was all about.

Dad was dreaming of relocating the family to Wisconsin—either Wausau or Merrill—where he would go, get a job, and then send for Mom. She would bring Bonnie and me by train to this new and idealized world, a reflection of the ongoing immigrant's dream of the Callen heritage. He wrote about his beloved fishing gear at home and asked that his dad be reminded to oil his rifles while he was away. He said he had not missed a hunting season since he was sixteen. Now he had missed three while enemy planes and submarines had been hunting him!

What Dad envisioned for our family's future was spelled out in the August 27, 1945, letter to Mom. It would be a wilderness Wisconsin fishing/hunting camp of his own. Dad wrote to Mom:

I've been seeing you in the kitchen at work during the day, going to and from the cottages cleaning them up for new customers, and in the evenings sitting next to me on the front porch. We just sit there looking out over the lake and the boat shed in the shadows of a small light for the warf. We turn our gaze up the hill a little to our left and the little white cottages gleam in the moonlight with the forest for a background. You can see several individual trees outlined against the glow of the sky. From the cottages to the lake are the white slag drives with the small pine trees growing alongside them.

Dad was a mixture of practical builder and poetic dreamer. His dream would be difficult to realize financially. We never made it to Wisconsin.

Neither of my parents came from wealthy families. Mom was struggling to support her two children, and Dad was trying to be frugal with the little that he was earning at sea. On September 1, 1945, he wrote to Mom about his money worries, reporting that the bonuses for the Merchant Marines were being reduced. He would not have much money to bring home. His advice to Mom: "Please, Honey, try to save every nickel you can. It is going to make it tough trying to get to Wisconsin on what little I'll have." Mom was working at the Arsenal outside Newton Falls and doing the best she could. At the time of this letter, his ship was near Manila in the Philippines and he was working hard in his spare time building a model of the ship he was on. He would bring it home with pride. He was unusually skilled with his hands—and a little nostalgic, even about the world of war he was anxious to leave.

Much frustration filled Dad's letters in the final months of 1945 and into early 1946. During his three-year tour of service, he found himself in the North Atlantic, India, Africa, Australia, and finally in occupied Japan, although mostly he was on the vast and dangerous seas of the world. He worried that his children were getting big and might not even know him when he got home. He was lonely on the long voyages and, on occasion, did some personal reevaluation. For example, he reported to Mom on December 4, 1945: "I want to be more considerate of you than I was before."

I have no idea what lack of consideration Mom had endured earlier. Later, I would know Dad as a very good man who nonetheless could allow himself to be preoccupied with his own hunting and fishing passions, sometimes in ways that seemed less than considerate to his family. He was hardworking and faithful, the American ideal of the self-made man who could make what was needed, fix what was necessary, and do whatever he thought best. He had dreams that would enjoy only minimal fulfillment.

My father had chosen to isolate himself from his church roots as a young man, and then he was caught in the whirlwind of history. I think he was conscious of having little control over his early life, something he intended to correct after the war. Forced separation was hard on a struggling new family. The circumstance was further complicated by the possibility that Merchant Marines, once home, might be drafted into the Army since their seaman's duty was not recognized as regular military service. Fortunately, that did not happen in Dad's case.

Dad was discharged in March, 1946, in occupied Japan, endured a long voyage to Seattle, and then found his way across the continent to somehow begin a new life at home. A proud family fact is that Dad's brother William was the first American to set foot on the main island of Japan. He was on the plane carrying General Douglas McArthur and exited first to be sure all was set up and the cameras rolling for the General's grand arrival.

Dad told me in 1963 that he actually had received an induction notice while sailing somewhere on the stormy North Atlantic. Disgusted by such a disregard for his dangerous service as a Merchant Marine, he sent the notice back to the United States marked "address unknown." He had no idea, he told me with a twinkle in his eye, exactly where he was (riding on one huge and unidentified wave after another). What he knew for sure was that he already was in harm's way for his country! He never heard more about this induction attempt. The reason he told me of his action was that I was about to go to a western Pennsylvania courthouse for a marriage license, the same building where he had been registered for the draft many years before. He hoped his circumstance would not prove any problem for me. It did not.

In his many letters from sea, Dad sometimes would ask about "the kids." On September 13, 1945, he said, "Tell Barry to take care of the chickens." On November 7 he wrote: "Barry has a tendency to learn quickly, so he should get along alright in school. I'd like to be moved and settled [in Wisconsin] before he starts to regular school." The following week this came to Mom from Dad:

> I've been thinking of you and the children in the woods. I'm going to teach those children and you, if you care to learn, what I know of the outdoors and everything that goes with it. There is nothing, to my estimation, that can beat mother nature. I want to teach Barry in particular woodcraft, guns, and the woods in general. I believe someday it will come in handy for him.

Dad managed some such teaching over his remaining years. I came to share some of his sensitivities to nature, even though my living space and professional career would never be focused that way. During my growing-up years, Dad and I often would hunt or fish together. I enjoyed it for the most part, although it did not become my life's passion. I honor his dream and desire to share his passions with me. I carry a small amount of sadness that I was not exactly what he had hoped. During my Christmas vacations home from college, I would go hunting with him; but I would carry a camera instead of a gun—if I got my "shot," nothing would die or have to be cleaned when we got home.

Once finally home from the sea, Dad was reunited with his family in Newton Falls, Ohio, and in "the Valley," the New Brighton area of western Pennsylvania where we all were born. He had undergone one operation while at sea, having a rib removed to treat pneumonia. He spent some days in a Pittsburgh hospital to have his tonsils out, a bullet removed from his arm, and considerable dental work done. Occasionally his ships had been strafed by enemy warplanes. When men were caught on deck and did not get fully under cover, a bullet strike was the frequent result. Once out of the hospital, as he had dreamed, and with Mom staying with her job and us kids, Dad was off to Wausau, Wisconsin, to scout future possibilities.

Money and housing were scarce, but Dad was determined. He found a job working at a small industry that assembled windows and doors. It paid him $28 a week. He worked by day and looked for housing in his spare time. These were discouraging days that demanded maximum patience. He could not find affordable housing to rent for a family in this relatively small town. He did not have a car and realized that possibilities for locating a fishing camp to buy lay farther north in the state. Practical problems piled up.

Dad wrote to my mother on July 8, 1946, two days before my fifth birthday, saying that "things are just plain tough." Soon he was forced to go "back east," the end of the Wisconsin dream. My parents ended up buying a summer cottage in Craig Beach on Lake Milton, about six miles from Newton Falls in northeast Ohio. It had to be winterized so that it was habitable for a family of four to use all year. Dad did the work himself. He always would have a fishing boat docked on the nearby lake, having built both the boat and dock himself. In 2011 Emeth Press published my novel *StarWalker*. It was my way of recalling and honoring those post-war years in that little lakeside village.

My father stayed busy for the next twenty-eight years working as a carpenter, mostly in the mills of Youngstown twenty miles from Craig Beach. He never did develop a fishing/hunting camp of his own. Over the years from 1946 until his death in 1974, Dad and Mom lived in Craig Beach in the same little home on Beach Lane. In addition to his main employment, Dad was a volunteer fireman, local landlord (built and rented one house, with me helping to carry, measure, and pound or pull nails), building inspector, flock-finisher, locksmith, saw sharpener, and gun dealer. He was a constantly busy and enterprising man in a relatively isolated little piece of the world. It was my growing-up world.

Dad returned annually to nearby Pennsylvania to hunt deer and bear. Places like "Tionesta" sounded to me like the land of fairy tales. It actually was a town in the heart of deer country. The book *Buck Fever* by Mike Sajna (1990) shares well my dad's outdoor passion. He hunted rabbits and pheasants around northeast Ohio. For a few years when I was between thirteen and nineteen years old, our family took a week each summer to fish at a camp on Deer Lake in rural Ontario, Canada—special memories for me. My parents finally did buy two or three acres of rural land a few miles from our home in Craig Beach and developed "the Ranch" by putting in a small lake and an archery range. Dad named the place "Flyin' Arro Aquarama" and invited friends to this special little place on Cable Road, Portage County. A few came at first, but not many. My sister and I often rode out there in the back of Dad's pick-up truck to help do various maintenance things. Our father was never afraid of work, but his vision struggled to touch reality. Only in fragmentary and fragile ways did his original Wisconsin dream ever come true. Even so, he never quit trying.

My fourteenth birthday was special, and in my mind a model of Dad's mostly-failed dream. Our family was on vacation, the usual fishing trip to Deer Lake in Ontario, Canada. Eric and Vinnie Wickander owned a lodge and six family cabins on this deep and fish-rich lake—exactly the kind of setting my father had longed to own in Wisconsin. The Wickanders had immigrated to Canada from Norway during the economic depression of the 1930s. Eric's aging mother now had her own little home opposite the lodge. She decided that she liked my company.

Realizing that it was my fourteenth birthday, the older woman asked if I would row her out among the islands, some as small as one acre, with tall standing timber and rocky shorelines. I was delighted to do so. She then announced that she would give me the island of my choice as a birthday gift! Amazed, I beached the boat on an attractive island. We looked briefly at this little wonderland, she approved my choice, and I rowed her home. What my dad had dreamed for his family after the war I now was being given—almost, that is. When her son Eric heard of this generous verbal deal, he got angry, said his mom was getting a little irresponsible, and put a quick end to my brief illusion of foreign ownership of a virgin paradise island. I had tasted Dad's dream and also what I assume was his subsequent disillusionment.

Fading visions are sad things. I have not shared Dad's hunting/fishing camp dream (my island aside), although at times the idea offers some romantic fascination. The cold embers glowed freshly just a little in 2000 when my son Todd got interested in fishing and started taking his son Ian (then five) and daughter Emily (then three) with him—Ethan was too small, but not for long. I keenly remember one day helping Ian cast his line again and again, and on another day renting a boat on the little lake at Aqua Gardens in Anderson, Indiana, and rowing Todd and Ian to interesting spots so that they could try their luck. I did not have a fishing license and was happy just to provide the transportation for two new generations of Callen fishermen.

That Christmas, my wife Arlene and I gave Todd a silly "singing" fish mounted on a wall plaque, with money in its mouth to help Todd purchase the fishing boat he wanted. My father, then already dead for 26 years, would have been delighted! I chartered a boat and captain to go fishing on Lake Michigan with Todd when he was in high school—and again in July, 2007, this time taking Todd and his two sons Ian and Ethan. We landed eight, including two king salmon weighing about sixteen pounds each. Nothing like that ever swam in Lake Milton where I grew up as a kid!

I have never lost touch with the vision of the oceans that carried my father around the world in very dangerous times. There has remained with me a keen interest in the sea battles of World War II (especially those involving submarines). This has been a personal quest to gain a more intimate sense of relationship with Dad. This quest was expressed in my 2009 submarine novel *In Deep Water* and in my vacation cruises on the high seas—especially the one to Iceland in 2012 that crossed the North Atlantic where Dad often had sailed.

I share the following wisdom of Roger Dingman, written as he concluded his 1997 book *Ghost of War*: "Only by welcoming the ghost of war past and listening to the truths it teaches can we hope to drive away the specter of wars yet to come" (p. 256). It would not be until 2003 that I would first venture onto the open sea. My wife Arlene had died and my second wife, Jan, and I boarded a giant cruise ship in Florida, one totally unlike the danger-filled liberty ships of my father's war years. Even so, I felt in touch with him again. Jan and I would be blessed to do this often in the years to follow. I often would think of my father as we sailed on the open seas of the world.

My parents, each born in 1919, were part of a very special generation. Journalist Tom Brokaw journeyed to Normandy in the northwest of France in 1984 and then again in 1994 to prepare documentaries for the fortieth and fiftieth anniversaries of the dramatic Allied invasion of occupied Europe. These visits changed Brokaw's life. He became profoundly grateful for what that generation of Americans had done.

Brokaw came to believe that my father's and mother's was the best generation that any society has ever produced. Having come of age in the

Great Depression, they answered the call to save the world from two of the most powerful and ruthless military machines ever known, Germany and Japan. When it finally was over, Brokaw observes, the millions directly involved

> . . . joined in joyous and short-lived celebrations, then immediately began the task of rebuilding their lives and the world they wanted. They were mature beyond their years, married in record numbers, and gave birth to another distinctive generation, the Baby Boomers. They stayed true to their values of personal responsibility, duty, honor, and faith. They became part of the greatest investment in higher education that any society ever made [the GI Bill] and helped convert a wartime economy into the most powerful peacetime economy in history (*The Greatest Generation*, 1998, xix- xx).

I now take pride in that amazing generation, and have much respect for my parents having been a small part of it.

We all, to some extent, are carried along by the times in which we find ourselves. Little did I know in the late 1940s that I, a boy in limited financial and educational circumstances, would one day write a history of those decades (*Seeking the Light*, 1998) and the history of a mid-western church university impacted by the return home of the GIs after World War II (*Guide of Soul and Mind*, 1992). That impact opened the door for me to pursue a career in Christian higher education.

While my world would be quite different from that of my parents, their generation paved the way. As a pilgrim, I would walk a different path. However, the light guiding my way has been partly the afterglow of the journey of Mom and Dad, and the millions who traveled with them. See *Appendix G*, a small family tree beginning with my grandparents from the 1880s to the present.

Blarney Castle, Cork, Ireland, taken by me in 2006. It is a symbol of my Scotch-Irish heritage.

My grandparents Mary and Charles Callen.

Robert C. Callen, my father, a Merchant Marine in World War II.

WAR RATION BOOK No. 3

763610 Q

HARRY   L   CALLEN

My Uncle Van and me, 1942.

Charlotte, my mother, and me.

Young Bonnie Lou and Barry Lee Callen, in a
frame made by Dad.

Robert C. and Charlotte M. Callen, my
parents, in 1944.

Callen family at Craig Beach. My sister Bonnie and I pouring for our mother, father, and grandfather, about 1960

Barry as patriotic little boy at the end of World War II

Chapter 2

The Lake and the Valley

Good places to be born and grow up

My two worlds until young adulthood were mostly what my family called "the Lake" and "the Valley," meaning Lake Milton and its Craig Beach village in northeastern Ohio and the Beaver Falls/New Brighton or the Beaver Valley area fifty miles away in western Pennsylvania. I personally started in the latter area and was moved westward to the former at about age two. I grew up "out west" in Ohio. Even so, I was always aware of and occasionally visited the Valley, later returning there to attend college and marry.

The Fifties: Decade of Games and Growth

The world of my childhood was the midwestern United States of the 1950s. Robert Ellwood says this about the generation of my mother and father that set the stage for the fifties:

> This was the generation, born chiefly in the 1920s, that endured depression childhoods, fought the greatest war in history through to victory, returned to receive unprecedented education under the GI Bill. . .and went on to create an America affluent and technologically advanced beyond anything the past had imagined outside of science fiction....

It was the generation that parented the "baby boom," already making for overflowing church and school nurseries by 1950 (*1950: Crossroads of American Religious Life*, 2000, x).

On the negative side, in the 1950s there still was a considerable amount of racism, sometimes an uncritical patriotism, and certainly much materialism, all functioning awkwardly along with much new church-going. My parents' generation believed that problems could be solved, even as they had been solved in the face of the awesome challenges of the war years of the 1940s. They hoped they were right since there were significant new problems to face.

On June 25, 1950, communist armies from North Korea poured south across the thirty-eighth parallel, an artificial boundary set up by the occupying Allied powers five years before. The question of that fateful hour was: Is this the beginning of World War III? If so, it surely would be an Armageddon-like showdown. Even if a victor emerged, there might be little left that was alive or not dangerously radioactive. There was fear everywhere.

President Harry S. Truman, who earlier had ordered the dropping of two atomic bombs on Japan, would not concede the whole Asian peninsula to communism. He wrote in his diary: "It looks like World War III is here—I hope not—but we must meet whatever comes, and we will." Some military veterans of World War II were called back into service, including my wife's uncle, Frank Barber, and many of them died in Korea. Fortunately, Frank survived and my father was not called.

But even with all this foreboding in the air, the 1950s turned out to be a great time to grow through my teen years. The 1950s (just before the social revolts of the 1960s) joined the 1920s (just before the Great Depression) as a nostalgic decade of games and growth. The 1920s had been a happy era of prosperity, popular Republican presidents, and zany fads (the Charleston dance and goldfish swallowing, for instance). The

1950s was much the same, with Hula Hoops, Davy Crockett hats, Barbie dolls, and barbecue grills in backyards. Unlike the 1920s, the 1950s were not years to be followed immediately by economic depression, a big bust after a bustling boom—although the 1960s, my college, seminary, and first teaching years, would be extremely turbulent in other ways.

I grew up in the midst of times of relief from war when the nation's self-confidence was high and there was an abundance of economic expansion and social optimism. Most of the young people I knew were members of families with modest financial resources and limited cultural advantages. Our parents still carried vivid memories of economic hardship and war sacrifice. These memories were shared with the next generation in varying degrees, although we children were now being reared in a different world, one with rapidly expanding expectations.

The Youngstown, Ohio, area near my home in Craig Beach was heavily dependent on the steel industry. It had been one of the economically hardest hit industrial centers in the nation in the 1930s (low demand for steel). That changed in 1940 when huge quantities of war materials were needed quickly. Facilities in the immediate Youngstown area soon were turning out one-tenth of the nation's total steel production. Women flooded the workplace, including my mother.

In contrast with the volatile 1930s and 1940s, the 1950s seemed in many ways like the whisper of a quiet summer evening. Hopes were high, times were good, and most doors were open. The right people had won the terrible war. Goodness had prevailed and there was expanding affluence across America. While my family lived from paycheck to paycheck, we were never hungry—and we saw on the new television screens what others had and what might come our way one day soon.

Now mighty abroad, the world's major postwar power, the United States determined to be mighty at home, with production and consumption booming. Eight of the ten bestselling nonfiction books in 1950 had how-to and self-help emphases. They included *Betty Crocker's*

Picture Cook Book and *Look Younger, Live Longer* by Gayelord Hauser. People wanted to make everything work well. The ideal of American society seemed to be "togetherness," particularly a cohesive family unit enhanced by the buying of one's own home. We owned ours in Craig Beach, modest as it was. It had been a summer cottage. My tiny bedroom had been the front porch. With all of its limitations, it was ours. Like the nation, my Dad kept working on it to make it better, and Mom did what she could to keep it livable inside.

Mine has been called the "Silent Generation." We were born in the mid-1930s through the mid-1940s (1941 for me). We were sandwiched between two better-known generations, born too late to be World War II heroes (the "Greatest Generation," our parents) and too early to be among the "Boomers," the bigger crowd that disrupted things in the 1960s. We came of age after World War II and tiptoed cautiously in a post-crisis social order filled with new possibilities. We rarely talked about "changing the system" and kept our heads down during the McCarthy era. We didn't have to wait for a depression or war to end. A booming post-war economy was ready for us to join right out of school. We were the "Lucky" generation, although a "Cold War" creeped across our sunlit times—something always does.

Americans were becoming fascinated with the new communication and entertainment medium called television. The number of TV stations in the nation skyrocketed from 6 in 1946 to 442 in 1956. In 1947, Burr Tillstrom went on the air in Chicago with "Kukla, Fran, & Ollie," one of the most loved children's TV programs of all time. By the middle of the 1950s, 66 percent of all American homes had television sets and bulky antennas rising awkwardly above their roofs. This dramatic development in family life was to alter social values and patterns significantly. It brought widely diverse people together for the first time in common cultural experiences.

I remember my first contact with television around 1950. A local Craig Beach family got a TV set and invited the little neighborhood to their living room to watch a late-evening boxing match (they charged a nominal admission fee to their house, probably to help pay for the set!). Boxers Archie Moore, Sugar Ray Robinson, Rocky Marciano, and Ezzard Charles became household names, as did the wrestler Gorgeous George. What a fascination it all was! On the first telecast of his *See It Now* program (November 18, 1951), Edward R. Murrow was able to show simultaneous pictures of the Brooklyn and Golden Gate Bridges, commenting: "We are impressed by a medium through which a man sitting in his living room has been able for the first time to look at two oceans at once." The times were amazing.

Disneyland opened to the public in July, 1955—not to me, of course, since California seemed like another world, and I was never more than fifty miles from our house, except for the fishing trips to Canada. It was a playground of welcome nostalgia, imagination, and innocent fun for the whole family. In many ways, Disneyland was a symbol of the 1950s. Teenagers of the time tended to focus their lives around the *Top 10* songs on the radio. Some of the most popular artists were Patti Page, Tony Bennett, Kay Starr, Bing Crosby, Eddie Fisher, Perry Como, Nat King Cole, Rosemary Clooney, and groups like the Ames Brothers and Andrews Sisters. Most popular songs were idealistic and sentimental portrayals of a dream world of love and romance. People were trying to forget war, although the "cold war" was always present and threatening.

High school students in 1956 were singing and dancing to Elvis Presley's *Love Me Tender*, followed the next year by songs of the Everly Brothers and new teen idols Paul Anka, Pat Boone, and Ricky Nelson. Dean Martin, from Stubenville, Ohio, near Youngstown, first teamed with Jerry Lewis in 1947 to become a leading comedy duo of the 1950s. Gene Kelly captured the postwar American mood. His clever and light-hearted dancing was never better than in the beloved 1952 movie *Singing in the Rain.*

The McGuire Sisters was a beautifully harmonizing trio from a Church of God pastor's home in Ohio. Their big break came in 1952 on Arthur Godfrey's *Talent Scouts* show, with "Sugartime" soon one of their songs that I and all my friends recognized immediately. Another hit song of the time was *Everything's Coming Up Roses.* At least in general, that is the way it really seemed to be in the popular culture. I absorbed it all. However, for financial, location, and religious reasons, I rarely participated in travel, school dances, or cultural events. Although certainly far from destitute, our family and our little village of Craig Beach were relatively poor and rather sheltered from "the world."

Our religious life was conservative, frowning on things like dancing and movies. Craig Beach, Ohio, sitting quietly on the western shore of Lake Milton, had little to offer culturally. There was no local library or theater, but soon there were television sets. By 1959, when I was a high school senior, the really popular TV shows were dominated by brash, frontier-crossing, good-guy westerns. There was *Gunsmoke, Wagon Train, Have Gun—Will Travel, The Rifleman, Maverick,* and *Tales of Wells Fargo.* These were joined by the slapstick comedy of *The Jackie Gleason Show, I Love Lucy,* and *The Red Skelton Show.* The nation was expanding, recovering, conquering, laughing, experimenting—and constantly driving. Only 84,000 cars had been produced in the U. S. in 1945 and there were gasoline restrictions on the use of cars for private purposes. But by 1955, annual sales of cars had rebounded to 7.9 million! And what cars they were.

Many vehicles of the 1950s had large V-8 engines, tail fins, and decorative chrome. These bloated Fords, Chevrolets, and Chryslers were signs of the times, carriers of the image Americans had of themselves. By the end of the 1950s, 77 percent of all American families owned at least one car, and there were many new places to take them. There was an expanding motel industry. There were drive-in movie lots. Banks and restaurants were opening drive-through service. In 1955, the first McDonalds started selling hamburgers in Des Plaines, Illinois. Even food became "fast" and car related. Dad always had a pick-up truck and we also had a modest car that my mother drove mostly, often taking my sister Bonnie and me somewhere (Dad was usually busy).

Those years in Craig Beach seemed relatively simple and carefree, but basically good even if sometimes boring and with little money in the pocket. I do remember sore knees from picking clover in our backyard to feed our rabbits—cheaper than buying commercial pellets. I remember "cleaning" rabbits that Dad had killed with a shotgun. Picking hairs off that sticky inner skin was a task I detested, especially when my fingers were numb with the cold. We village kids trick-or-treated around the local streets at Halloween with lots of homemade fun and little fear of danger in the dark. My boyhood friend Shirley Meeker found the Village of Craig Beach a wonderful place to grow up. In the summers she played on the lake and joined our classmates Delores Ward and John Steffans in operating and maintaining rides for children, a bowling alley, and concession stands in the local amusement park just two blocks down Beach Lane from my home. Years later, I would write *StarWalker*, a novel set in my little home village of Craig Beach.

Each summer, many families of the area would go to the nearby Canfield Fair, one of the bigger and best in the nation. Its 114th annual convening happened during the summer of 1959 just as I was graduating from high school and ready to start college. Some 50,000 cars were coming in and out of its parking lots each summer. The Canfield Fair proudly exhibited the life of the nation ever since its founding in 1846 as the Mahoning County Agricultural Society.

In the 1950s, the fair featured several firsts, including live television coverage, an air-conditioned exhibit, the General Motors Futurama Show, the Lennon Sisters of the *Lawrence Welk Show* singing to overflow grandstand crowds, and Gabby Hayes, veteran of many western movies. It was America on parade in northeast Ohio. Going there was a highlight of my summers. I remember how excited my grandmother VanArsdale would get when the band of a local high school would come marching by. She could not help but follow them.

The American population had shifted from surviving the Depression (1930s) to winning the war (1940s) to trying to win the peace (1950s). Every weekday morning beginning in 1952, Dave Garroway hosted the popular *Today Show* on television, ending each edition of the news with his right hand raised and his gentle voice offering to the viewing public the sincere benediction, "Peace!"

Americans surely hoped so. It was a fast-moving and still dangerous world. There were atomic bombs and a "cold war." I was still a kid, rather shy and busy with my simple distractions and private anxieties. I was fortunate to have around me good people who cared about me and guided me in mostly good ways, and that certainly included the church. I had a sturdy heritage from the "old world" and grew up in a fresh, expanding, even if a still troubled "new world."

A Wonderful Home Church

While we Ohio Callens always kept our family and Free Methodist church contacts in "the Valley," I was nurtured spiritually nearer to Craig Beach in a young and wonderful congregation of loving Christian people. My grandparents Charles and Mayme (Main) VanArsdale, had married in June, 1906. It was not until the 1940s that Grandpa began working in Newton Falls and first discovered there the congregation of the Church of God movement (Anderson). It was a new congregation meeting at first in the home of Elmer and Elizabeth Sowers on Jay Street. Elizabeth was shepherd for this little flock until circumstances shifted that role to her daughter Lillie.

The VanArsdales had a rich heritage in the Free Methodist Church, as did my other grandparents, Rev. Charles and Mary (Rose) Callen. Our arrival in Newton Falls was only because of the relocation of the Ideal Foundry from Beaver Falls, Pennsylvania, after a fire in the old plant. Grandpa VanArsdale kept his job and followed the company to its new location in Ohio. My mother got a job at the nearby "Arsenal," a large munitions factory built close to Newton Falls to support the war. A committed Christian layperson, Grandpa immediately searched for a new church home, soon tired of the drive to Warren where the nearest Free Methodist congregation was, and began testing the options in Newton Falls.

Grandpa chose the little Church of God congregation on Jay Street, primarily because of the inspiring biblical preaching of its young female pastor, Lillie (Sowers) McCutcheon ("Sister Lillie"). Until his death in 1967, he would remain a loyal and loved saint in this congregation. As quoted in my later biography of her (*She Came Preaching*, 1992), Sister Lillie recalled this about me and my family:

> It was a sunny Sunday morning many years ago when I first met Dr. Callen. While greeting people coming to worship in a humble little chapel on Jay Street in Newton Falls, I noted a saintly grandfather nearing the church entrance. Barry was a timid little boy tightly holding his grandfather's hand. Bonnie, his little sister, was grasping the grandfather's other hand as they all three entered the chapel. Beginning that day, Barry's family made the First Church of God in Newton Falls, Ohio, their church home.

This family did not include my father—he was a church-respecting but not a church-going person during my early years.

This exceptional pastor commonly called "Sister Lillie" had a profound impact on my life. All the while, however, my grandfather VanArsdale—and thus me—kept active touch with the Free Methodist Church "back home" in the Valley. Particularly relevant was the Free Methodist congregation in New Brighton, the city where I was born and the congregation pastored by my grandfather Callen from 1936 to 1940. The other religious site of significance to me was the camp grounds of the Free Methodist Church located in East Liverpool, Ohio.

There is a point in the beautiful Ohio Valley where a part of Columbiana County witnesses the Ohio River touch the intersection of the states of Ohio, Pennsylvania, and West Virginia. Some potters from England migrated there because of its rich clay resources. They nostalgically named the town Liverpool after their English home. In 1834 it was incorporated as East Liverpool, adding the "East" because a town in Ohio already had used the name Liverpool. It became known as "Crockery City." Early in the twentieth century, next to the city's scenic Thompson Park, the Free Methodist Church began building a camp grounds, a circle of about fifty private cottages with a large tabernacle in the middle. The Morrison Baker family from New Brighton and my VanArsdale grandparents were two of the first cottage owners dating back to about 1930.

This camp ground would later become sacred in my memory. I spent at least one week each summer of my early life in and around the VanArsdale cottage. It had several beds separated only by curtains hung on a network of wires. The little bathroom (no plumbing) contained only a "slop jar" that had to be carried daily down the little gravel street and dumped into one of the several holes in the men's outhouse. I took my turn carrying, heard many fiery campmeeting sermons in the nearby tabernacle, and finally accepted Christ as my own personal Savior at this camp meeting altar in East Liverpool. I was thirteen years old.

Ralph Page was one ministerial model that I looked up to in that setting. He was energetic, self-giving, warm, and loving. I did not know until many years later that, in his earlier life, he was a good friend of Evelyn Cooley, mother of Arlcne, my first wife. If Evelyn had married him instead of Donald Cooley, her life would have been so different! I was fortunate in being influenced toward Christ by Ralph Page and eventually marrying Evelyn's daughter.

Back at the Newton Falls church in Ohio, Austin Sowers, associate pastor and brother of Sister Lillie (the pastor), was much like Ralph Page, enthusiastic, self-giving, an excellent Christian role model for me. I was more blessed than I knew at the time. My life values, faith, and vocational direction were being set.

The Western Shore in the Western Reserve

Today, North Jackson, Ohio, is a small community of about one thousand people clustered around the crossing of Route 45 (north/south) and Mahoning Avenue (Route 18, west/east). It sits about eleven miles west of Youngstown, nine miles south of Warren, and five miles east of Lake Milton. While many of the surroundings appear primarily agricultural, the immediate area is heavily industrialized. Things have changed little since 1959 when I graduated from the local high school there. Exceptions are the building of the huge auto assembly plant of General Motors in nearby Lordstown, Lake Milton becoming a state park instead of the property of Youngstown, and the high school building I knew so well in North Jackson being torn down in 2010 and replaced with a new one located closer to Lake Milton.

North Jackson is named in honor of President Andrew Jackson. It is part of the old "Western Reserve" of the state of Connecticut. One publisher used "Everysmalltown, U.S.A." in referring to North Jackson. It is surrounded by farms and factories, recreational lakes and super highways. Of particular significance is the nearby resort area of Lake Milton. This lake, now a well-developed state park, has long been a summer playground for many Youngstown, Akron, Cleveland, and Pittsburgh residents. But in the 1950s it was the permanent home of only a few hundred people, including me as a boy. I grew up on the lake's western shore in the village of Craig Beach.

Lake Milton was originally formed by the construction of a dam in 1914-1917 intended to create an industrial water reservoir for Youngstown and provide area flood control. It was later used more for recreational purposes. A maximum of one mile wide and about five miles long, this lovely lake provided fishing, recreational boating, and attractive shoreline. By the 1930s there was an amusement park and public beach along the western shore at Craig Beach.

In my earliest years, there was still standing the big wooden roller coaster, then unused because there had been a death on it. Near the park's entrance was the grocery store operated by the parents of my high school friend Betty Baldwin. The store was a stop for the school bus. We were allowed to wait inside on cold winter days. The stop and store were just two blocks from my modest home, a winterized summer cottage like most in Craig Beach at the time. In the hot evenings of summer, I would fall asleep with my window open, listening to the music of the merry-go-round playing down the street. The room was a closed-in front porch, just large enough for a bed and facing dresser—which touched the bed so that the bottom drawer would barely open.

The population of Craig Beach (minus the big influx of weekend summer visitors) was 198 in 1940 and 569 in 1950. We Callens had added to this growth by four in 1946 when Dad located us there after his war years at sea. On weekends in the summers of the late 1950s, thousands of others joined the local residents to play at the beach and in the adjacent amusement park. The park and beach were the gathering points for youth from neighboring communities. Locals from my high school class sometimes would sit on the guardrail along the street between the park and beach and taunt carloads of cruising youth from out of town. Occasionally, the coarse fun took an ugly turn.

My classmates Charles Williams, John Steffans, and Frank Balent were once hanging around the dance hall in the amusement park on a summer evening. Two students from nearby Austintown were there. My Jackson-Milton friends "mouthed off," trying to intimidate the outnumbered visitors. This time it backfired. Before the evening was over, several carloads of young Austintowners pulled up and went into action. Charles was beaten badly. He was fortunate that bruises, cuts, and a little humiliation were all that he suffered. I often wandered through the park, but was careful to stay clear of trouble. I was shy and hardly a fighter. With little or no money in my pocket, and as instructed by my parents, I avoided the bowling alley where the smokers hung out.

Most Craig Beach families, including mine, were short on extra cash. I had to amuse myself by riding a bicycle when I had one and swimming when the weather allowed. I often threw a baseball straight up in the air on the street in front of our house. When no one else was available, I played catch with gravity, a companion always available to me! When little crabapples fell to the ground in our backyard, I cleared the place by throwing them into the little woods beyond Dad's shed, pretending to be a big-league pitcher. I was a fan of the Cleveland Indians baseball team and tried to hear most games on a radio when not in school.

Although my family did not have a television set until the early 1950s, I was aware that in 1948 Milton Berle had begun appearing regularly on the *Texaco Star Theater*. His would be a remarkable entertainment career, not ending until shortly before his death in 2002 at age ninety-three. "Uncle Miltie" was hardly the best moral model, but he surely was funny and I came to love him. His autobiography still sits on my office shelf, as does the 2001 one of James Arness (Marshall Matt Dillon of *Gunsmoke*).

Dad had hunting dogs and we sometimes raised rabbits for selling and eating. To save buying any unnecessary pellets for rabbit feed, I and my sister spent numerous hours on our knees picking clover from the yard—backbreaking work often leaving me with a bad case of frustration and poison ivy. Every summer I got painted pink with a lotion that was supposed to help my itching misery.

Our immediate neighbors included one family that had violence and alcohol problems. Another family had two autistic children that I often watched pacing about their little fenced-in front yard with uncontrollable body motions. The elderly Husteds lived across the street. Frank had a cancer operation that included placing a large metal plate in his protruding stomach—an arresting sight that I saw daily. Our village may have been a little place, but most of the problems that plague humanity resided within its boundaries.

The Husteds were Roman Catholics from the nearby St. Catherine's parish—and they had a television. These were the years before Vatican Council II. One day I, a nominal young Protestant, was surprised to hear that the local Lake Milton priest had directed his flock not to watch on television the preaching of a popular new Baptist evangelist, Billy Graham. That seemed to me quite narrow, defensive, and arrogant. My own association in Newton Falls with the Church of God congregation (Anderson) inclined me to be suspicious of anything Roman Catholic.

Catholicism had begun locally with the first mass of the St. James parish in North Jackson convening in the old gymnasium of the high school in 1937. More related to my family's religious heritage was the Methodist congregation in nearby Pricetown where I once attended a summer Vacation Bible School. I recall playing among the tombstones next to the church. Even more congenial to the ecumenical ideal of the Church of God movement (Anderson) was the First Federated Church located next to the North Jackson High School. It was the merger in 1929 of three denominations, and the home congregation of my high school friend Ian Worley.

Kids living in Craig Beach were on the outer edges of two school districts. In March, 1954, I began high school by being bused to Newton Falls seven miles from Craig Beach, with the next three years being taken by bus to North Jackson High School several miles the other way. Some of these long rides were quite eventful—noise, teasing, even an occasional fight that I tried hard to avoid. My sister Bonnie, two years behind me, was spared the awkwardness of these Newton Falls rides and changing high schools after only one year.

During my freshman year, I had no idea that there was a key meeting going on in nearby Warren that involved a man who later would be a very important person in my life. The occasion was a staff meeting for the guidance of the National Association of the Church of God (Anderson), a largely African-American organization that centered its life on the "Zion's Hill" camp grounds in nearby West Middlesex, Pennsylvania. The man was James Earl Massey, then a young pastor in Detroit, Michigan.

While I was trying to get settled in Newton Falls High School, the ministry of Rev. Massey was being criticized unfairly. In fact, at this Warren meeting, in the very presence of Rev. Massey, a key older minister accused him from the pulpit of teaching deviations from accepted truth. How painful for a proud and unusually gifted young pastor! But for me at the time, it was a complete non-event. Not until 2002, when I would be Editor of Anderson University Press and completing my work on the autobiography of Dr. Massey (*Aspects of My Journey*), did I first encounter this information about the 1954 meeting. By then he was my beloved friend and highly valued colleague. In later years I would edit and publish several books by and about him, including the celebrated *Views from the Mountain* that preserves many of his writings.

Relatively oblivious of the larger world, with all of its unfairness, I was preoccupied with the problems and joys very close to home. I vividly recall walking on hot summer evenings through the local amusement park to the stand by the road just opposite the beach. It featured fries sprinkled with vinegar—a wonderful aroma and taste that occasionally I could afford! There also were the cruising cars with radios playing and macho egos on display. I was not one of the "tough guys." Sometimes there was trouble enough without creating more. I remember vividly one frightening night when we realized that a home a few blocks away was ablaze—it was the home of my classmate John Steffans. Dad was a volunteer fireman, but nothing could be done to save that home

One day at the Pricetown elementary school (where I attended grades one through eight), I broke my collarbone playing pum pum polloway—our games at recess could get rather rough. When I was in eighth grade, the school sidewalk was covered with ice, a young girl banged into me from behind, and my fall left me with a broken arm (it was embarrassing to be "taken out" by a young girl). Before the cast came off, I suffered a case of the measles—a miserably itchy situation under a hot cast. Childhood diseases spread rapidly and immunizations were less common then. By my high school years, in addition to the measles, I lived through significant bouts of scarlet fever, mumps, chicken pox, and whooping cough, the latter leaving me with pneumonia that put me in St. Joseph's hospital in Warren, Ohio, for a week. This was the only time between my birth and my late sixties (cancer-related treatments) that I was ever a patient for any reason.

My cousin Cecil Scott was my teacher at the time of my early hospitalization. I was in the fifth grade at Pricetown. She brought homework to the hospital so that I would not get behind in anything. Her son, my cousin Bob, was my own age and a special friend. The Scotts also lived at Craig Beach beginning in 1946, having migrated westward from Pennsylvania after time in New Jersey during the war. George, Bob's father, had worked at a shipyard and at night taught welding to women who were urgently needed in the wartime work force. Then in 1952 the Scotts moved the six miles to Newton Falls where Bob attended high school. Those few miles kept our families from having frequent contact.

Although I felt a call to Christian ministry in the early 1960s, Bob Scott's call did not come until 1975. After he graduated from New Orleans Baptist Seminary in 1980, he and I had much in common beyond family ties and early boyhood memories. In 2001 he moved back to northeast Ohio, a mature Baptist pastor. I recall meeting him for breakfast in Medina in August, 2002, as I was passing through on my way to the West Middlesex Campmeeting where James Earl Massey was being honored by my release of his new autobiography—so different from that cloud of suspicion he had been under back in 1954. Bob looked old and tired to me, and clearly was anxious to make his last few years of ministry meaningful. We reflected fondly on our deceased parents. It had been quite a journey for them, and now quite the memories for us.

My family had migrated to Craig Beach in 1946 as part of the process of my father and mother putting their lives back together after the wrenching experience of World War II. They built a life in the village, with Dad usually traveling to the Youngstown area twenty miles away for his main employment as a carpenter. Dad's IRS tax report for 1948 records his employment by five area companies that year, for a total income of $3,400. He was initiated into the United Brotherhood of Carpenters and Joiners of America in October, 1946, and faithfully paid his required dues for nearly thirty years, even when there was no work and it was a hardship ($2.75 per month in the late 1950s, growing to $9.20 in 1969). He was loyal to his union, and I presume gained benefit from it generally, although sometimes there were many weeks in the winter when little construction was going on and he was unemployed.

Dad went deer and even bear hunting in western Pennsylvania when the seasons came, whether he had work or not. There was friction around our house when he went away with his guns in spite of work being available. The out-of-state deer license was not cheap, but the hunting culture was in his very being. My father certainly had a lifelong passion for hunting in Pennsylvania, where deer have been hunted since at least 14,000 B.C.

As a teenager, Dad managed to shoot a deer that he had to track for some distance before it died. Darkness soon settled in, forcing him to curl up under a pine tree, cover himself with pine needles, and stay with his deer for the night. The next morning he proudly approached his home, only to see police cars. He asked someone what was wrong and was told that some kid was lost in the woods. He volunteered to go inside, get a quick breakfast, and then help with the hunt—only to learn through the clear displeasure of his parents that he was the cause of all the trouble! On another occasion, he entered a barn to ask if he could be permitted to hunt on that property. Suddenly, a bullet from a 22 rifle entered his shoulder. He fled, the wound healed, and only later when a doctor was removing shrapnel from a wartime wound was the bullet again discovered.

Those who got home safely from war in 1945 and 1946 looked for a more normal life. Some headed back to the peace of the mountains and woods where forgetting global brutality came more easily. Dad was drawn to the wilderness. On the first Monday after Thanksgiving, the usual start of deer season in Pennsylvania, the "Pumpkin Army" (called this because of the bright orange hunting clothes) would descend on the region just north of the picturesque little town of Callensburg (founded by my ancestor Hugh Callen, Sr., with its history recorded by Arnold Kepple). In 1985, Pennsylvania had 1.1 million licensed hunters (second only to Texas), with many transplants like Dad joining the crowd from across the border in Ohio. They were in quest of big game, yes, but these servants of industries in the Pittsburgh and Youngstown areas also wanted to be soothed by the calming of the big woods and the experience of the heart-pounding rush of the hunt.

Americans treasure the image of pioneer hunters forging their way across frontiers and carving out of the wilderness the greatest nation of all times. That image fit Dad. He was part owner of a hunting cabin near Boone Mountain. I visited there with him only once—a memorable experience, something of a right of passage into manhood. I never joined the Pumkin Army, but my heart loves the wilderness.

Dad respected nature, killed for meat and not mere sport, and was a bit "macho." It was typical for the times. Men may have been tender inside, but they also were consciously self-made and independent. Mom and Dad were community-minded people, known and respected by everyone in the village of Craig Beach. Mom was a civil defense officer and helped with elections by handling paperwork at the voting place (the local fire station). She was the Craig Beach and Pricetown reporter for the weekly Newton Falls newspaper, and was sensitive to life at the local elementary school. This sensitivity can be seen in the poem she wrote when I was beginning the fourth grade. Called "A Challenge," Charlotte M. Callen wrote the following for the 1951-1952 calendar of Pricetown Elementary School:

> Let's make this a year of gladness
> For our children and our friends.
> We can work and play together
> Long before the school term ends.
>
> Not for fame or any honor
> Should we strive for, after all;
> But let a few good seeds be scattered;
> It'll be worth our efforts small.
>
> We will grow! Perhaps not in stature,
> But we'll show our spirit strong;
> Then our school will be the victor
> And they'll see us thrive 'ere long.

Dad served a term on the local school board, became the village building inspector, and was a volunteer fireman and Scoutmaster of Troup 66 in Pricetown beginning in 1951. "Callen" was a good family name locally.

I went through the full Cub Scout program with the support of my parents. I never had the opportunity to be a Boy Scout, although later, with my wife Arlene by my side and in our twenties when I was a seminary student in Anderson, Indiana, I would serve for two summers as the chaplain and dining hall manager of a large Scout camp in central Indiana, Camp Kikthawenund. Arlene was assistant cook. She was hardly the outdoors type, but the experience was mostly good. It even inspired in me the thought of being a military chaplain when I finished seminary. I think I would have enjoyed that role, but it was not to be.

While young and full of life, my first facing of death came on February 21, 1954. I recall playing ball on the street in front of our Beach Lane home in Craig Beach. Suddenly I had to move over to let an ambulance go by. It was an unusual sight that turned ominous when it went on for two blocks and turned into the driveway of the home of my grandparents. Soon I learned that my grandmother VanArsdale had suffered a massive cerebral hemorrhage and would live only a few hours in a Warren hospital. Mayme (Main) VanArsdale was born February 22, 1882, in Dempseytown, Pennsylvania, to Theodore Main and Margaret Maule Main and lived for seventy years.

Our family went back to New Brighton, Pa., "the Valley," my birthplace, for the funeral. It was a sobering experience for me, and also an enriching connection with my extended family. In fact, just one week later we were back in the same facility in New Brighton for the funeral of my maternal grandfather's mother, my great grandmother, Fannie Paulson, who was born in 1861 in Fallston, Pennsylvania, and died on March 6, 1954. In later years, we also returned to the Valley for the funerals of my mother's sister and brother, my aunt and uncle Evangeline and Laverne VanArsdale. Young's Funeral Home in New Brighton has been a place for the family to gather and grieve.

A decision was made that I should begin to spend evenings and overnights during the school week with my grandfather VanArsdale. He was now a widower and his house was only two blocks away. The intersection between our homes was where I caught the school bus. I remember his cooking oats every morning while he played records of gospel songs. I loved him, saw him cope well with his grief, and could not imagine that many years later I would be buying a little condo for myself in Anderson, Indiana, after my wife had died—and with my grandchildren living only a few blocks away. I piled too much sugar on my hot oats each morning, but also tasted the sweetness of Grandpa's spirit.

A North Jackson Blue Jay

I vividly recall being bused the seven miles to Newton Falls High School for my freshman year. I knew nobody at the school except my cousin Bob Scott. I was quite unsure of myself in the "big town"—population 5,000 compared to the 400 of Craig Beach. Soon I found myself in a carefully monitored crowd of students. We were taking an "IQ" test, the first time in my life. I was tempted to doubt my capacity to survive all of this, but I did. My score was well above average, I was told, not a genius, to be sure, but good enough to pursue any academic challenge I wished. Of course, I had no idea of all the academics that would be ahead of me.

I remember being introduced to the fascination of algebra and having our bus driver, a leather-skinned woman named Gertie, stop the bus one day on the country road and announce that we would just sit there instead of going on to school if the loud noise and wild actions did not stop. I was a little embarrassed and frightened. Many of us were intimidated by the "big town" school—only to learn later that some in Newton Falls were nervous about us, the mean country crowd suddenly joining them. I made one good friend, Roger Carrier. He came from a conservative Christian family and had a very gentle spirit, things I could relate to easily. We "lake kids" stayed at the Newton Falls school only one year and then were bused the other way to North Jackson for our final three years. It was a political decision. We just went where we were told. Now I would be a "Blue Jay."

The world was at peace in the sense of a lack of open international warfare. Unfortunately, school administrators at Jackson-Milton High School sometimes found themselves in conflict with some students—the petty little wars in which people regularly live. Superintendent John Rayburn was thought by some not to like the group of students from the Lake Milton area who had arrived for their sophomore year in 1956. That year, a young woman just out of college began and ended her teaching career. What happened to her was silly at first, and then very sad.

This new teacher came to Jackson-Milton with a prim-'n-proper elitist attitude and a sincere love for fine literature. Soon feeling uncomfortable with the lack of sophistication and expected academic seriousness of her class, she told us that we were products of a relatively primitive farming community, a description heard by the rascals in the class as "a bunch of ignorant farmers." They were offended and decided to get even. For the next few days, some of my friends (not me!) came to class with patches on their pants or skirts, straw in their hair, and even a little deliberately planted barn odor. Occasionally, they would unscrew classroom lightbulbs before her arrival and then, to our teacher's confusion and embarrassment, tighten them when she had gone to get janitorial help. For her, the whole experience was so disturbing that apparently she had a nervous breakdown and abandoned teaching. I would learn personally in a few years that teaching can be a real challenge, and that students are real people with feelings as well as limitations.

While none of my friends meant that drastic a result for the young teacher, they had no wish to be treated as stupid "country hicks." A few of them were capable of a little violence. Hardly a fighter by temperament myself, I had strong religious roots and tendencies more intellectual than combative. This is why I gained a lifelong friend in the gentle-natured Roger Carrier in Newton Falls and soon gravitated to Ian Worley in North Jackson. He was a brilliant young man whose parents were college professors at the university in nearby Youngstown. Decades later, both Roger and Ian would remain my friends, Roger with a career in the steel industry in Warren, Ohio, and Ian a professor of environmental science at the University of Vermont.

A few students in my high school class had part-time jobs and even their own cars. Most came to school in buses, including those of us from the Lake Milton area. One day Virginia and Freda began an eye-scratching brawl on the bus, for what reason no one now remembers. Most of the time class members spent their high school years figuring out who they were, what life's pecking order was, and what should come next. Many, like the gentle and delightful Delores Ward from Craig Beach, had no expectation of college, little academic inclination, and more interest in friends and extra-curricular activities.

Sports was big. John Steffans hated high school, but loved playing football for Jackson-Milton. Local sports fever was especially high in 1954 when the Cleveland Indians excited Ohio and the nation with one of the great baseball seasons of all time. Unfortunately, a hard lesson lay just ahead. This team of apparent destiny lost the World Series to the New York Giants in four straight games! The class of 1959 was learning about life, about both the thrill of victory and the agony of defeat.

We lived in an area that competed hard and was used to winning. Jim Brown carried the football 12,312 yards for the Cleveland Browns from 1957 to 1965, a dramatic career. Ohio State University went to the Rose Bowl three times in the 1950s, beating its West Coast rivals every time. Sports was something in which at least young men were expected to excel. I wore number "65" on the Blue Jays varsity basketball team. While my number was big, we lost more games than we won. My highlight game was in the 1958-1959 season when we beat Austintown in overtime, in part because of my career-high twenty-eight points. My athletic abilities were modest, but I really enjoyed the game and the team experience. I could have done without the fleet Richard Treharne, my teammate, calling me "Pussyfoot," a name somewhere between a tease and a taunt.

My high school certainly had its academic, cultural, and extra-curricular limitations, as did many of the homes from which we students came; but it also had its share of program diversity and opportunities for the setting and time. Latin was still taught as a foreign language, a holdover from a more classic curriculum. Taking two years of this language helped me in my later literary and teaching careers. There was a chapter of the National Honor Society to which I belonged during my junior and senior years. My induction was a symbol of important things to come in my life. The date of the all-school ceremony in the gymnasium was February 26, 1958. The sponsor of the local chapter of the NHS was Juanita Siesholts, an older woman on the faculty who taught me Latin in the classroom and now supported a public recognition of my academic achievements and potential. I'm in her debt.

Shirley Meeker, my classmate from Craig Beach who had strong theatrical interests, choreographed all of our school's staged events from 1957 to 1959. She has remained a friend to this day, living in Florida, serving older person's with mental deterioration and being a professional clown on the side (she was an amateur one in high school). I had a very small acting and group-singing part in one musical production in which, with almost teary-eyed nostalgia, we would sing "Red sails in the sunset, Way out on the sea, Oh carry my loved one, Home safely to me." I would never "act" again. It would be late in life before I would be part of any organized singing group. It would be the sanctuary choir of Park Place Church of God in Anderson, Indiana. I regret my lack of musical training when I was young, something that would frustrate me later since I love great music.

There were formal-dress dances on a few celebration occasions in my high school. The air would fill with popular songs like Tammy by Debbie Reynolds, *Twilight Time* by The Platters, and *Volare* by Domenico Modugno. Most students loved these school events as social highlights. Others, like me, lacked much in the way of dress-up clothes and ready transportation for evening events at the school six miles away. Further, I faced a religiously-based critique of the morality of dances—a good excuse to avoid what was socially awkward for me anyway. Even so, I heard the romantic longing in the words "Heavenly shades of night are falling, it's twilight time…. Each day I pray for evening, just to be with you, Together at last at twilight time." I was something of a closet romantic with two left feet.

A few members of my class of 1959 got beyond sports and personal identity issues and managed to focus on taking academics seriously. I was one of them. My parents were not college people, but especially my mother saw its value. They both were open to the possibility for me. In an English class I wrote a serious essay on the Hungarian Freedom Fighters, based on the daring and idealistic revolt in 1956 that was crushed quickly by the Soviet Union. My high school principal and English teacher, Mary Lucy Lauban, liked this writing effort. I think it was my very first. She spoke of it appreciatively to the class, and even made an effort to have it considered for national publication. This was the humble beginning of my literary career—launched in part by the high standards and active encouragement of a teacher. Now, in my late seventies, I am often called upon and more than happy to mentor young writers for a new generation.

In my boyhood home at Craig Beach, the phone number to be cranked by hand was three longs and three shorts. Usually, several people on the "party line" would quietly answer almost any call to check on whether the conversation was interesting enough to warrant extended listening. There was other "fun" and sometimes a little change in the pocket to spend at Baldwin's Market or Shultz's store, the two places in the village where food and a few other items could be bought.

Betty Baldwin was a quiet and gentle member of my class. She came from a conservative Christian home, so we had common values. We went to the senior prom together, riding with another couple, and dancing very little (I had no car and had barely figured out the simple Waltz pattern for my feet to follow). I remember justifying this dancing by reporting that our basketball coach said it was great training for the calves of the legs if one stayed on tip toes while doing the steps. It seemed legitimate to enhance my basketball skills. I was careful to limit the female contact.

Real trouble came on occasion. During our sophomore year, Frank Stroney was nearly killed. He was on his way to a dance with friends when he lost control of his car on an icy road and soon was being given the last rites by a priest. He did survive and was tutored by classmate Ian Worley in his effort to catch up with lost class work. Ian, active in the Civil Air Patrol, got Frank interested in flying a small aircraft locally. One day Ian took to the air with me as his passenger. We flew the little plane out to Lake Milton and circled over my home in Craig Beach. Mom knew what was happening. I could see her standing in the front yard leaning against the tree with one hand and pretending with the other to be throwing sedative pills into her mouth. The dramatic gestures were for my benefit and caution. She feared flying and later said she would never get on a plane unless I also was a passenger. She assumed that God was not done with me, so my safety would extend to her. Mom never left the ground in her lifetime, but I rejoice now to realize that she was right about God not yet being done with me.

The happenings on the world and national scenes were hardly in the consciousness of my high school class. Occasionally I had to hitchhike home from basketball practice. Those six country miles out to Craig Beach on the western shore of Lake Milton seemed like the whole world to me. My class- mates and I were far more conscious of superintendent John Rayburn and principal Mary Lucy Lauban than we were of the executive and congressional branches of the national government. There was, however, the senior class trip to Washington. While in the nation's capital, a handful of my classmates elected the sobering experience of standing in a long line in the Capitol Rotunda to view the body of John Foster Dulles, the deceased Secretary of State. The classic photograph of my class, seated in neat rows in front of the Capitol building, still hangs on a wall in my home. I am seated on the ground in the front row, next to my friend Ian Worley.

Some on our trip ingested too freely the drug of choice at the time, alcohol. I was not among them, being rather shy, having little money in my pocket, and not feeling the need to rebel against established authority. What I did do was use my little camera to take a photograph from the hotel window. I meant it to be of a national landmark, only to discover later that somehow I had double-exposed the frame with an accidental shot of the piping in the bathroom. I was nervous and inexperienced. While no one cared about my blunder, except as reason for a good laugh, the death of Dulles, so key a member of President Dwight Eisenhower's administration, was a blow to "Ike." The president was having much-publicized health prob- lems of his own during his second term. But my classmates and I focused more on personal diversions than on potential national dilemmas.

That is how it was. During our growing-up years in the 1950s, there was fun, danger, questions, hope, pranks, learning, and really good friends. It was quite a sheltered midwestern experience, I suppose, but for the most part it was good. At the time of the graduation of my high school class in 1959, the world was at peace (so far as we knew) and there was hope of a job for all. It soon would be time to get more serious about life. I did my growing and had tasted the potential of learning. I was ready to move on. My hope was college, but there was no transportation for commuting, and virtually no money for related expenses. Even so, God had a plan and it got worked out through a set of circumstances in my extended family. College was indeed in my future, in fact would become a centerpiece of my future.

My mother, Charlotte, father, Robert, and my grandmother, Mary Callen.

Sunday school class, First Church of God, Newton Falls, Ohio, 1954. I am second from the left.

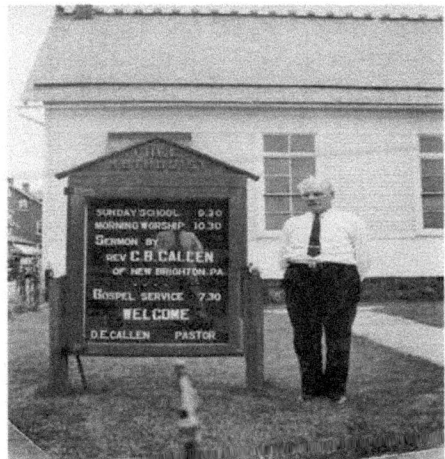

Grandpa Callen, visiting preacher at the church pastored by his son, my uncle, Rev. David Callen

Craig Beach Amusement Park, two blocks from my childhood home. Our backyard sheds at the Beach Lane home and nearby boat docks.

My friend Betty Baldwin and I at the prom.

My grandmother Mary Callen, wife Arlene, son Todd, and I visiting my boyhood home on Beach Lane in Craig Beach, Lake Milton, Ohio, 1968.

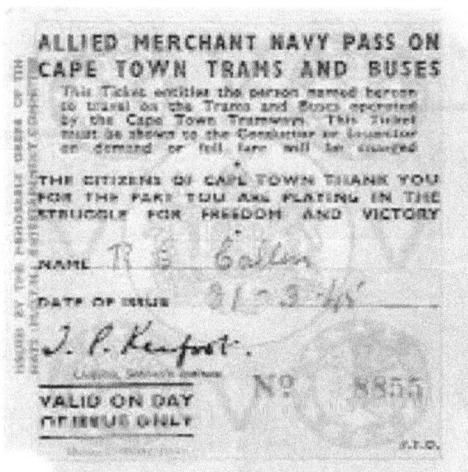

My father shipped into Cape Town, South Africa, in the 1940s to aid the Allied cause during World War II. I would return there in 2007 in the cause of combatting the AIDS pandemic. Dad and I each had our important world missions.

Mahoning County Public Schools

Jackson-Milton High School

This Certifies That

Barry Lee Callen

has satisfactorily completed the Course of Study prescribed by the State of Ohio for the Jackson-Milton Local High School a High School of the First Grade and is therefore entitled to receive this

Diploma

In Witness Whereof we have affixed our signatures at North Jackson, Ohio

June 2, 1959

My Jackson-Milton
High School basketball "Letter."

Certificate of Membership

National Honor Society
of
Secondary Schools

This Certifies that

Barry Callen

was elected a member

of the Jackson-Milton Chapter

of the

National Honor Society of Secondary Schools
membership in which is based on
Scholarship, Leadership, Service, and Character.

Given at Jackson-Milton High School

this day of February

An early beginning
of my academic career.

Chapter 3

Beside the Beaver Vale

Pro Christo et Patria

My college experience was in a surprising location, and was one of excellent quality. Geneva College is located on a bluff overlooking the Beaver River–thus the "beside the Beaver Vale" words in its alma mater. It is in the College Hill residential section immediately north of downtown Beaver Falls, Pennsylvania. The college is related to the Reformed Presbyterian Church, a small body of sturdy Christian believers committed to Christ and Fatherland ("Pro Christo et Patria"). My experience there would introduce me to a Christian fellowship quite different from my Free Methodist and Church of God (Anderson) heritages, and from the Free Methodist family heritage of Arlene Cooley, another member of the Geneva freshman class of 1959 unknown to me previously.

Arlene and I were at Geneva because of the presence and generosity of relatives. We met in the registration line on the first day of our college careers, dated for most of our four years on campus, and married shortly after our joint graduation in May, 1963. We found love and earned college degrees at the same time. For me, moving to Beaver Falls, the city neighboring New Brighton where I was born, was a little like coming home to a place I hardly knew. Looking back decades later, it's clear that God's gracious hand was very much in my college experience.

Families Made the Difference

Special attention must be given to relatives who lived next to the Geneva College campus in Beaver Falls during the four years that Arlene and I were students there. They were exceptionally significant to our experiences. My mother's siblings, Evangeline VanArsdale (my "Auntie") and Laverne VanArsdale (my "Uncle Van"), made all the difference for me. Neither was a perfect person (are any of us?), but they were hardworking and good-hearted people who chose to be generous to me by providing housing near the campus and friendly family connections for these crucial years in my life. Without them I may never have gone to college at all.

Lyle and Bea Flinner, Arlene's uncle and aunt, did the same for her. They were renting a two-story brick home from the college, located on the edge of the campus overlooking the football field. It was so convenient for the walking dates Arlene and I had (there were no cars at our disposal). Lyle was a professor of psychology and speech and a minister of the Church of the Nazarene who later would be the lead minister in my marriage to Arlene (along with my home pastor, Lillie McCutcheon and my grandfather, Charles Callen). Bea was a campus librarian.

And my host relatives? My mother's older sister, Evangeline, had been on a journey that became important for me. "Auntie," as my sister Bonnie and I called her, worked for the Treasury Department in Washington, D. C., from 1942 to 1944. She had moved there with friends from the New Brighton Free Methodist Church in Pennsylvania at a time when workers were needed badly by the government in wartime. Then she relocated to Roberts Wesleyan College in North Chili, New York, the Free Methodist school in that region that needed a secretary for its president. It is clear that being a loyal church person is what attracted her.

Soon after Auntie began her new work at Roberts, my mother got on a train with me and we went to visit—rare travel in my youth, a trip which I do not remember.. The irony was that, at that very time, Donald and Evelyn Cooley were also on this New York campus so that Don could prepare for Christian ministry. Their three-year-old daughter, Arlene, was right where I was visiting—although neither of us three-years-olds knew or cared. It would be another fifteen years before Arlene Cooley and I would really meet, this time as freshmen at Geneva College located midway between our homes, hers in Uniontown (southwest Pennsylvania) and mine in Lake Milton (northeast Ohio). How we got to Geneva is an interesting story since this church campus is related to the Reformed Presbyterian Church, not to either the Church of God or the Free Methodist Church.

Auntie made the decision to leave Roberts in 1947 to fulfill a similar secretarial role at Greenville College in Illinois, another Free Methodist campus. She loved the people there, but was single, made little money, and missed her family. In 1951 she decided to resign and go home to western Pennsylvania. She wrote to her older brother Laverne, who was a local banker and faithful member of the Kiwanis Club in Beaver Falls, announcing her big decision and asking him to keep an eye out for possible employment. One of the club's members was a staff person at the local campus, Geneva College. He commented that the school had an opening for a secretary, getting the quick response from my Uncle Van that one might be available.

Auntie came home, moved into a third-floor apartment in her brother's home which was within walking distance of the college campus. She went to work at Geneva, first as Assistant Registrar and then secretary to the president. That's when I came into the picture. Was it just a coincidence? Probably, although the irony is interesting, maybe providential. Given my Church of God affiliation in Newton Falls, Ohio, and the strong Free Methodist association of both sets of my grandparents, one would hardly expect that the college I would attend would be sponsored by a small Presbyterian denomination. But it was. It helped launch my awareness of and appreciation for the broader Christian family, and for a Christian community serious about the life of the mind.

The Geneva presidency of Edwin Clarke had begun in 1956. By 1959 his secretary was Evangeline VanArsdale, my mother's sister. I had no financial resources to enable my going to college, but my aunt in Beaver Falls lived alone in a third-floor apartment in my Uncle Van's home located two blocks from the campus. She offered me a bed in her apartment and alerted me to an available scholarship that would go to someone of "superior academic achievement by being graduated in the highest tenth of the high school class." The amount was $160 toward tuition for the first college year, renewable for three more years "if a high quality of work is maintained." My high school principal, Mary Lucy Lauban, verified to Geneva on April 24, 1959, that I would be graduated from Jackson-Milton High School on June 2, ranking third academically in a class of 54. I met the qualification and received the scholarship. So, with a family connection and good grades in high school, the pieces had fallen in place for me to attend college despite my family's lack of college experience and financial resources.

When this opportunity came to attend college, my thoughts about the future were a mixture of teaching and Christian ministry. I had seen good models of both. I became a history major and English minor and pursued courses in religion, an interesting experience since the Christian tradition of the school—the staunch Calvinism of the Reformed Presbyterian Church—was quite a contrast in some ways to the Arminian revivalism of my Free Methodist and Church of God backgrounds (e.g., Geneva's emphases on "closed" communion, predestination, and infant baptism). This made for some interesting classroom discussions! I learned to respect professors with whom I disagreed on some religious matters. I especially came to appreciate Dr. William Russell who was a frequent history professor of mine.

Remembering College Days

The fall of 1959 saw Geneva College entering its 111th year, but the first for Arlene Cooley and me. The Reformed Presbyterian Church, founder of Geneva College, is a small denomination of Scottish "Covenanters." Geneva began in Northwood, Ohio, in 1848. After the Fugitive Slave Act of 1850, making it a crime to assist slaves escaping northward, college personnel and local Northwood residents resisted the law. Northwood was strategically located on the Underground Railroad between the Ohio River and Lake Erie. These sturdy Christian believers would live by their faith—which disallowed human slavery. Like early generations of the Scotch-Irish Callen family, freedom in the new world was a high priority of Geneva College.

New circumstances encouraged Geneva College to relocate to Beaver Falls, Pennsylvania, in 1880. The campus now would be perched on a high bluff overlooking "the Beaver Vale," a river valley below that carried both the Beaver River through this highly industrialized area and a busy railroad line that runs along the river's western bank and then through the next small city, New Brighton, where I was born, and on to Pittsburgh. The Harmony Society, German Pietists living communally near Beaver Falls, was bankrolling the building of Beaver Falls in 1880. These people offered the attractive land above the river to the Ohio college in order to enhance the cultural breadth and religious roots of the emerging city. It was an arrangement of mutual benefit.

The first college basketball game ever played in the United States was at Geneva College on April 8, 1893. Geneva defeated the New Brighton YMCA. By 1959, when I graduated from high school in North Jackson, Ohio, and Arlene in Uniontown, Pennsylvania, Geneva had become a fine

Christian liberal arts college. One symbol of its excellence dates back to 1914. In that year, a tornado took the roof off of Old Main and severely damaged the chapel. The building was extensively remodeled, with the present stained glass windows installed. They feature the seals of Oxford and Cambridge Universities in England, with the Geneva seal pictured on them. This was a campus with a serious academic tradition and strength.

Arlene and I were part of about 300 new freshmen in the fall of 1959. Our class elected Gerald Kelly president, Nancy Elliott secretary, and Fred Martin treasurer— all good Reformed Presbyterians and friendly people. I met Arlene in our first registration line in the basement of the stately McCartney Library. Clarence McCartney, the "prince of American preachers," had died in 1957, but his legacy was left for our benefit. Within weeks of first meeting, Arlene and I had our first date, a campus football game in Reeves Stadium just behind the home of Lyle and Bea Flinner where Arlene lived.

Breathing was not always easy there because of air pollution. The Cork Works sat just beyond the south goal posts and had been belching out its smelly smoke since 1903. Arlene did not have a sports background, which allowed me to shine a little (so I thought). She asked me why there was one full-back and two half-backs, but only one quarter-back. It was such a simple question, but, unfortunately, I had to hesitate before I could figure out how to respond intelligently. Her thought was about numbers and fractions, but the answer lay in the relative distances from the line of scrimmage. She was perceptive, and my presumed brilliance learned a little humility. This young woman was attractive, smart, a gentle personality and deeply committed Christian in the Free Methodist tradition. There were possibilities for us as a couple.

What was more dependable than my embarrassed sports brilliance was school pride. We freshmen sat together in the stadium with our little green beanies on—a required mark of being new on campus. When our eyes were raised above the field, we saw in the evening darkness the flaming "G" high on Eastvale Hill beyond the Beaver River. An arrangement of stones, paint, and bright lights allowed school pride to gleam in the darkness across the Beaver Vale and warm all the Geneva faithful. Horror struck at the homecoming game in our freshman year. We were playing our big rival, Westminister College (the "liberal" Presbyterians). When the time came for the "G" to blaze and thrill the home crowd, a "W" appeared instead! Our sacred tradition had been violated.

By April of 1961 Arlene and I were both familiar parts of the local scene on campus. She did some wonderful artwork on a wall of her dorm room and I was playing basketball for the college. On April 24 there convened an all-college event, the first in the new Metheny Field House on campus. Rev. Willard McMillan, director of spiritual activities, offered a meditation on "Athletics in the Christian Arena" and I offered the prayer, "representing the men's basketball squad" according to the summer issue of the *Geneva Alumnus*. Our home games were now played on campus instead of at the Beaver Falls High School gymnasium. My teammates included Jim Irons, Pete Croud, and James Jackson. James was an African-American from Selma, Alabama, the first person of color I had ever known personally. Many years later, he and I would be selected to appear in a campus publication that featured seventy-five outstanding graduates of the college from its first 150 years. It was an honor to be chosen with him.

I recall fondly the evening downtown in Beaver Falls when I was playing in a junior varsity game for Geneva. At the buzzer to end the second quarter, I hit a hurried jump shot from center court. Arlene was my date at the game and had made a corsage that I proudly wore after my shower and during the varsity game. It won a prize for us. She was always artistic and thoughtful, and I surely enjoyed her attention. By our junior year, our dates were frequent, mostly just taking long walks around the residential streets on College Hill. Neither of us had access to a car and virtually no money. The steep stairs up to my Auntie's apartment, where I lived, one flight outside and three others inside, provided us a private place for lengthy and sometimes rather personal goodbyes. Love had bloomed.

A campus publication called *The Chimes* carried collections of student writings. Published by the English Club, the May 1960 edition carried two of my efforts, "The Destiny of America" and "Twilight," and one essay by Arlene titled "The Meaning of Patriotism." This is where the publishing of my writing began. I wrote rather poetically:

> Twilight is a time of dying light, of invading darkness; a time to remember remorse of the past, to dream of a far-off future; a time of peaceful silence with disturbed and haunting thoughts; a time bewitched and enchanted, yet simple and real; a time of vigil for man while nature is slipping into slumber; a moment when love blooms, eternal fascination; a time of beauty of the highest order wherein lies the revelation of God to a world of ungrateful creatures who are usually too preoccupied to hesitate at eve and meditate... Twilight is a sunrise anxiously awaited yet unseen, a sunset gone yet never forgotten.... It is an elusive fragment of absolute faith which the heart of each man yearns for, but has difficulty attaining in the dizzy rush of the modern world.... Twilight is truly God's time, surely man's time, and without doubt "the" time.

A mystical streak in my spirit already was struggling with a busy life that risks insensitivity. I saw this struggle on the national scene, saying in my other piece:

> America is a hope, an ideal, a symbol of faith in the everlasting desire of mankind for freedom.... America is at a

crossroads. She may take the path of least resistance and never fulfill her destiny. Then her morals would slip to a shameful level; and, worst of all, she would become complacent in her attitudes toward the rest of the world.... America can and should be a country by the people, of the people, and for a needy world. Her greatness will be multiplied only when she divides her wealth and knowledge with the lowly.

These were my words in 1960, reflecting my young self, my religious background, and the "Cold War" times in which I lived. I saw the dangers of unshared prosperity, defensive isolationism, and a misplaced faith in military might. Could serious writing be in my future?

How dramatic would be the coming 1960s for me and America! Some forty years later I would continue my concerns with the book *Seeking the Light: America's Modern Quest for Peace, Justice, Prosperity, and Faith* (1998). Arlene's essay back in 1960 was akin to mine. She said, "In order to have true patriotism, it is necessary to combine inward feelings of pride, respect, and love for one's country with the outward act of putting country before self." She and I were young "radicals" in a modest sense, morally sensitive, but lacking any particular political agenda.

Geneva College had 983 regular day students in 1961, 611 of whom resided in the Beaver Valley. The night school enrollment was 841. According to the *Geneva Alumnus* (fall 1961, 15), the secretary of Geneva's president, my Auntie with whom I lived, had been elected the president of the local Business and Professional Women's Club. In May of that year, she had traveled to Philadelphia, and in July to Chicago for conventions of this organization. She was active, outgoing, a networker, and outspokenly proud of her nephew on campus. Auntie was good to me, even if overbearing at times—to the distress of my mother. Auntie tended to be a little possessive, and was a bit jealous of all the time I happily gave to

Arlene. Meanwhile, Arlene's Aunt Bea and Uncle Lyle with whom she lived kept a close eye on her.

Traffic was a particular campus problem. State Route 18 came twisting through the community and went right in front of Old Main on its way downtown. Being an industrial area, there were many large trucks and city buses, slowed only by two 90-degree turns just before Old Main. When evening school classes took their break, dozens of commuting students would line the sidewalk in front of Old Main to smoke—a vice not allowed on the campus proper. So, as the public drove by, they saw the college as a line of smokers! Not until 2006 did the state and college agree to straighten the highway so that it would bypass the campus, adding to student safety and campus cohesion. But, when I was a student, things were loud and dangerous. Walking to school from Auntie's, I had to cross the highway, often several times a day.

I became something of a prominent personality on campus. August Conte was my opponent for president of the Student Senate in our junior year—I had become slightly more political. Our photos were featured on the front page of the April 27, 1962, issue of *The Cabinet* (campus student newspaper), where it was said of me:

> Barry Callen lives in Lake Milton, Ohio, and is a history major. He was a member of this year's *Genevan* staff and served for two years as a sports writer for *The Cabinet*. Barry was treasurer of his sophomore class and a member of the track and junior varsity basketball teams during his freshman and sophomore years. He stressed the belief that "the Student Senate represents that vital link between the student body and the administration which must be strong at all times if the administration is to function at the peak of efficiency and if the dominant sentiments of the student body are to be reflected in these policies."

The outcome of the election? Conte won, I think easily. I had mounted little or no campaign. Maybe I had spent too much time walking with Arlene. Apparently I was more eloquent in my views than successful in my politics.

In fact, words seemed to be natural for me. I remember looking with some shock at the graded final exam of my course on the history of England taught by Dr. Charles Akers. He had given me an "A-" on the big essay I had proudly written for him. I wondered, with a little wounded pride, how he could justify the "-" on my excellent writing. His only written comments were "Rather verbose" and "Who is 'they'?" These were perceptive comments indeed. My words probably were a little more numerous than necessary (which impresses most professors) and, of course, I would not have written "they" occasionally if I had really known exactly who I was talking about! This little problem aside, my speaking and writing skills were developing and did have a future far beyond my anticipation. Geneva was a good garden for my growing academics.

Getting Ready to Teach

Professionally, I pursued preparation for the vocation of public school teaching. My interest was history—after an initial journey into mathematics that became so abstract that I lost interest (and maybe had reached the limit of my ability). The chair of the History Department at Geneva was Dr. William Russell. While Drs. Charles Akers and George Coleman were also prominent in my college classroom experiences, it was the gentle nature and yet disciplined and systematic approach of Dr. Russell that especially attracted me. He was a Reformed Presbyterian scholar and gentleman whom I respected in every way.

I also recall fondly Drs. Norman Carson and Geri Bass in English, Dr. Willard McMillan in Christian ministry, Dr. Johannes Vos in Bible, and Byron Morgan, my basketball coach. Edwin Clarke, president from 1956 to 1980, was always a kind and competent presence. There also was David Carson in political science. Typical of the long tenures of faculty members, he joined the Geneva faculty in 1951, retired in 1992, and wrote the history of Geneva College in 1997. It is titled *Pro Christo et Patria* (for Christ and fatherland). These were strong and good people, serious about both Christian faith and quality academics. I am deeply in their debt.

I did my student teaching from September 4 through November 2, 1962, under Mr. Roger Alexis, a committed and creative teacher of American history at Beaver Falls High School, located about a mile from the campus which is up on College Hill. One had to go down the long hill and into the city to get to the high school, something I did often on foot since I had no car. The real problem, of course, was coming home when tired—it was up the hill at the end of the day. Professors Francis Hawthorne and John McIsaac represented the campus education department in my professional semester. The eight-week experience was intense. Each day I reported to the high school at 8:10 a.m., observed or taught until 3:00 p.m., and then tried to get to the campus as quickly as possible for the mandatory education seminar for student teachers that convened at 3:45!

I had a little help. This was semester one of my senior year and also that of Arlene Cooley. We were now intending marriage. She was completing her work in elementary education. Having more of an artistic eye than me, on one occasion she made a set of nice block letters that I could use to good effect on the bulletin boards of my classrooms. On another occasion, she and I traveled to her home in Uniontown, Pennsylvania, in the back seat of the car of her aunt and uncle, Bea and Lyle Flinner. I was facing a final exam in Chinese history when we got back, so Arlene drilled me on the details of all the dynasties of ancient China. She was anxious to help, and my final grade was more than satisfactory.

My student teaching included 160 students in six different classes assigned to Mr. Alexis. One student was a young man by the name of Joe Namath, a star quarterback on the high school's football team and later to go to the University of Alabama and then on to a legendary career in the National Football League as "Broadway Joe." In my classroom, however, he was a marginal student who came from what I heard was a troubled home. The 2004 biography of Joe by Mark Kriegel, called *Namath*, details the Beaver Falls life of a brash, "cool" young man who was gifted with unusual athletic ability and occasionally spent a night in jail for his outrageous pranks. Academic life was hardly his preoccupation. In my 2009 submarine novel, *In Deep Water*, I would build a character consciously modeled after Joe. Outrageous pranks on a submarine in time of war can be both funny and dangerous!

The journey of Joe Namath has become an important lesson for me. A teacher cannot know the potential of given students. Years later, in Anderson, Indiana, it would be my privilege to work closely with Carl Erskine, famed pitcher of the Brooklyn (now Los Angeles) Dodgers who was a native of Anderson. Greatness often comes when what appears to be only ordinary is nurtured by visionaries and blessed with open doors. I was the most minor of influences on Joe, but at least I tried to steer him and the others in the right direction. Carl came from humble beginnings and now, having reached the top of his sport, is a leading elder citizen of his hometown. I would work for years with Carl on the Anderson University Board of Trustees, he as member and I as Secretary. In 2011 my cancer treatments would be received in the "Erskine Center" in Anderson. Thanks, Carl!

Joe and Carl cause me to reflect on the tiny village of Craig Beach where I grew up. It was hardly a place designed to spawn visions of greatness in its young. Of course, greatness is hardly a proper adjective for myself. Even so, the open doors that have come my way over the decades seemed unimaginable when I roamed Beach Lane, the amusement park, and the shores of Lake Milton as a boy. Modest beginnings do not necessarily limit eventual horizons. Teachers can be so influential—and the grace of God is pervasive. I reflected on all of this in my 2011 novel *StarWalker*, set in Craig Beach. It features a young boy struggling to find his way in life (quite autobiographical).

On September 26, 1962, I was given full responsibility for three of the high school classes of my supervising teacher. By October 12 the whole schedule was mine to handle. Mr. Alexis observed some of the time, critiqued my lesson plans and proposed exams, and worked on his own audio-visual projects. I pushed video projectors around the halls, renewed bulletin boards each day, handled money collection in home room for various causes, and sometimes was pressed into service for other teachers when emergencies came up. These were busy and stretching weeks. One emergency was the eruption of the Cuban missile crisis, maybe the closest the world has come so far to World War III.

October 30, 1962, was parent visitation day at Beaver Falls High School. Mr. Meta was called away because of his wife's sudden illness and the school office asked if I would teach his four senior classes on "Problems of Democracy." I was totally unprepared, but said I would. The day's news saved me from not knowing exactly what to do. I led vigorous discussions of a dramatic event on the world scene and what its implications might be for American democracy. President John F. Kennedy had just ordered a naval blockade around Cuba, openly challenging the Russians and potentially precipitating all-out nuclear war. These were senior students, some of whom might be in military uniform within months. It was a growing-up day for me and them.

I later would write about this world event in my 1998 book *Seeking the Light: America's Modern Quest for Peace, Justice, Prosperity, and Faith.* So much changes over the years, and so much remains the same. In 2012, with the United States and Israel facing off against the growing and threatening nuclear program of Iran, one writer called the situation the

1962 "Cuban missile crisis in slow motion." The U. S. and the world had still not learned the depths of human sin, the limited capabilities of war to solve human problems, and the best way to justice, security, and peace. We felt the fear in those 1962 classrooms, the same fear that lingers yet today.

Geneva's class of 1963 in which Arlene and I shared membership had seen built on campus in its four years a new field house, additions to the Science Hall and Old Main, a renovated dining hall, and two new student dorms. It was growth time for us and Geneva College. The growth, of course, did not leave behind the old. There was still the Brigadoon, a quaint snack shop and student hang-out built in 1950 and named after the mythical village featured in the musical of the same name. I was in the Brigadoon on October 13, 1960, when—at exactly 3:36 p.m.—Bill Mazeroski hit the home run in the ninth inning of the seventh game that beat the New York Yankees and gave the World Series to the Pittsburgh Pirates. Suddenly, the Beaver Valley felt like the capital of the world!

The published "last will" of our class said that we gladly were leaving behind "the cork dust, muddy Beaver River, and noisy railroad." I was said to be leaving "disliking Chinese food, but very warm with Cooley!" Arlene (Cooley) left "her shovel [?] to any promising young education major." We also were leaving the beautiful "Beaver Vale," our academic bluff above the Beaver River. These had been growing years. I got a degree, a profession, a wife, and confidence in myself and the future. I also had fallen in love with the goals of a Christian liberal arts college, a love key to my future.

Leaving Our Alma Mater Behind

One wishes that college friends would remain close for all of life, but life takes people in different directions. I enjoyed my college friendship with

Richard Cunningham, so much so that he was a groomsman in my wedding. However, we soon lost touch altogether, reconnecting only in the year 2000 by internet and email. He then lived in Wayland, Michigan. While no longer a Reformed Presbyterian, he was still the same warm Christian man I knew in the early 1960s.

Two classmates would join me much later in being featured in a Geneva publication of select alumni from across the school's 150 years (*Profiles in Servant Leadership*, 1999). They were Faith McBurney Martin, an English major who had become an author and the Executive Director of the Reformed Presbyterian Woman's Association headquartered in Pittsburgh, Pennsylvania, and Dr. James Jackson, an African-American from Alabama who majored in biology, played college basketball with me, did his student teaching with me at Beaver Falls High School, and became a prominent high school principal in the Albany, New York, area.

I maintained some contact with five of my professors, Dr. William Russell (history), Dr. Geri Bass (English), Dr. David Carson (Political Science), Dr. Norman Carson (English), and Dr. Willard McMillan (Christian Studies). These were exceptionally good Christian people, each an excellent role model in the classroom and in the life of faith and service. I was with them all in April, 2002, when I returned to the Geneva campus to be featured in a "Geneva Authors Book Festival." The four aging men came to be with me on this occasion, and I visited Dr. Bass in her nursing home nearby. Life by then was moving on rapidly for all of us.

At one point in my college career I suffered a case of the bachelor blues—or was it just a bout of male ineptness? My aunt with whom I lived while a college student suddenly had a ten-day hospital stay to have a kidney removed. The little third-floor apartment was all mine for this time, including the tiny kitchen. I had an idea. I bought a beef roast and asked my girlfriend, Arlene, for a tip on how to cook it. She did a little guessing, I did some experimenting, and the result was a dense and rubberish blob that could not be penetrated by any ordinary fork or kitchen knife. Into the garbage it went!

By then the pressure was really on. Beyond the costly meat disaster was the fact that every glass, dish, and piece of tableware in my aunt's apartment somehow was now dirty and my aunt was coming home. I had to break the long dishwashing drought and bring a reasonable sense of order to the apartment before critical female eyes came from the hospital and viewed with dismay my disaster zone. While I much preferred books, basketball, and wandering College Hill on foot with Arlene, I managed to solve the problem that my lack of domestic discipline had created. It was a close call.

I am glad that I managed my studies much better. I graduated from Geneva College on June, 4, 1963. I was class valedictorian, ranking first academically in a class of 236. My soon-to-be-wife Arlene was right behind me in the rankings. She graduated with a degree in elementary education, preparation that soon would be very important for us out in Indiana. The "Who's Who" section of the 1963 *Genevan* (college annual) featured twelve members of our class, with Arlene and me the first two pictured. What a lovely symbol of things soon to come for us. We both had worked hard and done well.

Our commencement speaker was Robert E. Wilson, Commissioner of the Atomic Energy Commission of the United States. He had been born seventy years earlier just two blocks from the campus in Beaver Falls. He said in his address that he did not share the common perception of the business community of the time that "our universities and colleges are hotbeds of Communism or Socialism." He continued: "While I recognize that you graduates, like all of us, face many uncertainties in these troubled times, I do not think you either desire or deserve any sentimental sympathy when you have had the opportunity, given to only one in a hundred in this war-torn world, of getting a first-class college education in a free country."

Dr. Wilson was right. I had received a very good undergraduate education at Geneva College, had met a wonderful young woman who soon would be my wife, and had doors opened before me that I had the freedom to pursue the best way I could. Arlene and I had very little money, but we did have real opportunities, and thus deserved no sentimental sympathy. We somehow would find our way forward.

The first ten years after college graduation day would be volatile and troubled indeed for the nation. For me personally, going directly to seminary to pursue graduate education for Christian ministry would keep me out of the military and likely service in Vietnam. Avoiding the military was not my primary motive, but it was a welcome byproduct. I moved from a "2S" (college student with good grades) to a "4F" ministerial category of the Selective Service. I was not a conscientious objector formally, although my religious commitments and personal values leaned that way. My father had joined the Merchant Marines to stay out of a foxhole in Europe. Maybe, at least in part, I turned to the Christian ministry to render my service peaceably.

One death in 2007 was particularly symbolic for me. I had met Jim Irons only once since our years as basketball teammates at Geneva College beginning in 1959. He was a fierce rebounder, a native of Monaca, Pennsylvania, where my first months of life were spent in a little house "back of Monaca." Jim had stayed in "the Valley" after college to pursue a successful coaching and teaching career at East Liverpool (Ohio) High School (where earlier I had been converted to Christ at the Free Methodist campgrounds) and Freedom (Pa.) High School where my Uncle Van had launched his banking career. Jim finally returned to Monaca High School to complete his career, staying home as a loyal and highly competitive man. He and I remained on the same team over the years, at least in the sense that we had similar roots in "the Valley," were proud Geneva graduates, were rebounders and educators, and were loyal to family and callings. We differed in that I was called to Christian ministry and would stray west to Indiana. In my heart, however, the lovely Beaver Vale lying below the Geneva College campus would never leave my heart.

Looking back on my college experience from later years, it appears that I had been given a special opportunity, a solid beginning. By contrast, both of my parents had reached for a dream that never quite materialized. Dad longed for the freedom and joys of the great outdoors, but spent most of his working years in the dirty environs of the big steel mills of northeast Ohio. Mom longed for a rich family life and the adventure of travel, but spent much of her time trapped in our small home on Beach Lane in the little village of Craig Beach. Dad's preoccupations (work, hunting, and fishing) and limited dollars virtually stranded her for decades.

I am grateful to report that a similar experience would not be mine. I married my college sweetheart, Arlene Marie Cooley, on August 10, 1963 (detail and photos in chapter eleven). I would not be stranded in a private world of frustration; in fact, I would travel the world and find an amazing number of doors opening to me. I would never feel stranded anywhere in life. Yes, I would have to work hard to pass through these doors, but the bigger reality always involved the giftings of divine grace that made things possible.

Sometimes my mother put her frustration into words. The local newspaper often carried news reports and poems she had written. In the *Newton Falls Herald* (December 22, 1964), for instance, she spoke of the nostalgia of Christmas. The paper's preface said that "Mrs. Callen of Lake Milton was feeling the nostalgia deeply. Attending Anderson College (Indiana) at the time were her son Barry, a graduate ministerial student, and daughter Bonnie, a college senior. Barry's wife of just one year, Arlene, was a fifth-grade teacher." Here are some lines of my Mom's published poem, titled "My Kids Are Home," with the "we added one" comment referring to Arlene.

> My kids are home for Christmas.
> Oh, lucky, lucky me!

I've wondered how that I could wait
For them to trim that tree.

So many times throughout the year
How lonesome I would seem.
If only I could hear "him" scold,
Or hear "Miss Bonnie" scream.

Oh, my kids are here for Christmas
And we added one, you know.
I really didn't lose a son;
Marriage makes a family grow.

The pumpkin pies are steaming now;
Tom Turkey's good and brown;
The stuffin' never smelled so good—
Oh, this place is upside down!

Well, it's just a week or two until
My kids 'll be up and away;
But we'll have had the best time yet
On this year's Christmas Day!

This poem says much. In 1964 Arlene and I were newly married. We each had good educations from Geneva College. I was attending Anderson University School of Theology to gain preparation for Christian ministry and she was teaching the fifth grade in nearby Chesterfield, Indiana, to keep food on the table while I studied. My sister Bonnie was an undergraduate senior on the same Indiana campus—none of us knowing that we all would stay in that Hoosier city of Anderson for our lifetimes. My parents were still in Craig Beach and Arlene's mother was still in Uniontown, Pennsylvania. Each mother would come in turn to Anderson to live out their final years with us after their husbands were gone. Having been born in western Pennsylvania, reared in northeastern Ohio, and educated back in "the Valley," we now were living and serving "out west" in Indiana.

Located on "College Hill," Beaver Falls, Pennsylvania

Ariel view of Geneva College, with a busy state highway twisting through campus. Not until 2007-2008 was this road straightened and the campus finally unified. The arrow marks the home of my Uncle Van and Auntie where I lived.

Evangeline VanArsdale, my "Auntie,"
and secretary to President Edwin Clarke.

Dr. William H. Russell, Professor of
History, key teacher in my major.

(above) Geneva's
Great Books
Discussion Group.
I am standing in
the center, with
Professors David
Carson standing
left and Norman
Carson seated
right.

(left) Staff of the
Genevan. I am
standing in the
center.

WHO'S WHO

Class of 1963

ARLENE COOLEY

Arlene has shown good scholarship in her field of education and leadership and participation in many activities. She is a member of P.S.E.A., the Chemistry Club and the Great Books Discussion Group.

BARRY CALLEN

A History major and well known on campus in many capacities, Barry is a member of the great Books Discussion Group, and is on the *Cabinet* staff. He also was a member of the *Genevan*, and of the track and basketball teams in his freshman and sophomore years.

JUNIORS

Barry Callen
Lake Milton, Ohio

Richard Lang
Bergenstown, Pa.

Gloria Caskey
Chromelo, Iowa

Donald Chionte
Beaver Falls, Pa.

Sharon Christmann
Valencia, Pa.

August Conte
Aliquippa, Pa.

Arlene Cooley
Uhlestown, Pa.

Sandra Creighton
Beaver Falls, Pa.

Richard Cunningham
Beaver Falls, Pa.

Some of the Geneva College class of 1963, in our junior year. I am pictured upper left; Arlene M. Cooley is lower left. August Conte was my political opponent and Richard Cunninghbam would be in our wedding 1963.

My marrying Arlene Cooley brought into my life her mother Evelyn (Jeffreys) Cooley and Evelyn's siblings Robert (wife Mary), Ruth (husband Frank Barber), Bea (husband Lyle Flinner), and Juanita (husband Richard Cramer). Below are Evelyn (left) and Juanita and Dick with my second wife Jan and me (bottom). My transition from college to seminary was influenced greatly by Austin E. Sowers (pictured to the right with his sister, Lillie McCutcheon, the Newton Falls pastor of my youth).

Chapter 4

On the Way to Vocation

Life in response to God's call

I believe in the concept of being called by God to a life's work. Now, in my late seventies, I can look back and, with the perspective of the years, affirm that such a calling has been my personal experience. As I remember my faith journey and vocation, I have many reasons to rejoice!

The highest privilege in life is not going "to work" every day, but having the opportunity to happily invest oneself in pursuing a divine calling. I often said this during my many years at Anderson University: "Even if they didn't pay me, I would come every day anyway as long as I could somehow support my family." Discerning a call, however, is not always immediate or easy. Often the light dawns slowly through discovering the gifts one has and recognizing the doors that open and close along the way.

God called me to Christian ministry as a young man. In all my human frailty, I answered and was helped to find the way to this vocation, one stage at a time and with the help of one wise person after another. Sometimes God calls in part through the opportunity to observe the faithfully lived vocations of others. Early in my life, the ministry models I knew were those of special family members, dedicated teachers, and outstanding ordained ministers. They made all the difference for me.

Finding the practical means of fulfilling a calling, however, came rather slowly.

Work and Church Beginnings

I remember well one Christmas vacation in the early 1950s. I was a student at Pricetown Elementary School near my home in the village of Craig Beach in northeast Ohio. My father's parents had retired from a lifetime of pastoral ministry and moved to our village in retirement. They had no social security account and no home, having always lived in church-owned parsonages. Dad bought a little house in the village for them and located part-time employment as janitors at my school. My Callen grandparents were proud, honest, and hardworking Christian people. During that particular vacation time, I helped them strip floor wax and clean the whole building, moving hundreds of student desks back and forth. It did not seem right to me that they had to work so hard at their age.

We tried to find a little fun in this difficult physical labor. For instance, I was free to pull the big rope in the front entrance that rang the bell high up in the school tower—a daring little fun break from hard work. My precious Callen grandparents are gone now, and so is that school building, but good memories of them as godly vocational models are not gone. Charles and Mary were wonderful models of being "called" to serve regardless of cost.

Early secular employment in the summers brought a few dollars to help me through college. I briefly hayed on Schlisher's farm outside Pricetown—my sister joined me and got a bad sunburn. I interviewed to be a caddy at the Lake Milton golf course, but failed to get the job (I had never hit a golf ball, let alone help someone else play the game). I worked one summer in a machine shop in Craig Beach, punching out buckets full of metal pieces for screen doors. Another summer my father arranged for me to work as a laborer at a big steel mill in Youngstown—I rode the twenty miles with him each day, allowing me to get as close to him as I ever did. I adapted to the work, and I think he respected me for being a good laborer. Even so, that was hardly my "vocation."

For the summers of 1962 and 1963, I pumped gas into speedboats on Lake Milton, walking daily to the little Ashland marina about a mile from our Beach Lane house. It was vigorous work, mostly pleasant, and helped pay college bills. My campus sweetheart, Arlene Cooley, once came to visit and meet my family. Surprisingly, she impressed my father at the dinner table when he asked her to pray before we ate. She did, quietly, after which Dad said to her, "I couldn't hear you." Without hesitation, she looked right at him and said, "I wasn't talking to you!" He liked her instantly. Down at the marina, she and I drank cold pop together in the heat and continued our courting between arrivals of boats at my dock. I was rather dark brown at our wedding in August, 1963. The summer sun had done its annual work on my fair skin. These various "jobs" were only momentary employment activities, not my vocational future.

The future for me lay with the church. The local congregation of my youth, the First Church of God in Newton Falls, Ohio, was an exceptional place for the nurturing of young Christians. The brother and sister pastoral team of senior pastor Lillie (Sowers) McCutcheon and her associate, Austin E. Sowers, inspiringly conveyed biblical content, lived servant lives that modeled integrity, and paid special attention to young people. When pastors are enthusiastic about the gospel of Christ and sensitive to individual needs, immature seekers are encouraged to risk in faith and grow in grace. I certainly was one of the immature ones.

My own conversion to an experienced faith in Jesus Christ came when I was thirteen. It was at the tabernacle altar on the Free Methodist campgrounds in East Liverpool, Ohio, where my VanArsdale grandparents had a cottage. These grounds are across from Thompson Park and sacred to me. There were tears at that altar, release of my sense of guilt, and a fresh life beginning in the liberating love of God. My grandfather Van Arsdale was right by my side. Once back in Craig Beach, I remember being out in our backyard on a quiet summer evening looking up at the stars. They sparkled above like never before. I felt clean and wonderful inside.

I remember Sister Lillie, my home pastor, once visiting the East Liverpool camp grounds just because our family was important to her. Within a Sunday or two of my conversion, my home church had me behind the big Newton Falls pulpit to read the morning Scripture before some six hundred people. I was very nervous. My eyes glazed as I began reading the assigned psalm. Soon unable to see the words in my Bible, I was too embarrassed to stop, so I went on—making up biblical verses until it seemed that the right amount of time had elapsed! No one ever admitted noticing my desperate diversion into the world of biblical authorship. Whatever I did then or later, the very best face was put on it by church leaders and I was launched forward to risk bigger tasks and opportunities. That was first-class mentoring.

I was blessed much more than I could realize at the time. Christian ministry was modeled before me and suggested itself in relation to my own future. My pastors were most encouraging. The Sunday morning worship bulletin in Newton Falls for August 28, 1960, included this:

> *HEAR BARRY CALLEN TONIGHT!* We are so glad God has called Barry into His sacred ministry. Tonight Barry will preach his *first sermon*. We are praying for the Holy Spirit to bless him and use him in a special way.

My first sermon! I am not sure who wrote these words or what my sermon was about. I'm sure that I was again very nervous. No matter. Encouragement and appreciation were in the air at the Newton Falls church and I breathed in deeply.

On that Sunday of my first sermon, Rev. Austin Sowers was in Houston, Texas, with some of the congregation's young people at the International Youth Convention of the Church of God. For many reasons, I missed such occasions. Back at the home church before I preached, Caroline Ackerman sang a solo. Soon she also would be on her way to ministry, spending many years as a missionary nurse in Kenya and Tanzania, East Africa, always loved and supported by this congregation until her retirement in 2007. Her brother John would live in Haiti and carry on a longterm medical ministry in that deeply troubled land. Caroline, John, and I are only three of more than fifty young persons who went into ministry from this one small-town congregation over the years. I once compiled a list of these church leaders in my biography of Sister Lillie (*She Came Preaching*, 1992, 323-324).

Although jumping ahead in time, it's appropriate to note here a special moment in August of 2006. Convened in Nashville, Tennessee, was a Strategic Planning Conference of the Church of God—140 selected leaders from across North America searching together for the future that God intended for this reform movement. Church historian Merle D. Strege was speaking at one point and chose to illustrate his concern for mentoring a new generation of leaders by noting that one congregation in the past had done a superb job of ministerial mentoring. His evidence? He pointed out that four prominent participants in that very conference were all from the Newton Falls, Ohio, congregation: Jeannette Flynn, an executive leader of Church of God Ministries; Ryan Chapman, head of the program of national prayer ministries for the church; Robert Moss, newly elected chair of the General Assembly and Ministries Council of the Church of God; and myself, just retired from thirty-nine years at Anderson University, then serving as Special Assistant to the General Director of Church of God Ministries and functioning at this conference as its recording secretary.

The Newton Falls congregation had begun in the home of Elmer and Elizabeth Sowers on the corner of Center and Jay Streets. In 1948 the cornerstone was laid for a new church building on West Broad Street. Dedicated in 1949, by 1954 the church celebrated a service of mortgage burning. The special guest speaker was Robert H. Reardon, then Executive Vice-President of Anderson College in Anderson, Indiana. He was an unknown person to me. I had no idea that in years to come he would play a great role in my life, and I would write his biography (*Staying on Course*, 2004).

What was clear at that 1954 mortgage-burning occasion was the significance for me of this congregation and its pastors, people, and teachings. The hymn sung in that service of my first sermon in 1960 was "The Solid Rock." That is a metaphor of how this congregation functioned for me. It was foundational. Years later, the same could be said about the campus of Anderson University and its president, Robert H. Reardon. It was hard in the closing weeks of 2006 to see him slowly dying of cancer—he was finishing well, just as he had lived and helped me live.

Young people from the Church of God congregation in Newton Falls, Ohio, regularly went off to all of the colleges of the Church of God movement around the country. For instance, Jeannette Flynn went to Gulf-Coast Bible College in Texas, Robert Moss to Warner Pacific College in Oregon, and pastor Lillie McCutcheon's own son Ray and me, my sister Bonnie, and numerous others to Anderson College in Indiana (in my case, only to the Anderson seminary since my undergraduate years were spent at Geneva College). Strength and support always were available to young people from "home" church. Jeannette Flynn put it this way: "I always got the feeling that Lillie knew my life, saw real potential in my life, believed in me, and was calling me to be all I could be." I felt exactly the same way.

Sister Lillie expected people to serve, and proceeded to inspire them to do just that. She had a way of generating new servant leaders, both through personal modeling and direct encouraging. For any one of her own young people, her loyalty seemed to know no bounds. In my case, she traveled to Pennsylvania in 1963 to assist in officiating at my wedding, to Indiana in 1973 to give leadership in my ordination service, and again to Indiana in 1974 to lay hands on me and pray when I was installed as dean of Anderson University School of Theology in the annual convening of the General Assembly of the Church of God. Reversing the direction, I returned to Newton Falls with my wife, Arlene, in 1988 for Sister Lillie to officiate at the twenty-fifth anniversary renewal of our marriage vows. She was a highly valued and constant "presence." So was her brother Austin.

With Austin to Anderson

My focus as a student at Geneva College had been high school teaching in the area of history; Arlene's focus had been elementary education. Upon graduation, it turned out that professional preparation for Christian ministry was our goal rather than my seeking a teaching position in some high school setting. My thoughts turned to Asbury Theological Seminary in Wilmore, Kentucky. Even so, and surprisingly, our journey together moved next, not to Kentucky, but to Anderson, Indiana.

For me, getting to Anderson was full of destiny and the result of a complex set of circumstances. I had decided to attend seminary after graduating from Geneva College in May, 1963, and thought primarily of Asbury Theological Seminary. In large part, centering on Asbury was because of its visibility in Free Methodist circles and its reputation as a fully accredited and vigorously conservative seminary in the Wesleyan/Holiness tradition (which, of course, the Church of God shares with Free Methodists and others). At the time, the seminary of the

Church of God was new, founded in Anderson in 1950, and still unaccredited. So I applied to Asbury, was accepted with the offer of substantial scholarship assistance on the strength of my college record, and journeyed south with Arlene, about to become my wife, to seek a teaching job for her in central Kentucky. While there were openings and favorable contacts, timing became an issue. Affirmative action initiatives in Kentucky blocked public school officials from employing a white teaching candidate except late in the summer when it was clear that no appropriate non-white candidate had turned up. We needed a position to cover living expenses and were held in limbo.

Austin E. Sowers, one of my home pastors in Newton Falls, was anxious for my future leadership to be in the Church of God movement. "Brother Austin," Lillie McCutcheon's actual brother and longtime ministerial associate, is the one who took the initiative in 1963 to drive me to Anderson, Indiana, introduce me to leaders of the Anderson campus, encourage me to enroll in that seminary, and even helped me get an interview that led to Arlene securing a teaching position in Chesterfield (near Anderson). This position made our decision to come to the Anderson campus instead of Asbury in Kentucky—which likely would have led to a lifetime apart from the Church of God movement.

Brother Austin had the same nurturing vision as Sister Lillie, and plenty of energy to back it up. What a team they were in Newton Falls, and what encouragement to young people they always gave! In later years I would have opportunity to minister briefly with Austin when he was a missionary in Australia. I also played leadership roles in the funerals of his brother Vern and then Sister Lillie herself. Each occasion would be a labor of love, an act of gratitude occasioned in part because of Austin taking me to Anderson to make the contacts that led to a lifetime of ministry in the center of the life of the Church of God movement.

By the way, teaching contracts did come for Arlene in Kentucky late in the summer of 1963. That was too late. We already had committed ourselves to Anderson University School of Theology. God's providence pervaded the timing of events and Brother Austin was God's agent. In May, 2018, as he was dying under hospice care, I had opportunity to recall all of this for him and thank him.

Gaining a Foothold in Anderson

Earl and DeLoma Gadberry purchased the little grocery store on the corner of Fifth Street and College Drive in Anderson, Indiana, in 1943. It sat across the street from the "Old Main" of Anderson College. Until the late 1950s they operated Gadberry Grocery and Lunchroom where many college professors and students would stop, eat, and visit. Finally driven out of business by the growing chain groceries, the building was converted into small apartments (always having a roach problem—likely from the building's earlier food-storage years).

Arlene and I moved into one of these apartments, 1005 1/2 East Fifth Street, in August, 1963, right after our marriage and brief honeymoon at her grandfather's cabin in the mountains above Uniontown, Pennsylvania, her hometown. Our tiny apartment was located across College Drive from the dramatic new Park Place Church of God structure, and across Fifth Street from Old Main, then the heart of the life of Anderson College. "Granny" Campbell lived alone next door to us, a constant friend of international students.

Arlene and I had come to Anderson for me to attend seminary, while she taught school to support us. Two doors from us were Ronald and Joyce Fowler, also new seminary students from northeast Ohio. Soon the Callens and Fowlers became lifelong friends and ministerial colleagues. Neither Ron nor I had any idea that not too many years later he would be chair of the board of trustees of Anderson University while I was dean of the School of Theology, then dean of the College, vice-president for academic affairs, and corporate secretary of the school, writing the minutes and many reports to and for the board Ron was leading. He and I learned our biblical Greek together under the instruction of Boyce W. Blackwelder. We two couples were living on meager incomes, but with God's rich call on our lives.

My academic experience at the School of Theology was excellent—as was Ron's. The graduate school gained full accreditation while we were students. My time included commuting to Earlham School of Religion an hour from Anderson to take two courses with the famous Quaker scholar David Elton Trueblood. His sophistication and teaching style inspired me, and he complimented my writing. In fact, my 2007 book *Caught Between Truths* carries his personal endorsement. The Anderson professors were well prepared and wholesome in their attitudes toward academic life and pastoral ministry. I was not aware that this graduate education was only a beginning for me; in fact, in a few years I would have earned my third graduate degree and be leading the seminary that had just nurtured and graduated me.

For the summers of 1964 and 1965, Arlene and I had jobs at a regional Boy Scout camp near Anderson, Indiana. Camp Kikthawenund was a busy place for about ten weeks each season. I needed employment and had seen a notice at the seminary for a chaplaincy opening. With Dr. Hollis Pistole's help, I had become camp chaplain and administrator of the dining hall operation in which Arlene worked as assistant cook. I found challenging and fulfilling my roles of daily planning and conducting an evening worship service on the hillside that had a picturesque A-frame chapel at its base. These were ecumenical experiences that I hope had meaning for the hundreds of boys who participated. They surely had meaning for me, actually tempting me to consider military chaplaincy as a Christian vocation.

What also would become meaningful for Arlene and me was the successive generations of our family that would be enriched by this camp. She and I were there in the 1960s. Our son Todd worked there one summer in the early 1990s just before he was married, and his son Ian had his first outdoor experience there in August of 2002—including canoes, archery, swimming, and weaving. Maybe some year Ian's son or daughter will have the next chance. I hope so. For me, it was an early source of administrative experience and a taste of ministry "in the field." The camp environment was hardly Arlene's ideal world, but she coped and worked effectively in the kitchen. We were a good team and carried away good memories.

My graduation from seminary approached, with me expecting to seek pastoral placement. This was in spite of the fact that the mid-1960s was quite an anti-institutional and socially rebellious time. Several of my classmates were involved in para-church and social action ministries and not particularly respectful of the typical local church. I was more conservative in this regard, having come from a healthy congregation. But another path suddenly surfaced, one that would be the leading edge of my future ministry.

Dr. Gustav Jeeninga, a Bible scholar and archaeologist on Anderson's undergraduate faculty, was granted a full-year sabbatical leave for 1966-1967. The college was looking for someone to teach his courses and supervise the little museum of Near Eastern artifacts that he maintained in his office and advertised in a newsletter. I had done very well academically in my seminary work, and even had taught a few classes part-time while on campus (Bible for Professor Marie Strong and English writing for Dr. Vila Deubach). They had sought my help on recommendation of Professor George Kufeldt, my Old Testament teacher in the seminary. I learned only later that he had reported that I was an exceptional student and writer. His judgment was generous. I am grateful to this good man for his kindness behind the scenes.

To my surprise, campus president Robert H. Reardon took me to lunch at the Anderson Country Club—a place that I certainly had never been before! He asked me to be Dr. Jeeninga's temporary replacement.

At Geneva College, I had qualified to teach American history at the high school level and, of course, now had tried my teaching wings on the Anderson campus. Arlene thought that staying in Anderson for a year was a reasonable idea, I was flattered, and no particular church placement was in view yet. So I told the president "yes," and soon received a contract for $6,000 and much responsibility for the coming year.

The Jeeninga office I inherited was on the fourth floor of Old Main, with no elevator, of course. I scrambled every day up and down the many steps, staying only one step ahead of my students in my reading and lectures. Later, I was told that my youth, obvious love for the Bible, and pure enthusiasm combined to overcome my rookie ineptness. Through all of the anxiety and rush, it felt right.

It was a dramatic year. Arlene was still teaching fifth grade in Chesterfield. I was a temporary college professor and my wife was pregnant! Most days, our excitement was tempered by Arlene's delicate health. We had moved from 1005 1/2 East Fifth Street to a rented house on Cottage Avenue just two blocks away and right behind Park Place Church of God where we were now attending. Not a driver herself, Arlene always rode to school with others, often taking a baked potato for her lunch—that and Sprite were sometimes all she could keep down. Since we had lived on her salary before, we now put mine in the bank as a hedge against the future. It was a good thing because, late in the year, I received another "free lunch" from president Robert Reardon. This one would set the path of my professional future.

Completing My Education

The extraordinary growth of American higher education in the 1960s was being experienced on the Anderson College campus, leading to the need for the expansion of facilities and faculty. A direct beneficiary of this circumstance, I was offered a full-time position in Bible and religious studies. I accepted on one condition. I needed more graduate education to really be qualified. President Reardon and dean Robert A. Nicholson agreed to a two-year educational leave, with my returning to Anderson in the fall of 1969 with a second masters and doctorate in hand. Financially, Arlene, I, and our coming baby would live on my banked salary for the first year ($6,000) and on an Anderson College loan for the second. It would be difficult, but possible. Here was the chance to attend Asbury, my original intent right out of college. Our son Todd was born in July, 1967. Only weeks later, we three were on the road in the heat of August, in a car not air-conditioned, headed to Kentucky and our future.

While I was a masters-degree student at Asbury Theological Seminary in Wilmore, Kentucky, 1967-1968, I had the opportunity to study under several excellent professors. In the process, I became more sensitized to the world of the Wesleyan/Holiness theological tradition that would be the religious world of my future. This knowledge would be critical in a way I did not expect at the time. Under the supervision of Dr. Harold B. Kuhn, I wrote a masters thesis on the Church of God movement titled "A Study in Ecumenical Idealism." This was a good time and place to think through who I was theologically and come to understand the Church of God movement in a larger historical frame. This fine theological school in Wilmore brought to me a welcome broadening of many perspectives, and several important new relationships. One was Clyde VanValin, pastor of the Free Methodist congregation that we attended.

Wilmore, Kentucky, is an interesting little town, historic in the American holiness movement. Arlene and I rented half of a modest duplex from the seminary, with a high-speed train track practically in our backyard. I walked to classes. We got a tip from a neighbor and went to Nicholasville to buy at a discount price half of a cow to be butchered and frozen. I grilled it, steak by steak, over the months, good eating on a very restricted budget.

One day a large snowstorm paralyzed the town. Word was brought to me that my grandfather Callen had died. With no phone of our own, I struggled to the community phone booth to make a sad call—there was no way I could get to the funeral in Pennsylvania. On several occasions, when the twisting roads to Lexington were clear of snow, Arlene and I would take Todd to a doctor. Recurrent bronchitis had no respect for our limited funds and no medical insurance. Even so, with Arlene now a stay-at-home mom, life went on, and my classes were mostly good.

One day a call came to the seminary from an official of Southeastern Christian College in the nearby city of Winchester. The school had an emergency need for a part-time teacher of Christian ethics for the winter quarter of 1968. Harold B. Kuhn, a key professor in my masters program, had recommended me for the role. Although my schedule already was busy, and Arlene and I had our hands full caring for an active baby in our little seminary duplex (we had no relatives nearby to provide any assistance), it seemed right to accept the challenge. I needed the teaching experience and the few extra dollars. At the time, we were living on our savings from both of us having taught the previous year in Anderson, and we were about to move on to Chicago for my doctoral program, to be funded entirely by borrowed money from Anderson College.

I did not welcome the necessity of taking the Graduate Record Exam to complete my Chicago application. Since I had no choice, I drove anxiously to the University of Kentucky in Lexington, took the exam, and later learned that I had scored higher than the minimum standard for doctoral admission. Gratitude prevailed at our house. However, before I could get to Chicago, there were two big developments. One nearly changed my goal altogether, and the other enriched it greatly.

1. Almost to Roberts Wesleyan College. In part from the brief Kentucky teaching experience at Southeastern, my earlier year of teaching at Anderson College, my rich family background in the Free Methodist

Church, and a stimulating year of advanced study at Asbury seminary where Free Methodist students were prominent, another opportunity suddenly came along. Arlene and I had no telephone, so I had to be informed by messenger that president Ellwood A. Voller and dean Paul L. Adams of Roberts Wesleyan College in North Chili, New York, were trying to reach me. I recall walking to the little business district of Wilmore where there was a public telephone booth. They called me there at an appointed time.

These educational leaders, whom I had never met, expressed strong interest in my considering a full-time appointment to the religion faculty of their campus. Roberts had been an active educational center of the Free Methodist Church since its founding as Chili Seminary in 1866. In 2006, my friend Howard A. Snyder would publish a major biography of Benjamin T. Roberts, the school's founder and one of the more influential and sophisticated leaders of the American holiness movement in the nineteenth century. Of course, when I was on the phone in the winter of 1968, I knew virtually nothing of B. T. Roberts, his story, or his school. Still, I was flattered, tempted, and confused by the conversation.

I already had a long-term teaching appointment at Anderson College and was on a two-year leave of absence in order to complete my graduate education at Asbury and then at Chicago Theological Seminary. But this offer was fresh and had unusual ties to the Free Methodist heritage of myself and my wife. In fact, we later learned that, when Arlene and I were each about three years old, both of us had been on this New York campus, maybe at the same time! For me, it had only been a brief family-related visit. For Arlene, the campus had been her home for a short time while her father studied for the ministry (which never happened because of his mental illness). Suddenly, we faced a pivotal decision time in our lives.

I agreed to be flown to Rochester, New York, and formally interviewed. It was a good experience. I recall noting that one of the New Testament classes at Roberts was using a textbook by Adam W. Miller, a former dean of the School of Theology in Anderson. This was a surprising and welcome circumstance, a symbol of how this campus could be a merging of my two church traditions, the Free Methodist Church and the Church of God (Anderson). The result of my visit was a formal offer for me to assume a full-time teaching position upon the completion of the intended Chicago doctorate in another year. I made clear to my interviewers that the money to make the next year possible was coming from a financial loan from Anderson, something that would be repaid over five years. President Voller responded by saying that Roberts would pay for the year of doctoral study, with no obligation on my part to pay any of it back! Roberts Wesleyan had just celebrated its centennial and was in an expansionist mood. Voller was an activist and not afraid to spend money where he thought it would be productive. I was being seen in the category of future productivity.

How good it was to be wanted as a young and virtually broke professional. I said I would give the Roberts offer serious consideration. Once back in Wilmore, I went to the same telephone booth and placed a call to Robert H. Reardon, president of Anderson College. I told him of the offer, thinking that only fair. He said, "Barry, do you have a car?" "Yes," I said. "Then get yourself to Anderson right away and we will have a good talk about all of this." I did just that, a little tense about gas money, the car's condition, and having to leave Arlene and Todd alone with no transportation.

Robert Reardon, Robert A. Nicholson, dean of Anderson College, and Gene W. Newberry, dean of its School of Theology, met me, treated me to lunch, and talked about my four good years on the Anderson campus, three as a seminary student and one as a full-time teacher. They spoke glowingly about the future of the campus and how well I fit. Anderson was a known thing to me, they said, as opposed to the risk of how things might work out on a campus that I had visited only twice, once as a toddler and once while being recruited by administrators. These good Anderson men intended for me to stay on track to Chicago and then come back to Anderson.

I returned to Kentucky alone in my car, reflecting on it all. Arlene and I talked and prayed. A decision was made. Anderson was the known quantity, including numerous people whom we trusted and loved. Roberts Wesleyan was viewed by us as much less known, and possibly president Ellwood Voller was an overextending administrator who might not manage to follow through for us on what seemed an extravagant offer of financial assistance. So I turned down the offer from Roberts and proceeded to complete my Asbury work and pursue the Anderson plan, going on to Chicago and into debt to do it. Arlene was comfortable with the decision, even though her heritage was singularly Free Methodist. She was careful with money and wondered whether the leaders at Roberts were being realistic. We closed that door. I would pay the price and remain with Anderson College and the Church of God.

My Asbury year was exceptional, with outstanding men as my mentors, including professor Harold B. Kuhn (teacher at Asbury from 1944 to 1982) and Frank B. Stanger (president of the seminary from 1962 to 1982), William Arnett, Wilbur Dayton, Kenneth Kinghorn, Dennis Kinlaw, and others. I had been tempted to move back into the Free Methodist world, but had not. Many other Church of God seminarians would attend Asbury Theological Seminary over the years, often tempted to pursue ministry outside their home tradition. In October, 2007, forty years after my student days at Asbury, I was sent back to the Kentucky campus by Church of God Ministries to visit with Church of God students and encourage them to value their home church heritage. How good it is that one's personal history can be used for the benefit of a new generation.

Interestingly, the issue of Roberts Wesleyan would come up again. I functioned in the summer of 1971 as the teaching evangelist at the Tri-State Camp Meeting of the Free Methodist Church located in East Liverpool, Ohio, the very setting of my personal conversion seventeen years earlier. I well remember the day in the middle of that week when I woke up, realized that it was my thirtieth birthday, and half-seriously wondered if my credibility had just left me! Following the radical 1960s, it was common to hear that no person over thirty had any relevant wisdom left.

Everyone, however, didn't think that way. A leader of the camp spoke about my ministry to Lawrence R. Schoenhals, then president of Roberts Wesleyan College. Schoenhals wrote to me on August 2, 1971, to inform me of a key retirement on campus and the search for a replacement. He wanted to explore the matter with me and actually visited with Arlene and me in Anderson, Indiana, that November. Soon he and dean Donald D. Kerlee invited me back to the campus in New York state to actively candidate for a faculty position in religion and philosophy. In a letter to president Schoenhals dated November 24, 1971, I said that "for a variety of personal, professional, and financial reasons, it appears unwise for me to pursue our conversations further at this time." The matter was ended—again.

Actually, another Roberts Wesleyan contact with me came up in February, 1988, when I received a letter from the dean's search committee at Roberts. It invited me to apply for the deanship. The timing was ironic since I was in the process of leaving my many years in the deanship at Anderson to return to full-time teaching and writing. I respectfully declined the invitation. By this time my wife Arlene was well integrated into the Anderson, Indiana, community, as was our son and Arlene's mother who by then was living with us.

Then a few years later, while at an annual meeting of the Wesleyan Theological Society in Nampa, Idaho, a man approached me and expressed sincere appreciation. At first I thought his reference was to my work as editor of the *Wesleyan Theological Journal*. In fact, he was the man who had accepted the teaching position at Roberts Wesleyan College back

in 1968 after I had turned it down. Now retired, he said that he owed
me a debt of gratitude for his chance to teach!

My final contact with Roberts Wesleyan College was in March, 2004.
I was newly married to Jan after Arlene's death the year before. The
annual meeting of the Wesleyan Theological Society was convening that
year on the Roberts campus, which I had not visited since 1968. Jan
traveled with me to learn about this group of scholars so important in my
life. We stood in front of old Carpenter Hall and looked at the steps
where I had stood when only three years old, at the very time when
Arlene was living inside with her parents. Somehow, this was one of those
surprising cycles of life that was full of nostalgia and gratitude, a Roberts
Wesleyan cycle that now seemed complete—finally.

2. To the Middle East. Just before my graduation from Asbury
Theological Seminary in the spring of 1968 with the Master of Theology
degree, I was contacted by Gene W. Newberry, dean of Anderson School
of Theology. He told me that the Lilly Endowment of Indianapolis was
funding a major trip to the Middle East for the Anderson religion faculty.
They would be sending the group to Cyprus, Israel, Jordan, and Lebanon
to visit numerous archaeological sites where there would be world-famous
biblical scholars present to lecture to the visitors. All expenses would be
covered by the grant—and, said Newberry to me, one of the Anderson
faculty preferred not to go. Would I want to go in his place? What an
opportunity! Had I accepted the Roberts invitation, this would have not
come my way.

I had never been outside the United States except for those few
fishing trips to Ontario, Canada. Now my problem was that the Chicago
doctoral program began in the summer of 1968 with a required "plunge"
on the streets of Chicago designed to sensitize one to the plight of the
urban poor. I contacted Chicago Theological Seminary to request that I

be allowed instead to plunge into the plight of new Palestinian refugees in the sprawling camps just set up because of the 1967 war won by Israel against its Arab neighbors. Permission was granted and the way cleared for me to take the trip of a lifetime.

Arlene and Todd stayed with her mother, Evelyn, in her home in Uniontown, Pennsylvania. I called there from New York just before the departing international flight and learned that Todd had just taken his first steps, and I had missed them! Even so, my family was in a comfortable setting and I was headed for many dramatic learning experiences with five men and one woman who had been my teachers in Anderson and soon would be my teaching colleagues there.

I took many slides and kept a careful journal for my own record and the Chicago summer assignment. I saw, feared, and was awed as we traveled from place to place. I learned so much that would enrich my teaching for decades to come. My second wife Jan and I would join a group of Messianic Jews and my rabbi friend Jeff Adler to travel back to Israel in the summer of 2005. It was a third time for me and a first for her. How fortunate we were!

Finally, I was home from that amazing 1968 journey and it was time for the big move to Chicago. Our actual arrival was a little shocking. Once in our third-floor apartment a few blocks from the quadrangle of the University of Chicago, and complete novices in a big city, we heard explosions out in the dark. Rather than a gun battle, we learned the next day that it was the fireworks for Hubert Humphrey who had just been nominated by the Democrats for the presidency of the United States. Later that next day, however, there was considerable social unrest, leading to riots, and in a few weeks even the taking over of the University of Chicago administration building by student radicals. Police were in abundance, as were gang graffiti and the fiery preaching of Christian activist Jesse Jackson. He was a recent graduate of the school now new to me.

My family and I were no longer in little Wilmore, Kentucky, that would not permit a fast-food chain in town for fear of providing a parking lot where rowdy youth might gather. From the conservative Wesleyan/Holiness seminary in Wilmore, and by way of a summer in the smoldering of a recent war in the Middle East, Arlene, Todd, and I were now on the southside of volatile Chicago. My new seminary setting, Chicago Theological Seminary, was hardly conservative; it was focused on a "liberal" faith in action in a world of urban turmoil. My sensibilities and insights were being stretched to the limit! That is, in part, what education is all about.

I was a member of a doctoral cohort of fifteen students, ranging from a Jesuit priest and Presbyterian minister to a few Baptists, Methodists and me. I was next to the youngest, and maybe the only one not previously soured on life in conventional Christian congregations. Occasionally, I was pressed hard to question traditionalism, reevaluate my personal past, and forge a fresh and more socially radical future. I stretched some and resisted even more. This was a world-class intellectual bastion with a streak of outright arrogance (so it seemed to me). The only attitude not to be tolerated was strong conviction, unless it was the conviction that tolerance of much diversity is to be valued highly. My classrooms were made hazy with the pipe smoke of the professors—very different and uncomfortable for me.

Arlene was uncomfortable socially and nervous about the traffic everywhere. She spent most of her time caring for Todd and me and doing a little babysitting in our apartment. We rarely went to the downtown Loop because of the time and cost involved. I recall at least two occasions, however, when we did go. Once it was to see two astronauts on parade, fresh home from space, and once to see the river turned green in honor of St. Patrick's Day. Chicago pulsated with life, which for the most part I found fascinating and stimulating. The late 1960s were surely a socially revolutionary time.

I worked hard on my classes, sometimes being a little intimidated by the setting, often being enlightened in fresh ways. My professors may have leaned far to the "liberal" side of things, but they were true professionals with high standards. Arlene and I joined a grocery co-op and on many weekends drove the busy freeways to Gary, Indiana, where I preached for the Greek Church of God. My sermons were in English, but they prayed and taught in Greek. I successfully urged them to merge with a nearby "American" congregation before they lost all of their young people. The merger finally happened. I often have teased that I closed my first church!

The year in Chicago went quickly. The weekend pastorate was fulfilling and the qualifying exams exhausting, but completed successfully. My mother and "Auntie" from Geneva College came to see me celebrate graduation in my red robe, now as "Dr. Callen" with my Doctor of Religion degree. The time had come to leave the city and return to my teaching appointment back at Anderson College. It had been a "heady" and stretching experience done on borrowed money.

Back Home Again in Indiana

Arlene and I returned to Anderson, Indiana, in the summer of 1969 after being away on special study leave for over two years. I remember driving down the rather quiet and tree-lined East Fifth Street on the south edge of the picturesque campus of Anderson College and wondering with some momentary anxiety about what was happening in the world (as though I no longer was in the midst of the real action once removed from the turmoil of war in the Middle East and the social upheaval in Chicago). Wilmore, Kentucky, had been small and academically stimulating, my weeks in the Middle East right after the big war of 1967 sobering indeed, and then the year in Chicago during the dramatic social turmoil of the late

1960s quite an experience for a little boy from Craig Beach, Ohio! With the help of so many, I had grown up.

Arlene and I had managed to live for two years on about $9,000, with the baby and including educational books and tuition. We had benefited from subsidized school housing and a generous scholarship from Asbury Theological Seminary. The out-of-pocket expenses of half of our two-year experience had been covered in part by what Arlene and I had saved in 1966-67 when we both taught in Anderson. The other half was covered by a $4,400 loan from Anderson College that we would repay in full by payroll deduction during the first five years that we were back on campus. It was not easy, but it was well worth the sacrifice. Anderson College had played its part and Arlene and I knew how to live with relatively little. We considered ourselves fortunate to have had these special growth opportunities, a foundation for a lifetime. Our arrangement was that, once my education was complete, she would not need to teach again. She never did.

Now the question was, where would we live? With more help from the college for a downpayment on a modest house on Gaywood Drive in Chesterfield, Indiana, we tried to settle down with our two-year-old son Todd, our debt, and very little furniture. We ordered a new couch, and for many weeks had a little picture of it taped to the living-room wall. It was in the Chesterfield elementary school that my wife had provided a real gift for our futures by her earlier four years of teaching. Now I would be the bread-winner and she a stay-at-home mom. Financially, it would never be easy. In our early months back in Indiana, we had to replace the furnace, an $800 expense we had not counted on. We were in debt to the college and my salary was modest. But it was enough and we managed.

When the weather warmed, Arlene's ministry instincts took over. We opened our garage door and she ran a neighborhood Bible school for the many children on our street in Chesterfield. The fence of our backyard also served as the centerfield fence for a baseball field of the local park.

Occasionally, a well-hit ball would land in our yard and even bounce against the house. Remnants of the July 4th fireworks settled dangerously toward our roof. A plumbing problem required the digging up of our front yard. But we still managed and even served.

Returning to Anderson College in the summer of 1969 was a little like trying to relocate to the country farm after once having seen the bright lights of Paris. My annual report to dean Robert A. Nicholson, dated June 4, 1970, reported on the "conversion factor." Arlene and I had left Chicago's fast pace, its intense academic atmosphere, and the visibility of a wide range of Christian and other lifestyles. Now we were in Anderson's lessened air pollution, seemingly slow-motion pace, more restrictive environment of Christian belief and practice, and somewhat lower academic expectations. Anderson was a Christian liberal arts college serving mainly students from blue-collar Midwestern homes. It had many students who were the first in their families to attend college, let alone experience the University of Chicago, one of the elite academic centers of the world.

I vividly remember the first task given me on my return to the Anderson campus in 1969. Even before the fall semester began, a group of about seventy-five African-American pastors had gathered on campus for days of continuing education. Most of them had not completed high school. There was an emergency need for someone to deliver a lecture to them and I was asked on very short notice. Still in my Chicago academic mode, I delivered a rather sophisticated lecture titled "The Phenomenological Dimensions of an Oxymoronic Ministry." It was much too academic, too Chicago-like. My hearers were gracious—but I was embarrassed! In fact, it took a few years in the classroom for me to relax, become vulnerable to students, and stop acting like the world's resident expert on all things. Appropriate humility of the teacher opens the door for the more likely learning of beginners.

Living in Chesterfield was not ideal since Arlene did not drive. For occasional campus evening events, it would be necessary for me to make three trips to Anderson, one to get the babysitter, one to go to the event, and then another to take the babysitter home, each lap about five miles. We finally decided to give up owning a modest home and rented a two-bedroom apartment near the campus. Beginning October 1, 1970, our residence became apartment N5B at 1823 East Eighth Street (Vickers Apartments). The third floor was not always the most convenient for carrying groceries, etc., but it served us well. In fact, I owe words of great appreciation for Arlene's willingness to live through the transitional years 1963 to 1970 when we married, moved often and lived on very limited funds. Our first seven years of marriage were stressful, but yielded a son, two masters degrees, a doctorate, and a teaching position at Anderson College. Arlene was faithfully and resourcefully by my side all the way. While never easy, it had been necessary and got done.

The "conversion factor" back to Anderson College involved more than the struggling transitions in our personal lives. It was an historic time on the Anderson campus. "Old Main" had been constructed by church pioneers when they first came to Anderson, Indiana, from Moundsville, West Virginia, in 1906. Now in 1968 the old cornerstone was removed and the wrecking ball began to swing against this massive stone structure that had first become the home of Anderson College in the 1920s. In its place would be an impressive modern structure called Decker Hall.

When I returned to campus in 1969, the big construction project was underway. It required the temporary housing of many administrative and faculty offices in a network of house trailers. I moved into one of them with a philosophy professor, Dr. Sander Kleis. He and I shared what would have been a little bedroom in our assigned trailer. He was brilliant but eccentric, with a passion for endless conversations with campus athletes who would sit on his desk to chat. My desk was squeezed tightly against his. I reported the following to dean Robert Nicholson after that 1969-1970 school year:

> I say it in candor and in kindness: I can imagine physical arrangements more likely to encourage professional growth (especially in its more quiet and reflective aspects) than sharing a trailer office with Sander Kleis. He is a wonderful, intelligent, and dedicated man, but he is also highly gregarious! A major blessing of the year was his sabbatical second semester.

In later years, the Kleis daughter Avis and her husband David Liverett would be dear friends of Jan and mine.

Even my face had a certain "conversion." When in high school and college, I wore a "burr cut." Short hair was practical for basketball and a fad of the time. I didn't join the youth rebellion of the 1960s that often was marked by very long hair on young men. I did, however, develop a new appearance in 1971. I was spending a month in Japan leading a group of Anderson College students in the TRI-S program (student summer service). While living in the missionary home of Nathan and Ann Smith, Ann suggested that I try growing a beard. She said it would improve my appearance. I did. Once home and beyond the scrub stage, I decided with some hesitancy to wear it to the campus for my fall classes. In one version or another, I have kept the beard ever since. Missionaries can be very influential people! It would not be until 2011 and my temporary loss of all head hair because of chemotherapy treatments that I returned to the short-hair style of my youth. In 2012 I enjoyed watching my grandson Ian experimenting with hair styles. His was a head full of reddish curls dangling about his ears and eyes and covering well a very active brain! I had a brain, but never curls.

My Pastoral Ministries and TRI-S

Even though I pursued and completed two masters degrees and a doctorate between 1963 and 1969, and although I had been drawn by interest and circumstance into full-time college teaching, the pastoral ministry was never far from my mind. Nor, on occasion, was it separated entirely from my actual functioning. I always have been a churchman in the midst of my academic pursuits. In fact, when I hung my degree diplomas in my several campus offices over the years, above them always was my certificate of ordination to Christian ministry—the copy that Sister Lillie, my beloved home pastor, had bronzed for me. Actually, I did function as a preaching minister on a few occasions over the years.

While still in my three years as a seminarian (1963-1966), I accepted the role as interim preaching pastor of the Church of God congregation in Danville, Illinois. Some of the long trips there in the winter were harrowing, but always rewarding. Here were people genuinely appreciative of my sometimes fumbling and experimental efforts to minister on their behalf. Then I was tempted not to leave central Indiana after seminary graduation. The Tillitson Avenue Church of God in Muncie sought me as their pastor. I had been a guest preacher and admired their high commitment to well-educated Sunday school teachers. The church was very close to the campus of Ball State University. Its pastoral search committee said that I could do doctoral work there if I wished. It was good to be wanted by a fine congregation, but I felt drawn to Asbury Theological Seminary and Chicago Theological Seminary. I made the hard decision to turn them down and never regretted the decision.

While living in Wilmore, Kentucky, Arlene and I attended the local Free Methodist congregation pastored by the gentle and wise Clyde VanValin. Once we had made the big move to Chicago, I balanced my preoccupation with the doctoral work and my young family with a call to be the weekend preaching pastor of the Greek Church of God in Gary, Indiana. This was a wonderful group of loving Greek people struggling to maintain their ethnic heritage while their youth were slipping into the dominant culture around them. I urged them to merge with a much larger Church of God congregation located close by and where their young people were already active socially with their high school friends. The merger finally did happen, I think to the benefit of all. Sometimes, success in pastoral ministry is defined as helping people see their real circumstance and become willing to move on.

There also was my year as the interim pastor of the Maple Grove Church of God in Anderson, Indiana. I had returned with my Chicago doctorate in hand and rejoined the active membership of Park Place Church of God, then being pastored by Hillery C. Rice. Clifton Brashler had pastored the Maple Grove congregation in Anderson since 1963. By 1970, having led this small body of believers to new facilities on eight attractive acres along East 38th Street, he left to pastor in Tampa, Florida. Hillery Rice assisted with the recruitment of a new pastor and recommended me as the interim preaching pastor. Although a busy young professor on the Anderson campus, I accepted the call and for many months enjoyed a productive weekend ministry at Maple Grove. I still have a list of the sermons I delivered from February through June, 1971.

I was blessed at Maple Grove with laypersons like Dr. Paul Breitweiser, who was on the music faculty of Anderson College, and a young person, John Howard, who soon would become a seminarian under my deanship and in the 1990s my educational colleague when he was the chief operating officer of Gardner College in Camrose, Alberta, Canada. My sister Bonnie and her husband Rex attended this church at the time. My wife Arlene was active in the direction of a Bible school for the youth.

My role at Maple Grove ended when missionaries Paul and Nova Hutchins were caught at home because of a political problem in their Asian field of service. With my encouragement, Paul was called to Maple Grove as the new pastor. Arlene and I stayed for a time as laypersons at Paul's request, but finally chose to return to Park Place Church. Paul and Nova became lifelong friends. In the 1980s, they would be serving in Kenya, East Africa, and act as my gracious host when I journeyed to this special land. As dean of Anderson College at the time, my task was to work with the Church of God school in Kenya in relation to its quest for accreditation (now Kima International School of Theology). I was pleased to have been able, many years before that, to have functioned as a bridge person that assisted with Paul's transition to pastoral ministry in Anderson, Indiana.

A busy academic career was now in process for me. By the fall of 1969 I had completed my first three graduate degrees (a fourth was still to come from Indiana University). Although with very limited finances, Arlene and I were settling back into life on the Anderson campus after living for a year in Wilmore, Kentucky, and another year in Chicago, Illinois. My salary was low, but our family debt load was reasonable and the opportunities for future growth and travel were very good. Already I had participated in the 1968 Holy Land seminar in Lebanon, Jordan, Israel, and Cyprus. In 1971 it became my special privilege to lead a TRI-S group of campus students to Japan. It probably was the most personally profitable of my several TRI-S trips over the years to come.

Japan is both an ancient and modern place. Our World Airways charter flight from Seattle to Tokyo had problems over the Pacific Ocean with leaking aviation fuel. We arrived very late and missed our connecting flight to the south island. Missionary Trish (Bentley) Janutolo met us and saved the day by arranging alternate transportation. Once in the home of missionaries Nathan and Ann Smith, we were totally exhausted and slept on floors all over the house. In later decades, Trish and her husband Blake would be close campus colleagues and personal friends back in Anderson.

We TRI-S people helped build a retaining wall behind the missionary residence, visited Zen Buddhist temples, and went to Nagasaki, one of two atomic bomb blast sites at the end of World War II. I preached with the help of a Japanese interpreter and taught English pronunciation to Japanese teachers of English. We experienced the Smiths as superb Christian witnesses, culturally sensitive, with Ann especially able to speak excellent Japanese. Superb also were Phil and Phyllis Kinley in Tokyo, whom we visited after a cross-country trip in a "bullet" train. Years later, and back at Park Place Church of God in Anderson, Indiana, the Kinleys and Smiths retired as missionaries and became active laypersons and our personal friends, "our" first being Arlene and me and then, after her death in 2003, Jan and me. The memories of my Japanese sojourn are many, nearly all good.

I have always been a fan of Anderson University's TRI-S program. One sees the church and one's own country in a new light when outside them. This is a great way to engage in a culturally rich liberal arts education. My sadness is that Arlene did not travel with me. It would have been very stressful for her because of the air travel, heat, and strange food. To bridge the gap of our immediate experiences, I brought home Japanese clothes for her and Todd, a lovely tea set, many pictures, and numerous tall tales that she heard patiently on various occasions. Also during the 1970s, I would benefit greatly from other TRI-S trips, including the ones I led to Australia and England. Again, what a set of experiences for a little boy from Craig Beach, Ohio!

The year 1972 was an eventful one for me. For the first time I was named one of the year's "Outstanding Educators of America." In the January Term of that year I co-led with Dr. Gustav Jeeninga another campus group, this time to Italy, Greece, and Israel—it was his sabbatical that I had covered to launch my teaching career in 1966-67. Later, I would edit and publish through Anderson University Press his autobiography, *Doors to Life* (2002). I now was writing occasional pieces for the national periodical of the Church of God, *Vital Christianity*, including an article inspired by my Italian sojourn ("Among the Ruins of Pompeii," July 8, 1973).

The Center for Pastoral Studies was founded on campus in 1972. By then I was the chair of the college's Department of Bible and Religion and was named the Center's founding director—president Robert Reardon expressing faith in my administrative potential. It was my privilege to work with skilled educational persons like Jerry C. Grubbs, T. Franklin Miller, and Fredrick H. Shively to conceive, organize, and operate the Center in its first years. Robert Reardon is to be credited for initially dreaming the Center's dream. It fell to me and then others to make it an operational reality.

I was ordained formally to the Christian ministry on November 28, 1973, in a moving service at the North Anderson Church of God, then located on North Broadway in Anderson, Indiana. This was the congregation in which I had interned during one of my seminary student semesters in 1965-66, with pastor Marvin Baker as my wise mentor. In my mind and in the judgment of others, it was clear by 1973 that my educational and administrative responsibilities on campus constituted significant Christian ministry. Accordingly, Dwight McCurdy represented the Indiana Assembly of the Church of God at this ordination occasion. Following the opening hymn, "To God Be the Glory" (identified on the printed program as "a favorite of Dr. Barry Callen"), the sermon of ordination was preached by James Earl Massey, campus pastor whom I greatly admired as mentor and model in ministry and who would be a lifelong colleague and dear personal friend. I then was introduced formally by my home pastor, Lillie S. McCutcheon, who had traveled to Indiana from northeast Ohio for this occasion. Within days, and as a personal gift, she had my ordination certificate bronzed and delivered to me.

Geneva College

Anderson School of Theology

Anderson College, Anderson, Indiana

Asbury Theological Seminary
WILMORE, KENTUCKY

The Chicago Theological Seminary

CERTIFICATE OF ORDINATION

This is to certify that

Indiana University
School of Education

My superb ministerial mentors included Lillie and
Glenn McCutcheon (standing middle) and Austin and Nancy Sowers (seated).
Sons Ray (left) and Bob McCutcheon have been lifelong friends.

HOLINESS UNTO the LORD

My conversion to Jesus Christ happened in this tabernacle
on the Free Methodist campgrounds in East Liverpool, Ohio.

MOVING DOWN SALVATION'S ROAD

"Salvation" should mean being rescued from all that is false and destructive and then being transformed into the fullness of the new being that God intends. The tragedy of life is not that eventually we all will die. It's that, prior to our deaths, what is supposed to be wonderfully alive in us never gets born! Being "holy" is moving on down the salvation road by being truly re-born, re-formed, re-engaged, re-related to a holy God in ways that begin to show in how we think and act.

Barry L. Callen
Catch Your Breath! (2014, p. 33)

**The VanArsdale family cottage,
East Liverpool, Ohio, Free Methodist camp grounds.**

The Anderson School of Theology faculty, 1967. Most were my seminary teachers and in just six years would be the faculty under my deanship. Dr. Gene W. Newberry, whom I would follow as dean, is seated near left.

I was surrounded by outstanding leaders of the Church of God who nurtured and encouraged me. Shown here in 1976 are Drs. T. Franklin Miller (left) and Robert H. Reardon (right).

The door next to the bicycle was our little student apartment at 1005½ East Fifth Street in Anderson, Indiana. Just beyond is the tower of Park Place Church of God.

Dr. Gustav Jeeninga and I took Anderson College students to the ancient Mediterranean world.

Dr. Jeeninga, Professor of Religion, member of the A. C. faculty since 1960, founder of the A. C. Museum of Bible and Near Eastern Studies. Did research in the Near East in 1952-1953 and during his sabbatical leave 1966-67, at which time he participated in excavations with the American School of Oriental Research and traveled extensively in the Near East.

Dr. Callen, Assistant Professor of Religion at Anderson College and of the School of Theology, completed his doctorate at Chicago Theological Seminary (1985) with a concentration in the relationship between the Christian Faith and Cultures of the past and present involved in this study and contemporary in its location. Callen's study (1986) of biblical archaeology and the ancient civilizations of the Middle East.

Chapter 5

Leading the Church's Seminary

Educating young ministers for excellence

It had been a longer stay than anticipated. Arriving in Anderson, Indiana, in 1963 to begin my seminary education was intended to be a three-year period of graduate-level ministerial preparation. How surprising that, ten years later, I would still be in town and, most surprising of all, functioning as acting dean of Anderson School of Theology. That decade would be only the beginning of a much longer career on the Anderson campus.

By 1973 I was chair of Anderson College's Department of Bible and Religion, director of the new Center for Pastoral Studies, and acting dean of the seminary from which I had graduated in 1966. This fast track in Anderson had begun when I was twenty-two years old and had landed me in the dean's chair of a graduate school at age thirty-two. All of this happened because of an unusual set of circumstances and key people who put faith in me. All of it, of course, was being supervised by the graciousness of divine providence, a quiet working that often cannot be recognized except with the passing of time.

A New Day for the Seminary

The faculty members of Anderson School of Theology received a presidential summons in 1971. President Robert H. Reardon was a man of action and wanted to talk to them very seriously. The sponsoring Church of God movement had no formal educational requirements for ordained ministers. Seminary enrollments in Anderson were low and it was time for change in the direction of increased practical relevance to the church. The president laid out a general plan for the seminary's future. In faculty minds, his vision placed in question the continuance of the standard three-year Master of Divinity degree program being offered on campus. Since the M. Div. was the traditional heart of a seminary curriculum, they were nervous and defensive.

President Reardon argued that wisdom lay with new, versatile, shorter masters programs (forty-five instead of ninety semester hours) and more coordination with the undergraduate college's religion faculty and curriculum. There was need, he announced, for a new Center for Pastoral Studies to facilitate practical and continuing ministerial education not offering formal academic credit. It also would be helpful to enter cooperative relationships with seminaries like Christian Theological Seminary in Indianapolis and Asbury Theological Seminary in Kentucky. Reardon even hinted that, depending on the outcome of such changes, all current seminary faculty members might not be needed in the future. The immediate result of this meeting was confusion and even anger. The faculty viewed the three-year Master of Divinity as the basic seminary program. Now they wondered about its future—and their own. I was the new chair of the undergraduate religion department at the time and was not in the meeting, but I heard much from those who were. It was a very awkward and uncomfortable time.

The intent behind these presidential announcements was to highlight the need to act boldly by embracing creative innovation in the face of persistent enrollment problems. The president was ready to put programmatic specifics to the general thinking that already had been done by a Joint Committee on Theological Education appointed in 1969 by the administration. This committee had been charged to look at the entire campus program of ministerial education, break down old walls between Anderson College and its graduate School of Theology, revise the curriculum as needed, and deploy the teaching resources of the campus to the best advantage—sometimes exchanging graduate and undergraduate professors and courses. I was an active member of this crucial committee, my first real taste of institutional thinking, administrative leadership, and political strategies. It was tense and demanding. Much was at stake. I found myself right in the middle.

The strategy of the proposed new "seven-year track" on campus was to identify ministerial students early, accelerate their professional education at the undergraduate level, and retain them on campus for the Anderson seminary. Some introductory graduate courses could be satisfied at the undergraduate level, with the potential for electives thereby increased in the seminary. The length of time required in seminary would be shortened for many students by requiring only half the usual number of academic credits (down from ninety to forty-five in the new programs). There were to be "covenant churches" identified as practical places to support academic education. A minister-in-residence program would be launched to bring effective pastoral ministers into the academic setting.

It was a bold set of fresh initiatives, largely envisioned by a president who cared deeply for the church and the relevance and thus continuance of its seminary. I was quickly engaged in the detailed work of designing the particulars of the new graduate programs and helping to think through the interrelationships of college and seminary faculties—their reporting lines, specializations, teaching loads, etc.

The seminary community, while appreciative of these desired goals, resisted what they judged the inevitable "watering down" of graduate courses to accommodate underprepared college students. Particularly did they oppose the feared dilution or even deletion of the standard M. Div. program that they considered the heart of a true seminary. The volatile situation intensified when Buford Norris, president of Christian Theological

Seminary, sought to finalize the formation of the "Foundation for Religious Studies," a proposed ecumenical enterprise to be based in Indianapolis. Major foundation funding was anticipated for realizing the cooperation of several seminaries of differing theological traditions, thus making available to all of their students a wider range of faculty and curricular resources. The foundation funding appeared to hinge in part on an "evangelical" seminary being part of the envisioned consortium. So, Anderson School of Theology, the closest such seminary to Indianapolis, was being urged to participate through cross-registration of students, open library access, limited faculty sharing, and even possible relocation to Indianapolis.

A meeting of the Anderson board of trustees convened in March, 1972, and heard the strong support of president Robert H. Reardon and seminary dean Gene W. Newberry for participation in the new Foundation for Religious Studies. They also heard about the new Center for Pastoral Studies, new degree structures, and other innovations. The board also listened carefully to strong objections from seminary faculty and student representatives. Finally, the decision was made, not for seminary relocation, but for relationship with the new consortium, a new Center for Pastoral Studies, and the new degree programs to be called Master of Ministry and Master of Arts in Religion (with continuation of the three-year M. Div.). I quickly was engaged in the hard work of discussing with Indianapolis officials how we would proceed with cross-registration of courses offered by several seminaries—it would be a complex process to say the least. I was both intrigued and a little overwhelmed. Was this to be the future?

Having begun initial implementation, negative reaction to some of the changes was heard from numerous Church of God ministers. Some felt that the seminary was being compromised, either because the M. Div. program appeared threatened (the concern of seminary graduates) or because a small Roman Catholic seminary was involved in the consortium. Some ministers announced with near panic that future Church of God ministers would now be educated by Roman priests. After vigorous debate in the 1972 General Assembly, a 499-422 vote rejected the appropriateness of involvement in the Foundation for Religious Studies and called for a quick end of it. A study committee was authorized to bring a report to the 1973 Assembly containing "recommendations for the continuation of a *Church of God* seminary, responsible to the General Assembly."

Out of this painful conflict, the Church of God movement was beginning to claim real ownership of "its" seminary. The perceived threat of loss to outside forces had heightened awareness of the graduate school and the willingness to find resources to enable its continuance apart from a consortium relationship. Prior to this time there had been no general church funds designated specifically for the seminary. It had been launched in 1950 by Anderson College and funded by the Anderson campus and student tuition. With lowered enrollments in the late 1960s and early 1970s, it often was heard that the seminary was being funded out of the pockets of undergraduate students. This had to change.

I was selected to be the renovated seminary's young new leader, first as director of the Center for Pastoral Studies beginning in 1972 (administering the seminary coordinately with the dean, Gene W. Newberry, confusing to say the least), then as acting dean in 1973 (while Newberry was on sabbatical in Kenya, East Africa), and finally as dean beginning in 1974. On the very day of my election to the deanship by the board of trustees, a letter went from president Reardon to all North American pastors in the Church of God. It announced this key decision. Citing my six years of faculty service, my current directorship of the Center, my having authored the 1973 book *Where Life Begins* (my first book), and my current role as acting dean of the seminary, the president extended this generous evaluation of me to the pastors: "Surely the Church is fortunate that a young and gifted man like Dr. Callen is available to assume the responsibility as Dean. I know you will rejoice with me in his election, and will want to give him the support he needs and deserves."

I was unusually young for such a major leadership role. I did have strong academic credentials, but very limited administrative experience. I would have to rely on God for the necessary gifts and trust that I would be supported well by hundreds of national leaders, many of whom I did not even know. I would also need the trust of the seminary faculty who were objecting to some of the curriculum and relationship changes. Time would prove my confidence in this faculty's graciousness well-founded. Gene Newberry had been my dean and teacher in seminary; now he would complete his distinguished career by teaching and writing under my administrative leadership. It would be an honor for me and, I hoped, a joy for him. It worked out just that way, concluding with his retirement in 1980 and our personal friendship extending well into the twenty-first century.

In the year 2000, Dr. Newberry published his autobiography titled *A Boy from Lewis County*. In it he says this in his typically gracious way about his sabbatical time in East Africa: "I wrote the Board of Trustees at AC and asked if I could conclude my twelve-year deanship with this teaching in Kenya. Barry Callen was so capable and available to follow me" (p. 109). The board agreed and I assumed the dean's chair.

The 1974 election by the board of trustees that placed me in the deanship of Anderson School of Theology required the formal ratification vote of the General Assembly of the Church of God. That vote was 93% affirmative (621 to 47). My initial term of office was three years, and my total tenure as dean would turn out to require two other ratification votes, 1977 (95.6% affirmative) and 1980 (91.1% affirmative in an Assembly filled with controversy related to the Anderson campus but not specifically seminary related).

So, in 1974, I was the new dean of the graduate school, charged to lead the significantly new School of Theology. Being only thirty-two years old at the time of ratification, I was the youngest dean in all of the seventy accredited seminaries in the United States and Canada. In addition, being only eight years away from my own graduation from the Anderson seminary, I now was to be the administrative leader of the same faculty members who had just been my teachers! This would not have worked had these people not been a special group of well-intentioned and gracious human beings. To my good fortune, they were. Among them was Gene W. Newberry, whom I was succeeding as seminary dean and who had been my first teacher of theology. Also included was John W. V. Smith, my teacher of church history who now became associate dean at my request.

In my young and administratively inexperienced hands, president Robert H. Reardon had placed a senior graduate faculty. Why choose me for this big assignment and not one of them? As I recall his private observations to me, the president wanted a fresh beginning, not some extension of the old assumptions and procedures that had not worked very well. Also, it was his judgment that there was little administrative ability resident among the seminary faculty. I had caught his eye as a young scholar on campus who had strong church roots, quality academic credentials, and already had risen to be chair of the undergraduate Department of Bible and Religion. He had also been impressed that I had chosen to return to Anderson after my doctoral work out of loyalty to the school, in spite of having had in hand a much better financial offer (Roberts Wesleyan College). School loyalty was important to Robert Reardon who had been part of the Anderson campus since the 1920s.

The combination of my conservative background (my pastor being Lillie S. McCutcheon of the Newton Falls, Ohio, congregation) and my broad academic credentials (including a second masters from the "conservative" Asbury Theological Seminary and the doctorate from the more "liberal" Chicago Theological Seminary) meant that the faculty would be comfortable and the General Assembly of the Church of God likely would have no quarrel with the choice. President Reardon went with his instincts, a typical way for him to proceed. He had a reputation for "shooting from the hip," and he usually was right. I surely hoped that his reputation for wisdom was warranted in his choice of me to lead the seminary into the future! I was sobered by the challenge and honored by the trust being invested in me.

When the Center for Pastoral Studies was established in 1972, it was used for a brief time as the structural home of both the seminary and college religion faculty members on campus. Jerry C. Grubbs was appointed in April, 1973, to replace Irene Smith Caldwell in the seminary's Christian education chair. According to his letter of invitation, Jerry was "to become a member of the Center faculty, with your primary base of operation being the School of Theology." He was the first of many faculty members whom I would be privileged to recruit to the campus over the following seventeen years (although the only one under the Center canopy). As seminary enrollment began to grow, organizational distance again developed between the graduate and undergraduate units of ministerial education on campus. This seemed functionally inevitable even if not theoretically desirable. In 2016, with seminary enrollments down again, they would be joined into one school.

In addition to Jerry Grubbs, I brought to the seminary Lester Crose and later Douglas Welch in Christian mission, Dwight L. Grubbs and Fredrick H. Shively in pastoral ministries, Theodore A. Stoneberg in pastoral care and counseling, Harold L. Phillips and James Earl Massey in New Testament and preaching, Walter Froese in church history, Gilbert W. Stafford in Christian theology, and Merle D. Strege in historical theology. These appointments were in response to five retirements, one sudden death (Boyce W. Blackwelder), and two new positions created in response to enrollment and program growth. I was blessed that these marvelous people were available to be gathered around me.

President Reardon had made clear to me from the beginning of my administration that I was inheriting a senior faculty and my biggest task in the first five years would be to appoint a new generation of faculty members. Looking back many years later, it appears that I did bring to the seminary a great group of Christian educators, all of whom became valued colleagues and close personal friends. A much longer list of undergraduate professors would be added to the list of my appointments when later I would serve as dean of the College (about sixty faculty members in all). As I write, I note that all of these I brought to the seminary faculty are now retired or deceased. Time does move on! I appointed a new generation and now I have watched dean David Sebastian and Mary Ann Hawkins do it again, and do it well.

The 1973 General Assembly of the Church of God received and approved twelve recommendations designed to affirm and strengthen the School of Theology and achieve increased financial support for the seminary and its students. This strategy soon yielded real fruit. The 1974 General Assembly approved a five-year plan of new seminary support through the church's World Service budget, a total of $200,000. That same Assembly proceeded to adopt a proposal for the national church to join with the Anderson campus in raising an annual fund to help defray the tuition costs of Church of God seminarians at Anderson School of Theology. This fund, soon to be known as the Boyce W. Blackwelder Seminary Tuition Fund, would be the vehicle for raising and distributing directly to seminary students in excess of one million dollars over the following years. Dr. Blackwelder had been my teacher of biblical Greek and then had served as a faculty member under my deanship. After his sudden death, I was privileged to help arrange to have his name associated with this significant support of future seminarians. It was a small way of expressing gratitude. Another way was my editing the book *Listening to the Word of God* in 1990, a scholarly tribute to Boyce Blackwelder.

In that same 1974 Assembly, I was formally installed and commissioned as the seminary's new dean. I stated the following to the Anderson board of trustees in June, 1974, in my first official report as dean:

> The Church of God in general and this board of trustees in particular have found it necessary to search relentlessly for the most appropriate and feasible model for educating ministers in a context of excellence, without destroying meaningful bridges to the sponsoring church and without compromising the integrity of the school itself. This process to date has proven time-consuming, painful, and profitable in ways often unanticipated.

The outcomes of this relentless search were several. One was establishing the premise that seminary education should proceed within the organizational framework of the Church of God movement. A cooperative ecumenical enterprise such as the Foundation for Religious Studies in Indianapolis was not acceptable to the church. Another outcome was drawing attention to the importance of seminary education for coming generations of ministers.

The School of Theology would now function with a much greater accountability to and support from the Church of God movement. Its dean would stand for General Assembly ratification, a seminary line item separate from that of Anderson College would appear in the World Service budget of the church, and the several undergraduate colleges of the church would work toward curricular coordination with the School of Theology in ministerial education. The graduate school in Anderson was to be recognized as the church's only seminary. In fact, the church's Commission on Christian Higher Education produced a major report titled "Theological Education and Ministerial Training in the Church of God." Proposed successfully to the 1976 General Assembly by the Commission was the following, quite a step forward for a free-church body like the Church of God movement:

We propose that the General Assembly recognize seminary training as the *normal*, the *ideal* level of initial preparation for the future young minister, and that the Assembly continue to authorize an annual appropriation of funds whereby this level of ministerial training can be made available to eligible students who give evidence that they will use their educational experiences for the good of the church.

It had been a long road from places like Oberlin seminary in Ohio in the 1930s and 1940s, where a few key Church of God persons experienced seminary education for the first time, to a formal recognition that such education should be recognized as "normal" and "ideal" in the Church of God movement—with the movement having its own accredited seminary. Such advanced education was aspirational, of course, and in no way mandatory. But at least it now was an approved statement of intent, and I was recognized formally as the new leader for this very new day.

A Busy Academic Administrator

Before I began my exciting and sometimes exhausting activity as seminary dean (although I had been acting dean for over a year), there was the formal establishment of my call and commission to academic and institutional leadership. The date was June 19, 1974, one of the more memorable days of my life. I was asked by president Robert H. Reardon to come and stand before the 1400 ministers and lay leaders of the General Assembly of the Church of God convened in annual session in the sanctuary of Park Place Church of God in Anderson, Indiana. This was my formal service of installation as the new dean of Anderson School of Theology. In my pocket was a Western Union telegram just received from Kisumu in Kenya, East Africa. It was from Gene W. Newberry, the man still on sabbatical leave whom I now was officially replacing as dean. It read: "Barry, congratulations. Best wishes for a rewarding deanship. Sorry to miss the occasion." Gene was about to rejoin the School of Theology teaching faculty and was bowing out of the deanship with his usual graciousness.

The large assembly of church leaders was adding congratulations and best wishes. My wife Arlene and son Todd (then seven years old) were present and asked to stand to be recognized. The faculty of the School of Theology and the six presidents of the Church of God colleges in North America surrounded me as I sat on a chair in the middle of the platform. President Reardon named the three deans who had gone before, read Dr. Newberry's telegram, spoke of the awesome responsibility I was assuming, and recognized Ronald J. Fowler, pastor in Akron, Ohio, and my dear personal friend, to read Ephesians 4:4-13. Ray Keith, chair of the Anderson board of trustees, delivered the official charge to me. I responded with a few comments of humility and commitment. Former seminary dean Adam W. Miller offered the dedicatory prayer just before president Reardon said the following as the act of installation:

> Dr. Barry Callen, faithful servant of the Lord Jesus Christ, inasmuch as you have responded to the call to service and declared yourself today before this Assembly, I proclaim you to be Dean of the School of Theology. May God inspire and instruct many mighty sons and daughters under your care so that the church may be nourished and led into greater ministry in the days ahead. Go forth to the task before you in the power of His might, and may the memory of this day return again and again like a heavenly benediction to refresh your soul.

Of course, I have never forgotten that day. What a responsibility it was to have the sons and daughters of the church under my care! Following the hymn "Renew Thy Church, Her Ministries Restore," and just before my own beloved home pastor Lillie S. McCutcheon offered the benediction, Dr. Reardon asked the crowd to respond in unison as he said: "We love you Barry…. We trust you Barry…. God bless you Barry." This was an especially moving thirty minutes in my life, followed the next day by a full reporting of the event and my photo appearing in the local *Anderson Herald* newspaper. As the president hoped, I have been refreshed often by the memory of this day, including now as I write, remember, and rejoice again.

The program changes in the seminary, particularly the new emphasis on internships, preaching, evangelism, ministers-in-residence, and the founding of the Center for Pastoral Studies, were applauded widely. While the Master of Divinity degree program was retained, masters programs requiring only half the number of hours now were in place to serve persons who otherwise might not have been able to attend seminary at all, or who had ministerial goals other than pastoring. Additional new programming soon was added in relation to preparation for missionary service with the 1976 launching of the Master of Arts in Religion: Christian Mission degree program. President Reardon was pleased and supportive. He spoke this way to the board of trustees in June, 1974, about the Center for Pastoral Studies that now was flourishing:

> It is an ingenious vehicle which, if managed carefully, can bear an enormous amount of freight. The impulse to tradition is strong—perhaps nowhere so strong as in academia. It would be easy for us to lapse back into traditional separatist concepts—with the college and the seminary each rebuilding its own walls. I think such a direction would be not only

cowardly, but would be to turn away from one of the most promising developments anywhere on the horizon.

With a quarter of a century of the seminary's service celebrated in 1975, a new era for the graduate school had begun. Student enrollment rose significantly. Major new student aid dollars were now available, the seminary's visibility in the Church of God was much higher than before, and its programs had a new vitality and flexibility. The semester one headcount enrollment of 68 in 1972 rose dramatically to 188 by 1977, nearly a tripling of the seminary. I was attempting to steer a fast-moving train!

A beautiful new chapel and badly needed library space beneath it were constructed in 1974. The chapel was named for the beloved former dean of the seminary, Adam W. Miller. Worship finally had a prominent architectural statement right in the midst of seminary academic life. The whole project was a dramatic development indeed, a public sign of the seminary's progress. During the winter of 1974 the front of the building was removed and covered with a plastic wall, requiring students to wear coats to class. Never before had I been so closely involved with such a construction project. My father, then recently deceased, would have been proud of me. I was supervising carpenters as Dad had, if not actually being one myself.

We decided that the interior of the chapel would be dignified and plain, except for a large stained-glass "window" in the front (backlit and not actually on the outside). My wife Arlene and I developed the general design for this Willhardt Memorial Window. It then was engineered by the Willett Company of Philadelphia. It seeks to portray a universal expression of the Christian faith, with its artistically executed theological assumptions and symbols particularly sensitive to emphases experienced and proclaimed by the Church of God movement—biblical authority, holiness, healing, and unity. Over the years I helped orient new students to the seminary by interpreting for them the window's intended symbolism. In fact, in the back of my book *Contours of a Cause* there is a color photograph of the window and my essay of interpretation.

My personal calendar from 1973 to 1983, the years of my seminary deanship, was filled with meetings of the seminary faculty and the Academic Cabinet of the School of Theology, staff and budget committees of the campus generally, and the Division of Church Service and Commission on Christian Higher Education of the Church of God movement. I served as secretary of both the Division and Commission, constantly broadening my range of personal relationships and understanding of the workings of national church life. I chaired and wrote minutes of all School of Theology faculty meetings, trying to keep the right issues on the table and their handling preserved for the future.

I participated occasionally in activities of the Cincinnati Council on World Affairs, especially in the Council of Deans that directed its work on behalf of the supporting colleges in Indiana, Kentucky, and Ohio. Beginning in 1973, I made annual tours around North America and the Caribbean to represent the seminary on each of the campuses associated with the Church of God. This increased my acquaintance with the histories, programs, and personnel of the church's liberal arts and Bible colleges. One result was my authoring the 1988 book *Preparing For Service: A History of Higher Education in the Church of God.* I later prepared an updated and much expanded version of this book (*Enriching Mind and Spirit,* 2007).

From June 29 to July 3, 1977, I was the main speaker for the Man-Dak Church of God Campmeeting in New Rockford, North Dakota. This annual gathering billed itself as the only truly "international" campmeeting of the Church of God ("Man" for Manitoba in Canada and "Dak" for North Dakota in the United States). Under the theme "Lord, I Believe," I was identified on the published program as an "author-educator-evangelist." Featured with me was the Canadian concert tour group and song evangelist John Swindells of Alberta Bible Institute (later Gardner College). Prominent among the participating ministers, and secretary of the camp's planning committee, was John Howard, then pastoring in Winnipeg, Manitoba. He had graduated from Anderson School of Theology under my deanship. I had helped him be placed in Canada after his seminary years, and he would become a lifelong friend. In later years, John and his wife Nancy would move west to the church's Canadian school, Gardner College, where he would serve as a teacher and then dean and president until his retirement in 2006.

Reuel Tiesel was another seminary graduate under my leadership with whom I became a close friend. It was a sad day for me in March, 2007, when Reuel died of cancer at age 56. There were so many others. Several couples were invited to our home for a reunion lunch during the annual Anderson campmeetings. Each of the men was a prominent graduate during my years as seminary dean. As I now write so many years later, I rejoice that they are continuing to serve as key church leaders. Included are Craig F. Frank in Arizona, Stephen M. Stull in Indiana, and G. Lee Wallace in Tennessee. Larry A. Logue pastored for many years in Missouri before his untimely death in 2011.

On several occasions, partly at John Howard's initiative, it was my privilege to be on the campus of Gardner College in Camrose, Alberta. Sometimes I was representing the seminary in Anderson, Indiana, or attending an annual meeting of the Commission on Christian Higher Education of the Church of God, or delivering the Belter Lectures, or speaking at the school's commencement and teaching at an area pastor's conference. I came to love this little school on the western Canadian prairies. Sadly, it now has closed its doors after more than seven decades of service to the church. Baker Book House in Michigan and Pater Noster Press in England jointly published my book *Authentic Spirituality* in 2001. I note in the introduction that its writing had begun with my Belter Lectures in January, 1987, at Gardner College (January is a cold month to be in Alberta, Canada!). This book, one of my better ones, was republished under the same title in 2006 by Emeth Press. I owe a debt to kind brothers and sisters in Canada—and I hope that I added something of value to their lives and ministries over the years.

Balancing Family and Professional Lives

My family life had its dramatic developments while I was engaged in this flurry of professional activity as seminary dean. My father, Robert C. Callen, was a carpenter, locksmith, and building inspector who lived in the same little house in Craig Beach on the western shore of Lake Milton, Ohio, from 1946 until his death from intestinal cancer in 1974. When he was dying at home, Lillie S. McCutcheon and her husband Glenn came to minister to him. They and I were joined by my mother Charlotte, grandmother Mary (Rose) Callen, and wife Arlene. We stood by "Bert's" bedside on that dramatic day while Sister Lillie gently instructed, comforted, and finally baptized him. She shared with him the gospel story of the saving Christ, holding in her hands the big ring and wooden keys that she often used in her lectures on the Book of Revelation to dramatize the keys of the kingdom of God. One key at a time, before the eyes of this dying locksmith, the gospel of Christ was portrayed with unmistakable clarity.

Dad, of course, knew the gospel well, having grown up in a pastor's home, but he had stayed at arm's length from it for most of his life. Then, at his funeral in the Newton Falls, Ohio, church where she pastored and I had grown up, Sister Lillie delivered what the family judged a masterpiece sermon about the process of building a home in heaven by the quality of one's life on earth. She preached to honor a deceased carpenter who now had arrived at his final and best construction site—one already completed on his behalf by divine grace. No wonder I loved this good woman of God and wrote her biography (*She Came Preaching*, 1992). In many ways, her story is crucial to my own. While Dad was not ready to sit under a woman's preaching for most of his life, Sister Lillie had finally become important to his life story.

In November, 2000, I received an email from Craig Callen, a prominent Ohio dentist and one of the sons of my Uncle Bill (William Callen). He told me some things I had not known before. When Craig was about fourteen and his father was dying of cancer, they had talked about life in general. Uncle Bill shared that Bert, his brother and my father, occasionally working as a pile driver for bridge construction—including the interstate bridge that currently crosses Lake Milton near Craig Beach, had done something I never knew. He had refused opportunities to travel the country and make good money with his special skills. Apparently Dad had turned them down because he wanted to remain home with his family. Craig's report ended with this:

> My dad [Bill] said that he told Bert he was crazy. Bill had spent his life away from his family working way too many hours in the restaurant business, and lost his family through divorce in the process. As Bill later looked back, it was he who was crazy. Bert was the smart one!

Shortly after Dad's death, I was the baccalaureate speaker for Anderson College and School of Theology. It was Father's Day, an emotional hour for me in the pulpit of Park Place Church of God where the service was held. Not a perfect father, Dad had been faithful and honest, hardworking without the curse of runaway greed. I am very thankful.

In the months after Dad's death, my mother Charlotte struggled alone in the little house in Craig Beach. She was burdened with grief, loneliness, and very little money. Dad had not left much except the modest house, which she soon managed to sell for a mere $17,000 on her way to moving to Anderson, Indiana, and completing her life with

Arlene, Todd, and me. She came in 1976 and died on her sixtieth birthday in 1979. We buried her alongside Dad in the cemetery near Palmyra, not far from the old home in Craig Beach, Ohio. The previous year, Grandma Callen had died (Nov. 12, 1978) and was buried in Mt. Vernon Cemetery, Elizabeth Township, Pennsylvania. As had been the case with Grandpa Callen's funeral, circumstances kept me away. I wish I had been there. She was a special woman with her disciplined German ways and her big heart filled with the Spirit of Jesus Christ.

I wish that things would have been better for my mother in her last years. She lived in the little apartment in our home at 1703 Falls Court, but was in poor health and generally depressed. Working for some time on the Anderson College campus as a secretary in the security department, she was the sociable sort and saw the campus community as the bigger world that life had denied her previously. Mom went to a few college basketball games with me, excited by the opportunity right across the street from our home, but she had great difficulty climbing the bleachers. Her knees were bad, her heart weakened, and her will to live declining. She loved our son Todd. I am proud to report that she attended a two-day seminar in April, 1978, and earned a certificate for "Improving Office Skills." During World War II she had been a skilled typist employed at the Arsenal in northeast Ohio. Mom was a very loving person who had a lust for life that circumstances had kept boxed in for the most part. She got just a little out of the box near her life's end.

Arlene and I tried to attend to Mom's basic needs, remembering how well she had cared lovingly for her father during the last year of his life in a little bedroom in the Craig Beach house. When Grandpa VanArsdale died in 1967, her total inheritance from his estate was one social security check for $122. There was always far more love than dollars in our family. My mother helped Arlene and me with the downpayment on our home in Anderson. We were pleased that it became her home also, at least for the brief time she had left. Soon after Mom's death in 1979, that apartment became the final home of Arlene's mother, Evelyn, who migrated to us from Pennsylvania in 1982.

As I look back, I hope that my very busy academic and administrative lives, with all of their meetings and travel, did not cause me to be less of a son, husband, and father than I should have been. Balancing one's personal and professional lives is not easy. Many roles and groups were competing for my limited time. God's grace now covers whatever failures may have been mine in leaving something important only partially done. One failure was limited involvement in the life of my sister Bonnie and her family. She also lived in Anderson, Indiana, not that far away. This failure would change for the better in later years, especially after the death of my wife Arlene in 2003 and my marriage to Jan.

Special Privileges Come My Way

My role as seminary dean made me a high-profile person in the church. Accordingly, some special privileges came my way. One of particular note was the invitation for me to be one of five persons representing the Church of God movement in North America at the Congress on World Evangelization convened by the Billy Graham Association in Lausanne, Switzerland, in the summer of 1974. Joining about 5,000 Christian leaders from over one hundred countries, I heard Billy Graham, Carl F. H. Henry, Corrie Ten Boom, and others exploring how to share the Christian faith across the cultures of the world. I read Corrie's book *The Hiding Place* and sorrowed again at the great suffering caused by World War II. I remember standing in the crowd singing "The Lord's Prayer," with those around me joining in multiple languages, but nonetheless truly one in Jesus Christ. These were moving moments I have never forgotten. During free time, I wandered the streets of the French-speaking Lausanne, visited nearby Geneva, namesake of my college alma mater, and took a train into the mountains to see the spectacular Matterhorn. It was all very impressive.

Beyond traveling, I also turned to serious writing. My first book came in the early 1970s (*Where Life Begins*). It was a little book on the Christian life designed to support a unit of the Sunday school curriculum published by Warner Press. In the years immediately prior to 1980, I assembled and published through Warner Press a series of paperback books. They gathered the heritage of the Church of God movement into a mini-archives of historic materials under the general title *A Time To Remember*, later republished in two large hardbound volumes titled *The First Century*.

In part because of this publishing work, and because I now had gained national prominence in the church as the dean of its seminary, I was elected in 1977 for a three-year term as a member of the Program Committee for the International Convention of the Church of God that met annually in Anderson, Indiana. For 1977 I served under the leadership of Arlene Hall, formulating the program theme "Live By the Word." For the following two years, ones consciously preparing for the big centennial convention in 1980, I chaired this key committee, establishing the themes "Behold, God's Church Alive!" for 1978 and "We Hold These Truths" for 1979. Then, for the sake of continuity, I was retained as a consultant to the committee for one year beyond my elected term to support the unusual planning task related to the 1980 convention. This would be the centennial gathering that included a World Forum, the first International Dialogue on Doctrine, which I convened at Anderson School of Theology, and the centennial celebration convention itself.

Probably because of my involvement in these years of planning, my leadership role in the seminary, and my publishing activities related to the church's heritage, it was determined that I should be the keynote preacher for the big International Convention convened in Anderson, Indiana, in 1980. What a privilege to stand on such an historic occasion and represent the Church of God movement's century of witness and outreach! This probably was the most dramatic setting in which I have ever been the featured preacher. My privilege and significant task was keynoting the large international gathering in Warner Auditorium—about 9,000 people in attendance representing many nations. I remember the Japanese delegation receiving instantaneous translation through headsets they wore—an innovation at the time.

The hours just before I was to stand before that special crowd were not comfortable, to say the least! The General Assembly of the Church of God had begun its annual sessions in Lewis Gymnasium on the Anderson campus—an unusual location used only this once because of the expanded size of the crowd (about 1,500 in the Assembly and about 15,000 on the grounds). It was a troubled scene. There were angry voices with complaints against the Anderson campus that had been stimulated by an "open letter" sent widely just before the Assembly convened. The letter criticized one or two faculty members and the existence of a class on human sexuality. The process was chaotic and not constructive, a poor display before the world church in attendance.

I was seated in the front row of that historic and chaotic Assembly, and I suffered, especially when my home pastor, Lillie McCutcheon, made some harsh comments about my president, Robert Reardon. I was caught in the middle, a poor way for me to prepare to preach to the centennial crowd an hour later. I slipped out early and took a long walk, ending at Warner Auditorium where I was expected. I had to clear my mind of conflicted church politics so that I could preach an historic sermon on Christian holiness and church unity. I was troubled by the irony of it all—celebrating unity with a swirl of turmoil.

The centennial sermon began with my acknowledging that, partly because of my beard, I knew I looked like Daniel S. Warner, the primary pioneer of the church movement. I was surprised by the extended period of loud laughter in response to my opening comment. Humor sometimes involves saying what others are thinking when they assume that you do not know what they were thinking. This broke the ice and helped me to relax and focus on my sermon and not on debates in the General Assembly and the big international crowd seated before me. I had come a long way, having once been a young teenager in Newton Falls, Ohio, so scared in front of a crowd of six-hundred that I had to make up Bible verses to avoid embarrassment. When God calls one to a demanding assignment, God also provides whatever is necessary.

On July 28, 1980, when all had returned to normal in Anderson after the big centennial convention, I received a gracious letter of appreciation from T. Franklin Miller, a key organizer of the centennial events. He spoke of my "invaluable assistance," referring to my heritage series of books (*A Time To Remember*), the School of Theology having sponsored the first International Dialogue on Doctrine, and my June 24 keynote sermon. His final paragraph pleased me most:

> Some of the younger men from other countries told me how refreshing and encouraging it was to hear you say some of the things that were in your message. They felt there really is hope for the Church of God throughout the world when they could hear someone boldly enunciate the truth as you did in your sermon. God certainly used you and I am deeply grateful for your courage, your willingness, and your ability to preach this sermon.

That sermon had been a highlight moment in my life. I was honored for the opportunity to have served on such a large stage.

One colleague and I mirror each other's time on the Anderson campus. Robert A. Nicholson (b. 1923) has been a friend, colleague, and mentor of mine since the mid-1960s. Our long careers at Anderson University have some interesting parallels. He was a student on the campus in the 1940s and then became a young faculty member in that same decade. For me it was a similar situation, only in the 1970s. "Nick" was asked by the president, John A. Morrison, to begin a touring choir, largely to counter considerable negative pubic relations between the campus, national church, and conservative local churches across the country. Later, I became Dean of Anderson School of Theology and was asked by the president, Robert H. Reardon, to begin a Center for Pastoral Studies, largely to reverse a negative trend in the church that was leaving the campus seminary in a very weakened condition.

Nick became campus-wide academic leader in 1958, and I replaced him in the same role in 1983. Both of us loved the church and campus deeply and pioneered new programs and relationships intended to relate the two more constructively. I was privileged to publish his autobiography in 2006 and deliver an honoring tribute to him at his funeral in 2018.

My seminary deanship had become a base from which I could grow, serve, write, and genuinely affect the church's life in helpful ways. God was being especially gracious to me. I worked hard, very hard. Sometimes I was a little "over my head," but I stretched, survived, and proceeded in faith and

Anderson University School of Theology deans, 1983. (Left to Right) Gene W. Newberry, Jerry C. Grubbs, myself, and Adam W. Miller, holding a portrait of Earl L. Martin.

Appreciation paperweight given
for my financial and other gifts.

Painting (left) which hangs in Tallen
Hall of Anderson School of
Theology and Christian Ministry.

Preaching the keynote sermon, centennial of the Church of God movement,
1980.

Anderson University School of Theology deans, May, 1997. David L. Sebastian, James Earl Massey, Jerry C. Grubbs, myself, and Gene W. Newberry.

Robert H. Reardon and I planning the future of Anderson School of Theology, 1975.

Chapter 6

Moving to the Larger Academic Scene

Frontiers of Christian higher education

The years 1973 to 1983 had been great ones for Anderson School of Theology, and certainly very stretching and fulfilling ones for me. So much had changed on the campus and with me personally during that eventful decade. Much more change was already in the wind. In part, it was coming because of additional institutional change, and in part it was because of my own personal educational initiatives.

I was privileged to be the dean of the seminary, then the only graduate school of Anderson University. I grew comfortable in the role. The many repetitive tasks became almost routine. I found myself a little restless by the late 1970s. Although I was not aware of it at the time, God was quietly calling me toward a large new set of challenges. Fresh doors were opening and I was willing to walk through them.

A Dissertation on Faculty Freedom

By the late 1970s I was feeling the need for some additional graduate education, especially in the area of educational administration. I had prepared for pastoral ministry and classroom teaching, but found myself functioning as an academic administrator, mostly learning on the job. I looked for a program of continuing education with flexibility that might be accessible to me while I carried all of my regular responsibilities. I found Nova University in Florida that was ahead of its time in offering doctoral programs for busy professionals in higher education. So, in May of 1978, I was accepted into this university's external degree doctorate for community college faculty.

My first venture with Nova was a summer intensive course that was convened in the Diplomat Hotel in Hollywood, Florida, August 2-9, 1978. While the specific course content was not all applicable to much that I was doing at the seminary in Anderson, it surely was educationally stimulating. I registered for a course with Nova's Chicago cluster group, commuting to Chicago for one intense weekend per month. The course was taught by a nationally famous man in higher education who flew to Chicago from Stanford University for our monthly classes. Again, the experience was stimulating, but so community-college oriented that I chose not to pursue additional courses with Nova.

Looking back on these years, I am a little surprised that I was persistent in pursuing additional graduate education. My own campus was more than satisfied with the three graduate degrees I already held. There was no particular position in view for my future that pulled me toward another degree designation after my name. It was just that I had interest and found myself reaching for more. Sometimes I would tell an inquirer that I had learned administration on the job for years and now was interested in what others thought I should be doing. Having left the Nova program, I began commuting to nearby Ball State University. After two or three courses there in higher education, I shifted to Indiana University, took some courses at the IUPUI campus in Indianapolis, and was encouraged by officials there to formalize my candidacy for a Doctor of Education degree.

Soon, with considerable advanced credit granted for course work done for my other graduate programs, I was at the dissertation stage. The chair of my Indiana University dissertation committee was Dr. Gerald Preusz, a gentle and wise man who was genuinely interested in my research topic and was most helpful. I began the introduction to the dissertation with this:

> It is assumed by many educators, and even some church persons, that the phrase "church-related liberal arts college" is an awkward way of trying to identify what may be an inconceivable institution of higher education. The very combining of "church-related" and "liberal arts" often has been seen as a joining of contradictory concepts. An institution so described lacks basic educational integrity because the institutional adoption of a particular religious stance is presumed to be in direct opposition to the goals and methods of a classic liberal arts education.... In many cases, the root problem is the difficulty in discovering a constructive way to relate the Christian faith and the goals of higher education in the midst of a socially and religiously pluralistic culture.... How can one be genuinely free to *seek* the truth in an institution which presumes in advance that it already *knows* the truth?

I proceeded to focus specifically on the issue of faculty academic freedom as it was defined and had actually functioned in twenty-three colleges selected randomly from the sixty-nine institutional members of the Christian College Coalition (each college being liberal arts in orientation, regionally accredited, and affirming the significance of Christian faith for institutional mission).

Anderson College was in the selected research group. I noted that Anderson presented a clear example of the supposed dilemma of the joining of faculty academic freedom and the beliefs of a campus-sponsoring church. After a year of intense self-examination, prompted in large part by a series of critical questions from persons within the shcool's church constituency, Anderson College had published in 1981 a key statement that I had authored. Titled "Anderson College: In Partnership with the Church," it affirmed that:

> . . .curricular design and community life combine the honesty and rigor of academic inquiry and the perspectives and mission emerging from biblical revelation. It [the college] lives in an atmosphere of free inquiry, even while it affirms that all knowledge is understood most fully in the light of God's redemptive activity in Jesus Christ as that is interpreted through the historic witness of the Bible and the contemporary ministry of the Holy Spirit.

My dissertation said: "There appears to be an inherent tension with the presence of the free questing of the traditional scholarly life, on the one hand, and, on the other, the institutional acceptance of a pattern of divinely revealed absolutes within which the questing should proceed." I attempted to explore the application of this paradoxical circumstance in a population of colleges which, by self-declared definition, live daily with this paradox at the center of their educational programs. I surveyed the 1,325 full-time faculty members in the sample colleges. The eventual survey return rate of 77.2% was considered exceptionally high by my dissertation committee. The subject obviously was thought significant by the numerous faculty members who responded to me.

The general finding of my research was that the colleges and their faculties provided general affirmation of the worthiness and workability of the central paradox inherent in the Christ-centered, liberal arts colleges of the Christian College Coalition. Using wording from the 1982-83 catalog of Barrington College, I argued that "Christian belief is not a restraint to the academic process, but rather the basis for an integrated world view." As soon reported in the *Chronicle of Higher Education* (December 7, 1983), my study showed that "these colleges have combined the free questing of traditional scholarship with their religious views to produce more of a dynamic and creative tension than a debilitating dilemma."

I am pleased to report that my dissertation was nominated as "dissertation of the year" in the School of Education of Indiana University. Then the publication *Christian College News* (November 18, 1983) said that it was "believed to be the most comprehensive survey ever conducted on the subject of faculty academic freedom in Christian colleges and universities." Local press coverage in Anderson, Indiana, included a feature story, with photo, on November 20, 1983. The headline was: "Christian Faith, Education Compatible: AC Official."

I was flattered by the press coverage of my research and findings and hoped that the whole effort would enhance the perceived viability of Anderson College in its future student and faculty recruitment efforts. In 2004, in my role as Editor of Anderson University Press, I was pleased to edit and publish a booklet by a friend, Richard Hughes, that I titled "What Makes Church-Related Higher Education 'Christian'?" Richard had shared this material with the Anderson faculty earlier and it had been well received. I was pleased to make his thoughts available more widely.

Changing of the Guard in Anderson

The year 1983 saw more than the completing of my Indiana University doctoral dissertation. There was a major changing of the guard on the Anderson campus that initiated a sequence of events leading to the adding to my name the new titles "Dean of the College," "Corporate Secretary," and "Vice-President for Academic Affairs." The opening of this big new door for me meant, of course, that a significant chapter of my life was ending. My decade of administrative leadership at Anderson School of Theology ended and was recognized by the seminary giving me the School of Theology's 1983 "Distinguished Ministries Award."

Dr. Jerry C. Grubbs followed me as seminary dean. I remember well that he was my first appointment to the faculty in the early 1970s. He had come from a pastorate without his doctorate, but with an agreed plan by which the institution would assist his completing it in his first few years on campus. That was accomplished successfully. Soon I named him to an administrative post I had pioneered in 1973 (Director of the Center for Pastoral Studies). Then in 1983 the new campus president, Robert A. Nicholson, and I had judged that Jerry should succeed me as dean of the School of Theology. Jerry agreed and was so elected by the board of trustees. I left a major responsibility I had grown to love in order to tackle the demands of a larger academic scene, including all undergraduate academic departments, campus registrar and library functions, and more.

Why had I left the seminary? The new president, Robert A. Nicholson, had invited, even urged that I replace him as Vice-President for Academic Affairs, Dean of the College, and Corporate Secretary—a tall order since Nicholson had prominently and competently held these major posts since 1958, the entire presidency of Robert H. Reardon. Now Reardon had retired and Nicholson was moving only thirty feet away into the neighboring president's office in Decker Hall. Part of the new president's reasoning in choosing me related to the campus having faced a critical problem in campus-church relations in 1980-81. Elevating me to such prominence was thought to be a welcome message to the church about the campus being prepared to vigorously reaffirm its church relatedness.

I struggled with my response to the new president's call, having mixed feelings about leaving the School of Theology where I was comfortable and successful—even if a little restless. My wife Arlene feared being placed in the institutional limelight as a high-profile social hostess. President Nicholson came to our home and patiently heard and spoke reassuringly to her concerns. She was satisfied enough to agree to my accepting this huge new responsibility. We both were a little anxious about what might be ahead.

With my positive decision made, the new president released the news to the public. I would head the academic programs of all departments and disciplines, along with the support services such as library and registrar. Named to vice-presidencies with me were my friends Ronald Moore (development and finance), Duane Hoak (administrative services), and Cleda Anderson (student life and human resources). I remember that early into our new roles we vice presidents were asked to take the Myers-Briggs Inventory and then, as a group, have the results reported and interpreted. It could have been awkward and threatening, but we all knew and respected each other in advance and the process went well. President Nicholson was anxious to affirm our diversities and build a close-knit administrative team on the base of our congeniality and compatibility. It worked well for the years immediately ahead.

I made the following statement of educational philosophy to the Anderson College faculty and students during the chapel service in which I was installed as the college dean (October 27, 1983):

The key questions are: Education, of what kind, and for what reason? We live in an affluent society and in very troubled times. Jobs are harder to get; human values are being violated on every hand. Cut-throat competition reigns in higher education—whatever students want is being provided on many campuses, no matter how shortsighted. What do students want? Jobs! But they also want fulfillment, a personal happiness which must have some meaningful rootage in relationships and implications for personal destiny. The mission of a college should be more than job preparation. The ultimate justification for an institution of Christian higher education lies in what Warren Martin has called the "synoptic function." General education, professional education, teaching, and research are to be brought into contact with each other "so that the social, political, moral, and ethical ramifications can be held up for sustained investigation" (*A College of Character*, 46).

This occasion of installation for my new deanship was one with full academic attire, convened in the sanctuary of Park Place Church of God. My wife and son were present and asked to stand for recognition and greeting. These were proud moments. In their presence, and with the faculty and student body seated before me, I shared elements of my educational philosophy. My conclusion was that the wholeness of truth can lead to wisdom in human affairs, especially when the quest for truth is informed by a particular perspective, one that transcends and holds the others together. I announced the perspective that I assumed was foundational at Anderson College. I quoted Colossians 2:2-3 that speaks of love leading to the riches of understanding. They lead to knowing the mystery of God, namely Jesus Christ, "in whom are hidden all the treasures of wisdom and knowledge."

A Very Full Datebook!

A new chapter in my professional career had begun in 1983, and I was consciously putting it in terms of what I understood to be good educational philosophy and biblical teaching. I intended to be an academic leader in the context of Christian faith. I was a minister wearing an academic robe—the very paradox I had explored in my Indiana University dissertation. This new journey was full of uncertainty, but at least I trusted president Robert Nicholson, whom I would serve on campus, and I believed in my Lord, whom I was seeking to serve with my whole life.

An immediate sacrifice I had to make was attending the 1983 World Conference of the Church of God about to convene in Nairobi, Kenya. I was all set to go when my new responsibilities emerged on campus.

Now it was impossible to leave Anderson. I arranged for Douglas Welch, former missionary in Kenya, to go in my place. I would attend all the other World Conferences after that, however.

Beginning in 1983, the volume of meetings on my calendar increased, something I hardly thought possible. Now there were regular meetings of the college faculty, the school deans, department chairs, budget and honorary degrees committees, the executive committee and full sessions of the board of trustees, Joint Staff Luncheons with the leaders of the national agencies of the Church of God, and annual meetings of the Commission on Christian Higher Education of the Church of God and the Coalition of Deans of church-related colleges in the Midwest. For most of these, including all faculty and trustee meetings, I was responsible for managing agendas in advance and producing formal minutes afterwards, in part because I now convened the faculty meetings and was the elected Corporate Secretary of Anderson College and School of Theology.

For the entire academic enterprise of the campus, I was to be the strategic thinker and planner and, of course, the crisis manager. There were numerous other duties. I managed the campus calendar, determining almost alone the beginning and ending dates of semesters, the dates for vacations and commencements, etc. An early initiative I took was to address the procedures and standards for determining recipients of honorary degrees, and setting a strategy for reviewing this process in a way that included a "concurring" role for the faculty prior to final trustee decisions. My fresh formalization of this program is still functioning today, virtually unchanged. I professionalized the full-time librarians to full faculty status.

Within the first year in our new roles, the Nicholson-Callen team oversaw the establishment of a new liberal arts curriculum and an extensive structural redesign of the undergraduate college—both had been under scrutiny for some time. I recall especially the meeting on August 25, 1983, when I met with all department chairs to explain the new academic structure. President Nicholson had been working on a major restructuring plan for the undergraduate college before he assumed the presidency, a plan that would expand the academic administration and accommodate a growing range of programs. As I came into the dean's office, I was handed a sketch of the tentative plans and given relatively free reign to finish the details and launch the new organization. Something of that magnitude would naturally suffer from early confusion and resistance.

Three "schools" were created, each with its own dean to function under my direct supervision. I chose and the president affirmed Drs. F. Dale Bengtson, James Macholtz, and Darlene Miller to fill these key new roles. I selected Dr. Blake Janutolo to replace Jim Macholtz after his untimely death in 1985. This restructuring required careful rethinking of all reporting relationships, policies, procedures, forms, etc. It was a demanding process, complicated because there were faculty members resisting the changes, thinking that it was too much organization requiring too much money. Time has made clear the wisdom of the move, painful though it was at first.

Especially in the first two years of my deanship, the undergraduate faculty meetings were often tense and debate-filled. Within the first semester of my academic leadership I had to conduct a voting process on whether or not to accept into the revised liberal arts curriculum a "Freshman Seminar." It was a centerpiece of the proposed plan of curricular revision that dean Nicholson had overseen for two years prior to my arrival in his chair. There came that fateful hour in the fall of 1983 when I called for the faculty vote on the Freshman Seminar. It was by secret ballot. The votes were counted during the meeting and the alarming news was handed to me. The result was a tie and I would have to cast the deciding vote! Not only was that a politically explosive way to begin one's deanship, but the issue at hand was not one about which I knew very much. I took a deep breath, tried to gather my thoughts and feelings, and then noticed a faculty member coming forward to hand me a ballot that had not gotten noticed and counted. The conclusion was approval of the proposal by one vote, and it did not have to be mine. Even so, it was hardly an ideal way to establish a key component of a revised curriculum, or for me to be fully appreciated by all faculty members.

The years ahead would be characterized by occasional faculty bickering, maneuvering, and often unspoken unhappiness about the decisions of 1983. Even so, student enrollments grew and eventually most faculty energy was expended in other directions. Robert Reardon once defined a faculty member as "someone who thinks otherwise!" There is some uncomfortable truth in his cynical definition. My task was to heal, guide, and build. I was reasonably successful, although a personal price had to be paid.

Looking back at my datebook to recall my main activities during the months of May and June, 1983, makes me a little dizzy. I was orienting Jerry Grubbs into his new role as seminary dean (replacing me) while busily seeking to grasp the multiple dimensions of my many new roles. Keith Huttenlocker was concluding his pastorate at Park Place Church of God to become the Executive Director of the Division of Church Service for the Church of God nationally. It was my responsibility as secretary of that Division to explain the search process and present nominee Huttenlocker (then my pastor) to the Executive Council of the Church of God on May 5.

During that frantic May, I scheduled two-hour meetings with each of the chairs of the eighteen academic departments of the college in order to orient myself and open good lines of communication. I also was meeting weekly in Indianapolis with Gerald Preusz of Indiana University to complete my doctoral dissertation. In June, I flew to Cleveland, Ohio, for a three-day meeting and soon after drove to Memphis, Tennessee, for another. I conducted the annual School of Theology planning retreat, prepared for the undergraduate fall faculty sessions, made charts and wrote position descriptions for the new academic structure and its leaders, recruited and oriented the needed three new school deans, etc. This was administration in high gear. I was fully engaged—and hoping I was not in over my head. Frankly, I think I was a little, and I tried to make up for that with hard work. I learned, grew, failed, and succeeded, depending on the task and day.

Meanwhile, I was meeting regularly with the Design Committee preparing for the major 1984 Consultation on Mission and Ministry of the Church of God (trying to set goals for the church to the end of the century). That September I preached the annual ordination service of the Indiana Assembly of the Church of God, and in October functioned as a conference leader and preacher at the Midwest Ministerial Assembly of the Church of God convened in Kansas City. The fall meeting of the Anderson College board of trustees was October 6-8. I developed the agenda and hosted the meeting of the board's Educational Policy and Personnel Committee. I then functioned as secretary for the meetings of the Executive Committee and the full board. The president and I had helped to set in place a new committee structure to make more efficient the work of the trustees. The campus and board were maturing, in part because of the vigorous leadership of president Robert Nicholson.

On went the very full schedule. I was formally installed as dean of the College on October 27, 1983. In December I was in Detroit installing Larry Green in his new pastorate. In early January, 1984, I was on the campus of Warner Southern College in central Florida for the annual meeting of the Commission on Christian Higher Education of the Church of God. In November, 1983, Anderson School of Theology hosted on campus the annual meeting of the Wesleyan Theological Society. The irony is that, although years later I would become deeply involved with this academic society and travel all over North America to attend its meetings, in 1983 I was so busy that I did not have time to walk to a neighboring building on the Anderson campus to attend the annual WTS meeting.

Possibly the most troubling of my many new responsibilities was having to decide by 5:00 a.m. on a very cold and snowy winter morning whether or not campus employees and students could stay in bed for the day or have to brave the elements and come to school. On only three occasions did I pull the plug on all campus operations. There would always be unhappy calls to my office, whatever I decided. The public schools would close more readily than a campus that had some sixty-five percent of its students resident in dorms rather than needing to wait for buses and make dangerous rides over country roads. When the publics closed and the campus did not, it seemed that I was hardhearted and did not care about the safety of people. When I did close the campus, some felt that they had paid for their classes and should not be cheated out of them.

A complication evolved that was not the case in earlier decades. Many faculty members no longer lived in the immediate neighborhood of the campus. If half of the faculty could not make the necessary drive, it would not help much that most students could successfully walk to their teacherless classrooms. I had a special code to use as I contacted local radio stations, identified myself, and announced what should be said to the public about whether or not the campus doors would be open. It was a thankless task. Such are the "joys" of administration!

I knew that I needed more personal linkage with the life of the city of Anderson. Previous presidents and deans of the campus had been prominent in local service clubs. So, in 1984, I decided to become a member of the Suburban Rotary Club. We club members teased that we were the young professionals as opposed to the "old timers" who gathered in the larger downtown club as the money-controlling "movers and shakers" in town. I hoped to continue the tradition of building bridges between "town and gown." Although Arlene and I had lived in Anderson for some twenty years, our primary contacts with the city were through her having taught in the school system in the 1960s (Chesterfield), our son Todd having gone through the city's educational system from Park Place

Elementary School to East Side Middle School and then to Highland High School. We did know a few city leaders, either through our membership at Park Place Church of God or participation in events that brought many local people to campus. Now that I was the academic leader of the campus, it seemed that I must broaden further my involvements with life in the city.

From 1984 until my resignation from the club in 1997, I functioned as an active member of Suburban Rotary. For three years I edited the club's newsletter. Primarily through my financial giving to "Polio Plus," the multi-national effort of Rotary International to eliminate polio from the planet through mass inoculations, I became a "Paul Harris Fellow"—an honored status carrying the name of the founder of Rotary International. My eventual club resignation was because, toward the end of the century, I no longer was functioning as an academic administrator and had other preoccupations that limited my ability to be involved actively as I had been for years. In the 1980s, however, I chose to be deeply involved on a weekly basis and benefited greatly from the many friends and contacts I enjoyed through membership in a worthy service club. We were encouraged to meet with other Rotary clubs when traveling. I recall visiting the original club in downtown Chicago, a club in Honolulu, Hawaii, and the club in Lake Wales, Florida, when I was visiting Warner Southern College.

President Robert Nicholson's vision and energy level were both very high. The pace of activity and institutional change was intense in the 1983-1988 period. He was appropriately sensitive to the importance of the institution's continuity with its history and traditional mission; he also saw that the world of higher education was changing and he was convinced that it was time for significant realignments to better prepare the Anderson campus to compete successfully in a new time. I was close by his side across these years, sometimes out of breath trying to keep up.

There were many important developments. For instance, a unique and widely admired new partnership developed by 1984 between Anderson

College and Purdue University. This alliance was encouraged by president Nicholson, guided on Anderson's part by myself as dean, and implemented especially by Michael Collette. At our invitation, Purdue, a large state-supported university in Indiana, established a base of operations on the Anderson campus and began offering an associate degree in applied science in 1985. This marked the first time in Indiana that a state-supported university had contracted in this way with a private church-related college. Purdue judged this the most efficient way to meet a real public need, the retraining of many in the workforce of the city of Anderson in the face of a declining automobile industry. This partnership continues to this day.

In my published history of Anderson University, I say this about campus life in the 1980s: "Much expansion, resource gathering, strategic planning, and partnership in building programs, structures, and vital relationships had taken place" (*Guide of Soul and Mind*, 375). We seemed out of breath most of the time. I was in the middle of it all, sometimes a bit overwhelmed, often stretched and rewarded, and usually quite weary at the end of the day. Such is the life of an academic dean on a prospering campus.

Milestones on the Journey

By the middle of the 1980s, my schedule was unrelenting, with occasional events of tension and sadness intruding on a pattern of vigorous institutional progress. One tension-filled event was the 1986 national church study of the controversial subject of "speaking in tongues." This ecstatic spiritual experience was not traditionally part of Christian life as taught in the Church of God movement, but it had appeared in some congregations, usually quite disruptively. In addition to my role as recording secretary of the church's national study committee on this divisive subject, I made presentations to it titled "Historical Perspectives on Glossolalia" and "Biblical Guidelines: Glossolalia in the Life of the Church" (the latter becoming part of the study commission's final report to the General Assembly of the Church of God). I may have been an academic dean, but I was still a Christian minister and committed churchman. Sometimes it was difficult being active on so many fronts at once.

I recall the moment when shocking news was brought to the "tongues" study committee in the midst of its meeting in a hotel near the airport in Indianapolis. Lillie McCutcheon, my home pastor as a boy, returned from a break time and told the whole group what she had just heard on the television in her hotel room. The United States had launched its space shuttle Challenger and it had exploded! As we went on to struggle with the divisive issue in church life that was our assignment, we now carried another heavy burden. The U.S. space program had just suffered a tragic loss of life, and with this loss came national disgrace and maybe the confidence of the public in the supposed prowess of science and technology. Americans had put men on the Moon in the 1960s. Now in the 1980s we could not dependably get a crew safely out of Earth's atmosphere. It was a sad and sobering day.

The study committee went on with its work and reached a broad consensus. I prepared the document for presentation to the 1986 General Assembly. It was received with appreciation and its biblical guidelines, observations, and recommendations were commended "for careful study and guidance throughout the Church of God." That moment of approval was special for me. I had participated in a crucial process that brought quiet to what had been significantly troubled church waters. Our full committee report was published in the church's national periodical, *Vital Christianity* (a sign of its significance), and otherwise circulated widely over the following years. Later, I would include the central portion of this report in my documentary history of the Church of God movement

(*Following the Light*, 300-303). It was an historic piece of church diplomacy and of God's supervising Spirit.

While formally addressed in this way, the "tongues" issue did not go away. In February, 2000, Arlo Newell and I were called to be crisis consultants to a large congregation, the Dayspring Church of God in Cincinnati, Ohio. These people were experiencing considerable difficulty with this very issue. Our role was to hear the people express their pain and confusion and then interpret to them the meaning of the 1986 document of the General Assembly. The leadership of the congregation had judged that this church should stay with the larger Church of God movement and needed to understand, adopt, and live by this 1986 report. When our work was done and revealed by the presentation of a long report which I read to the church, some people immediately left the congregation. Even so, its stability was regained and on July 8, 2001, I returned to preach the installation sermon for the new pastor, a personal friend, Timothy Kufeldt. It was a day of celebration. The turmoil had subsided, a new and loved young pastor had been called, and a new day had dawned.

I will not forget that moment on July 8 when I was invited to the pulpit of Dayspring. I put my Bible down on the lectern, looked up, and saw some 400 people standing and vigorously applauding my presence. It was a moment of catharsis for the congregation. Their time in the valley of dark shadows seemed to be over. They were rejoicing and ready to move on for God. In 2007, Judy (Sowers) Hughes joined the pastoral staff of this church. She is a lifelong friend who would benefit from the difficult and successful 2000 intervention of Dr. Newell and myself. As I remember this, I again rejoice about the healing grace of God.

Another event of sadness and celebration was the death of my former teacher, associate dean, and personal mentor and friend, John W. V. Smith. The funeral was held in Park Place Church of God in Anderson, Indiana, on November 23, 1984. I was one of the pallbearers who carried John's remains to their resting place in Maplewood Cemetery just across from the seminary in Anderson that he had served so long and well. I loved this good and wise man whom I had chosen as associate dean during my decade of seminary administration. Twenty-two years after John's funeral, when I was at Penney Farms in Florida to conduct the funeral service of Dr. Gustav Jeeninga, I renewed my acquaintance with Margaret Smith, John's beloved widow then living there. A generation was passing away, the one that had mentored me. Even more was this the case in 2017-18 when I delievered tributes at the funerals of dear colleagues and personal mentors Robert Nicholson, Austin Sowers, and James Earl Massey.

There were also great times of celebration. For instance, the days July 11 and 12 of 1987 were special for me. One of the historic congregations of the Church of God movement is in St. James, Missouri. John A. Morrison, president of the Anderson campus from 1925 to 1958, knew this as home. Celebrating its one-hundredth anniversary, this church invited me to drive to the picturesque Ozarks to do the preaching. It was a personal delight. The Sunday afternoon service was designed for nostalgia and rejoicing.

An old-style grape arbor had been constructed to provide some seats in the shade. My pulpit was a large tree stump, the old-fashioned way to do things. We conducted a baptism—the only one of its kind in my experience. The candidate was a large gentleman in a wheelchair. I and others carried him and the chair into the Meramec River where we slid him out, baptized him, and put him back in. He was thrilled! So was I. Never have I forgotten his joy, nor the faith and sacrifice of several generations of pioneer believers in that good place. Some of the story is told in the warmly personal autobiography of John Morrison (*As The River Flows*, 1962). Morrison begins that work with this:

> The River Meramec is a winsome old stream—one of nature's
> most enchanting gifts to mid-America…. On long and lazy

summer days, the Meramec is the picture of peace and quiet and rest. I love to linger on her bank and hear the music of her waters. They seem to be singing about the meaning of things. Men have come to her banks, and men have gone from her banks, but she just keeps rolling quietly along. And in her music there seems to be reason as well as rhythm.

That is what I was learning about life. With all the coming and going, there is threaded through things a reason and a rhythm that comes from beyond the human sphere.

I carry similar memories of quiet waters. They come from my growing up along the western shore of Lake Milton in northeastern Ohio. Sometimes as a boy I would reflect on things as I watched the waves and pondered what might lay just out of sight beneath the often mysterious surface. One of my novels is about growing up in the beauty and tensions and mysteries around Lake Milton (*StarWalker*, 2011). I now am gone from those gentle shores, but the lovely lake remains, with its quiet beauty and mystery. Some of those qualities have taken residence in me, for which I rejoice. For instance, in 2007 I released my book *Caught Between Truths*. In its pages I detail the paradox and mystery resident in Christian faith. Rather than lament the dilemma resident in paradoxes, I celebrate the deep wisdom they capture. The paradoxes of divine truth, reaching beyond our limited rationality, sing of the simple and yet complex meaning of things.

Stressful Years for the Family

The beauty in life often must be seen and appreciated despite surrounding stress. Beauty comes in many forms, including the graciousness of colleagues. Anderson College professors William Farmen, Lee Griffith, Vern Norris, and Joe Womack had provided significant assistance as I designed and researched my Ed. D. dissertation at Indiana University.

Soon they would become important classroom leaders for my son Todd. I am in debt to these good men and dozens of others.

In 1983 I concluded the introduction to my I.U. doctoral dissertation with this reference to my family:

> Since freedom is a subject discussed at length in this dissertation, it is appropriate to refer to my immediate family in terms of freedom. Often, my wife Arlene and son Todd found it necessary to restrict their own freedom in order to grant me the time, energy, space, and, yes, the freedom required by a research project of this dimension. I am in their debt.

While I was finishing the research and writing in 1983, Arlene and I were still "band slaves." The marching band program at Highland High School in Anderson was demanding priority time from its many student participants and their parents.

During that summer, Todd, playing the bagpipes and the saxophone in this wonderful Scottish band, went on a trip with the band to Tennessee. On November 26 and again on December 20, there were Highland basketball games played in the Wigwam in Anderson, a 9,000-seat high school gym housing pageantry and excitement seen in few other high school settings in the United States ("Hoosier hysteria"). Todd played in the basketball band and his dad, an "old" basketball player himself, was pleased to be in attendance as often as possible.

Evelyn, my mother-in-law, now was living with us in Anderson and attending a local Free Methodist congregation. In the summer of 1983, I was pleased to take Evelyn to her fiftieth-year high school reunion back in Uniontown, Pennsylvania. She was alone otherwise, so I was her escort. On August 10 of that same year, Arlene and I celebrated our twentieth wedding anniversary. The years had been filled with much more than we had ever anticipated when we walked down the aisle in the Free

Methodist congregation in New Brighton, Pennsylvania, in 1963. We had been faithful to each other and life had been full, and mostly good. We were truly thankful.

In 1983 Todd was a teenager impatient with the restrictions of home life and more than ready for the freedom of college. My campus position meant that he qualified for a remitted tuition program that made Anderson University the practical choice for him. He graduated from Highland High School on June 5, 1985, and arrangements were made for him to move into Smith Hall as an Anderson College freshman. This residence hall, while located immediately across the street from our home on Falls Court, was adequately far away, functionally speaking, to provide the separate identity that he needed. Ironically, today Todd is living back in the Falls Court home with his wife Laura. He got his freedom in 1985, but did not stray far.

This move across the street began an excellent collegiate experience for Todd. He was bright, a questioner, seeker, and experimenter who needed both Christian witness and personal space. He found both on the Anderson campus, for which I am deeply grateful. As his dean, we had limited contact by mutual choice. He needed to find his own identity apart from me and his mother. After several personal relationships with young ladies, choices not always to the liking of his parents, Todd found Beth Hazen, who soon would be his wife and the mother of the first three of my grandchildren, Ian, Emily, and Ethan. Much more about grandchildren is found in chapter eleven!

While Todd was busy building his academic and social life on campus, there was no doubt about the intensity of my schedule. Just days before my venture into the Ozarks in 1987 to celebrate with an historic congregation, I had returned from a quick four-day trip to Honolulu, Hawaii, where I was negotiating a possible educational partnership between Anderson College and a local school there. I worshipped in the Church of God congregation near Honolulu and had the joy of having fresh flowers placed about my neck by a gracious usher. This was the church pastored earlier by David and Karla Telfer, family friends who were married the same day Arlene and I were. As Associate Registrar of Anderson College, Karla now was reporting to me. Unfortunately, divorce disrupted the Telfer family and Karla became discontent with her Anderson work and went elsewhere.

The Indianapolis Colts of the National Football League had begun staging their summer training camps on the Anderson campus—in fact, within a block of my Falls Court home (an interesting diversion to watch on occasion). I remember well the Saturday evening in August, 1986, when the Telfers hosted Arlene and me at a Colts game in Indianapolis— my first time to watch an NFL game in person. I met Peyton Manning when he first joined the team as a first-round draft pick, and in 2012 I lamented his being traded to the Denver Broncos after a hall-of-fame career in Indianapolis. This team became "mine" and finally won a Super Bowl in 2007.

The day after seeing a Colts game in 1986, I returned to the Indianapolis airport to meet P. J. Philip, an international economist and educator from India. I had made arrangements for P. J. and his wife to move to Anderson for a year while he taught as a visiting professor. Then, after only a few days home, I gathered my bags (expertly packed by Arlene, as usual) and with my son Todd flew to South Korea for the World Conference of the Church of God. Since I was leading a group, I earned the right for Todd to travel without cost, otherwise we could not have afforded his going. This trip was one of several results of my Anderson University employment that worked in Todd's favor.

The pace of my campus and church work remained hectic. What was evolving in my life was the need to maintain balance, to avoid burnout, to find renewing diversions. I lacked an enjoyable hobby unrelated to my work. Dwight L. Grubbs, a trusted colleague in the School of Theology whom I had recruited some years before on a trip to Houston, Texas, told me about a retreat opportunity at Gethsemani, a Benedictine monastery near Trappist, Kentucky. I went alone (an all-male environment), found a welcome silence and hospitality, and began a pattern of retreating there periodically.

I came to value the life and work of Thomas Merton, a famous monk who had resided at Gethsemani until his untimely death in 1968. I worked with some success at the spiritual potential of Christian contemplation. On different trips to Kentucky, I took along Dwight Grubbs, James Morehead, C. D. Oliver, and Paul Strozier, all good friends and Christian colleagues in Anderson. I wanted to share with others my treasured get-away place for spiritual growth. In my 2011 theology book *Heart of the Matter*, I weave through the pages many of the experiences and insights of Thomas Merton.

Another setting, this one in rural southern Indiana, was a welcome respite for Arlene and me together. It was the Abbey of St. Meinrad where she and I spent a wonderful weekend in March, 1986. After her death in 2003, my second wife Jan introduced me to Beahmblossom, the lovely hilltop "cabin" in the woods near Nashville, Indiana, owned by Ronald and Twila Beahm, members of the Cogitator's Sunday school class at Park Place Church of God in Anderson. They made the facility and their warm hospitality available for retreats of the class and other groups of the congregation. Since 2003, Jan and I have enjoyed this lovely location on numerous occasions.

I was given a special gift in 1984 as I was completing a preaching assignment with the Church of God people in Australia. It was a book titled *Poetical Works of Henry Lawson*. Lawson is said to have been "the first articulate voice of the real Australia." Two of the poems caught my eye as I browsed through the book on the long trans-Pacific flight home. In "The Vagabond" he says (p. 17):

A careless roaming life is mine,
Ever by field or flood—
For not far back in my father's line
Was a dash of the Gipsy blood....

A roving spirit in sympathy,
Who has traveled the whole world o'er—
My heart forgets, in a week at sea,
The trouble of years on shore.

Then there were these lines in "On the Night Train" (p. 47):

Have you seen the Bush by moonlight,
from the train, go running by?
Here a patch of glassy water,
there a glimpse of mystic sky?
Have you heard the still voice calling,
yet so warm, and yet so cold:
"I'm the Mother-Bush that bore you!
Come to me when you are old"?

I took these lines quite personally as I flew toward home. I was fulfilled in life, but tired, nostalgic at times, almost to the point of a little escapism. I was hardly old, only forty-three, but I could hear clearly voices of the past and the alluring calls to serenity. For me, time was moving on. I wanted it to move more slowly and flow more deeply.

In both May and October, 1985, I traveled to southwestern Ohio to enjoy the serenity of Hueston Woods State Park. Once Arlene and I went together and once I went alone. I recall the physical and spiritual pleasure of renting a little boat and rowing myself around beautiful Lake Acton almost to the point of delightful exhaustion. "Mother-Bush" was calling me. God wanted my attention in the midst of all my activity. But even while I was finding a little personal renewal, invitations were coming and my multiple commitments in Anderson were only being compounded by activities on the international scene. It seemed that I could not get off the road or out of incessant meetings.

The 1980s were eventful, stressful, and transitional for the Anderson campus and for my roles on the campus. I and the campus were moving toward ever larger pieces of the academic scene. For instance, I supervised the research and recommendation processes that led, with the excellent assistance of Michael Collette, to the launching of the division of Adult and Continuing Education in 1987. I also did research and wrote justifying documents that helped lead to the institutional name change to "Anderson University." Across these years, I was involved directly in rebuilding the undergraduate faculty, much as I had done in the School of Theology in the 1970s. I did interviews with and prepared first-year contracts for over fifty new faculty members.

Working closely with librarian Richard Snyder, we secured a major grant that allowed a merging of the two campus libraries (college and seminary) into an integrated and greatly expanded facility that was dedicated in October, 1989. Its new name now honors, quite appropriately, president Robert A. Nicholson. I was honored to be in the middle of these major campus changes.

In the process of all the above administrative activity that had begun for me in 1973, I had moved away from the actual task of classroom teaching, a lifelong love of mine. I was getting out of date with my own fields of academic specialization. As the Dean, my contact with college students usually was limited to passing judgments on difficult situations not solved at lower levels of administration. Arlene was becoming vocal about her concern for my health—she often saw me coming home rather late and very tired. I slowly began to realize that I was beginning to reach the limit of my toleration for the task, maybe even reaching the limit of my ability to be truly effective as the chief academic administrator of the ever-expanding university.

A significant and welcome change was not far away. It would come in relation to another change of presidential administration, as had been my big change from the School of Theology to the undergraduate college in 1983. This time the stimulus for change would be the retirement of Robert A. Nicholson and the coming of James L. Edwards to the presidential office. This transition became another milestone in my own journey.

Vice-Presidents of Anderson College, 1984 – Duane Hoak, myself, Ronald Moore, and Cleda Anderson. I enjoyed great colleagues.

Anderson College World

V O L   4   N O   7   M A R   8 3

Research examines academic freedom on Christian college campuses

It is a question that has challenged Christian higher education for generations: is academic freedom on Christian college campuses a myth or reality?

Dr. Barry Callen, dean of the School of Theology, may soon be in a position to give academia a definitive answer. His national research project, including an extensive faculty survey on the subject, is nearing completion, and is fully booked. He will share his preliminary findings with a national conference of Christian college deans.

Perhaps the most comprehensive survey ever conducted on the subject of faculty academic freedom in Christian colleges, the research is part of a doctoral dissertation in higher education administration that Dr. Callen is completing at Indiana University. Its title is "Faculty Academic Freedom in Member Institutions of the Christian College Coalition."

The research base consists of member schools of the Christian College Coalition, an alliance of about 70 Christ-centered liberal arts colleges and universities around the nation. The entire faculties of 23 of these member schools, including Anderson College's, were randomly selected to participate in the survey.

Although Dr. Callen points out that the results will yield dependable conclusions only for Christian College Coalition institutions (as opposed to church-related colleges in general), he is certain that the survey will produce some very reliable information because of the high rate of response we are receiving.

Dr. Callen's survey is generating a response approaching 75 percent. At some schools — including Northwestern, Anderson, George Fox — more than 80 percent of the questionnaires are being completed and returned.

Dr. John Reys, chairman of the psychology department at Anderson College, agrees with Dr. Callen that a response of that magnitude is exceptional.

"A return of 75 percent is very good," Dr. Reys concurred. "The normal return rate for a survey conducted through the U.S. mail is 30 percent."

The intent of the research is primarily descriptive, according to Dr. Callen seeking to "determine the actual

"Recent years have brought a resurgence of religious conservatism in the United States. To what degree has this trend been parallelled by a lessening tolerance of your campus administration for faculty members who might be judged as controversial by the college's church constituency?"

...Survey question

definitions, perceptions and implementation, of faculty academic freedom," in Christian colleges.

Asks a supporting document of the survey: "How can a college do justice to its avowed purpose as a Christian institution, a purpose which meshes with a commitment to a set of beliefs, and at the same time maintain the freedom of inquiry which most academic people think is necessary for good education?"

Dr. Callen's data has yet to be fed into the computer, and his dissertation won't be published until August, but he has been asked to give a progress report to a national conference of the deans of Christian College Coalition institutions meeting in Washington, D.C., March 26-27.

Dr. Barry Callen

President Robert A. Nicholson and me, during my inauguration as vice-president for academic affairs, Anderson College (University), October 27, 1983.

Douglas Nelson and I, giving
Coretta Scott King her honorary doctorate, 1986.

Dwight L. Grubbs and I, giving
Ronald J. Fowler his honorary doctorate, 1986.

A major step forward for Anderson University was the linking of the undergraduate Wilson Library (left) and the graduate School of Theology (right) with a large underground area. The physical merger included moving to a common cataloging system. Smiling at the left, I rejoiced at this major development in my area of campus administration. The result of this linking was the Nicholson Library honoring president Robert A. Nicholson (second from the right).

Thomas Oden   C. S. Lewis

Roger Olson

Thomas Merton

Prominent

Rosemary Reuther

Christian Leaders

Clark Pinnock

Geoffrey Wainwright

Engage in

Eleven Conversations

James Massey

Donald Bloesch

About All Central

Theological Issues

Elton Trueblood

Georigia Harkness

Barry Callen

Henri Nouwen   James Cone

EMETH PRESS
www.emethpress.com

The back cover of my 2016 book *Heart of the Matter.*
While on the road, I've met some amazing Christian leaders!

Chapter 7

Going on the Road

A pilgrim in God's very wide world

O ver the years I have enjoyed the gentle voice, sly humor, and homely subjects of journalist Charles Kuralt. In the 1960s he went to the president of CBS News and asked for permission to wander around the United States and do feature stories on whatever local life he happened to find of interest. Mr. Salant half-heartedly agreed and told him to keep the budget low. Kuralt found many fascinating American places and people ignored by the mass media. The interviews and commentaries turned into hours of arresting television viewing. His 1985 book *On the Road with Charles Kuralt* was a bestseller. I have sampled my copy many times. According to Kuralt, he "tried to go slow, stick to the back roads, take time to meet people, listen to yarns, notice the countryside go by, and feel the seasons change" (p. 14).

My earliest years were lived mostly along the back roads of American culture, with no one from CBS ever coming to Craig Beach to see if there was anything worth reporting. I stayed close to home in northeast Ohio and western Pennsylvania. Beginning in the late 1960s, however, I began to feel a little like the Charles Kuralt of the Church of God. From my new base on the Anderson College campus in Indiana, I joined many wonderful, worldwide ventures that transformed my little world. I have mentioned some of these ventures in the previous chapters. Now I want to expand on the report, telling a little of what I saw and learned while "on the road."

Around North America

Until after my college graduation in 1963, I had rarely been more than fifty miles from Craig Beach, Ohio. Then came marriage and seminary out west in Indiana. After seminary graduation in 1966, the travel pace picked up considerably. In just the three years 1967, 1968, and 1969, Arlene, Todd, and I lived in Indiana, Kentucky, Illinois, and then back to Indiana after I had finished my formal education. Our residences included the tiny town of Wilmore, Kentucky, and the urban sprawl of Chicago. This was just the beginning, especially for me. Most of our family traveling over the years was to Uniontown, Pennsylvania, and/or to Craig Beach, Ohio. Many Christmas celebrations in Uniontown enabled me to become a true member of Arlene's extended family. I grew particularly close to Dick and Juanita Cramer, and their daughters Cheri and Karyn and their husbands John Truskey and Dale Wayman.

My move into seminary administration in 1973 created tasks that took me on the road regularly. As seminary dean, I began a practice of visiting each of the Church of God colleges in North America at least every other year. As a member of the Commission on Christian Higher Education of the Church of God, I always attended annual meetings, which rotated between Anderson, Indiana, and the college campuses. This contact led me to love these schools and write their histories, first in *Preparing for Service* (1988) and then in *Enriching Mind and Spirit* (2007).

The memories collected from these travels are many. I recall experiencing a temperature of 40 degrees below zero in Camrose, Alberta, Canada, when the Commission was meeting at Gardner College. I remember attending, in bright and warm sunshine, a Rose Bowl game in Pasadena, California, when the Commission met at Azusa Pacific University. I would be on that West-Coast campus several times in later years, once delivering the Robertson Lectures and three times representing the Church of God movement in the Wesleyan-Holiness Study Project.

That "Project" would evolve into the Wesleyan-Holiness Connection and its Aldersgate Press for which I would serve as Editor beginning in 2011 various occasions when I was in Portland, Oregon, Houston, Texas, Lake Wales, Florida, Kendleton, Texas, Oklahoma City, Oklahoma, and Camrose, Alberta. On two occasions I was in Trinidad visiting the little college there. Canada, the Caribbean, the United States, all were becoming my homes away from home.

I did some traveling with my family. Once Arlene and I crossed the continent on an Amtrack train so that I could attend the West Coast Ministers Meeting of the Church of God in Sacramento, California. In the room next to us on the train were Arnold and Sylvia Levy, an older Jewish couple from Chicago who ate with us several times along the way and became our treasured friends until their deaths many years later.

On another occasion, Arlene, Todd, and I took to the rails more northward on our way to Seattle, Washington, and then by ferry to Vancouver Island, this time for a vacation. On the way west, we went through the Wisconsin Dells that we had visited earlier by car. Todd got bored as we crossed the endless state of Montana. He was so active that I took him to the observation deck and encouraged him to sit quietly and watch the passing land for an albino buffalo, "rare but existing" I said. This diversion gave Arlene and me a little peace for a few hours, although he decided before the trip was over that I had tricked him with the albino business. Many years later, Todd's son Ethan helped me "trick" Todd again, this time taking him to a location in Pennsylvania where a "white buffalo" actually had been born! My integrity was restored, accompanied by much laughing!

On a third occasion, Todd attended the National Youth Convention of the Church of God in Florida. He rode the bus of Park Place Church of God while Arlene and I trailed along in our car. Arlene was not much of a traveler, so our trips together were relatively few. To her, a Holiday Inn was the desired limit of her "roughing it." Ironically, the result of my traveling was that I had visited at least as many countries as states in my own nation. My second wife, Jan, later teased me about this irony and we took two wonderful bus trips to the national parts in the western states.

Far From America's Shores

My first significant travel beyond North America had been that amazing experience in 1968 in the Middle East discussed above. The countries visited were Israel, Lebanon, Cyprus, and Jordan. Beginning in 1972, there would come a burst of additional international activity, despite a young family, limited finances, and heavy involvement in campus life in Anderson, Indiana, and church life around North America. The travel would take me to nearly all points of the planet, often in relation to the TRI-S program of Anderson College and various ministries of the Church of God around the world that called for my services.

The Church of God movement has convened a series of multi-national gatherings to enable acquaintance and dialogue about the beliefs, mission, and ministries of the movement globally. They typically were made possible by the financial support of the church in United States and enabled by the church's administrative offices in Anderson, Indiana. I was privileged to be present in many of these gatherings, including those in Anderson, U.S.A (1980), Seoul, South Korea (1987), Wiesbaden, Germany (1991), Sydney, Australia (1995), and Birmingham, England (1999).

A key component of five of these gatherings was the adjacent convening of International Dialogues on Doctrine. I convened and chaired the first of these in 1980 as Dean of Anderson University School of Theology, and either convened or acted as recorder for the others. I served as keynoter for the 1980 and 1995 world gatherings and in my *Following the Light* detailed the processes and outcomes of all the World Conferences, World Forums, and international Dialogues on Doctrine,

1955-2000. Unfortunately, the horrific terrorist attack on the United States in 2001 ("9/11") ended these gatherings, but not the growing need for them. By the 1980s the constituency of the Church of God movement had become larger outside then inside North America. That trend has continued.

I said this when keynoting the 1995 World Forum: "The Church of God now is a worldwide movement that must learn increasingly to profit from its diversity, not be paralyzed by it." I was echoing what my colleague Douglas Welch had said to the 1980 World Forum: "The Scriptures challenge us to take seriously the total interdependence of the community of faith. This is not optional. It is urgent that we sit down together to discover new wineskins for the new wine of the Spirit flowing in this age."

In 2018 Jim Lyon, then General Director of Church of God Ministries in North America, was urging a renewed International vision of the church and its ministries. He noted the significant advance in communication technology now offering new feasibility for extensive international contact of the church's world leaders. One initiative was my drafting for wide consideration new language for the identity and mission of the Church of God movement in today's world. It needs to be rooted in the movement's heritage but not dominated by the particular religious culture of the Movement's origin in nineteenth-century America. It needs to be thoroughly biblical, intentionally global, and designed to stimulate a fresh togetherness in mission that bridges national and cultural borders.

Now for a glance at my international experiences that include but extend far beyond the global needs of the Church of God movement.

1. Japan. My father had been a part of the Allied occupying force in Japan in the mid-1940s as the world war concluded. It was involuntary frustration for him. In the 1970s, by contrast, I happily returned to the islands of the Rising Sun. It was a land that helped my cultural life to rise much more in fascination than frustration. Just a few years after World War II, Ann and Nathan Smith had gone to Japan as Church of God missionaries. Now they were comfortable with the land, culture, and language and ready to be our hosts. They lived in Futsukaichi on the southern island of Kuyusu.

With myself as group leader, nine of us flew from Seattle, Washington, in 1971 to begin this Anderson College TRI-S trip. Daniel and Verna Rinker were on their honeymoon. Dennis and Emily Carroll were key group members, with Dennis later becoming a respected judge in Anderson, Indiana, and member of the Anderson University board of trustees. Our chartered World Airways plane leaked fuel, causing us a long delay in departure. We missed our connecting flight from Tokyo to southern Japan. Young missionary Trish Bentley kindly met us and, in all the scheduling confusion, helped us find our way to a new domestic flight. She, and later her husband Blake Janutolo, would be valued friends and colleagues of mine back in Anderson, Indiana, for the rest of my life.

The Smiths had begun a Christian Center next to their residence in Futsukaichi. My group braved the heat and helped build a large stone retaining wall behind the property. We were introduced to public baths, Shinto and Zen Buddhist temples, the museum in Nagasaki commemorating the horror of the atomic bomb dropped there, the "bullet" train to Tokyo, the educational and pastoral ministries of Phil and Phyllis Kinley in the huge capital city, and so much more. I preached with a Japanese interpreter in a Church of God congregation in Saga City, taught English pronunciation to Japanese teachers of English, and had a three-day home-stay where no English was spoken (leads to interesting situations!). At the suggestion of Ann Smith, I began growing a beard, and have worn it ever since in one form or another. She said I would look better with it. I hope she was right! Being one of the more saintly persons I ever knew, she probably was.

This full month in the Japanese culture, both very ancient and very modern, was a life-changing experience for me. Once done, my mother met my plane in Pittsburgh and drove me to Uniontown, Pennsylvania, so that I could be reunited with my wife and son and then drive them back to Anderson for the opening of another semester at Anderson College. I brought with me Japanese clothes for Arlene, Todd, and myself, and a quality tea set for Arlene to use with pride.

For me, Japan serves as a metaphor of the constant change in life. My father sailed into Manila harbor in the Phillipines in 1945, only then learning that the war had formally ended. His ship carried war material that the crew had transported thousands of miles at the risk of their lives. They were ordered to dump it into the harbor and to dock, giving the ship to the Japanese—who had been granted permission to use it to transport their sick and wounded home to Japan. What a dramatic change, fighting an enemy and suddenly giving that enemy your tools of war!

The Japanese had bombed Pearl Harbor in 1941, bringing the United States into the war. Four decades later, I traveled to Honolulu, Hawaii, on business for the Anderson campus. I soon realized that many of the big hotels along the famous Hawaiian beaches were now owned by Japanese companies. What Japan had once failed to conquer in wartime it now had bought in peacetime. Japan, an ancient culture devastated by war in the 1940s, had become very modern and prosperous by the 1980s. Things change constantly. We must learn to change with them, and also be wise enough to know the few things that should never change.

2. Greece, Italy, and Israel. Gustav Jeeninga was the professor whom I replaced temporarily in 1966 during his sabbatical. He and I were soon full colleagues at Anderson College and partners in an unforgettable January Term course in 1972. We called it "The Classical and Biblical World," charged $775 for participation, recruited a wonderful group of twenty-five students and college staff, and planned "to gain understanding of and appreciation for the central tenets of the Christian faith by a study of its beginnings in the life of Jesus and in the first decades of the church's expansion." The course was convened in Israel, Greece, and Italy. Gus and I designed readings, hymns, scriptures, and lectures to support all the touring. I was featured as the bright young scholar and Gus the seasoned biblical archaeologist—a combination that attracted the participating group. Credit could be earned for any one of seven college or four seminary courses.

This experience was exceptional for me, including the curricular coordination with the School of Theology that soon would balloon into far more than I could have imagined (I would be the acting dean within a year). A humorous and embarrassing story is told in Dr. Jeeninga's autobiography, *Doors to Life* (2002, 235-239). Gus and I were fooled on the streets of Athens, Greece, leading us into a brothel that almost cost the group its trip to Corinth the next day—I had all the cash for the bus in my pocket. While all turned out well, it was an hour never to be forgotten! Nor was the trip in general, with most experiences far more enriching than embarrassing. Stepping inside St. Peters in Rome nearly took my breath away. Walking around the ruins of ancient Corinth fired my imagination. Making my way through Hezekiah's water tunnel in Jerusalem was humbling, to say the least. Eating the eyeball of a lamb at a community celebration in Irbid, Jordan, was an unforgettable day for me. I was identified as the honored guest, meaning that no one would eat until I had enjoyed the delicacy—at least as defined locally. There was no choice!

One more breath-taking experience was later reported. Donald Collins was in our traveling group, a young pastor in Anderson, Indiana, who would be a respected colleague of mine well into the following century. In his 2010 autobiography titled *There Were Angels Along My Way*, Don reports: "Visiting the sites with which I was familiar from the years of reading *Egermier's Bible Story Book* was indescribable. The highlight was climbing through a farmer's tomato patch to the top of the Mount of the Beatitudes. I sat undisturbed and read much of the Book of Mark. The panorama was before me: the Sea of Galilee, Capernaum, the mountains where Jesus had gotten up a good while before dawn to go to pray. It was a transcendent hour" (p. 70).

In 2005 I would be privileged to take my wife Jan as we traveled around Israel with a group of Messianic Jews and our rabbi friend Jeff Adler from Indianapolis. There were many transcendent hours, especially for Jan who had never been to the "Holy Land" before. This experience deepened my interest in Jewish-Christian relations, helping to lead to my 2012 book *Beneath the Surface: Reclaiming the Old Testament for Today's Christian.*

3. Switzerland. No single event ever moved me more than the 1974 International Congress on World Evangelism called by the Billy Graham Evangelistic Association. This ten-day event convened in the huge international convention center in Lausanne, Switzerland. I suppose it was because I was the relatively new dean of Anderson School of Theology that I was invited to go as an official observer. Fifteen people were in attendance from the Church of God movement, with only myself, James Earl Massey, William E. Reed, and Charles Tarr representing the United States. The Congress brought together some 4,000 Christian leaders from 150 countries to demonstrate unity and find better ways to accomplish the great commission of our Lord—go into all the world and preach the gospel. "Evangelical" Christians had the reputation of being sectarian, clannish, and culturally and doctrinally narrow. But here we were, representing many cultures, styles, languages, and doctrinal slants, and yet united in hoping to carry out better the mission of the church that belonged equally to us all.

This was my first opportunity to meet Billy Graham and various other prominent Christian leaders from all over the world. One day we massed in the nearby Olympic Stadium to hear Graham preach—a way of being evangelistic to the local city population. On another day, designated as free time, I took the train into "Heidi country" to sample the beauty of the Swiss mountains. It was a long walk across the city from my hotel to the convention center; sometimes I took a bus, an interesting process in a French-speaking city. Before leaving, I bought a wall clock, Swiss made and hand-painted. It remains a family treasure to this day. Taking no risks, I carried it home myself, snuggled between my feet on the plane for safety. In my heart, I brought home much more than a clock!

4. Australia. I was attracted to the great land "down under" partly because Austin and Nancy Sowers were ministering in Sydney as missionaries sponsored by my home church in Newton Falls, Ohio. They were like personal family. Their daughter Judy (Hughes) became one of eighteen students who comprised my TRI-S group from Anderson College. Also included was Trish Bentley (Janutolo) who earlier had been of assistance to my Japan TRI-S group while she was a missionary there. Flying from and to Los Angeles (Aug. 1 and 22, 1976), we were off to tour, build relationships, do heavy labor at the Church of God camp called Berachah, lead worship services, and teach Bible classes in Fairvale High School. Judy and I stayed at the Sowers home when in Sydney, having a little Newton Falls reunion in the fascinating world of kangaroos. My family remained in Anderson, Arlene not exactly an adventuresome long-distance traveler, although she knew well and loved Austin, Nancy, and Judy. We exchanged several letters and phone calls during these three wonderful weeks.

I marveled to see again the big servant heart of Brother Austin. Many in his Matthew Avenue congregation were women, some without transportation. Before and after a church service, he would drive his van a considerable distance to shuttle his needy flock from and then back to their homes. I met and learned to love local church leaders Len and Dot Bradley, Lloyd and Ruth Chilvers, and Jack and Madeline Haines. There also was the Hughes family. Ron and Pam had two sons, Malcolm and Chris. In a few years, the whole family would be living permanently in Ohio, Judy and Mal would be married, and the unanticipated and unwelcome day would come in 2003 when Chris, at my request, would wear his Scottish kilts and play "Amazing Grace" on his bagpipes. The sad occasion would be my burying my beloved Arlene in Maplewood Cemetery in Anderson. We would be together again in 2018 at the funeral of Austin Sowers.

Back to 1976, death met me the moment I returned home to Anderson from Australia on August 24. Arlene told me that Dr. Boyce W. Blackwelder had just died of a heart attack. As dean of the School of Theology, I suddenly was without a New Testament professor just as the fall semester was about to begin! In the midst of jet lag, the joys of Australia still vivid in my mind, I was met with the sometimes harsh realities of a working dean. I am so glad that Harold L. Phillips was available to step into the gap.

Eight years later, in September, 1984, I was back in Australia, this time traveling alone. My role was guest speaker at the annual Australian Leader's Retreat and Family Camp held at Berachah, the rural church camp outside Sydney where my TRI-S group had worked so hard in 1976. I greatly enjoyed these days, preaching, counseling with young church leaders, and especially discussing with the church its dream of a school. There were excellent universities available in Australia to meet the needs of the church's young–except for specialized training in Christian faith, life, and ministry. There also was a large gift from an individual for a new church school. I projected the model of a school that would convene only during university vacations and featured the very best of guest teachers from the Church of God around the world. I wanted the gift to be converted into a permanent endowment that would fund all travel and housing costs for these teachers longterm. There was excitement about this idea, but little local leadership to organize and implement such an enterprise, even when fully funded. The dream failed to materialize and the money was used in other ways. The Australian church would continue to struggle from lack of educated leadership.

As a way of encouraging the small church in Australia, the Church of God movement staged its 1995 World Conference and Forum in Sydney. I was again present "down under," enjoying this great city once more, seeing my Australian friends, and convening another International Dialogue on Doctrine as part of the larger Conference. Short histories of the several Dialogues on Doctrine, World Conferences, and World Forums of the Church of God are found in my book *Following the Light* (2000). I delivered the keynote address to the World Forum in Australia. It was titled "Celebrating Our Church of God Heritage" (a summary is found as "Honoring the Six R's of Heritage Celebration" in *Following the Light*, 2000, 403ff). Afterwards, several of us formed a tour group and flew farther south for a wonderful week traveling around New Zealand, one of the more beautiful places I have ever seen, rivaled only by the fjords of Norway that my wife Jan and I would be privileged to cruise in 2006 and 2012. We also would travel together back to Australia and New Zealand.

5. England, Ireland, and Scotland. In August, 1979, I led a group of six Anderson College students to England. Bad weather confused flight connections, but we managed to get to our little hotel in London and begin serving the Church of God congregation a few underground stops away—our "go-as-you-please" tickets were great! So was the new building the church was enjoying, although its educational space was very limited. When more than eighty active and undisciplined children from the neighborhood showed up for the Bible school that we were to conduct for a week, we had our hands more than full. I remember students Rose

Wounded Arrow and John Skipper giving all they had. With the help of three laypersons from the congregation, we improvised and made the week quite successful. No curriculum was available, and virtually no handcraft supplies, so we went shopping. The final program presented by the children was to a standing-room-only crowd in the church. Most adults were immigrants from various Caribbean countries.

Being the dean of the seminary of the Church of God, it was natural that I would be asked to serve in other ways. On our second day in London, I was requested to co-officiate with the pastor, Martin Goodridge, at a wedding (total strangers to me). How interesting to watch, prior to the ceremony, the ministers and couple go to a private room to meet with a public official in a white powered wig and sign the registry—the legal wedding. Each evening for one week, I led discussions with congregational members on the history and doctrine of the Church of God movement. Being a group of West Indian immigrants, they had many questions about the racial problems in the United States and how the church was addressing them. I also was asked to conduct a day-long clinic one Saturday for the church leaders, focusing on questions around major Christian doctrines. The final week was reserved for independent travel. I traveled alone, as did most of the others. It was my first time to see England. With little money in my pocket, but with a rail pass, I could get around well. The balance of service and touring, the dual purpose of the TRI-S program of the Anderson campus, was welcomed by all.

The next summer there was the rare opportunity for independent travel without ministry responsibilities. Arlene, Todd, and I went back to the British Isles, this time for personal pleasure. This was the only time that Arlene traveled internationally with me, so I tried to make it as comfortable as I could. We attended the theater twice in London, seeing "Annie" and "The King and I" with the famous Yul Brynner on stage at the London Palladium. The three of us left London for day trips on the fine trains, and finally took an overnight train to Inverness, Scotland. Our stay in a bed and breakfast next to the river downtown was a delight. One day we took the tour by small boat on Loch Ness, a dramatic inland lake. We did not see the legendary Nessie, but Todd looked hard and the setting was beautiful.

My third visit to England was to participate in the Eleventh World Conference and Sixth World Forum of the Church of God movement. They both convened in the international convention center in Birmingham, England, July 22-25, 1999. There were the inspiring worship sessions of the conference and then the major presentations and discussions of the Forum. Perceived commonly as worldwide church concerns were integrity in leadership, biblical principles for the family, and Christ as Lord of the nations. All proceeded under the general leadership of Edward L. Foggs of the United States.

My formal role was to function as recording secretary of the Forum. When it was over, my next role—a real pleasure—was to lead, along with a professional guide, a major tour called "Scottish Highlands." Forty-four of us, including my good friends Arthur and Judy Kelly from the United States and John Campbell from Canada, spent twelve days traveling north by bus. We visited the great Stirling Castle, spent time in Glasgow and Edinburgh, Scotland, visited Loch Ness and much more. These were wonderful times with special people. I remember Gibb Webber of the Anderson University faculty taking a trip outside Edinburgh in search of the "Holy Grail." ." He found only rumors of its whereabouts.

There were three other visits to the British Isles, all different. In 2003, just months before our marriage, Jan Slattery and I were part of a TRI-S group from Anderson University that toured in England, Ireland, and Scotland. Then in 2006, three years into our marriage, Jan and I struck out on a wonderful cruising adventure. It began and ended in Heathrow airport in London. We went by bus to the eastern port of Harwich from which we sailed on a cruise ship to France, Ireland, Scotland, and Norway. The fjords of Norway were as spectacular as advertised. One stop for our ship was in Plymouth harbor, England, from which the little Mayflower had sailed long ago for the new world. Jan and I had come from the new to enjoy the old. Frontiers are fine, but so is heritage.

There was yet another cruise, this time in 2012 sailing 4,000 nautical miles from Southampton back to Southampton, England. Jan and I journeyed on the sea to Iceland, the Faroe Islands, and a return to the fjords of Norway. We crossed in luxury the North Atlantic waters sailed by my father in the terrible war years of the 1940s. The Norwegian coast had been home to 240 German U-boats that had hoped to bring England to its knees and send to the freezing deep the American convoys supplying the English. My father survived that time, and now I had survived also. In my case, the danger had been the cancer and chemotherapy treatments the previous summer that might have made this trip impossible for me. However, the doctors were good and God was very gracious.

6. Kenya. In the early 1980s, officials of Kima Theological College in Kenya, East Africa, corresponded with me directly and through missionary Paul Hutchins about the possibility of Anderson College "accrediting" KTC. I was invited to come as the KTC commencement speaker and discuss in depth this possibility with the school's administration, faculty, and board of governors. All of this was accomplished during my visit to Kenya, August 14-28, 1985. I sought to acquaint myself in detail with KTC and the higher education scene in Kenya, including the African accrediting body, laws, and schools similar to KTC. I visited Daystar University in Nairobi and spoke at length with the KTC Board of Governors. The accreditation didn't happen, but the school persisted and is known today as Kima International School of Theology. For nearly two decades now its class in Christian theology has used as the main text my book *God As Loving Grace*.

I especially enjoyed preaching in the "cathedral" at Kima, the center of the large Church of God population in that country. A rainstorm came up and pounded hard on the metal roof, causing me to almost shout out the gospel of Christ while my interpreter seemed to repeat my words even more loudly in Swahili. What two hours these were! Paul Hutchins was my primary host. He got me around and showed me a range of African culture. We visited a Massai village. I preached in a rural church where I was presented with a "rungu," the weapon and scepter of a ruling chief. I also was guest preacher in a large Anglican church still under construction. The people were raising money—and expected a substantial gift from me as the honored guest! I was unprepared for that (and got solicitation letters from the bishop for several years after). A marble slab was installed in the brick wall near the front door that carried my name and that of Anderson College. This was an unusual honor indeed.

I did more than preach and consult on this trip—I caught a very large fish, a Nile perch weighing 116 pounds! Missionary Paul Hutchins and I were in the harbor of the city of Kisumu, enjoying ourselves on Lake Victoria, being hosted by John Nicolle, an Australian missionary who often took other missionaries fishing for their mental health. Back at Kima, my fish was "butchered" and shared with various families. It was much fun. I had gained substantial bragging rights—and, I hope, assisted the Kenyan church and school a little. In 2010 I would be back in Kenya, not fishing but helping to plan a new ministry to assist AIDS orphans in several African nations through Horizon International. I helped found this significant ministry in 2001 and have served as its Corporate Secretary from the beginning (see below).

7. Panama, Trinidad, and Jamaica. On two occasions my wife Jan and I transited the Panama Canal in cruise ships, marveling at the engineering that made this special place possible. Those trips were for pleasure. Some trips to the Caribbean were mission oriented. For instance, I journeyed twice to Trinidad and Tobago during the 1970s and 1980s. Both times my hosts were Carlton and Theodosia Cumberbatch. My purpose was to relate helpfully to West Indies Theological College led by the Cumberbatches and others. In 1986 I convened on this small Caribbean campus a consultation exploring the future of WITC. My more extensive contact with the Church of God in the Caribbean, however, was in Jamaica. The 2007 book *Enriching Mind and Spirit* carries my written histories of the Church of God colleges in both Trinidad and Jamacia.

In April, 2000, I was privileged to be the primary preacher for the week-long annual gathering of the Church of God in Jamaica, convening on the grounds of the historic Ardenne High School. It was hot in Kingston, but the people were wonderful and made all of my perspiring more than worthwhile. Wilmer Jackson, who had been a seminarian at Anderson School of Theology years before under my deanship, hosted me and took me to visit Port Royale where legends of pirates still haunt the grounds and old fort.

I had become an admiring colleague of Melvyn Hester (d. 2000) who had migrated from Kingston, Jamaica, to Anderson College in the 1950s, eventually to become a key minister in the Church of God movement and executive administrator of Human Resources for New York City. I participated as he was granted an honorary Doctor of Divinity degree and then delivered the baccalaureate address at Anderson University while he was dying of cancer. Shortly after that, I would be editing and publishing through Anderson University Press the autobiography of James Earl Massey. In it, he tells the story of the church school in Kingston, Jamaica, along with the migration to the United States of another Jamaican, Samuel G. Hines, who brought superb leadership to the North American church and with whom I was privileged to labor.

The second of my visits to the lovely island of Jamaica was with my wife Jan in 2007. This time we were hosted by Lenworth Anglin as the Church of God of Jamaica officially marked its first century of existence and ministry. We had come as the guests of the church to join the great week of celebration. It was a truly wonderful and sometimes exhausting time—a night street meeting in the public square in Port Antonio, a parade through the city's streets, a reenactment of the arrival of George and Nellie Olson in 1907 (the first Church of God missionaries to the island), a meeting in a mountain town with Donald and Lori Doe from Arizona and their group—they were building a pastor's manse, a centennial cruise of Kingston harbor, being formally received by the Governor General of Jamaica, and my preaching the official thanksgiving service in the "mother" church in Kingston. God's people were celebrating, and Jan and I were privileged to be guest leaders in their midst. Very prominent with us was Dalineta Hines, widow of the deceased church leader Samuel G. Hines from Jamaica. For her it was a joyous return home.

8. South Korea, China, and Hong Kong. Church of God leaders from fifty-two nations gathered in Seoul, South Korea, in the summer of 1987, with all conferences, rallies, lodging, and food services under one roof, the Seoul Hilton International Hotel. Never before had so many nations been represented in a world gathering of Church of God people. There were 700 North American delegates, with another 300 from other countries. Major evening rallies grew in attendance to about 2,000 to celebrate the theme "Strengthening Our Unity." All travel arrangements were made by Norman Beard of the TRI-S office of Anderson University. The traveler with me was my son Todd, who ventured during the conference on a tour to the demilitarized zone between North and South Korea—a highlight experience for him. He and I went together on a boat excursion to communist China, then flew by way of Tokyo to visit Hong Kong on the way home. Todd, much like his mother Arlene, is not the greatest of world travelers. Nonetheless, I doubt that he will ever forget 1987 in the Orient with me!

9. Haiti. My dear friends John and Jodie (Gross) Ackerman moved to Haiti in the 1980s to serve as Christian missionaries—I had officiated at their wedding at Park Place Church of God in Anderson, Indiana, in 1976. Both graduates of the Anderson campus, John served as a nurse and Jodie a teacher. They would rear their two daughters in Haiti and call this troubled land their home. I was sent to them in the late 1980s by the Missionary Board of the Church of God to troubleshoot a problem needing addressed. I had never seen such poverty in my life. John and Jodie were placing their lives on the line for the love of their Lord and suffering humanity.

In April, 2006, my wife Jan and I returned to Haiti on another assignment, this time for me to be guest leader for the annual retreat of the Church of God missionaries in the country. We lived for the week in the Ackerman home on a mountainside above Port-Au-Prince. We "bounded" along the local "roads" and twice worked with John in his rural medical clinic. Jan is a good traveler and happily joined in the work, a natural missionary at heart.

Years later, on one of the last days of 2011, Jan and I again saw Haiti, this time from the sea. We sailed by in a cruise ship, watching only barren hillsides and knowing that this poor land was still struggling with the awful devastation of a recent earthquake. John and Jodie Ackerman, our dear missionary friends, were still there healing and teaching. One of those unanswerable questions is why some of us are so blessed while others suffer so greatly. Jan and I have been among the blessed!

10. Germany. I had two wonderful opportunities to travel and minister in Germany, the first in 1991 and the other in 1993. The first occasion took me to Wiesbaden for the World Conference of the Church of God, and then to the lovely little city of Fritzlar where the German Bible School is located. My role as guest leader was to make several presentations to the European Minister's Conference being hosted in Fritzlar. I loved this little town, a classic small city on a hill, surrounded partly by a medieval wall. I especially was delighted to spend time with my friend Willi Krenz, a German pastor who had assisted many touring groups from Anderson College over the years.

In 1993 I was invited back to Germany, this time to the northern city of Hamburg to help celebrate the centennial of the Church of God movement in Germany and speak to the seventeenth European Theological Conference for pastors and their wives. Among other things, I was asked to speak about Islam and Christianity—a large influx of Muslims into Germany was raising problems in the society and fresh opportunities for the churches. I read much before going and my presentations were later published in *Missions* magazine. Beginning in 2005, my wife Jan asked me on occasion to discuss Islam with her senior classes at Anderson High School—before she retired in 2012. Given the violence so much in the news, many students assumed that every Moslem is a terrorist. I tried to counter such a serious misconception.

On this 1993 visit, I rode on the famous autoban, experiencing those amazing speeds. I marveled at the beauty of the Bavarian mountains. I saw lovely countryside, including the little town of Hitzrode, the place from which some of my ancestors came to the new world. I remember walking in the large city of Hamburg and stopping in a city park to observe a concrete bunker about three stories high. It had been used during World War II to shoot at Allied aircraft that were swarming overhead to bomb and end the war. I felt strange, seeing the stark crudeness of the site and remembering that in 1944 the husband of my first wife's Aunt Bea had been shot down in the area and presumed dead.

Jan and I had another trip to Germany planned for the summer of 2011. I had edited and published the autobiography of Rev. Willi Krenz of Germany (*Always Looking Forward*, 2010). In gratitude, he had volunteered to be our host and guide. My cancer treatments, however, aborted this plan, a genuine disappointment. This loss was corrected in 2015 when Jan and I did a river cruise through Germany.

11. **Kenya, South Africa, Uganda, Zambia, Zimbabwe.** My first visit to Kenya is noted above. Another opportunity would come my way. Having been corporate secretary of Horizon International since its beginning in 2001, opportunity for related travel came in November, 2007. This ministry focuses on AIDS orphans in six African countries, Kenya, South Africa, Ethiopia, Uganda, Zambia, and Zimbabwe. My wife Jan and I initially traveled to three of these nations with Horizon's president, Robert Pearson, and ten others, including young pastors Chris Denney and Troy Scott. We experienced natural beauty, such as Victoria Falls in Zimbabwe and wildlife in South Africa's Krueger National Park. We also saw human desperation at its worst, much because of widespread death from AIDS. We managed the challenges of four days in Zimbabwe, a nation in economic and political collapse at the time.

Our primary goals were to witness for Jesus Christ, learn about other cultures, explore additional ministry opportunities, and serve human needs, especially those of the many hundreds of dramatically disadvantaged children then under Horizon's care. I had opportunity to preach in Harare, Zimbabwe, and co-lead a pastor's conference in Lusaka, Zambia. Jan and I rejoiced when we met our thirteen-year-old boy in rural Limpopo Province, South Africa, whom we had sponsored through Horizon since 2005. We met Horizon staff doing heroic work, held orphans in our laps in "the bush," and traveled about as a blessed people in a great land where a few are rich and many are barely surviving.

As Jesus directed, through Horizon we were doing what we could in the midst of a pandemic—serving "the least of these" one child at a time. In 2010 Jan and I were back in Africa visiting and serving two other of Horizon's nations, Kenya and Uganda. The hundred pastors we helped teach in Fort Portal, Uganda, were so hungry to learn and such a joy to serve! An orphan choir sang and danced for us, expressing their gratitude for Horizon having given them a chance at life and a heritage of faith. The relationships made and information gathered on this and the previous trip to Africa helped enable me to write the history of this great ministry (*Hope on the Horizon*, 2010). In the years that have followed it has been my monthly responsibility to detail for the African partners the money coming to comprehensively care for the children.

12. The World At Large. In my first few retirement years, and especially after my wife Jan retired in 2012, she and I were blessed with the time and funds to enjoy several cruises to various parts of the world. We sailed the Caribbean Sea, the Mediterranean Sea, the North Sea, the Baltic Sea, the Adriatic Sea, the Inland Passage of Alaska, the Arctic Sea, and more. We walked the streets of great cities like Amsterdam, St. Petersburg, Athens, Jerusalem, Cairo, and Alexandria. We wandered through the stunning remains of Pompey in Italy and Ephesus in Turkey. We watched for whales near Anchorage, Alaska, panned for gold near Fairbanks, rode in a pirate ship off the shores of Honduras, cruised through the Panama Canal and on the rivers of Europe, and visited sites related to the novel *Anne of Green Gables* near the shore of the Gulf of St. Lawrence on Prince Edward Island.

We helped in a medical clinic in Haiti, sang gospel songs along the shores of Jamaica, walked through the lava fields of Iceland, bounced in a little boat along the sea cliffs of the Faroe Islands, and taught pastors in Uganda. We sailed down the east side of South America and around the southern tip at Cape Horn, almost being able to see the ice-pack of Antarctica. We then ventured to Ushuaia, most southern city on Earth, before going up the west coast of Chili to visit the world of penguins. Jan and I were being privileged to see God's amazing world and people. We were blessed well beyond any deserving.

The traveling involved more than moving about the globe. I also was blessed to venture far outside the Church of God movement (Anderson), discovering and serving with God's people in many of the faith's traditions.

Venturing Outside the Church of God

Given the church-unity vision of the Church of God movement, it was relatively easy for me to move freely among Christian believers with many associational labels (although a strain of "sectarianism," even in the Church of God tradition, did cause hesitation and unjustified suspicion on occasion). My own opportunities and instincts caused me to look hopefully outside the Church of God (Anderson)—not leaving it, just representing it ever more widely in the Christian community. This brought much richness to my own life of faith.

Venturing into the larger Christian world followed some natural paths for me, beginning with my exposure as a college student to the Presbyterian tradition. It accelerated over the years with great models entering my life, all-church leaders like James Earl Massey, Kevin Mannoia, David Han, and Jim Lyon.

As a Protestant, I eventually looked toward what may have been lost in its historic break from the Roman Catholic Church. Many leaders in the Church of God had spoken harshly of Catholicism, including my home pastor, Lillie S. McCutcheon, and her book *The Symbols Speak* that links Catholicism to the "beast" in the Book of Revelation. The Church of God had its own historic roots in a combination of the Wesleyan and free-church or Believers Church traditions. My life would move deeply into both wings of this root system, in part to better understand my own heritage and to enrich it.

As a boy growing up in northeast Ohio, I didn't realize that I lived between Grand Junction, Michigan, and North Chili, New York. I had no idea that these locations were historic centers for the Church of God movement and the Free Methodist Church, and that eventually both would be very influential in my life. In fact, one day I would be the biographer of the primary pioneer of the one church, Daniel S. Warner (1842-1895), *It's God's Church!* (1995), who is buried in Grand Junction. My friend Howard Snyder would be the biographer of Benjamin T. Roberts (1823-1893, *Populist Saints*, 2006), founder of the Free Methodist Church.

While I grew up in a Church of God congregation, it was the strong family history of both myself and my first wife, Arlene (Cooley), in the Free Methodist Church that made for interesting dialogue early in our courtship. When we first began dating as freshmen at Geneva College, Arlene's mother, Evelyn Cooley, was cautious about me, an unknown young man who came from the "Church of God." What she had heard about groups with this name made her uncomfortable. Evelyn was very serious about her Christian faith (the particularly conservative variety she knew growing up in the Free Methodism of Uniontown, Pa.). She did not want her daughter sidetracked into anything unorthodox or cultic. Although not known at the time to Evelyn or me, I would explore in my 1969 masters thesis at Asbury Theological Seminary the troubled relationship between leaders of the Church of God movement and the Free Methodist Church in the late 1800s. Evelyn gave me a wonderful "Selectric" typewriter to do this work (primitive by today's standards but the very best at the time).

Free Methodist leaders around the beginning of the twentieth century called the Church of God movement the "no-sect sect," and Church of God leaders responded by identifying the "F. M. sect" as sufficiently akin to the "Evening Light" (Church of God), and yet so fundamentally different at the key point of the unity of God's church, that it was an especially dangerous and subtle trap of sectarianism. Both were revivalistic holiness bodies, but only one was highly sensitive to the dividedness among Christians, and thus very anti-denominational. The other considered the presence of denominations inevitable and even necessary for the sake of maintaining the faith's integrity and disciplined programming. I wrote at length about this awkward relationship between church bodies, both so important to me. My essay, based on the earlier thesis I had written at Asbury Theological Seminary, was published in the spring 2002 issue of the *Wesleyan Theological Journal* under the title "Reconciling Clashing Ecumenical Visions." Especially during my early adulthood, this clashing and reconciling was going on inside me!

Soon after our courtship had begun, I had opportunity to meet Arlene's mother on a visit to Uniontown, Pennsylvania. She lived alone because her husband Donald Cooley had been hospitalized for many years with a severe mental disorder. She kept the little house at 100 Chaffee Street in perfect order, with the outside landscaping on the sloping corner lot obviously done by someone with an artistic eye and disciplined hands. Evelyn and I liked each other. She pinched pennies, worked hard, made her own clothes, and was highly disciplined about everything. It looked like she and I could get past the problem of church labels.

It helped a little when Evelyn learned of my own Free Methodist heritage, and when Arlene and I decided to attend regularly with my "Auntie" (Evangeline VanArsdale) the New Brighton Free Methodist Church while we were college students– although Auntie had no car and we all had to depend on transportation of friends for the long ride through Beaver Falls and across the river.

My paternal grandfather, Charles B. Callen, had once pastored this New Brighton congregation and various family ties still existed (it was the city of my birth). Since I had been present each summer of my early life at the Free Methodist camp meeting in East Liverpool, Ohio, New Brighton families like the Morrison Bakers were well-known to me and much appreciated. Another "safeguard" for Evelyn's concern was that Arlene was living on the edge of the campus with relatives, much like I was with my aunt. Lyle and Bea Flinner, Evelyn's younger sister, were providing Arlene's college home. Evelyn trusted them to keep a careful eye on Arlene's studying and dating practices.

I soon was asked to teach a Sunday school class of young adults at the New Brighton church. I agreed and it was a good experience involving some wonderful people, including my special friend Arlene. She once counted how many times during one teaching session I used the word "now," wanting to sensitize me to an annoying speech pattern I had. That ended the "nows"! The pastor, Harold Mitchell, eventually requested that I formally join the Free Methodist denomination—implying that this was only appropriate (required?) if I were to keep teaching in his congregation. I resisted on principle what seemed to me denominational arrogance (a reflection of my Church of God sensitivities), but finally I did accept a formalized relationship that soon earned me an "exhorter's license." It was renewed automatically for several years even though I never really used it.

Arlene and I were married in the New Brighton Free Methodist Church on August 10, 1963, just weeks after we each had received our degrees from Geneva College. This was our mutual home church during college and it was located between my family in northeast Ohio and hers in southwest Pennsylvania. Of necessity, we were very concerned about convenience and economy. The three officiating ministers were Lyle Flinner (Arlene's uncle with whom she lived during college and a minister of the Church of the Nazarene), Charles B. Callen (my grandfather, then a retired Free Methodist minister), and Lillie S. McCutcheon (my beloved home pastor of the Church of God congregation in Newton, Falls, Ohio). I remember well that seated on the center isle for the ceremony was Dr. Edwin Clarke, president of Geneva College. The picture was an ecumenical one, with three ministers from three different holiness church bodies and one Reformed Presbyterian leader. Such was a symbol of things to come.

Following is a glance at six dimensions of my "ecumenical" life. It has been relationally rich indeed.

1. A Protestant with Deepening Roots. My own spiritual journey took an unexpected road. I was reared in a wonderful congregation in Ohio where the pastoral leadership was exceptional. The spiritual nurture was so rich that more than fifty young people from that one small-town church entered full-time Christian ministry during the congregation's first fifty years. I am one of them and have expressed my gratitude by writing the biography of Lillie S. McCutcheon, the woman who was the senior pastor of my home congregation for more than four decades (*She Came Preaching*, 1992). I addressed her funeral crowd in 1999 and then her brother Austin's in 2018, expressing deep appreciation for both. One theme I heard stressed on occasion in that childhood congregation was *the church as God intends it*. Sometimes this ideal was highlighted by using the failures from the long history of the Roman Catholic Church as a reminder of what can go wrong.

This Church of God (Anderson) congregation featured a "radical," free-church, Wesleyan-informed theological mentality, but one with little historical perspective beyond reacting to a perceived long pattern of church apostasy. To help address this deficiency, I would edit and publish in 2009 the volume *The Church that God Intends,* a collection of relevant articles from the *Wesleyan Theological Journal* which I served as Editor for many years.

From my home church I absorbed the love of good pastoral leadership, an appreciation for nurturing young leaders, and a vision of the church as much more than any flawed human institution. After some years of my own ministry, however, my spiritual need led me—of all places—to a Roman Catholic monastery! Beginning in the 1980s, I became a periodic Protestant retreatant in a bastion of historic Roman Catholicism. The location was the longtime home of the famous Thomas Merton. The Abbey of Gethsemani has sat quietly in the hills of rural Kentucky since 1848 as a spiritual oasis carrying on a ministry of hospitality, providing spiritual retreats characterized by solitude, silence, and Christian reflection.

In one way, making this Abbey a spiritual home was quite a turn from my free-church Protestant upbringing (although over the centuries monasteries have been home to numerous Roman radicals); in another way, it was a growing up into the wider church without denying anything precious from my youth. My home pastor and Church of God heritage had called for an elimination of denominational walls and a unity of believers based on relationship to Christ. I was practicing this radical call, and was much the better for it.

The monastery environment, contrary to common perception, is not intended to disdain the world—as the writings of Thomas Merton make clear. The point is an intentional holding still, being in touch with oneself and God. It is a cherishing of the long tradition of God in the world, actually practicing prayer and God's presence, relishing the sweet sounds of silence, and finally realizing that true value lies first in *being* rather than in *doing*. My book *Authentic Spirituality* (2002, 2006) highlights the several historic streams of Christian spirituality, including the contemplative. The greatest richness comes in a combination of these streams.

Does my Gethsemani retreating make me a Protestant or Catholic? Neither exclusively. I now am a Christian who belongs to the whole church, protests on occasion, and chooses to be "catholic" in the best sense. I am reaching for the wider stream of Christian riches, benefiting from all and bound by none. This journey has only begun for me. I am a pilgrim still progressing. Nonetheless, at least the corner has been turned! I have been helped further by involvement in a decade-long dialogue between the Church of God (Anderson) and the Independent Christian Churches/Churches of Christ, both bodies having much in common with the Believers Church tradition. The book highlighting the process and results of this dialogue is *Coming Together in Christ* by James North and myself (1997).

I have had to shake off the assumption that all church history is darkened with apostasy and useful only as a foil for teaching the current ideal. The Church of God movement (Anderson) saw itself early as a fresh move of God beginning in the 1880s to restore the true church in the "evening time" of history. For the pioneers of this movement, looking back to the sadness of church history was a means of setting the stage for understanding the significance of the "final reformation" in these last days. This restricted view began ending for me when I encountered Charles E. Brown, the church historian who in the 1950s saw the Church of God movement as an extension of the "radical" tradition of Christianity. The restricted view further deteriorated for me in the 1960s when I became a part-time student at Earlham School of Religion to study with David Elton Trueblood, famed Quaker scholar, and when I became deeply involved in the scholarly world of the Wesleyan tradition in the 1980s.

I dedicated myself to widening the Church of God movement's concept of itself, linking it closely with the Believers Church and Wesleyan traditions. I consciously continued Charles E. Brown's work (*When Souls Awaken*, 1954) with my own 1999 book *Radical Christianity: The Believers Church Tradition in Christianity's History and Future*. Along with my friend Luke Keefer of the Brethren in Christ denomination, I shared the burden of several current representatives of the Believers Church tradition who are tending to lose their distinctive identity and witness in the overwhelming presence of today's establishment "evangelicalism" (usually Calvinistic and sometimes "fundamentalistic" in orientation).

2. A Leader in the Wesleyan/Holiness Tradition. I have been blessed by a dual and rich church heritage. First, the Free Methodist Church and then the Church of God movement (Anderson). They combined to be my ecclesiastical homes. They have their few contrasts, but at their hearts they are so much one. This oneness is well described in Howard A. Snyder's book about the founder of Free Methodism. Titled *B. T. and*

Ellen Roberts and the First Free Methodists (abridged ed., 2011, p. 244), he reports: "B. T. stood in the mainstream of historic Christian orthodoxy... and blended with these doctrines a set of radical accents which B. T. believed were essential to restore Christianity to its New Testament authenticity and vigor." Much the same could be said about Daniel S. Warner, primary pioneer of the Church of God movement (I authored his biography, *It's God's Church!*, in 1995). The particular "radical accents" differ somewhat from Roberts to Warner, but common to both is the goal of restoring Christianity to its New Testament authenticity and vigor. If I have contributed even a little to such a restoration, my life and ministry have been more than worthwhile.

Early ministerial involvements began to center in the life of the Church of God movement (Anderson) since my seminary experience at Anderson University School of Theology from 1963 to 1966 focused my attention and appreciation on this heritage. I continued to receive in the mail the annual renewals of my Free Methodist exhorter's license, but I just put them in a file until early in the 1970s when I formally requested that this modest denominational relationship be ended. In the meantime, I was unsuccessfully recruited to join the faculty of a Free Methodist college (Roberts Wesleyan near Rochester, New York), explored in depth the relationship between the Free Methodist heritage and that of the Church of God movement (in my masters thesis at Asbury Theological Seminary, 1967-68), and was a guest preacher and teacher at two Free Methodist camp meetings.

The first of these camp meetings was the Kiski Valley Camp Meeting near Apollo, Pennsylvania, in July of 1970, and the second the East Liverpool Camp Meeting in nearby Ohio in July, 1971. In each case, I delivered a series of sermons titled "Searchlights on the Church from the Life of Christ." At the Kiski camp, the "Reflections" from Roberts Wesleyan College came as the special singers—an irony for me since that was the college where I had almost gone as a faculty member. These were good and growing experiences, keeping me in close touch with Rev. Ralph Page who had been instrumental in my own Christian conversion at the East Liverpool camp back in 1955.

I recall vividly waking up on July 10, 1971, in our VanArsdale family cottage on the East Liverpool camp grounds and realizing that I had just turned thirty years old. It was common then for the revolutionary young generation to say that no person thirty or over had any wisdom or could be trusted. In my sermon that day, I confessed my birthday and thus the sudden onset of crippling ignorance! They let me stay anyway. The picture of me in the 1970 camp meeting program is of a clean-shaven young man, an establishment type. My beard would first appear the following year while I spent some wonderful weeks in Japan.

In August, 1993, I would function as the preaching evangelist for the Church of God in Ontario, Canada, convened on the Free Methodist camp grounds in Thamesford (Maple Grove Retreat Centre). Two years later the General Conference of the Free Methodist Church convened in Anderson, Indiana, on the campus where I taught. The FM bishops asked that I participate as an "ecumenical" member of the four-person Findings Committee that witnessed the Conference process, advised the bishops as the Conference proceeded, and prepared a formal report after the fact. I wrote a brief essay titled "Observation: Dynamics of Contextualization" that the committee decided should appear in its entirety with the final report.

That final report was drafted by the committee chair, David L. McKenna, recently retired from the presidency of Asbury Theological Seminary. He identified me in the report as "a recognized Biblical scholar and Wesleyan historian. . .[and] a clergy member of the Church of God (Anderson) who brought the invaluable perspective of an objective observer to the committee." While none of us is ever really objective, someone from outside a given context does bring a fresh perspective.

In the 1980s and 1990s, in a similar spirit, the officers of the General Assembly of the Church of God in North America brought to various annual Assemblies "fraternal guests" from a range of denominations. They were asked to observe the Assembly process and then bring formal remarks to the Assembly near its conclusion. Eventually, I gathered and edited these guest perspectives in a brief essay (see my *Following the Light*, 2000, 323-326). It was a valuable exercise in openness and Christian unity, one I applauded.

I tried becoming involved with the National Association of Evangelicals, attending one annual convention in Phoenix, Arizona, unexpectedly enjoying there the Formula One auto race staged on closed city streets adjacent to my hotel. Soon, however, I gravitated to the Christian Holiness Association—a body dating back to the nineteenth century and more reflective of my own Christian tradition than the establishment and Calvinistic NAE. This gravitation was a pivotal move for me.

In 1993, after participating for some years in the annual meetings of the Wesleyan Theological Society, the academic arm of the Christian Holiness Association (later changed to the Christian Holiness Partnership), I was approached about my willingness to be a candidate for the editorship of the *Wesleyan Theological Journal*. I agreed, recognizing the high honor and sobered by the large task. The Journal was seriously behind in its publishing schedule and the Society was in a weak financial position, so much so that its future was being questioned. I could not conceive how much hard work and how many rewarding events and relationships would follow my accepting this editorship that I held until my resignation in 2015.

Key materials that I edited and published over the years mostly originated in papers delivered at the Society's annual meetings. Note this list of the Society's themes and host institutions from the first of the many years that I have attended these great gatherings.

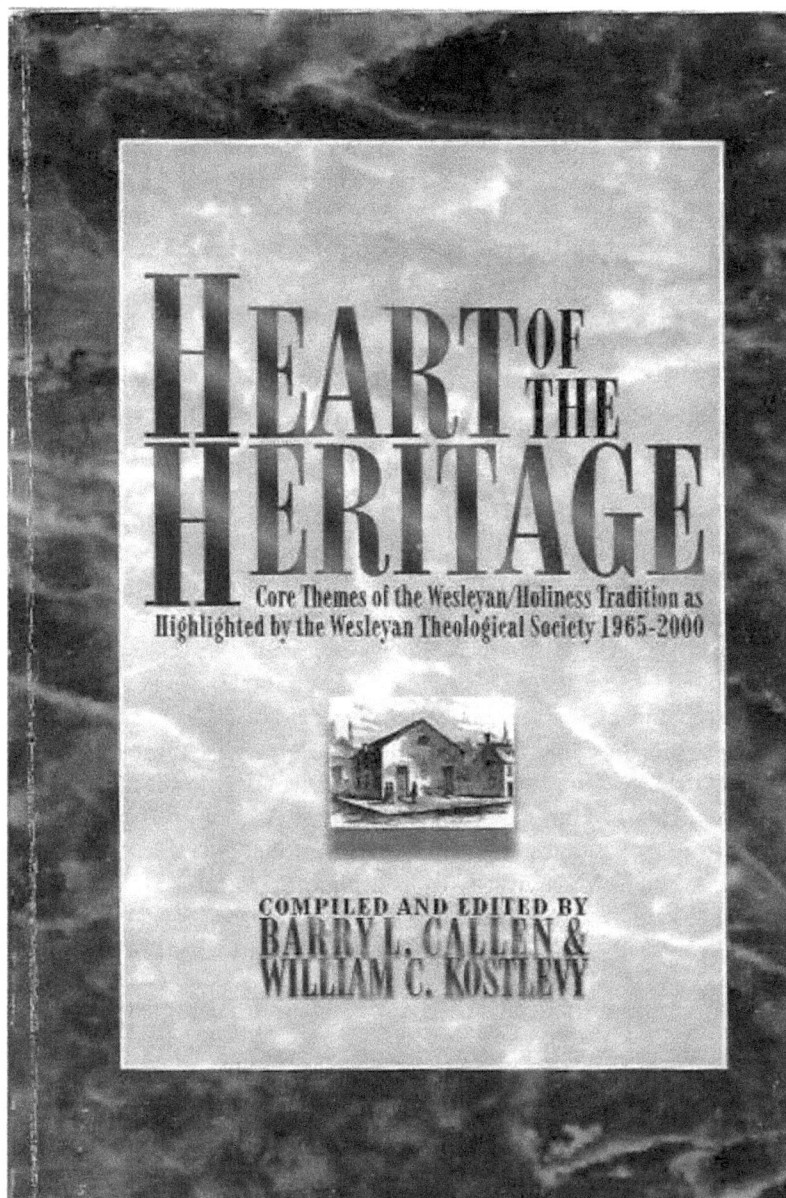

A compilation of the best academic work by notable scholars of the Wesleyan Theological Society, 1965-2000. Much of this work was published during Barry L. Callen's editorship of the *Wesleyan Theological Journal*.

Wesleyan Theological Society
The Annual Meetings in Which
I Was Personally Involved

Dates	Program Themes	Host Institutions
1991	Gospel for the Poor	Western Evangelical Seminary, OR
1992	Wesleyanism and Modernity	Ashland Theological Seminary, OH
1993	Wesleyanism and Eschatology	Southern Nazarene University, OK
1994	Asserting Our Biblical Heritage	United Theological Seminary, OH
1995	Sanctification and New Creation	Northwest Nazarene University, ID
1996	The Worship of God	Wesley Theo. Sem., Wash., D.C.
1997	Facing the Future	Mt. Vernon Nazarene College, OH
1998	Purity and Power	Church of God Theo. Sem., TN
1999	Wesleyanism/Postmodern Age	Southern Nazarene University, OK
2000	The Holy Trinity	Azusa Pacific University, CA
2001	Power and Reconciliation	Indiana Wesleyan University, IN
2002	Mission in Wesleyanism	Hobe Sound Bible College, FL
2003	The Wesleyan Traditions Today	Bahamas Wesleyan Fellowship, Nassau
2003	Wesleyanism and Pentecostalism	Asbury Theological Seminary, KY
2004	Practicing Wesleyan Theology	Roberts Wesleyan College, NY
2005	The Church—the Body of Christ	Seattle Pacific University, WA
2006	Friendship and Hospitality	Nazarene Theo. Sem., MO
2007	Suffering and the Holy Life	Olivet Nazarene University, IL
2008	Science and Creation	Duke Divinity School, NC
2009	The Centrality of Christ	Anderson School of Theology, IN
2010	The Future of Scripture	Azusa Pacific University, CA
2011	Empire, Church, Mission Dei	Southern Methodist University, TX
2012	Wesleyanism/World Religions	Trevecca Nazarene University, TN
2013	Holiness	Seattle Pacific University, WA

Some of the annual meetings of the Wesleyan Theological Society were particularly significant occasions for me. For instance, at the 1993 meeting I was first elected Editor of the *Wesleyan Theological Journal*. In the 1997 meeting I had my first personal encounter with Clark H. Pinnock, who was the keynote speaker that year. In 2000 I released my intellectual biography of Pinnock (*Journey Toward Renewal*), published by Evangel Publishing House in cooperation with the Wesleyan Theological Society. In 2001 the book *Heart of the Heritage* by William C. Kostlevy and myself was released.

It captures the core themes of the Wesleyan/Holiness tradition as highlighted by the Wesleyan Theological Society from 1965 to 2000. In 2008 I met our special guest Jürgen Moltmann from Germany, one of my theological mentors. He and I exchanged our books being released at that time and I read a paper critiquing his major presentation. In 2013 my colleague Don Thorsen and I released our co-edited *Heart & Life* book that is dedicated to the membership of the Wesleyan Theological Society.

These many settings, and particularly my many years as Editor of the *Wesleyan Theological Journal*, so important to the well being of the whole Society, likely led to an unexpected honor. Stanley Ingersol in Kansas City initiated in 2006 an internet polling of the persons judged most influential on the Wesleyan/Holiness tradition in the last one-hundred years. I was pleased to see three Church of God names nominated, James Earl Massey, Susie C. Stanley, and myself.

My highest honor was when the Society gathered in Anderson, Indiana, in 2009 and granted me its coveted "Lifetime Achievement Award." How privileged I felt to be identified as one of the most prominent scholars in and contributors to the modern Wesleyan/Holiness tradition of Christianity! As a member of the Executive Committee of the Society that does the voting each year, I have had a voice in every choice of honoree—except for myself (they held a secret meeting behind my back!). I am pleased that the list of recipients of the Lifetime Award has come to include the same three of us from the Church of God named earlier by Kostlevy. They are James Earl Massey (1995), myself (2009), and Susie C. Stanley (2012).

The years 2004 to 2007 saw the "Wesleyan Holiness Study Project" functioning annually on the Azusa Pacific University campus in California. Conceived and implemented by my good friends David Bundy, Donald Dayton, Kevin Mannoia, and Don Thorsen, the project was funded by eight concerned holiness denominations. I represented the Church of God movement. The concern was the great need to bring the holiness message back to life and perceived relevance in today's churches. A key document we produced and distributed widely was "The Holiness Manifesto" (for the full text, see *Appendix D*).

I was pleased to publish in the *Wesleyan Theological Journal* (Fall 2007) Don Thorsen's presentation of the history and significance of this Wesleyan/Holiness Study Project and his "Holiness in Postmodern Culture" (Fall 2008). Soon this beginning would mature into the forming of the Wesleyan Holiness Connection, guided by a national Steering Committee and Board of Directors, and also then its founding in 2011 of Aldersgate Press. With Kevin Mannoia as the chief visionary and catalyst, I was named Secretary of the Steering Committee and Board of Directors and founding Editor of Aldersgate Press. The Connection's web address (*HolinessAndUnity.org*) is a direct reflection of the central burden of the Church of God movement (embracing Christian holiness as a means of enhancing Christian unity). I was very much at home and pleased to serve in this amazing multi-denominational and international setting.

3. Apostolic Roots and the Believers Church. My awareness of the "Believers Church" Christian tradition began with my reading the book *When Souls Awaken* by Charles E. Brown (1954). I vowed to extend his exploration of this historical root of the Church of God movement, and finally did so with the book that James North and I wrote together, *Coming Together in Christ* (1997), and especially with my book *Radical Christianity* (1999).

My direct relationship with the Believers Church tradition began with the "Quaker connection." This pleasurable linkage was launched in 1964 when I traveled weekly from Anderson to Richmond, Indiana, to study with the great Quaker philosopher-theologian David Elton Trueblood. This was part of my Master of Divinity graduate program at Anderson School of Theology, at times a stressful part, but one that I now treasure. Trueblood was generous, caring, and intimidating, all at the same time.

Then in 1967 Arlene and I moved to Wilmore, Kentucky, with our new baby Todd. There I earned a second masters degree under the mentoring of the brilliant Quaker theologian Harold Kuhn. For a time in the 1990s my son's family functioned as Quakers in Anderson, with their son Ian dedicated at the First Friends meeting in Anderson in 1995.

My major relationship with the Believers Church tradition began in the 1980s with my beginning to attend periodic national conferences of leaders of this tradition. I first heard of these from Harold L. Phillips who had participated in the 1967 conference at Southern Baptist Seminary in Louisville, Kentucky, where the theme was "The Concept of the Believers Church." I have identified all of these conferences in my book *Radical Christianity*, with the first in which I participated convening at Ashland Theological Seminary in Ashland, Ohio, in 1992.

I recall a rainy day in October, 1997, when I drove to Louisville, Kentucky, to be a guest leader on the occasion of the 50th annual assembly of the Kentucky Council of Churches. I and my friend Donald Dayton (prominent scholar of the Wesleyan Church) had been invited to form a panel to function on the topic "Receiving the Gifts of Others." The central issue was how a classic "old" council of churches could become more open to the potential contributions of bodies of Christians (like the Church of God) which, while deeply concerned about Christian unity, were not inclined to participate formally with such councils.

The panel in Louisville was moderated by Michael Kinnamon, then dean of Lexington Theological Seminary (Disciples of Christ) and a prominent ecumenical figure on the world scene. He had played an important role in initiating the multi-year dialogue between the Church of God and the Independent Christian Churches/Churches of Christ that resulted in the 1997 book *Coming Together in Christ* by James North and myself. Kinnamon referred to this book as "a milestone publication in the field of Christian unity." This decade-long dialogue was my most intense and sustained involvement with the Believers Church.

In July, 1993, I was a guest conference leader at the North American Convention of the Christian Churches/Churches of Christ convened in St. Louis, Missouri. My assigned topic was "The Quest for Holiness: Our Continuing Imperative"—significant given the historic resistance to "holiness" language and "revival" methodology by this large Campbellite tradition (rooted in the ministries of Thomas and Alexander Campbell). My good friend James North of Cincinnati Bible College and Seminary was present to introduce me and help with the discussion.

Elizabeth H. Mellen of the Graymoor Ecumenical and Inter-religious Institute in New York City wrote about an ecumenical vocation for the Wesleyan/Holiness tradition. She noted two holiness writers, James Earl Massey and myself, who had written "quite eloquently" about Christian unity. She referred to Massey's book *Concerning Christian Unity* (1979), quoted approvingly from my book *Contours of a Cause* (1995), and called "a significant volume" *Coming Together in Christ* (1997) by James North and myself. She noted my "firm faith" that the brokenness in the Christian community is "not beyond the reach of God's reconciling power in Christ" (*Wesleyan Theological Journal*, Spring 1999, 101, 116). Such faith, what I called an "ecumenical idealism" in my Asbury master's thesis in 1969, grows directly from the teaching tradition of the Church of God movement.

I was the guest leader in 2001 for the fourth annual Pastor's Conference convened at Earlham School of Religion, the Quaker seminary in Richmond, Indiana, where I had studied in the 1960s under David Elton Trueblood. The conference subject was "Radical Christianity in a Postmodern World" and the entire focus was on the contents of my 1999 book *Radical Christianity*. Four faculty members, having studied my book in advance, made overview and analysis presentations in successive sessions and then gave me time to respond (I had seen nothing in advance!). This was exceedingly stimulating academically, with pastors and faculty members offering practical observations and posing questions to me. I had a good time with the Quakers who were saying that my book was an excellent presentation of the stream of Christianity that they represented—and also is represented by the Church of God movement (Anderson).

I delivered the 2007 Schrag Lectures on the campus of Messiah College in eastern Pennsylvania. The subject was the "radical" Christian tradition in a "postmodern" world. This fine campus represents the Brethren in Christ denomination. Its publishing house, Evangel Press in Indiana, had published several of my books, beginning in 1996 with *God As Loving Grace*. The only negative of my lectureship at Messiah was that I was stranded for three days by a freak spring snowstorm. A positive was that my lectures were later published in the journal *Brethren in Christ History and Life* (August, 2007) under the title "Postmodern Openings for 'Radical' Christianity." I was sure that there were such openings. One, of course, is avoiding arrogance by being respectful of the potential wisdom in the traditions of others.

4. Living in the Evangelical "Big Tent." I first met Clark H. Pinnock personally when he came as keynoter of the annual meeting of the Wesleyan Theological Society that convened in 1997 on the campus of Mt. Vernon Nazarene College in Ohio. I first met Roger E. Olson at the annual meeting of the American Academy of Religion/Society of Biblical Studies in Orlando, Florida, in 1999. Stanley J. Grenz came to my classes on the Anderson University campus as a lecturer and then I was with him in Nashville, Tennessee, at an annual meeting of the Evangelical Theological Society. It was there that I substituted for the absent Clark Pinnock in a session with Millard Erickson on "How My Mind Has Changed." In 2008 I met and responded to a paper by the world-famous Dr. Moltmann of Germany at a joint meeting of the Wesleyan Theological Society and the Society for Pentecostal Studies convened at Duke Divinity

School. These outstanding "evangelical" scholars were gracious to me and helped open to me the larger evangelical community.

In 2002, for instance, Roger Olson invited me to sign the "The Word Made Fresh" statement calling for renewal of the evangelical spirit and "deploring a present tendency among some evangelicals to define the boundaries of evangelical faith and life too narrowly." It called for "peace and harmony among equally God fearing, Bible believing, Jesus loving evangelical Christians who may find that they disagree about many secondary matters." I gladly signed. A good article on this statement appeared in *Christianity Today* (June 10, 2002). In 2010 I was privileged to be the co- keynoter with Roger Olson in a major conference on Arminianism convened on the campus of Andrews University in Michigan (Seventh-Day Adventist). Our presentations later appeared in the *Wesleyan Theological Journal* (46:2, fall, 2011)

I published in the fall 2002 issue of the *Wesleyan Theological Journal* an insightful article by Stanley Grenz titled "Concerns of a Pietist with a Ph.D." He was trying to set a better balance between the experiential and doctrinal dimensions of "evangelical" Christian faith. My intellectual biography of Clark H. Pinnock (*Journey Toward Renewal*) was released at the annual meeting of the Wesleyan Theological Society convened at Azusa Pacific University in March of 2000. It was published by Evangel Publishing House in cooperation with the WTS. At that meeting, Donald Dayton, then of Drew University, had four copies of my new book autographed for scholar friends, Henry Knight of the Methodist seminary in Kansas City accepted the assignment of writing a review of the book for publication, and Randy Maddox of Seattle Pacific University left the meeting with two copies on his way to a lecturing assignment in Australia. See *Appendix C* for my essay on "open theism" that was inspired by Pinnock.

My books now were crossing denominational and national borders. They had been published by Warner Press (Church of God, Anderson),

Abingdon Press (United Methodist Church), and College Press (Christian Churches/Churches of Christ). Later, the publishing list would lengthen to include Baker Book House (general evangelical), Westminster/John Knox (Presbyterian), Emeth Press (Wesleyan tradition), Pater Noster Press (Roman Catholic), Schmul Publishing (Wesleyan/Holiness tradition), Francis Asbury Press, Aldersgate Press (Wesleyan Holiness Connection, for which I serve as founding editor), Wipf & Stock (Cascade Books), and Anderson University Press for which I also serve as founding editor. I certainly had ventured far beyond the Church of God!

The national and language borders crossed included some of my books being translated into Spanish, Japanese, and Swahili. The book *Color Me Holy* was gifted in Swahili to all pastors of the African Gospel Church in Kenya (some 1,500). My first attempt at an audible book, a popular new medium, came in early 2019 with the audio conversion of *The Prayer of Holiness-Hungry People*. More on my writing ministry is found in chapter eight.

5. Serving African AIDS Orphans. Robert W. Pearson was a seminarian during my deanship of Anderson School of Theology. In the 1990s his ministry brought him to the great responsibility of being the General Director of Church of God Ministries in Anderson, Indiana. Leaving this position in 2002, he soon was sensitized while in South Africa to the tragic pandemic of AIDS. Feeling called of God to address this circumstance, he turned to a local businessman, Eric Dwiggins, a Church of God national executive, Jeff Jenness, and myself to join him in forming a new ministry organization. Called Horizon International, with me as corporate secretary, Horizon quickly became a significant Christian organization that is ecumenically based and focused on the dramatic needs of victimized children in Kenya, South Africa, Uganda, Ethiopia, Zambia, and Zimbabwe, all orphaned by the dreaded AIDS disease.

Robert, Eric, Jeff, and I were soon joined by the African-based staff partnership of Jenny and Cassie Carstens. What happened next was only by the hand of God. By the end of 2007, Horizon was active in providing the housing, health, clothing, and educational needs of more than 1,200 victimized children. This ministry had become widely known and appreciated in medical, church, and governmental circles in southern and eastern Africa. Congregations across the United States, foundations, and individuals were providing nearly $2.1 million dollars of funding per year. By 2018 the number of sponsored children had increased to nearly 3,000 with annual funding exceeding $3 million dollars. I was privileged to be one of the four pioneering founders of this international ministry of compassion.

My wife Jan and I traveled to Africa in November, 2007, to see much of this amazing ministry in operation. We were back there in 2010 to minister in Uganda and help open Horizon's ministry in Kenya. I taught in a conference of about one-hundred pastors in Fort Portal, Uganda, while Jan functioned as registrar. I then was privileged to assist with the launching of a formal relationship between Horizon and the African Gospel Church in Kericho, Kenya, before participating in the annual commencement of Kima International School of Theology related to the Church of God. While Horizon was providing valuable assistance to thousands of children in African nations, these very children were adding much to our own lives.

I recall a September, 2006, chapel session at Anderson University when Horizon's Kuyasa Kids Choir from South Africa was in concert in Reardon Auditorium. Tears of pride and gratefulness came to my eyes as these thirty children, many alive only because of the intervention of Horizon, dazzled privileged youth from North America with their rhythm, enthusiasm, and faith. Tears also came when I thought of the role of my first wife Arlene. She had supported my early involvement in Horizon. After her pre- mature death in 2003, I remarried. Jan and I encouraged all the people at our wedding who wished to give a gift to make it a check to special loves of our former spouses. For Jan's Phil Slattery, it was the organ fund at Park Place

Church of God. For Arlene, we chose the African Gift Shop of Horizon. In Arlene's name, we were able to give over $3,000 to purchase the initial inventory. In 2006, with a change of the shop's status, I approved a shift of the money to a permanent endowment fund that allows a few of our older orphans to attend an African university. That endowment fund now exceeds $500,000. After her death, Arlene became an "African missionary," a perfect honoring of her memory.

I too had become something of a missionary. While traveling only twice to our Horizon African ministry locations, Jan and I sought to be useful resources from our home base in Anderson, Indiana. She became a hostess in our home for many of the quarterly meetings of the Board of Directors. We have been close personal friends of the president, Robert Pearson, including in times of great stress that he has had to face. A key role I have played beyond that of corporate secretary is being the organization's historian. As Horizon approached the completion of its first decade of ministry, I was commissioned by the Board to research and write *Hope on the Horizon* (2010). It was a joy, even if very hard work.

The sudden death of Chadd Bain in South Africa caused me to dedicate my historical work to his memory and the ongoing Horizon leader- ship of his wife Kate among the Zulu children and beyond. Clearly the most difficult circumstance I wrote about was the brutality of the government in Zimbabwe. I was frank about it in the book, requiring us to try to keep the book from the eyes of that government to protect Horizon's leaders in that troubled land.

A key event was Horizon's 2018 Strategic Partner's Conference in Indiana. Jan and I hosted in our home Moses Sakala of Zambia and cele- brated the presence of Tatenda Gunguwo of Zimbabwe, two key African partners of Horizon. In their presence I was able to give the lead gift to launch a new Literature Endowment Fund, joining the University Scholarship Fund launched by the lead gift of funds from my wife Arlene's funeral in 2003 (mission money requested instead of flowers). This was another step in fulfilling Horizon's mission "to create a world of hope through AIDS orphans."

I have been privileged to go a long way on the face of the earth and on the roads of Christian service, learning their joys and sometimes suffering their agonies.

Just to See the World

My marriage to Jan in 2003, and then my retirement from the Anderson University faculty in 2005, gave me inspiration and opportunity to travel the world without business or ministry assignments necessarily attached—like leading student groups for Anderson University, going to World Conferences of the Church of God, or doing other church work internationally. Jan loves the road and has been a wonderful traveling companion. We have not spent heavily as tourists typically do; we have gone to enjoy each other and see this amazing world—not to buy its expensive trinkets and carry them home!

This new travel for pleasure began in the summer of 2003 with Jan and me joining the faculty/staff tour of Anderson University in Scotland and Ireland. I proposed marriage to Jan just before we left, and also a series of times in various romantic spots along the way. I had lost Arlene, my wife of thirty-nine years, and was starting life over in many ways. My family heritage includes the Scotch-Irish dimension. Jan and I thoroughly enjoyed this trip. Traveling companions Robert and Marilyn Smith had arranged secretly with my son Todd to be our "chaperons." In Dublin, I bought Todd what he really wanted, a quality Irish drum that occasionally he would play in church in years to come.

Our honeymoon cruise in late 2003 covered the eastern Caribbean and included a submarine ride off St. Thomas. Subsequent cruises enabled us to watch whales off the Alaskan coast, transit the Baltic Sea for a wonderful visit to St. Petersburg, Russia, go through the Panama Canal twice, sail among the Greek islands with stunning stops in Venice, Italy, Dubrovnik, Croatia, and biblical Ephesus in Turkey, and see the wonderful fjords of Norway on two occasions, and the dramatic scenes of Australia and New Zealand on another.

Our journey to Israel was a life highlight for Jan. So were our several journeys to Africa with Horizon and Anderson University. Memorable indeed were our travels with church friends, a river cruise across Europe, and ship cruises in the northeast of North America and the extreme southern region of South America. We knew we were privileged people. We were pilgrims in God's church and world.

Jan and I began the practice of reviewing all photos that I took on each international trip and choosing one to have printed, framed, and hung prominently in our home. They include a scene of the Jordan River in Israel, one of the canal business district in Copenhagen, Denmark, one of the fjords in beautiful Norway, wildlife along a waterway in Costa Rica, sailing the canal in downtown Venice, Italy, camels on Egypt's desert, a sunset in South Africa, and approaching the locks of the Panama Canal. I have enjoyed photographing God's good creation. There have been so many lovely people and amazing scenes along the way!

I am presenting a copy of my book *Hope on the Horizon* in 2011 (with my bald head during chemo therapy) to Kate Bain, Horizon International's Project Director for Izulu orphan projects in South Africa. Joining Kate and me is Robert Pearson, Horizon's president. The book is dedicated to Kate's husband Chadd, tragically killed in a traffic accident.

HORIZON
INTERNATIONAL
creating a world of hope for HIV/AIDS orphans

Dr. Barry L. Callen
Board Member, Corporate Secretary

C (765) 621 3003 | E-Mail: blcallen@anderson.edu
www.horizoninternationalinc.com

Dalineta Hines and Lenworth Anglin (left), and Jan and me (right), meeting with the Governor General, 2007, in Kingston, Jamaica.

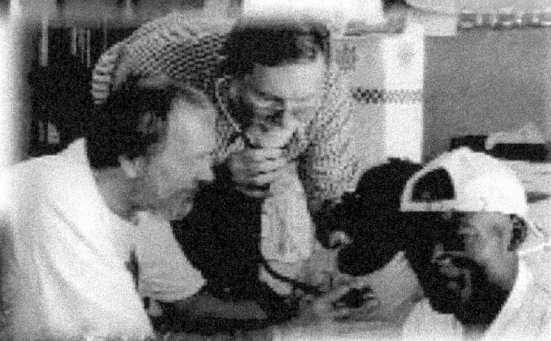

"Dr. Barry" in Haiti, 2006. With nurse John Ackerman, I was examining a girl with a serious heart defect.

In 2007 I met with leaders of the Church of God in Zambia on behalf of ministry to AIDS orphans and ministerial education. (L. to R.) Stan Hoffman, Robert Pearson, Mailesi Ndao, and myself.

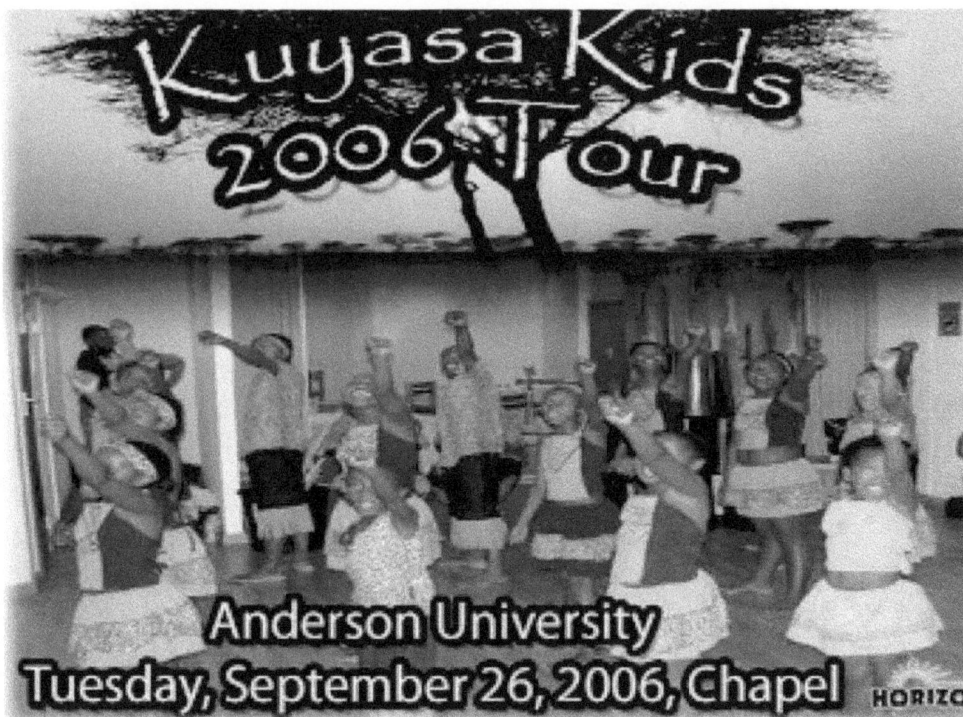

Kuyasa Kids, Horizon's orphan choir from South Africa.

Horizon's president, Robert Pearson (left), me, and
ministry leaders from Zimbabwe, Africa, Alick Phiri and Tatenda Gunguwo.

I led this group through Germany and Austria in 1991.
I am standing in the upper row, right of center.

Arnold and Sylvia Levy, a Jewish couple from Chicago, became dear friends of Arlene and me. We first met on a train traveling across the United States.

The famous David Livingston statue standing in Victoria Falls, Zimbabwe. A group of us from Horizon International visited this famous site in 2007. In my small way, I too was seeking to make a positive impact on this troubled country.

香港觀光紀念

VICTORIA PEAK HONG KONG

I rejoiced with my church friends Jack and Madeline Haines in Sydney, Australia, (upper right).

I (upper center) in Japan, 1971, leading a TRI-S trip for Anderson College. Bonnie (Callison) Newell stands center front.

Some of the recent presidents of the Wesleyan Theological Society. I was privileged to serve with all of them in my role as editor of the *Wesleyan Theological Journal*. Left is Carl Campbell (Bahamas). Next to Carl is Randy L. Maddox. Howard A. Snyder stands upper right.

In Rome, Italy, in the 1970's, I was a young seminary dean encountering ancient ruins with current messages for the wise who can hear.

Holding my 116 lb. Nile Perch caught in Kisumu harbor, Kenya, East Africa, 1985.

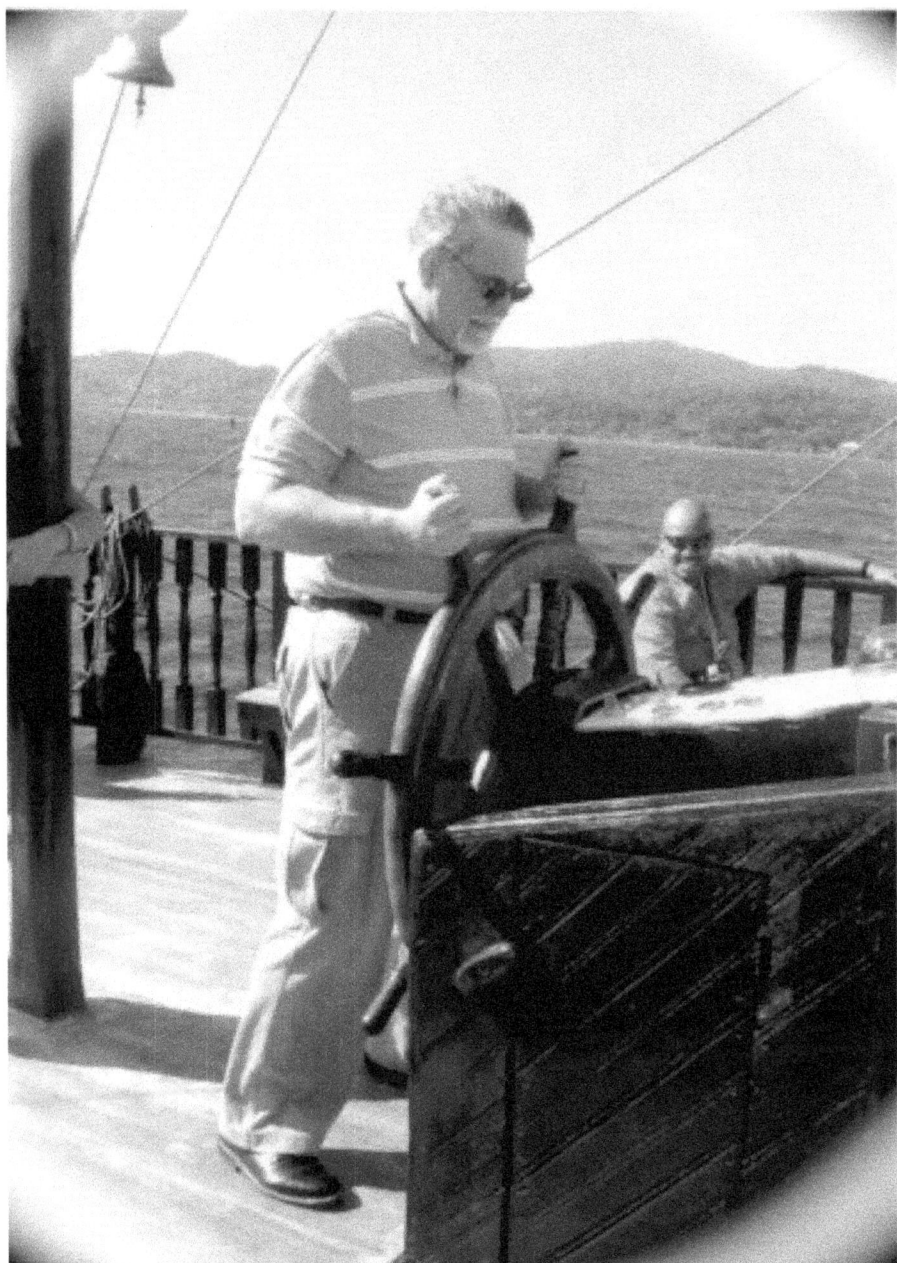

Piloting a pirate ship in the Caribbean Sea off the coast of Honduras (built especially for tourists). It is hard to steer with vigorous wind and waves having minds of their own!

Docked in a fjord in Norway, this was the cruise ship on which Jan and I sailed in 2012 to England, Iceland, the Faroe Islands, and Norway. There is so much beauty in God's world!

In Lausanne, Switzerland, 1974: Charles Tarr, Barry L. Callen, William E. Reed, and James Earl Massey. We were the U.S. representatives to the Billy Graham conference on world evangelization.

Jan and I sailing the dramatic coast of Chile.

Chapter 8

Thousands of Published Pages

My ministry of writing and editing

According to Benjamin Franklin, "if you would not be forgotten as soon as you are dead and rotten, either write things worth reading or do things worth writing." I hope that I have written and done a few things of lasting worth. Of note is at least the sheer volume of activity.

Writing can be an act of arrogance. For me, I hope it has been more a manner of self-expression than a tool for self-advancement. I identify with the following from Henry Wadsworth Longfellow's "The Ladder of Saint Augustine":

> The heights by great men reached and kept
> Were not attained by sudden flight;
> But they, while their companions slept,
> Were toiling upward in the night.

Writing and editing are hard work and I have spent a significant portion of my adult life in these strenuous tasks.

I wish to be clear. I identify with the above lines of Longfellow, not because I foolishly think of myself as among the "great men," but because I have toiled over the years when some others have slept. There is a price to be paid for getting results. I hope that I have paid this price more than my family, who sometimes had to be patient with my toiling. Especially between 1963 and 1975 when we had to move five times while I was earning my first graduate degrees and then getting settled back in Anderson, Indiana, my wife Arlene was very patient.

After Arlene's death and when Jan Slattery and I were courting in 2003, our dear friend Rev. James Earl Massey agreed to do a little marriage counseling for us, in addition to that done by Rev. Ronald V. Duncan who would officiate at the ceremony. James said to Jan in my presence, "Are you sure you are ready to be married to a scholar? Sometimes he will lock on a project and you will have to be very patient." She said she was ready, fortunately, and she has been nothing but patient and helpful ever since.

At least in my thought world, the one who knows me best is the one who has read me most. My writing is intentionally self-revealing. I never set out to write so extensively. It just happened. I have accepted writing and editing as a gift that I have been given, a gift that, by its very nature, must be shared. Using this gift has been intertwined closely with my ministerial identity and teaching profession. As I write, I think, pray, and witness.

Writers Never Die

Reflecting on the Benjamin Franklin quote above, I wonder and hope. If I have done relatively few things "worth writing," I pray that at least I have written some things "worth reading." The other aspect of this quote is about not being "forgotten as soon as you are dead and rotten." This was brought home to me in 1973 by Robert H. Reardon, then president of Anderson College. He had just named me the next Dean of Anderson School of Theology. With just the two of us in his office in Decker Hall, he gestured out his big window, pointing north to Maplewood Cemetery in the distance. He said to me: "Who out there among all the graves is still alive?" Before I could think of some rational response, he answered his own question. "Only those who wrote!"

Reardon made clear to me that I should write during my lifetime and thus be kept alive forever. I took his advice seriously, even though writing is not always done easily in the swirl of demanding administrative and teaching responsibilities. It was not that I was overly anxious about becoming immortal by producing a stunning literary output. But I could write, I was in a stimulating intellectual environment, and there was much that I thought needed to be said. So I followed Reardon's advice.

It is not easy to get started in the publishing field. First, one needs something important to say; then one needs to be able to say it well. Finally, one needs the necessary connections for the actual publishing and distribution of the written material. Hosts of writers fail at the locked door of publishing houses that are market driven and name sensitive. I made my earliest attempt in a high school class in 1958 when I wrote about the Hungarian Freedom Fighters and their failed rebellion in 1956. The subject was important and my handling of it apparently was good enough that my English teacher, Mary Lucy Lauban, made some effort to have a national magazine consider it. The attempt failed, but her telling the whole class that it merited a try was a great encouragement to me.

Soon I was a college student and privileged to study with quality literary people like Drs. Eben and Geri Bass. During my freshman year at Geneva College, two little pieces of mine were published in the May, 1960, issue of the *Chimes*, a product of the English Club. In one, titled "The Destiny of America," I announced that America was at a crossroads. Later, I would expand greatly on this theme in my social history of the recent decades of life in the United States titled *Seeking the Light* (1998). My second piece, titled "Twilight," saw me working poetically with the symbolic significance of the twilight metaphor. I was an eighteen-year-old busy with the books, beginning to fall in love with my classmate Arlene, and trying to come to terms with the issues of vocation and faith.

While a seminary student in Anderson, Indiana (1963-1966), there naturally were many papers and essay tests to be written. Since all the classes were completed with the result of "A" grades, apparently I developed the reputation among the faculty for having writing ability. This soon had an important practical implication. Vila Deubach, chair of the college's English department, called the seminary and asked for the name of a graduate student who was good with the English language. She had an English composition class that needed to be taught by some part-time person. Within weeks, I was teaching at the college level while still a full-time graduate student.

The opportunities kept coming. Shortly I would be away from the Anderson campus for two years completing my education (a second masters degree at Asbury Theological Seminary in Kentucky and a doctorate at Chicago Theological Seminary on the edge of the University of Chicago campus). Much class-related writing was again required, including my thesis at Asbury about the history and teaching tradition of the Church of God movement (Anderson). In fact, other than the two small pieces I had done for the *Chimes* at Geneva College, the first time I ever saw my name in print in relation to something I had written was in the major periodical *Christianity Today* (November 21, 1969). In the "Current Religious Thought" column, my Asbury mentor Harold B. Kuhn referred specifically to me and my master's thesis done under his guidance. He noted that it "traced the development and the idealism of the Church of God (Anderson)." Brief as this reference was, it was an appreciative nod in my direction by a man I admired. It was a signal that in coming years I would be exploring often and in great detail that particular tradition of church reform and idealism.

Another early signal of things to come was the first book review that I published in a significant journal. The *Christian Scholars Review* (fall 1971) carried my review of Vincent P. Miceli's *The Gods of Atheism*. I said that this Catholic author's work was "a manifesto flying in the face of contemporary tendencies to 'do theology' via introspection within the context of non-transcendent categories." Earth-bound theologians were exhibiting "a total preoccupation with the human, a continual reduction of God to the being of man—which makes theology a mere anthropology." I was defending a more orthodox faith, and doing so with vigorous conviction and rather high-sounding words. In 2004 I would explore this core subject extensively in my book *Discerning the Divine*.

By the end of the socially and theologically erratic 1960s, I had emerged with relatively conservative theological instincts and heightened concerns about the necessity of the social relevance of Christians. The former is reflected in my critique of Miceli's 1971 book. The latter is seen in my participation in the publication *Colloquium* that was launched as a monthly in the fall of 1969 and appeared for three or four years as a fresh vehicle of communication by deeply concerned persons (mostly young and well-educated Church of God scholars). It was much like the journal *Sojourners* that emerged at Trinity Evangelical Divinity School at about the same time. Arlene, my wife, typed the copy for most of the *Colloquium* issues, copy written by several of us who had gone on to additional graduate education beyond our seminary days in Anderson. The names included Roger Hatch, James Marshall, and Frank Watkins, who has had a significant relationship with Jesse Jackson in Chicago over the years.

Mort Crim, a prominent radio and television journalist with strong connections to the Anderson campus, wrote this to the *Colloquium* editors (November 1969 issue): "As a Christian and a newsman, I have a huge appetite for sharp, crisp commentary which effectively relates the ancient truths to contemporary situations. Your paper turned out to be a feast. Keep it up. Don't let anybody turn you around or tone you down." One pastor tried to turn us around with this from his critical letter to the editor printed in the March, 1970, issue: "Do not send any more issues of this communistic-socialistic paper which has been brought into being not to unite through Christian love, but to further divide our nation." While he misjudged our intention, we had gotten his attention!

The nation surely was divided in those Vietnam war years, but we who wrote differed on what would heal or further divide. By then chair of the Department of Religious Studies at Anderson College, I responded vigorously to this critical pastor with my own letter in the April, 1970, issue of *Colloquium*. I insisted that his "blunt judgment" was neither "constructive nor justified." I invited him to join rather than obstruct the dialogue, and I said that it certainly did not help anything for him to lash out with "unsubstantiated and aggressive words."

I wrote several pieces for *Colloquium*, a welcome vehicle for my convictions as a young professor and minister. One major piece (September, 1970) I called "Gamaliel Revisited." In light of my own travel in Lebanon, Jordan, and Israel in 1968, just after the history-altering 1967 war, and in part influenced by my respected colleague Gustav Jeeninga who was critical of Israel, I addressed the "Palestinian Problem." I said that it presented pressing moral dimensions for the Christian conscience, and that "Christians too often have displayed that fatal ability to sleep through revolutions." In this same issue, forty-two signatures, mine included, endorsed a statement supporting those young persons in the Church of God who were taking the unpopular position of conscientious objection to participation in the killing aspects of war. My college status and then ministerial credentials had kept me out of military service. While never a proclaimed conscientious objector, I doubt that I would have accepted any killing role.

During 1973, while I was breathlessly functioning both as the founding director of the Center for Pastoral Studies on the Anderson campus and acting dean of the School of Theology, somehow I managed to invest little pieces of time in writing more than letters, reports, and sets of minutes. I began writing for the North American periodical of the Church of God, *Vital Christianity* (formerly the *Gospel Trumpet*). I published one guest editorial (June 10, 1973) followed by three articles. The editorial was titled "Cherish the Heritage!" and reflected a theme that would be the subject of several of my books in later years.

The Church of God movement was then nearly a century old. I asked, "Has the day of great causes and great leaders passed? Are we now to be led by faceless and forgettable bureaucrats who excite no one to any great cause?" I expressed concern that the movement had reached a state of "tired blood and clouded vision," and I reminded readers that there was a Consultation on Doctrine in process and that the new Center for Pastoral Studies was at work in the right direction. I ended this way:

> I for one choose to be part of a "radical" Christian fellowship. No getting trapped by the moods of the moment. No getting sidetracked by artificial traditions. No apologies for calling others to basics. No settling for the passivity of the general landscape. The fellowship of Christians must be free, free to be innovative with Christ for our time, and free to respect and cherish the heritage which is ours!

Prior to my moving across the Anderson campus to the School of Theology in 1973, I had published what I think was my first piece in *Vital Christianity*. It was called "Palm Sunday," and appeared in the April 2, 1972, issue. It grew directly out of my experience of travel in Israel in 1968. I had photographed old Jerusalem's temple mount, looking west from the Mount of Olives. I then had crossed the valley and photographed the Mount of Olives looking east from the temple mount. These photos had been framed and hung in my office on the second floor of the new Decker Hall. They had both historic and devotional meaning for me. About them and the Jesus behind them, I wrote the following from the perspective of the Jerusalem wall looking eastward.

> We stand where the archer stood,
> Poised to repel the advance of any foe.

Take your ease, the Mount of Olives is
but a harbinger of peace,
A gentle hill with a garden of prayer.

To arms! Over the brow of the hill comes an army
With its general—on the back of an ass!

He comes, they say, to shatter our pretensions,
To lay low the walls of our pious defense,
To break our strong arrows of manliness
into the feeble darts of lovingkindness.

Resist him!! But how hard it is to hit him
With that encircling crowd of militant admirers.
He's out of my range now, and off that ass finally.
We have him on a cross!—But he still comes at me!!

I'm trying to resist him. But I'm weakening.
I clutch that bleeding side and hear those words,
"Father, forgive." I'm a traitor to my own cause.
My post at the wall is abandoned.

Chaos comes.
But, no! His army, now enlarged by one,
Marches on to where other weapons
Nervously guard other "peaceful" valleys.
I'm a captive of war! I'm a free man! JOY!

I am free to be what I am
And to become what he can make me,

And to enjoy things for what they are,
And to participate with him in reshaping things
Closer to the divine intention,
And to be free to probe
The liberating depths of servanthood.

I am no longer fearful of being a child,
For the wisdom of childhood is the door to the Kingdom.
I shall laugh, lay down my bow, pick up the towel,
And live as he lives!

Beyond writing for periodicals, the opportunity came for me to try writing a book. The book editor at Warner Press at the time was Kenneth Hall. He asked if I would write a book on the Christian life to support the church's Sunday school curriculum. Although teaching was a busy preoccupation and there was yet no such thing as a computer on my desk or in the faculty office, I readily agreed. Soon I had produced *Where Life Begins* (1973), complete with study questions and possible learning activities organized in thirteen units for use as an elective course for a quarter of a Sunday school year. I am amazed that this little book is still available this far into the twenty-first century.

Writing about faith and life, I began this first book of mine with questions. "Are traditional patterns of faith still believable in our kind of world? What has happened to the quality of living in highly industrialized and urbanized societies? Is there nothing left to life but growing, working, raising a family, retiring, getting hardening of the arteries, and dying?" (p. 5).

In the early 1970s I was a young professional, well credentialed in academic terms and just about to be ordained formally to Christian ministry. Already I had begun the administrative part of my career, functioning as a department chair and being named the founding director of the Center of Pastoral Studies on the Anderson campus. Warner Press had added the following on the back of my 1973 book: "Callen has taught in the Middle East and Japan." I and five of my Anderson colleagues had comprised a significant study tour of the major archaeological sites in the Middle East in the summer of 1968, and I had just led a group of Anderson College students on a serving and cultural learning month in Japan. In both cases, I learned much more that I recall teaching anyone! Even so, this early internationalism of mine looked good on the back of the book

President Robert H. Readron gave me an important piece of advice as I began my greatly expanded administrative role in 1973 as Dean of Anderson School of Theology. The word of wisdom was that a leader cannot avoid criticism; therefore, integrity and sanity demand that I choose my own guiding star and follow it faithfully. When being true to oneself, you have selected your critics—which means that they can be tolerated and sleep comes more easily at night. Over the years, when recalling Reardon's advice and his strong encouragement for me to write, I have to keep an eye on my own star and keep writing worthy pages. Others will judge their enduring worth.

When you read these words, I may or may not still be breathing. If I am not, check out my grave in Maplewood Cemetery in Anderson, Indiana, sample my published works, and decide for yourself whether or not I am really dead! If I am not, it is by the grace of God. If I am, God's grace will still be sufficient for me.

Accelerating the Publishing Pace

The years 1974 through 1980 were ones of accelerating enrollment growth for Anderson School of Theology. My deanship was being blessed and my writing ministry becoming more active. I functioned as founding editor of *Centering on Ministry* in 1976. The campus needed a new vehicle for assisting church leaders to communicate helpfully with those engaged in Christian ministry. The first issue (spring 1976) was sent without cost to all ministers registered in the 1976 *Yearbook* of the Church of God. The subject was the Bible and its centrality for the several disciplines of the seminary's curriculum.

After my introductory article as founding editor, the inaugural writers of *Centering on Ministry* were James Earl Massey, George Kufeldt, John W. V. Smith, Jerry C. Grubbs, and John M. Vayhinger. I enjoyed this manner of enabling my faculty to set their wisdom before the church at large. In some of the subsequent issues, I wrote short articles, including "The Peril of Persuasion" (fall 1977), "A Centennial Caution" (spring 1978), and "The Ethics of Power" (winter 1978). In the spring 1977 issue, I wrote about seminary education and Christian ministry in a free-church tradition like the Church of God movement.

Meanwhile, I had become a regular contributor to *Vital Christianity*, the periodical of the Church of God in North America. The editor, Harold L. Phillips, was a friend of seminary education and welcomed my work. My regular column in 1974-1975 was called "Reflections." It sought to discover the meaning and message of Christian faith in today's world. Popularly written for lay readers, the subjects of my columns included the nature of faith, the nature of the Bible, and the adequacy of the Christian gospel. I was seeking to model an academic administrator who cared about communicating meaningfully with the church. In the March 2, 1975, issue, my piece was a little different. It was called "Most Artists Die." I began by admitting that I had been reared in a small Ohio village where the only local "culture" centered in the amusement park in the summer and on rare occasions some minor event at the fire station. Fortunately, the years since had brought me many enriching experiences that had helped me notice the death of several prominent artists in 1973.

In that one year, I reported, death had claimed W. H. Auden, Pearl S. Buck, Pablo Casals, Noel Coward, and Pablo Picasso. Assuming that politics can be considered an "art form," dead also in 1973 were David Ben Gurion, architect of modern Israel, and Lyndon B. Johnson, designer of America's "Great Society." I pictured this series of artistic losses as a symbol of an increasingly materialistic American culture losing touch with its soul. Jesus, I said, was an artist who took "love, an unconquerable and intelligent goodwill for all, and found the heartbeat of the universe. He chose an unlikely group of men and welded them into firebrands for a new world. He took the horror of a cross and transformed it into new life for you and me." Being careful not to list Jesus among the dead artists of 1973, I announced, "He lives and continues to create and recreate life in the image of God. Hallelujah!"

The years 1977-1978 saw my regular writing shift to a section in *Vital Christianity* called "Views and Voices." I addressed the issues of biblical authority and interpretation, church mission, and the meaning of a true theologian. In the April 4, 1976, issue I even used the dean's chair of the seminary to offer a pastoral exhortation titled "Be Where You Are." Between 1977 and 1980, thirty-five articles appeared in *Vital Christianity* under my name. The most commented on were my two-part article on the Bible and "tongues" (Jan.-Feb., 1979) and "The Dilemma of Divorce" (June 8, 1980). I dared to address "hot" topics head-on.

After twenty-six years of service as Editor of Warner Press, a role of central significance in the history and life of the Church of God movement, Harold L. Phillips retired in June, 1977. I was in the last year of my first three-year term as Dean of the School of Theology. Things were going very well for the seminary and president Reardon had made it clear that he was anxious to nominate me for a second term to begin in 1977. Robert Nicholson, Dean of Anderson College, was chair of the selection committee for a new Editor of Warner Press. Herschell Rice of Pomona, California, an officer of the Publication Board, initiated a private conversation with me during the Anderson Camp Meeting in June, 1976.

This was an important conversation for me. Rice expressed his personal interest in my candidacy for the editorship and wanted to know if I would be open to considering this possibility if formally contacted. I was flattered and responded cautiously and ambiguously, not wanting to open or close any doors to such an important possibility. In my follow-up letter to Rice on July 2, I reaffirmed my commitment to the School of Theology and said that "I do not regard myself as a candidate. . .nor at the present time am I willing to be so considered by others." I was still being ambiguous with the "do not regard myself" and "at the present time."

Not surprisingly, my letter did not end the matter. On November 16, 1976, I wrote to Dr. Nicholson after a member of the selection committee had called me on November 7 to urge that I not eliminate myself and that I agree to a formal interview. I declined the interview and repeated to Nicholson my stance of not considering myself a candidate. Having shared this letter with president Robert Reardon, Nicholson sent me a handwritten letter (Nov. 22) urging me to close the issue of my possible candidacy more definitively since "it is no secret that you are the choice of the key officers of Warner Press." He concluded with this:

> What to do? Take yourself out of the race. You have accepted before the Lord, and the whole church, one of the most crucial responsibilities we have to offer. The seminary is beginning to flourish and come into its own under your leadership. This is the time to reaffirm your own deep commitment to the vocation you are just beginning, and I fully intend to be in a position to ask the [college] Board to elect you to a new term in June. You are aware, Barry, I know, of my love and confidence.

The very next day I sent a handwritten letter of reassurance to president Reardon and one to Donald Noffsinger, president of Warner Press, ending any consideration of my candidacy. I would not leave the seminary.

My wife was relieved, not wanting to face another big transition. Arlo F. Newell soon was chosen as the new Editor. He would become a supportive colleague of mine and of the seminary and serve well in the editorship, although after some years he and president Noffsinger of Warner Press would experience relational difficulties within the company structure, one phase of what was to be a major company crisis. Did I make the correct decision? To this day, Donald Noffsinger says that he should have insisted on my candidacy more strongly than he did. The following years were very good ones for the seminary. Hindsight suggests to me that wisdom prevailed. Even so, the issue did not die entirely.

When Arlo Newell retired from the editorship in 1993, I again was asked to be interviewed as a candidate. I did so reluctantly. Now being back in the classroom after sixteen years of academic administration, I consciously presented myself to the search committee in a way that was true to myself and that I knew did not fit the company's then-current preoccupations. David Shultz was the eventual choice. He did his very best, but went on to suffer the necessity of suspending the publication of *Vital Christianity* after more than a century of continuous ministry. He returned to the pastorate since the company was in financial emergency and voted to eliminate the office of Editor altogether—something unthinkable to the church until that time. I was spared being in the middle of all this. My wife had always opposed the idea of my leaving the campus. She was right. As I remember all of this now, I rejoice that God guided me throughout. Surprisingly, other editorships would be ahead for me.

Quite apart from the issue of the Warner Press editorship, publishing doors kept opening to me. Two letters to the editor appeared in the March 25, 1979, issue of *Vital Christianity*. Carl Reynolds of Springfield,

Ohio, said that my two-part article on "tongues" (Jan. 21 and Feb. 11, 1979) should be put in booklet form and distributed in every Church of God congregation. Benjamin F. Reid of Los Angeles, California, reported that the January 21 issue, including my article, was "a classic!" While there was considerable appreciation and distribution, the subject itself did not go away, and called me into more involvement in the following decade. I also wrote an article on homosexuality in the summer of 1979 and submitted it, but it was judged too volatile to deal with in that lay-oriented journal, at least at the time. My article "The Dilemma of Divorce" did appear in the June 8, 1980, issue.

Publishing opportunities often arose for me because of my anticipating unique circumstances well before they arrived. I did this several times. Beginning in 1974, almost as soon as I officially became Dean of Anderson School of Theology, I realized that the late 1970s would be a time for special focus on the heritage of the Church of God movement. With the movement's centennial celebration in 1980 fast approaching, I envisioned a major literary project and worked methodically on my own to gather and organize a large quantity of key heritage materials. My colleague John W. V. Smith began preparing a narrative history of the movement (*The Quest for Holiness and Unity*, 1980). I proposed to Warner Press a series of smaller books, almost a personal archives of primary materials, under the group title *A Time To Remember*. They were titled *Beginnings, Testimonies, Teachings, Milestones, Evaluations,* and *Projections.* This all became reality during 1977-1979 with considerable churchwide publicity (for instance, a full-page advertisement in the January, 1978, special issue of *Vital Christianity,* including photos of all six book covers and myself with Warner Press president Donald Noffsinger and editor Arlo Newell).

Soon after the final volume was released, the whole set was sold out. Since there was still an obvious market for this material, and with my making only a few corrections and updatings, Warner Press moved quickly to a 1979 reprint, not now in the six-paperback format, but with all of the books combined in two hardbound volumes under the new title *The First Century*. Within a few years, the 1,000 hardbound sets were also gone. It was not until the year 2000, at another time of heritage sensitivity when a new North American ministry structure had just been put into place, that I was able to have published my volume *Following the Light*. It reproduced some of the 1979 material, but in a new setting that was fully updated and included much material not available to me in the 1970s. This book has become a standard reference work in the church.

Between 1979 and 2000, one interesting event occurred. Pastor Kozo Konno of Tokyo, Japan, had come to Anderson, Indiana, to help celebrate the centennial of the Church of God movement. He had felt wonderfully inspired and come into possession of a set of my *The First Century* books. He wrote to me in November, 1980, seeking permission to translate all of these 914 pages into Japanese to "let the people of the Church of God in Japan read it well." He envisioned publishing 1,000 sets in Japanese at a cost of "about several million Japanese yen," to be funded privately since the church there did not have such money. I passed the request on to Warner Press editor Arlo Newell, who subsequently corresponded with Brother Konno. Permission was given to proceed and a skilled translator, Noboru Tamaguchi, was secured.

In 1981 I received a package in the mail from Rev. Kozo Konno, then chair of the Church of God in Japan. Inside was a special gift for me, two red and leather-bound volumes printed beautifully in Japanese. *The First Century* was now in Asia, freshly published in a major regional language. I felt honored. Others of my books would later appear in the Korean, German, Swahili, and Spanish languages. I think of my father whose generation used the word "Jap" harshly. Now my words were appearing in that ancient language, with my permission and pleasure. Times and sensitivities change, in this case for the better.

Fortunately, I have not had to share the deep sadness carried by Charles ("Sparky") Schulz for much of his life. Even though he created "Peanuts" and was one of the more famous cartoonists of all time, he struggled with the realization that his mother never saw anything he published. Her cancer would not wait on his success. I once met Sparky when he visited Anderson College in the 1970s and provided generous support to the new fine arts building on campus. But I did not share his difficult memory. My father died in 1974 when only one of my books was out. I think he was privately pleased that I was doing something constructive and widely applauded. Even though my mother also would die relatively young (in 1979 at age sixty), she had proudly read several of my early books. My first wife's mother, Evelyn, was one of my biggest fans. In fact, when her alzheimers was overtaking her, she read some of my books multiple times—and they were new to her every time!

After all of this activity with *A Time To Remember* and *The First Century*, four other publishing opportunities came to me (rather than my initiating them). The first was in late 1978 when I received a letter from president Robert H. Reardon addressed to me as dean of the School of Theology. He observed that, in his judgment, the Church of God movement had lost its driving force in recent generations and very much needed a fresh and compelling statement of its core convictions, one that could newly excite people to carry the movement into its second century. In his view, the faculty of the School of Theology was the natural group to tackle this project, and he wanted the finished product on his desk by March of 1979!

The president had strong convictions, wanted his campus to provide leadership to the church, and had placed the assignment on my desk with a deadline. It would not be easy since the movement is not creedal in nature and the seminary faculty would be a difficult group to move to consensus on such a delicate statement. Nonetheless, I went to work, handled the process of drafting and revising what the president wanted, handled faculty complaints and contributions, and had the result on his desk when requested. It then was published by Warner Press as a very attractive booklet titled *WE BELIEVE: Statement of Conviction on the Occasion of the Centennial of the Church of God Movement.* My assignment was complete.

In the years to come, several hundred thousand copies of *WE BELIEVE* were produced and distributed around the world in multiple languages. Its initial release brought much mail to the campus and myself. From Walter Kufeldt of the Florida General Assembly of the Church of God came a letter of thanks which said, "The School of Theology is to be commended! It's a giant step that we need to take." Maurice Berquist of the Mass Communications Board in Anderson wrote this to me: "Certainly what your group has done in lifting out the basic concepts that have both precipitated and perpetuated the Church of God has brought a helpful statement." William E Reed, the Executive Secretary of the Executive Council of the Church of God, expressed his sincere appreciation and then observed that this statement "will provoke some wholesome discussion—and some painful allegations." He was right.

President Reardon and I had tried hard to head off the likely allegations by insisting that this statement was not a creed, but only a position paper seeking to stimulate fresh thought and vision. Nonetheless, some very conservative pastors clearly were nervous. Robert Lawrence wrote this: "If there is any incipient hope of ultimately giving birth to a creedal statement, I would oppose it violently. Creedalism is sin." Apprehension even came from sociology professor Val Clear of the Anderson College faculty. "One of the remarkable aspects of genius with which we have been blessed," he wrote, "is the absence of tablets written in stone…. The formalization of doctrine which this implies—even though it is self-consciously not official—will stifle that very important tradition …. Having said all of that, let me go on to express my appreciation for your sending me a copy, and the fervent hope that I am as wrong in this fear as I have been on some other occasions." Fortunately, as time now has shown, Clear's fear was largely unfounded. Faculty members can be wrong!

The second publishing project involved the updating and republishing of the book *Christian Theology* written originally in 1925 by Russell R. Byrum (1889-1980). It had been very influential in the Church of God movement since the 1920s, but by 1981 was seriously out of date in some of its language and illustrations, and in most of its footnote references. Warner Press decided to revise and republish it. I was assigned as revision editor for Part I on the existence of God. When this work was completed for the book's release in 1982, Robert Reardon said this on the paper jacket of the new hardbound work: "It was Russell Byrum who threw open the doors and windows of learning. He was the young scholar/teacher who encouraged his students to explore new frontiers and to drink at the great fountain of historic Christian thought." I felt privileged to help bring Byrum into the late twentieth century. In the next decade, I would put my hand to writing a fresh theology book of my own (*God As Loving Grace*, 1996, reprint 2018).

The third project came in 2005 and was something of a sequel to the *We Believe* booklet of 1979. This time, instead of the School of Theology faculty as a whole, I personally authored the booklet "What We Teach." The initial impetus came from the librarians of Anderson University. On occasion, someone would ask them for a copy of what the Church of God movement teaches—many campus students come from other Christian traditions. A brief "creed" is usually what they hoped for, although none exists, and full-length books on theology would not hold their attention for long. The older *WE BELIEVE* statement had aged and represented only a previous School of Theology faculty. So, I set out to create a helpful but brief tool that could answer the questions from the teaching tradition of the movement as a whole.

Studies by/of Prominent Church Leaders
In books authored or edited by Barry L. Callen

Leaders Remembered and Honored	Book Titles	Years Pub.
African-Americans (a range of individuals)	*African-Americans and the Church of God* (a social history by James Earl Massey)	2005
Blackwelder, Boyce W.	*Listening to the Word of God* (biography and essays)	1990
Holiness Leaders	*Heart of the Heritage* (lifetime achievement awards)	2001
Jeeninga, Gustav	*Doors to Life* (autobiography)	2002
McCutcheon, Lillie S.	*She Came Preaching* (biography)	1992
Massey, James Earl	*Aspects of My Pilgrimage* (autobiography)	2002
Massey, James Earl	*Sharing Heaven's Music*	1995
Massey, James Earl	*Views from the Mountain*	2018
Morrison, John A.	*Faith, Learning, and Life* (edited writings)	1991
Nicholson, Robert A.	*Faith, Learning, and Life* (edited writings)	1991
Nicholson, Robert A.	*So I Said, Yes!* (autobiography)	2006
Pinnock, Clark H.	*Journey Toward Renewal* (intellectual biography)	2000
Reardon, Robert H.	*Faith, Learning, and Life* (edited writings)	1991
Reardon, Robert H.	*Staying on Course* (biography)	2004
Saints, Church of God (27)	*A Time To Remember: Testimonies* (edited writings)	1978
Saints, Church of God (32)	*Wisdom of the Saints* (edited biographies and writings)	2003
Tasker, George P.	*Ahead of His Times* (biography by Douglas E. Welch)	2001
Warner, Daniel S.	*It's God's Church!* (biography)	1995

Material about many other persons of interest is found in additional books of mine, including:

Seeking Higher Ground (a centennial history of Park Place Church of God, Anderson, IN, 2006)

Enriching Mind and Spirit (a history of higher education in the Church of God, 2007)

The fourth project came to me in 2004 as a commission from the Church Council of Park Place Church of God in Anderson, Indiana, my home congregation since 1963. The year 2006 would mark the congregation's centennial and a major history of the church was needed. I resigned my role as corporate secretary of the congregation in May of 2004 in order to have more time to devote to such an extensive research and writing project. The final result, released on Sunday morning, March 26, 2006, was the book *Seeking Higher Ground*. I told the congregation during that service that the title comes from an old holiness song that speaks of "pressing on the upward way." This congregation, I said, has been a people "stretching to be all that God intends as we worship God with all our hearts, educate for mature discipleship, and reach out to the whole world with really good news." The cover features the great spire above the church stretching toward the distant sky.

It was in 1996 that I published my own systematic theology, *God As Loving Grace*. It was my way of reconceiving and articulating the central truths of the Christian faith. Maybe, like I had helped do for Russell Byrum back in 1982, someone in the 2050s will think of my work as worthy of being updated for continuing communication to later generations. This thought could be more ego that reality, but one never knows. The future is in good hands, ones much bigger than mine. I used my 1996 book as a basic text for several years in my "Introduction to Christian Theology" class at Anderson University. It worked well. I was pleased to learn in 2000 that Steve Rennick was using it in a similar way at Kima International School of Theology in Kenya, East Africa—and I learned during my visit to KIST in 2010 that it was still in use there. It has and is being used in other colleges of various denominations. Wipf & Stock placed it back in print in 2018 with a nice new cover.

There is a listing below of my books that have focused on appreciation for particular people and church traditions. I have disciplined myself to remember (the instinct for history going back to my Geneva

College days). In remembering, I have opened the doors to rejoicing. The cause of this joy has been the grace of God much more than my own gifts of service. Productive lives of ministry are a combination of divine grace and faithfulness to one's call.

One day, while surfing the internet, I came to *amazon.com*, the site that claims to be earth's largest distributor of books. Many of my books are found there. I noted that a professor of philosophy at Loyola Marymount University, a Dr. James K. A. Smith whom I have never met, had put online his personal review of my intellectual biography of theologian Clark H. Pinnock (*Journey Toward Renewal*, 2000). He said: "Barry Callen has put evangelical scholars in his debt with this intellectual biography of Clark Pinnock's theological development. Pinnock's own journey is a sort of 'microcosm' of evangelicalism itself.... Callen does an excellent job of distilling the key themes of Pinnock's theology and allowing us to glimpse how Pinnock's mind has changed.... Both Pinnock's work and Callen's account of it are exemplary." See *Appendix C* for an essay reflecting the views of Pinnock and myself.

I admit to a little pride in being noted and my work appreciated by important persons. I also admit to a conscious valuing of important persons worthy of being remembered. I have written biographies of several such persons, including Clark H. Pinnock, Daniel S. Warner, Lillie S. McCutcheon, and Robert H. Reardon. It also is an honor to be asked by publishers for the privilege of using my name on the covers of books they are releasing—usually in the form of an endorsement on the back cover. For instance, my evaluative comments are carried on the covers of William M. Greathouse's *Wholeness in Christ* (Beacon Hill Press, 1989) and Clark H. Pinnock's *Most Moved Mover* (Baker Academic, 2001).

Editing the Work of Others

Thousands of my published pages are not the original work of my own mind, but the work of others that I have valued, edited, and guided into print—often in my capacity as Editor of the *Wesleyan Theological Journal*, Anderson University Press, and Aldersgate Press. This working with the material of others started in the 1970s with my book series *A Time To Remember*. I wanted to make the work of others available again in convenient format, especially materials related to the Church of God tradition as it celebrated its centennial in 1980. A similar motive brought into being in 1991 my book *Faith, Learning, and Life: Views from the President's Office of Anderson University*. This is a collection of the wisdom writings of John A. Morrison, Robert H. Reardon, and Robert A. Nicholson, presidents of Anderson (College) University.

Several of my subsequent books were also works I edited to honor the wisdom of others. Prominent among them are *Sharing Heaven's Music* (1995, in honor of James Earl Massey), *Following the Light* (2000), and *Heart of the Heritage* (2001, with William Kostlevy). The 2001 volume grew directly out of my editorship of the *Wesleyan Theological Journal*, as did the major 2009 volume *The Church that God Intends*. This editorship was a major and long labor of love in which I take considerable pride. There also was the 2004 book *Reading the Bible in Wesleyan Ways* (co-edited with Richard P. Thompson and published by Beacon Hill Press of Kansas City). With particular reference to the Church of God movement, there was the 2003 volume *The Wisdom of the Saints* highlighting the ministries and wisdom of thirty-two of the "greats" of the Church of God tradition.

I was first elected the editor of the *Wesleyan Theological Journal* by the Wesleyan Theological Society in 1993. The journal at that time had not appeared for nearly two years and the Society was in difficult financial condition. I began working to produce two issues per year, each containing about 275 pages of thoughtful and fully documented material by about twelve different scholars from various countries and Christian traditions (United Methodist, Church of the Nazarene, Wesleyan Methodist, Free Methodist, Salvation Army, Roman Catholic, Greek Orthodox, etc.). I personally have kept bound sets of my edited issues, which have come to be a small library. I have provided another bound set to the library of Anderson University and helped facilitate in 2010 the first electronic disc carrying all *WTJ* issues back to the beginning in the 1960s. By 2014 I had edited and published 354 different authors, some several times.

The summer of 2000 saw another development that put me on the trail of more authors whom I could assist into print. Anderson University Press was begun, with me named founding editor by president James L. Edwards. In the following years, I edited for others significant personal life stories, including Douglas Welch's biography of George P. Tasker (*Ahead of His Times*, 2001), James Earl Massey's autobiography (*Aspects of My Pilgrimage*, 2002), Gustav Jeeninga's autobiography (*Doors to Life*, 2002), James Earl Massey's *African Americans and the Church of God* (2005), and Robert A. Nicholson's 2006 memoir, *So I Said Yes!* Of special note is the 2012 volume *Voices of Riley* that I published for Riley Children's Hospital in Indianapolis.

My own writing, of course, went on, supported by a range of publishers. For instance, in 2006 alone I had three books released. They were *Seeking Higher Ground: The Centennial History of Park Place Church of God* (published by the congregation), *Authentic Spirituality* (published by Emeth Press), and *The Scripture Principle* (with Clark H. Pinnock, published by Baker Academic). Coming in 2007 were a commentary I wrote on the New Testament book of Colossians (Wesleyan Publishing House), *Caught Between Truths* (Emeth Press), and *Enriching Mind and Spirit*, a history of higher education in the Church of God (Anderson University Press).

The year 2006 marked the 100th year of the Church of God movement in Anderson, Indiana, and the 125th year of the movement's existence. Having retired from my teaching role at Anderson University in 2005, I became Special Assistant to the General Director of Church of of God Ministries, Ronald V. Duncan. He asked that I chair the planning committee responsible for special events and products related to this 2006 time of celebration. One of the products was the book *Camp Meeting Favorites: Heritage Songs of the Church of God*, edited by Joseph Gregory. Interspersed among the seventy-five heritage songs are supporting paragraphs and quotations from early pioneers of the movement. I was not aware until I saw the finalized book that all the quotations are drawn, not from the original sources, but from my book *Wisdom of the Saints* (2003) that gathers the published wisdom of these people. It was an honor for my work to be used as the official source for locating the wisdom of the movement's pioneer teachers and preachers. I had worked hard to make such wisdom available to new generations.

In the recent years, my books have taken on quite a range of subject matter and even genre. I wandered into the world of fiction with three efforts, all enabled by Emeth Press. They were *In Deep Water* (a 2009 submarine novel set in World War II), *Coming Home* (a 2010 novel in search of religious identity set in the hills of Kentucky), and *StarWalker* (a 2011 novel of hope trying to emerge in one boy's life). Meanwhile, my interest in the "truth" (the non-fiction style, that is) did not abate.

Subsequent books of non-fiction (by six different publishers) were: (1) a layperson's guide to understanding the beliefs and practices of the Church of God (Anderson) (*Following Our Lord*, 2008); (2) a major history of Horizon International, a ministry to orphans of AIDS in Africa with which I have been involved from its beginning (*Hope on the Horizon*, 2010); (3) a commentary on the Lord's Prayer (*The Prayer of Holiness-Hungry People*, 2011); (4) frank conversations among great Christian thinkers on the major subjects of Christian theology (*Heart of the Matter*, 2011); (5) an attempt to reclaim the Old Testament for today's Christians (*Beneath the Surface*, 2012); (6) a collection of prayers from the patients, families, and caregivers of Riley Hospital for Children in Indianapolis (*Voices from Riley*, 2012, as editor-publisher); and (7) *Heart & Life*, co-edited with Don Thorsen and the first book published by Aldersgate Press.

For venturing the considerable capital required to put these books into print and e-book format, I am in debt to Anderson University Press, Emeth Press, Francis Asbury Press, Horizon International, Warner Press, and others. See *Appendix F* for a full listing of my published works. A particular honor and responsibility came to me in 2011 when the Wesleyan/Holiness Connection, a network of denominations, formed Aldersgate Press as its publishing arm and named me the Editor on its behalf. A publishing team and I began our attempt to help renew a holiness emphasis across the face of American Christianity.

The February/March, 2005, issue of *ONE Voice!*, then the national periodical of the Church of God movement, ran a half-page ad featuring three of my new books, *Authentic Spirituality* (Baker Academic, 2001), *Discerning the Divine* (Westminster John Knox, 2004), and *Reading the Bible in Wesleyan Ways* (with Richard P. Thompson, Beacon Hill Press, 2004). The headline was, "Callen Becomes Most Published Author in the Church of God." While clearly true, this status had never been my goal or expectation. Even so, I feel so privileged to have served in this very public way, trying to capture yesterday's wisdom for tomorrow's guidance.

MCM
Madison County Month

May
Vol. 3 Issue 9

NEW BOOKS
Callen becomes most published author in the Church of God

ANDERSON, IN— Since 2001, three major books have been released by Dr. Barry L. Callen of Anderson University making him the most published author in the history of the Church of God movement.

In *Authentic Spirituality: Moving Beyond Mere Religion* (Baker Academic and Paternoster Press, 2001), Callen calls Christians to move beyond both a lifeless orthodoxy and an amorphous liberalism, uniting Word with Spirit on looking fresh at sanctification and the Christian spiritual journey. Callen insists that the goal of any Christian congregation should not first be relevance, growth, or success, but being "alive in God's Spirit."

Callen's second book, *Discerning the Divine: God in Christian Theology* (Westminster John Knox, 2004), builds on his earlier book *God As Loving Grace* (Evangel Publishing House, 1996). It is "a reasoned and careful treatment of Christian teaching about God over the centuries," says Callen, "which ends by affirming the Trinity as the

distinctive Christian view." The book serves as an introduction to, and context for, entering vigorous discussions in Christian circles about the nature of God.

His third book is *Reading the Bible in Wesleyan Ways* (Beacon Hill Press, 2004). This new Callen volume emphasizes that reading the Bible rightly and interpreting its meaning for today requires openness to the past and present working of God's Spirit in bridging the ancient texts and illuminating the present readers. In this volume Dr. Callen and colleague Dr. Richard Thompson have assembled and edited a series of essays on this subject, each written by a prominent biblical scholar from the Wesleyan theological traditions. The book features emphases typical of the teaching tradition of the Church of God movement.

All of these books are beginning to be used as textbooks on college and university campuses, in seminaries and beyond the Church of God movement.

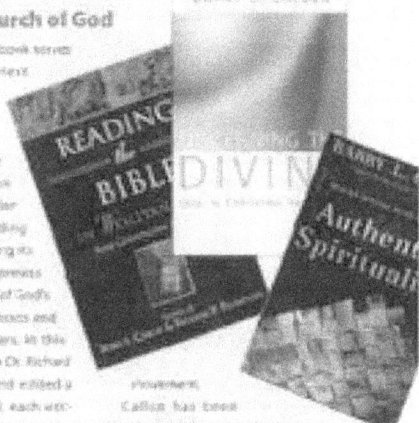

Callen has been a faculty member at Anderson University since 1966, serving as dean of both the former Anderson College and the Seminary. He has also been the international editor of the *Wesleyan Theological Journal* since 1992 and editor of Anderson University Press since 2001.

Some of the books published by
Anderson University Press, with me as Editor.
The mission of this Press combines those of the
University and the Church of God movement.
I was privileged to help honor some men
whom I admire greatly.

Autographing copies of my history of
Park Place Church of God, Anderson,
Indiana, 2006.

Wesleyan Theological Journals, produced by me as Editor.

With my pastor,
Lillie S. McCutcheon, 1979.

With my friends Arlo F. Newell and
Donald Noffsinger of Warner Press, 1978.

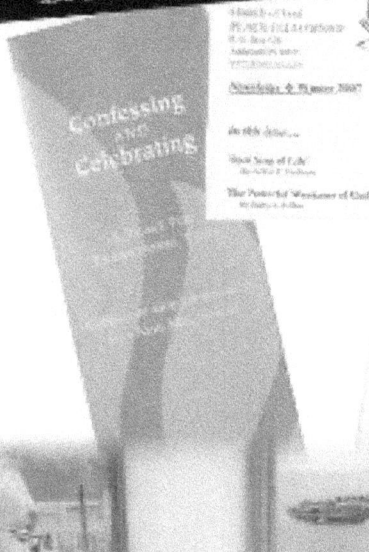

GALATIANS, PHILIPPIANS, COLOSSIANS

A Commentary for Bible Students

EARLE L. WILSON, ALEX R. G. DEASLEY, AND BARRY L. CALLEN

Enriching Mind & Spirit

A History of Higher Education in the Church of God (Anderson)

BARRY L. CALLEN

Confessing and Celebrating

WHAT WE TEACH

J. David Liverett, graphic artist, who assisted with several of my books.

Beneath the Surface

Reclaiming the Old Testament for Today's Christian

Barry L. Callen

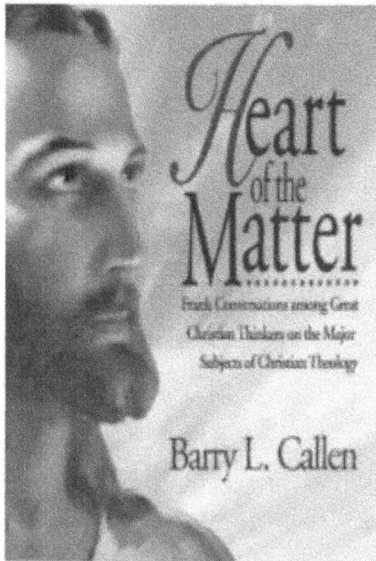

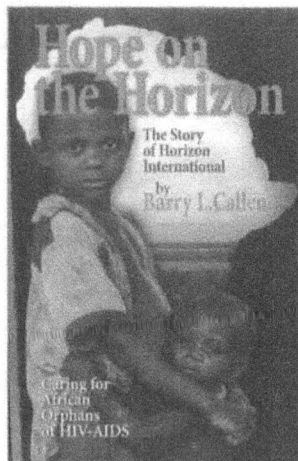

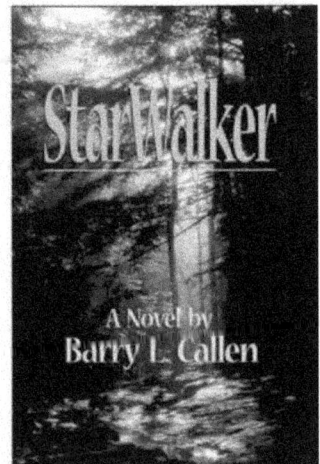

COMING HOME

A NOVEL BY
BARRY L. CALLEN

Heart of the Matter

Frank Conversations among Great
Christian Thinkers on the Major
Subjects of Christian Theology

Barry L. Callen

Heart & Life

REDISCOVERING HOLY LIVING

EDITED BY
BARRY L. CALLEN & DON THORSEN

In Deep Water

An Historical Novel of
Violence and Virtue,
Fear and Faith

Barry L. Callen

Hope on the Horizon

The Story
of Horizon
International
by
Barry L. Callen

Caring for
African
Orphans
of HIV-AIDS

StarWalker

A Novel by
Barry L. Callen

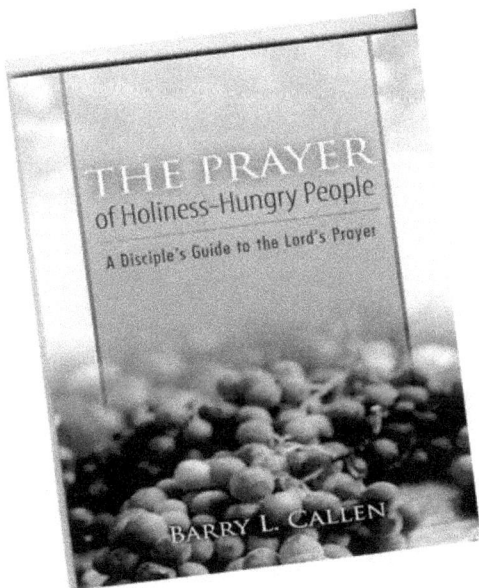

THE PRAYER
of Holiness–Hungry People

A Disciple's Guide to the Lord's Prayer

BARRY L. CALLEN

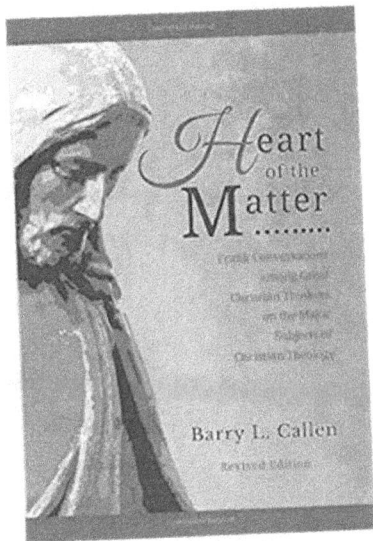

Heart
of the
Matter..........

Frank Conversations
among Great
Christian Thinkers
on the Major
Subjects of
Christian Theology

Barry L. Callen

Revised Edition

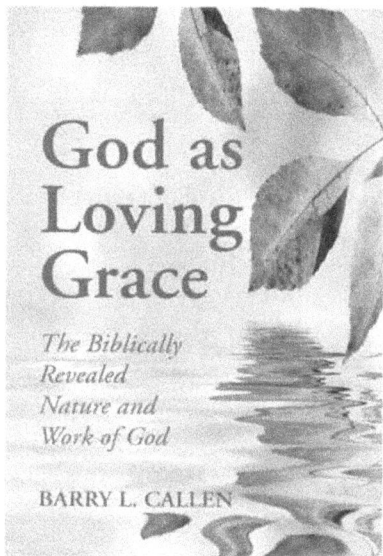

God as
Loving
Grace

*The Biblically
Revealed
Nature and
Work of God*

BARRY L. CALLEN

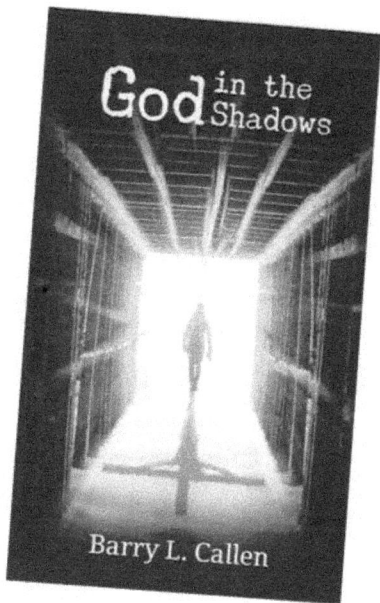

God in the Shadows

Barry L. Callen

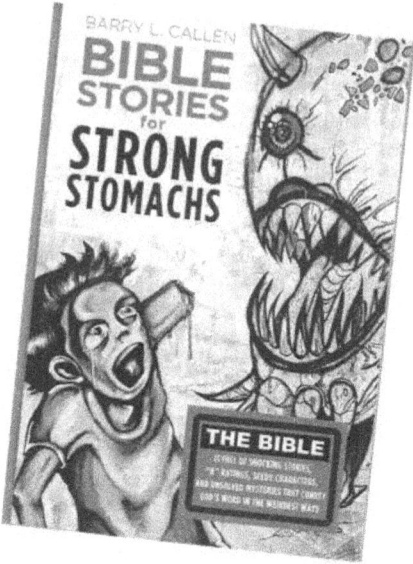

BARRY L. CALLEN
BIBLE
STORIES
for
STRONG
STOMACHS

THE BIBLE
IS FULL OF SHOCKING STORIES,
"R" RATINGS, SEEDY CHARACTERS,
AND UNSOLVED MYSTERIES THAT COMES
GOD'S WORD IN THE WEIRDEST WAYS

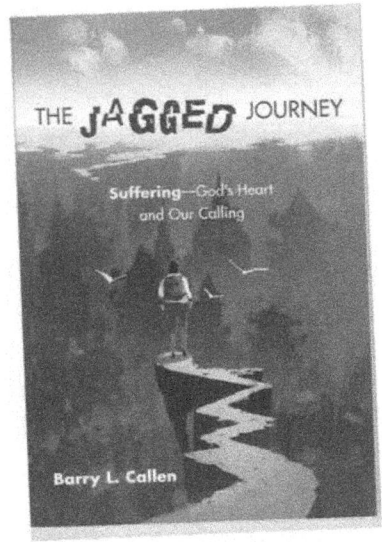

THE JAGGED JOURNEY

Suffering—God's Heart
and Our Calling

Barry L. Callen

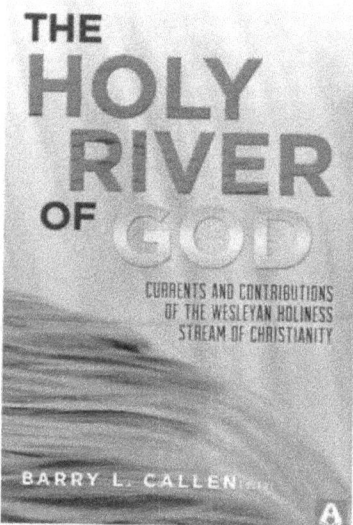

THE
HOLY
RIVER
OF GOD

CURRENTS AND CONTRIBUTIONS
OF THE WESLEYAN HOLINESS
STREAM OF CHRISTIANITY

BARRY L. CALLEN

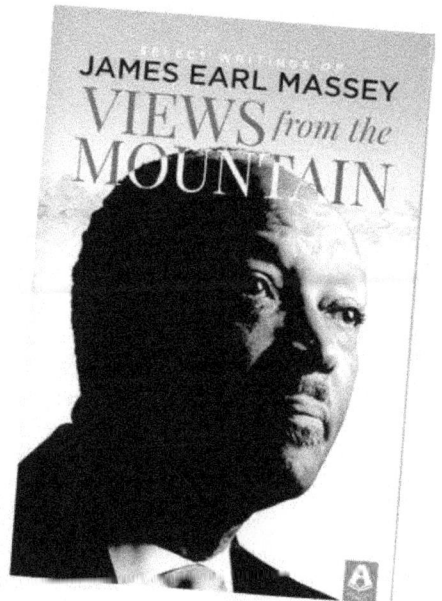

SELECT WRITINGS OF
JAMES EARL MASSEY
VIEWS from the
MOUNTAIN

Millennium Number Three

Journeying through times of transition

It was very early into the twenty-first century when I began an important practice that I have continued ever since. I began personal journaling, writing at least a paragraph for each day I lived, reporting events, thoughts, and occasional reflections. Of course, I had no idea when I began this in November, 2001, how eventful my life would be in the years immediately ahead. With the help of this journal, I now am able to be quite precise when it comes to the time and nature of many activities and personal thoughts. Looking back through the hundreds of pages now in this journal, I see patterns and connections of thought and action. Such insight is part of the wisdom of journaling. I have captured my experience of the early two decades of the third millennium after the earthly life of Jesus Christ.

Y2K and All That

When it was official that the calendar had begun the year 2000, it was likely that, at fifty-eight years of age, I had entered the last phase of my lifespan. My father had died at age fifty-five (1974) and my mother at sixty (1979). They had grown up during the Great Depression of the 1930s and entered adulthood with the world at war. Economic and military danger and near disaster on a global scale were things they had been forced to face. My generation was born early in World War II and grew up in the exciting and frightening post-war world of expanding materialism and Cold War, marked deeply by the Civil Rights movement and the long and tragic Vietnam War. I sought to recount this world of my generation in the book *Seeking the Light: America's Modern Quest for Peace, Justice, Prosperity, and Faith* (1998). By the end of the twentieth century, I and my peers had come to know a different kind of potential disaster, one that was conveyed through an unprecedented media blitz.

During 1999, one began to hear repeatedly "Y2K" (year 2000). The third millennium after the birth of Christ was both an exciting anticipation and a fearsome possibility. Popular films portrayed events that threatened to bring about the world's end by some malevolent force—asteroids in *Armageddon* (1998), aliens in *Independence Day* (1996), and dinosaurs in *Godzilla* (1998). I recounted in my 1997 book *Faithful in the Meantime* the mistaken Christian expectations of the world's end and the resulting confusion and despair of many Christian believers when 999 shifted without incident to the year 1000. Now I would be one of a small minority of humans to live during another millennium change. It was a symbolic and meaningful privilege, but one again surrounded by a widespread fear of doom (or the glory of Christ's return).

The fear in 1999 was heightened by two media preoccupations. One was suicide terrorists who might be targeting Americans with bombs all over the world—and such a feared disaster did strike on what joined "Y2K" as the fearsome "9-11." On that day early into the new millennium, large passenger planes were highjacked by terrorists and deliberately crashed into high-profile American buildings in Washington, D. C., and New York City.

The second media preoccupation was that cyber-terrorists likely were devising computer viruses that could create chaos in businesses and homes worldwide. There might be a technological Armaggedon as the calendars shifted to the year 2000. Computer chips and software now controlled the business records, utilities, military hardware, communication, and transportation by which most of the world was functioning. Unfortunately, most computer software had been designed without a change of century in mind, so that "00" might be read as 1900 instead of 2000—chaos indeed! The world literally spent billions of dollars toward the end of the 1990s trying to avoid this impending problem. In our mailbox in Anderson, Indiana, came numerous assurances that entities like our bank and local water plant were ready. Even so, we joined most others in planning for an alternate heating source in our home (a new gas unit in the fireplace that would run without electricity), buying bottled water, and having extra food and cash on hand. No one knew for sure what would happen.

On January 1, 2000, the weather could be very cold, and maybe nothing would be working. The front page of the December 26, 1999, edition of the Anderson, Indiana, city newspaper carried this announcement: "While police are normally busy during New Year's eve, a different set of circumstances this year—including paranoia induced by the millennium computer bug—has prompted local police to beef up their patrols throughout the last weekend of the century." "Paranoia" was too strong a word for the mindset of most people, but the uncertainty and general anxiety was definite. Never before had such a situation been experienced by humanity. Our fascinating new technologies could be our undoing.

One commentator put the uniqueness of the situation like this. Always before, the conveyors of religious prophetic warnings claimed to know in detail what would happen in the future; most, however, did not claim to know exactly when it all would happen. Now the computer technicians knew the precise second when the dramatic situation would occur, the moment the calendars rolled over to 2000; they just had no idea what would actually happen. Hopefully, there would be nothing highly unusual, at leasat nothing devastating.

Leading up to the fateful hour was my own family's 1999 celebration of Christmas, centered mostly around our three grandchildren and their excitement at receiving animated computer games (millennium bug free), a remote controlled race car, a very large doll that Emily named Miss Lulu, and much more. Ian was four, Emily three, and Ethan one. They were a joy to Arlene and me, although on some days we worried about what kind of world they would have to face. The two older ones already loved computers, knowing nothing of the big concerns surrounding their immediate vulnerability to the calendar hackers.

Arlene's mother—the grandkids called Evelyn "GG" (great grandmother)—was nearly eighty-four, had been living in the apartment in our home for almost two decades, and was increasingly feeble and frustrated as the new millennium approached. She had been so self-reliant, as had been the American culture with all its technical advances and wealth in the boom of the 1980s and 1990s. Big changes likely were coming soon, including the incapacity and then death of GG on November 15, 2004, and maybe even social chaos for the country and world. We tried to live each day more in faith than anxiety and, like everyone else, we waited and wondered.

While we waited on the new millennium, other changes came. Lillie S. McCutcheon (1921-1999), so significant in my personal and ministerial lives, died in March. I was asked by the Sowers/McCutcheon families to offer reflections on her life and ministry at her funeral in Columbus, Ohio, where she and her husband lived in retirement. My public comments were heartfelt and then published in *Reformation Witness* (fall 1999). In October, death also claimed Zella Hull Warren (1913-1999). During my first years as Dean of Anderson School of Theology in the 1970s, Zella was my faithful secretary and friend. Others close to Arlene and me also were lost to death in 1999, including Nancy Sowers in Dayton, Ohio, wife of "Brother Austin" who first brought me to Anderson, Indiana, and our dear Jewish friend Sylvia Levy in Chicago, Illinois. She and Arnold had sung "Sunrise, Sunset" at the wedding of our son Todd to Beth Hazen. Was the sun about to rise or tragically set on all humanity?

In November, 1999, Rev. Edward Nelson announced that he would be accepting a new pastoral assignment in Colorado. His tenure at Park Place

Church of God in Anderson had been controversial, partly because he was determined to make some significant changes so that the aging congregation could become attractive to a younger generation. His leaving added uncertainty to the earlier retirement of David L. Coolidge as minister of music, a vacancy not yet addressed. Being corporate secretary of the Park Place congregation at the time, the pastoral search process now needed would involve me directly. More than searching for another pastor or two, the congregation struggled to find unity within itself. There were many hurt feelings and conflicting agendas. The year 1999 was a difficult time of departures, deaths, and doubts about the future.

Ernest Gross died in Atlanta, bringing his family to Anderson for the funeral on December 28, 1999. His daughter Jodie, along with her husband John and their girls Jacquie and Jessica, stayed with us for two days and then returned to Atlanta on their way home in January, 2000, to their ministry assignment in Haiti. John would return to our home within weeks for knee surgery and several weeks of recovery. Ernie was laid to rest in Maplewood Cemetery, within blocks of our Anderson home. His burial place is adjacent to those of our dear friends John and Dora Batdorf. I joined James L. Edwards, president of Anderson University, in officiating at the brief committal service as the family huddled at the gravesite on a blustery winter afternoon. I was very conscious that the gravesite for Arlene and me had been purchased years before and lay not far away. We are called to minister to others while our own days remain uncertain. Arlene and I had no idea that she herself had only three more years of life. As it would turn out, I would have many more.

Meanwhile, I was completing three book projects that had absorbed my attention during a recent sabbatical leave that ended with the old millennium. In addition, I began some preliminary work on the first edition of this autobiography. I was careful to back-up the book files, not knowing what would happen to the campus computer system when 2000 finally arrived. In my annual report to Anderson University for 2000-2001, I noted having completed an especially heavy year of instruction, ranging from a freshman college class (Hebrew Roots of Christian Faith) to a doctoral class in the graduate School of Theology (quite a spread of students and subjects to teach at the same time!).

I had published two books that year and written a chapter for a third. I had served my first year as founding Editor of Anderson University Press and my eighth as corporate secretary of Park Place Church of God, where Fredrick H. Shively and I had been the primary designers of a major reorganization plan (part of the aftermath of the departure of pastor Edward Nelson). For the Church of God at large, I had served my thirteenth year as chair of the Bylaws Committee of the General Assembly and functioned as secretary of the small group that launched the Church of God Historical Society. I also had joined Arlo F. Newell as crisis consultants for the Dayspring congregation in Cincinnati, Ohio, that had suffered major controversy. Fortunately, this consultation was successful and in the years to come I would have additional contacts with this fine church as it rebuilt its ministries and staff. My life was anything but dull!

This intense activism had its downsides. I found myself musing over the culture that was all around me and already shaping my grandchildren more than I liked. Religious pluralism and rampant materialism were on all television screens one watched and in all the stores one visited. Obsessive capitalism and preoccupation with anything new seemed a mixture of genius and sickness. My book *Radical Christianity* (1999) helped me rethink a proud Christian tradition that dared to be counter-cultural, even at great risk. Our churches seemed to have strayed into the corrosive world of cultural accommodation. This is so easy to do; I probably had been a subtle part of it, although at least I tried to sound a warning.

I again had enjoyed a spiritual retreat in 2000, going as usual to the Gethsemani monastery in rural Kentucky. A professional journal I had begun reading in the 1980s is *Weavings: A Journal of the Christian Spiritual Life*. Its January/February 2000 issue featured the counter-cultural theme

"Poverty of Spirit." The editor's highlighted word was "exploitation." The signature of the culture of the 1990s had been the mindset of taking advantage—of opportunities, of natural resources, of neighbors, of strangers, of the weak and unwary, of those of other ethnic and religious backgrounds. The whole of the twentieth century in the West had been aggressive and scientific, warlike and opportunistic, bringing vast changes through an "appetite for ascendance" that often was willing to go for the jugular for profit or position.

By sharp contrast, the non-exploitative mind of Jesus did not even consider his unique relationship with God as something to be exploited. The "poor-in-spirit" followers of Jesus have no divine permission to secure themselves at the expense of others. Energy is to be spent on what is honorable, just, and loving. As the *Weavings* editor described true Christians: "Their hearts are not agitated by the booty of exploitation, but are stilled by the bounty of peace" (p. 3; see Phil. 4:4-9). So, "at this tumultuous turning point in our history," *Weavings* began the 2000 year with a new study of the Beatitudes, "landmarks for life in the Spirit." In this vein, I later would write a little essay titled "Please Don't Call Me Christian!" (see *Appendix B*). "The center of the Christin faith," I said, "is Jesus Christ, not a full identifying with all of the history, structures, and creeds that have carried the name 'Christian'."

I now was a mature minister in a professional sense, but less so in spiritual maturity. Part of my musing at the dawning of the year 2000 was my own track-record. My personality was irenic rather than abrasive, and I had been satisfied to be a minister-servant of the church, my students, and my readers. I did not think of myself as aggressive and competitive at the expense of others. I have never applied for any position, have been satisfied to serve as the supportive secretary in multiple settings, have been relatively conservative with money, not needing a lot of expensive items to live with. Even so, my scholarly pursuits and maybe even my workaholic inclination have not readily nourished a wholesome "pietism" that flourishes only when supported by sensitive spiritual disciplines. This may be one reason why the year 2000 would see me working hard to complete a book manuscript on Christian spirituality (*Authentic Spirituality*). As I wrote, I was searching, even while I was a committed believer. Writing had become my chosen spiritual discipline. Putting my thinking into well-chosen words helped me focus, organize, ponder, refine, and finally embrace and share.

Musings aside, the tense moment finally came. It started with the televised arrival of the year 2000 in Auckland, New Zealand, the new millennium's first appearance in the industrialized world—eighteen hours before it would circle the globe and arrive in Anderson, Indiana. I had enjoyed traveling widely in New Zealand in July, 1995, as part of the trip to Sydney, Australia, to participate in the tenth World Conference of the Church of God. Now I was pleased to see that the lights in Auckland did not suddenly go off when the reality of "2000" hit its computers. The threat of technological and social disaster lurked around the edges, but people danced in the streets nonetheless. This international spectacular went on all day, the last of the century and millennium. It was a magic rather than a tragic moment to be alive!

People everywhere were poised to party, ready for culturally rich celebrations that always included massive fireworks displays. The television network CNN brought the scenes to screens simultaneously around the world. Its reporters were rejoicing in the excitement and were poised to bring reports on any computer-related or terrorist-caused disasters. There were few if any. Things went well as hundreds of millions watched live scenes from the celebrations in China, Moscow, Bethlehem, London, at the pyramids in Egypt, and at the Vatican in Rome. Finally, the new year reached New York City and Washington, D. C. and the rest of the United States. Things had gone well, wonderfully well. The lights were still on. The year was 2000, with the future stretching forward, apparently to be real, although still uncomfortably unknown.

The big transition between millennia was paralleled in the organization of the cooperative work of the Church of God (Anderson) in North America. As chair of the Bylaws Committee of the General Assembly, it fell my lot to describe in writing the new structure (Church of God Ministries), detail its many specific relationships to the Assembly, and then present this writing formally to the Assembly for approval. Once this was done successfully in 1998, my attention turned to even more organizational matters.

There had developed a widespread concern that the Church of God movement was slowly disintegrating. I wrote an essay titled "Confession and Celebration" that appeared in the April/May, 2001, issue of *Communion*, in the fall, 2001, issue of *Reformation Witness*, and then as a free-standing booklet by Anderson University Press. I said: "Like all movements, the Church of God has been limited in its vision and effectiveness by its time and place in history. Nevertheless, it appears to me that the essential theological instincts of this reformation movement have been wise all along and remain timely for the opening years of this new century and millennium." Then I identified and explored five of these critical "instincts." I was gratified by the reception of this essay and pleased that my colleague Gilbert W. Stafford had published a book in 2000 titled *Church of God at the Crossroads* that deserved and received widespread attention. For my essay, see *Appendix I.*

My ministry came along during the years when milestones of the Church of God movement were being celebrated. Since some of my teaching and several of my books have focused on this reform movement, and since my ministry had become prominent nationally and internationally, it is not surprising that I became something of a "millennium man." A highlight of my life was in June, 1980, when the centennial of the movement was celebrated with a World Conference in Anderson, Indiana, and I was chosen to deliver the keynote sermon in the very large Warner Auditorium. The Church of God in Germany had celebrated its centennial in 1993, flying me there to speak in Hamburg. In 2002 the Church of God in India celebrated its centennial. While my teaching commitments made impossible my travel to Shillong for the requested preaching assignment, I sent written greetings to the crowd that I was told numbered nearly fifty thousand. It was an honor to have been invited.

In 2006 I led the planning that marked a century of the Church of God movement in Anderson, Indiana. That same year my book *Seeking Higher Ground* was released, a centennial history of Park Place Church of God in Anderson. In 2007 my wife Jan and I journeyed to Jamaica to share with the Church of God there its big celebration of one hundred years. I delivered the official thanksgiving sermon in the "mother" church in Kingston, with leaders of the nation's political parties in attendance.

Much was changing as these centennials were being celebrated. The 2001 academic and professional catalog of Evangel Publishing House (publisher for the Brethren in Christ denomination) was carrying photos of the covers of five of my books that it had published and was still marketing. I had enjoyed my relationship with the editor of Evangel, Glen A. Pierce, who soon would move to a mission assignment in Africa. His departure in January, 2001, opened the door for my longtime friend Joseph Allison who had much experience with Warner Press in Anderson and other publishers. That favored my continued relationship with Evangel Press. In 2005, when I retired from teaching at Anderson University and moved across the street to be Special Assistant to the General Director of Church of God Ministries, Joe was now on that scene directing publications for the Church of God—so our working relationship continued in yet a new setting.

The new millennium, while a large unknown, had its hopeful side. It also was exceedingly dangerous. When Wednesday, September 12, 2001, dawned, everything was changed. The sun rose over the absence of a New York national landmark, a smoldering ruin in lower Manhattan where the two gigantic World Trade Center towers had stood. In Washington, D. C., the Pentagon was still on fire and deeply scarred, along with the collective sense of American security. Thousands were dead. Terrorists had managed to use highjacked commercial airplanes as flying bombs to effectively bring havoc, suspend all air traffic in the United States, and force evacuations of U. S. facilities worldwide. President George Bush declared war on terrorism. This is exactly what had been feared at the beginning of the new millennium.

The shocking events of December 7, 1941, had changed the world into which I was being born. Now on September 11, 2001, the new millennium had begun with another Pearl Harbor, this time right in the heart of the United States. Something new suddenly entered daily conversation. It was frequent references to "9-11," the day the world shuddered and shifted. I first saw the New York devastation on a little television my colleague James W. Lewis had brought to his office desk next to mine in Hartung Hall on the Anderson University campus. The sights on that screen would never leave me. The pride of the United States was on fire! The country's heart mourned and was afraid. Somehow, however different it would be, life would go on. Mine would have to include a spiritual deepening.

Balancing Intellect and Spirit

While dramatic events had unbalanced the nation, I was still seeking balance in my own being. I had been the chapel speaker seven years earlier as the second semester of the school year 1992-1993 was beginning in Anderson University's School of Theology. I had been asked by the dean of the chapel, Dwight L. Grubbs, to share my personal testimony of spiritual journeying. The focus was to be on the task of balancing scholarship and Christian spirituality, a constant challenge for seminarians and their teachers. It had been my pleasure years earlier to bring Dwight to the School of Theology faculty from Houston, Texas. The previous summer he and I had participated in a spiritual retreat at the Abbey of Gethsemani in rural Kentucky, the Trappist monastery that was the longtime home of Thomas Merton. Seeing me as a strong academic, Dwight had expressed delight at my keen interest in spiritual questing. Thus, he had come to me with his request that I address very personally the subject at hand.

I began my chapel address by observing that my father, already long deceased, had not been an intellectual, but he certainly had been an intelligent and self-made man. He had exemplified the male stereotype of a rugged individualist who is practical and produces without showing much feeling. He was a carpenter. He made his own plans and generally was in control of at least his immediate surroundings. Although I was more academically inclined, a little of his style had found its way into the pattern of my life journey. The revivalistic, experience-centered orientation of the Free Methodist Church and the Church of God movement was my church heritage, but so was the more intellectual Presbyterian approach of my undergraduate experience at Geneva College. I was a church hybrid.

My graduate programs at the Anderson, Asbury, and then Chicago seminaries were contrasting experiments in balancing scholarship and spirituality, with emphasis on scholarship bringing richness and sanity to the shallow thoughtlessness of much church life. My doctoral work in the University of Chicago setting brought the temptation of a sophisticated arrogance. Now, years later, having waded through another doctoral program at Indiana University, why had I given priority to a place like the Gethsemani monastery? That's what Dr. Grubbs wanted me to share in the seminary chapel.

I tried to give those graduate students answers to what I thought were important questions, but I made clear that my I-have-the-answers focus had begun to shift. Maybe it was the mellowing of the years, maybe the distancing from my deceased father, maybe my deep and practical commitment to the church. I think it was these and more. It also was the fruit of the scholarship itself. Truth turns out to be less neat than it once seemed, no less real, just less neat. Philosophical systems, high sounding as they are, all have their vulnerabilities. The revered scientific method of our technological age has its limits—and sometimes even its demonic results. The Christian theological task continues because no "systematic" theology has proved or will prove fully adequate and enduring. Language and culture change, and so must theology if it is to remain meaningful to new generations of readers. Truth may be a fixed reality, but not our understandings and expressions of it.

I had come to appreciate the role of paradox in theology and to see wisdom in certain of its inevitable ambiguities. In fact, I would write a whole book on the subject (*Caught Between Truths,* 2007). Emil Brunner once said that "Christian truth is a bird in flight between two opposites." One does not have to be dogmatic to be conservative. In reaction to classic liberalism, I had grown up much like the typical fundamentalist prepared to package the faith in a set of rational propositions, preach them as articulated absolutes, and protect them from all comers. Now I had come to see truth more in a person, Jesus Christ, than in any abstract and absolute proposition about that person. For me, this has added focus and richness and a relaxed flexibility to my faith.

Faith and understanding grow in living relationship to Jesus Christ as much as in rational inquiry. Granted, without rational inquiry and criticism, faith often grows in random and perverted ways. Nonetheless, the role of real and intimate relationship is crucial. I smile approvingly at a cynical but wise comment attributed to Winston Churchill: "A fanatic is one who can't change his mind and won't change the subject." My 2011 book *Heart of the Matter* would focus the believer on relationship with the person of Jesus rather than the tangle of ideas that swirl around him. Its revised edition in 2016 only strengthened this belief.

In reaction to Protestant scholasticism, Pietism was an inevitable and important movement in church history. Great spiritual awakenings, such as the nineteenth-century holiness movement and the modern charismatic movement, all evidence a critical corrective. My own journey has made me increasingly sensitive to such a corrective. As I became immersed in the scholastic, my heart had cried for the pietistic, not instead of, but in addition to. "Love God with all your mind," yes, but also "with all your heart." Given the differing right and left brain functions, maybe the verse should be paraphrased, "Love God with all your brain."

I hope that saying all of this was helpful to those young seminarians back in 1993. I was trying to mentor them, just as many valued mentors have nurtured my professional and spiritual lives.

My Spiritual Mentors

My heroes in this quest for balancing scholarship and spirituality have included the following twelve giants who have crossed my path in helpful ways. How blessed I have been! Some have been more "famous" than others, but fame is hardly the issue.

1. John Wesley (1703-1791) was a classicist searching for personal assurance. He was a high-church Anglican running class meetings to insure the integrity of spiritual transformation among the English common folk of the eighteenth century. The Wesleyan tradition he spawned is shared by the Church of God movement and the Free Methodist Church, and my long involvement with the Wesleyan Theological Society has been crucial for me. Wesley's combining of reasoning and spiritual experience, along with church tradition and biblical authority, has been a pattern I have sought to probe and follow. See Henry Rack, *Reasonable Enthusiast: John Wesley and the Rise of Methodism* (1992), Randy L. Maddox, *Responsible Grace* (1994), and Kenneth J. Collins, *A Real Christian: The*

Life of John Wesley (1999). Randy and Ken have been valued personal friends.

2. Benjamin T. Roberts (1823-1893) was a sophisticated and politically active religious leader in the American holiness movement of the nineteenth century. He was founder of the Free Methodist Church, the denomination so central to the lives of both sets of my grandparents and the family of my first wife. His namesake, Roberts Wesleyan College, was nearly the site of my collegiate teaching career. I honor who Roberts was and much of what he stood for. See Howard A. Snyder's 2006 biography titled *Populist Saints: B. T. and Ellen Roberts*, which I successfully nominated for the 2007 Smith/Wynkoop Book Award of the Wesleyan Theological Society. Howard has been a valued personal friend.

3. Daniel S. Warner (1842-1895) was the primary pioneer of the Church of God movement, the church body so central in my life and ministry. In the face of the tendency of human institutions and agendas to dominate church life, he sounded a warning against rampant denominationalism and heralded the centrality of spiritual experience and the ministry and gifting of the Holy Spirit. Occasionally, I was teased about looking like Warner, and actually did a little acting, playing him in various settings. My 1995 biography of him is titled *It's God's Church!* See the chapter on Warner in my book *The Wisdom of the Saints* (2003). Although Warner died about the time my grandparents were being born, his legacy has remained very alive for me. My little booklet *The Top Ten* highlights the ways he is still relevant.

4. Lillie S. McCutcheon (1921-1999) was my personal pastor from my childhood, a woman of God who gave her life loving and nurturing a congregation in the little town of Newton Falls, Ohio. She had opportunities to assume "important" national positions in the church, but chose to stay home, pastoring as many as five generations of the same family over a period of forty-three years! Her influential *The Symbols Speak* (1964) shared her view of the prophecies in the New Testament book of Revelation. I dealt with her view over the years, often not agreeing, but always respectful. While uneducated formally, she was highly gifted and actively encouraged the education of others. See my 1992 biography of her, *She Came Preaching: Life and Ministry of Lillie S. McCutcheon.* See the chapter on McCutcheon in my book *The Wisdom of the Saints* (2003). She was a gift of God to me—and to so many others. I would be remiss not to name her brother and longtime associate pastor, Austin E. Sowers.

5. William H. Russell (1923-2009). Born in Indiana and reared in Chicago, Dr. Russell served in World War II and then received a high-quality education at the universities of Chicago and Wisconsin. He came to Geneva College in Pennsylvania to teach history in 1954. I first met him in a classroom when I was a Geneva freshman in 1959. Dr. Russell was an excellent teacher, the chief mentor for my history major, and a model Christian gentleman active in the Reformed Presbyterian Church locally and nationally. I was impressed by his eye for detail, his disciplined approach to academics and Christian faith, and his gentle way of relating to people. He became Dean of Geneva College in 1963, the year that Arlene and I graduated and married. Bill nurtured in me a call to teaching and how that teaching could be coordinated with a call to Christian ministry. I came to be in his debt more than he was ever aware.

6. D. Elton Trueblood (1900-1994) was my teacher. He was both a Quaker and a Harvard philosopher. He was transformed by the idea of God as "person" and the rational credibility of simple Christian faith. He helped open for me the doors to the intellectual enterprise that should be pursued by serious believers and to the validity of prayer, even intercessory prayer in our scientific age. One of the more important interpreters of Christian faith in the twentieth century, Trueblood encouraged my early writing efforts, supplying a foreword for my 2007 book *Caught Between Truths* (he had died without ever seeing the finished product). See his 1974 autobiography titled *While It Is Day*. It encouraged me to write this autobiography while it was still day for me.

7. Robert H. Reardon (1919-2007) was my president and mentor as I served from 1973 to 1983 as dean of Anderson School of Theology. He believed in me, opened doors for me, and stood firm on basic principles in very volatile decades. Reardon reflected wisely and sometimes humorously on the early years of the Church of God movement in his books *The Early Morning Light* (1979) and *This Is the Way It Was* (1991). He was a warm and sincere Christian believer who was the president of Anderson University for twenty-five years, championing the crucial combination of faith and learning. I gratefully recorded his life and wisdom in my 2004 biography of him titled *Staying on Course: A Biography of Robert H. Reardon*. See the chapter on Reardon in my book *The Wisdom of the Saints* (2003) and throughout my book *Faith, Learning, and Life* (1991). See also the dedication page in his honor in my book *Enriching Mind and Spirit* (2007) that records the history of higher education in the Church of God worldwide. Bob was a wise man and a dear friend who believed in me from early in my career.

8. Robert A. Nicholson (1923-2017) was my educational colleague when we were fellow deans at Anderson College, and then my president as I served as vice-president for academic affairs and dean of the college beginning in 1983. A strong Christian believer, he built a quality faculty and a wide range of academic programs on the Anderson campus beginning in 1958. He did so with a servant heart, while always active in church music, publishing, and strategic planning. He and I became "family" in a new way when his granddaughter Jenni married my stepson

Jordan in 2004. Nick's life story is in his 2006 autobiography titled *So I Said Yes! A Personal Memoir* that I was privileged to publish through Anderson University Press. In his final year he was nearly blind. I visited him weekly to read aloud editorials in the *New York Times,* his favorite news source. See the Nicholson materials throughout my book *Faith, Learning, and Life* (1991).

9. James Earl Massey (1930-2018) was one of my successors in the deanship of Anderson School of Theology. A superb writer, pastor, educator, musician, and lecturer, Massey is known as a "prince among preachers." Prominent especially in the African-American church community, he also has been an articulate ambassador of Christian integrity and unity across racial and denominational lines worldwide. I had the privilege of editing a 1995 volume in his honor, *Sharing Heaven's Music,* and editing and publishing his 2002 autobiography titled *Aspects of My Pilgrimage: An Autobiography.*

In my 2011 book *Heart of the Matter*, I included this wise man as one of my theological conversation partners featured throughout—along with C. S. Lewis, Thomas Merton, Clark H. Pinnock, D. Elton Trueblood, and Thomas C. Oden. Although he returned to Alabama in retirement, Dr. Massey and I kept in regular touch, especially through his final struggle with cancer. I was honored to offer a tribute at his funeral in Detroit and co-edit the volume of his select writings, *Views from the Mountain* (2018).

10. Gustav Jeeninga (1924-2006) was a Dutchman who had been a Nazi prisoner of war and then in 1947 immigrated to the United States to prepare for Christian ministry at Anderson College. Joining the faculty in 1960, he became a widely-traveled and well-known biblical archaeologist. Superb photographer and teacher, Jeeninga opened the minds and imaginations of thousands of young people to the rich history behind the biblical text. Beginning my teaching career as a substitute for him while he was on sabbatical in 1966-1967, we became colleagues, close friends, and fellow travelers to the biblical lands. I had the privilege of editing and publishing his 2002 autobiography titled *Doors to Life: The Stories of Gustav Jeeninga*, and then conducting his funeral in Florida in 2006. "Gus" was a special colleague and friend.

11. Gene W. Newberry (1915-2009) was my first seminary teacher of Christian theology and then my predecessor in the deanship of Anderson School of Theology. Always a practical and dedicated churchman, for decades he combined a graduate professorship with writing and teaching an adult Sunday school class at Park Place Church of God in Anderson, Indiana. He remained my mentor and close friend throughout his long life, always calling me "Dean," always emphasizing the positive. Gene was not a scholar's scholar, but he had and encouraged intellectual integrity. He was not an emotional revivalist, but his faith was personal, rich, and deep—a great combination. The Newberry autobiography of 2000 is titled *A Boy from Lewis County*.

12. Clark H. Pinnock (1937-2012) was one of the leading Christian theologians of the last fifty years. He challenged "evangelicalism" to avoid being overly defined by fixed theological systems of another time that risk losing the vitality of the Spirit's current witness to biblical meaning. The mission of Jesus Christ in today's pluralistic world demands authentic life in the Spirit and openness to fresh biblical insight. I prize my personal relationship with this wise and precious Christian man. I value his many books, including *Flame of Love* (1996) and *Most Moved Mover* (2001)—my name and endorsing statement appear on the back cover. I was privileged to author his intellectual biography, *Journey Toward Renewal* (2000), contribute the biographical chapter on him in a book of essays published in his honor, *Semper Reformandum* (2003), and co-author with him *The*

Scripture Principle: Reclaiming the Full Authority of the Bible (2006). Pinnock graciously wrote an endorsement of this autobiography of mine (see the cover). Clark was a tall man with poor eyesight. When in his presence, I grew taller and saw more clearly.

All twelve of these outstanding men and women were skilled in their differing ways at balancing the sophisticated and the practical, the world of the mind and the ways of the world. They were scholars and ministers, leaders and servants. Church of God movement pioneers like Daniel S. Warner were not so much anti-intellectual as ultra-supernaturalist. They were possessed by a sense of immediate divine presence and activity. God was here and on the move. God's current cause caught them up and carried them along.

Historians and biographers like myself now have analyzed the perceptions of these amazing people and found categories in which to place them. However, I caution that we always are in danger of losing their sense of the reality of a transcendent God who is with us to make a difference in us, the church, and world. Scholarship is called to serve, not supplant or subvert such immediacy of experience. Christian spirituality, made more wise through the disciplines of the mind, insists on experiencing and embodying what scholarship helps to clarify

One of my books is titled *Guide of Soul and Mind: The Story of Anderson University* (1992). Another is *Enriching Mind and Spirit* (2007), a history of higher education in the Church of God. This mission of guiding both soul and mind is part of the genius and challenge of a church-related campus like Anderson University. The goal is both to dignify scholarship and nurture spirituality, assuming that neither is healthy without the gift of the other. During its early years, the published slogan of the Anderson campus was "Where Spirituality Predominates." Today, some of the particulars of that early spirituality would not appeal and would even be amusing to us (no coffee, dancing, or sports on Sunday).

But the goal should endure, not over against but in league with serious scholarship.

What about me? I have learned that I must *be* as well as *do*. I must pray as well as research and write. It helps occasionally to be silent in a Trappist monastery as well as talk in classrooms and pulpits and on paper. I must *love* as well as *teach*, *learn*, and *write*. I need to be *in touch*, yes with good theology, historiography, and exegesis, but also with good personal religion, real faith, and simple trust.

While reading theological works, I have come to value the biographies and autobiographies of those producing the works. Knowing the life setting of the writer enhances real understanding of the writing (one reason for me to write this autobiography). I need to know contexts and be in touch with my feelings, faith, and sisters and brothers with whom I can journey. I need to be *in the books* and *in Christ* and *in the church* in order to approach adequacy as a man and a minister in this troubled world. I need to be still and know, to touch and see that the Lord is truly good!

I reflected this perspective in my February 1, 1976, article in *Vital Christianity* titled "Christian Scholars." I then was Dean of Anderson School of Theology and working hard at telling the church that seminary education, properly conceived, is crucial to the church's life. I wrote:

> Surrounded by a wealth of information and trained in the art of objectivity, the scholar has been accepted as something of a twentieth-century knight in quest of an elusive thing called "truth." There is honor in the quest—and there is also much danger. The danger? It is always possible to become so fond of fact-collecting that there is no room left for wisdom. Surrounded by computers, we may know so much that we don't understand anything! The church of today is crying for Christian scholars, men and women whose hearts are as

warm as their heads are full. Bring on the humble people who have a vision of truth that adds wisdom to the facts. Open the doors to the educational work of the Holy Spirit!

I concluded that seminary chapel address back in January, 1993, with the announcement that I had made progress on my spiritual journey, but I still had a long way to go. I asked that my friends and colleagues be patient with me—and join me. I was and am a pilgrim in progress, and these present pages are but an interim report.

When the year 2000 arrived, I was still on the journey, had just used the journey image as the subtitle for my 2000 intellectual biography of Clark H. Pinnock (*Journey Toward Renewal*), and had selected the title *Following the Light* (2000) for my documentary history of the Church of God. Soon I would choose *Following Our Lord* (2008) for a another book title on the history of the Church of God (Anderson). I was still journeying myself, trying to follow the light of Christ into the new millennium and the final phase of my earthly life. In fact, I called the last chapter of my (2016) book *Heart of the Matter* "Tramps for the Truth," saying that "we are all movers, brothers and sisters on a continuing faith journey.... The God who first called us to the journey also walks by our sides, showing us the way."

Approaching the Academic Classroom

It was in college and seminary classrooms that I sought constantly to balance intellect and spirit. I first was prepared to teach American history at the high school level. Geneva College was the scene of this preparation and an excellent educational place for me. My supervised practice teaching at nearby Beaver Falls High School was superb. However, my calling turned out to be quite different. After my practice teaching in 1962-1963, I would not enter a high school classroom again until 2005 when my wife, Jan, asked me to lecture on Islam to her world literature classes at

Anderson High School. So, I taught in high school in two different millennia, but very little in either. Most of my work was at the collegiate and graduate school levels. Some comments about that work are in order.

I recall what I said on October 23, 1976, at the memorial service for Dr. Boyce W. Blackwelder that was convened in the Adam W. Miller Chapel of Anderson School of Theology where I then was Dean. Boyce had been my seminary teacher of New Testament and Greek; I had become his Dean and soon I would edit a 1990 book in his honor (*Listening to the Word of God*). Now, suddenly, he was dead from a heart attack. I stood before the filled chapel and said this:

> Just a few years ago I was a green and frightened ministerial student, just married and out of college, anxious about my capabilities for handling the demands of graduate study, particularly concerned about my ability to deal with a vigorous study of the Greek language. So I slipped into the office of my academic advisor, Dr. Blackwelder, who had just joined the School of Theology faculty. He was humble, encouraging, impressive, soon to become my friend and teacher. I remember his passion for precision, his saying that "a scholar is a person who is careful with the facts." I remember the paradox of his style, both his gentle and humble simplicity and his tendency to forget the restricted size of a classroom, his voice booming his insights, with the tone of his words having borrowed from the biblical text a note of authority and finality. I remember that he remained a student himself, persistent in his own quest for truth, often saying that "no man's opinion on a subject is any better than his information on that subject." I remember how he cared for me as an individual student. I remember the seeds he sought to plant in the minds and hearts of his students—discipline, a love for God's Word, a

respect for the pulpit, a loyalty to the task. I remember Boyce, my teacher, and I praise God for my memories!

Over the years I tried to put into practice the teaching keynotes I admired in Boyce. He and I were different, but not that different.

Late in my teaching career I developed a pattern of writing my own class textbooks. These included *God As Loving Grace* (theology), *Faithful in the Meantime* (eschatology), *Authentic Spirituality* (Christian spirituality), and *Discerning the Divine* (seminary class on the doctrine of God). These books and others, like *The Scripture Principle* (2006, written with Clark H. Pinnock) and *Caught Between Truths* (2007) remain in use as textbooks in various colleges in the United States, Canada, Kenya, Germany, and elsewhere. Many of my students took pride in their teacher having written the textbook. Occasionally, a student would reflect negatively on this, saying that it would be a broader experience to hear from someone else. I never used my books alone, of course, and always included in the syllabus a long list of other relevant materials, some of which were required reading.

Students at Anderson University always completed formal evaluations of classroom experiences. In my classes, as in those of others, responses to the same class varied widely—"I learned very little" and "The best college class I ever took!" I cherish some evaluations that were both positive and deeply felt. In her written evaluation of my spring 2001 college class "Introduction to Christian Theology," Erin Moss said:

> This marks the beginning of my theological journey.... As knowledge often does, this class has left me with a greater appreciation for my own ignorance.... I need to establish a theology that is really my own.... The Wesleyan Quadrilateral has given me a grid with which to balance my ongoing learning.... Remembering a lecture from the beginning of the

class, I am challenged to love my faith, truly believe it, really experience it, and always progress in it. I plan on doing just that for the rest of my life.

All students do not relish their classroom experiences, but Erin is one of many of mine who did, and she verbalized well several things that I hoped to stimulate in my students over the years. She's now a Michigan pastor and trustee of Anderson University.

A teacher is also evaluated periodically by colleagues. In December, 2000, Dr. Merle D. Strege, my department chair at the time, prepared a biennial evaluation of my performance, saying in part:

> To his classroom work Barry brings the added dimension of his widening involvement in Wesleyan and Evangelical circles. He is Editor of the *Wesleyan Theological Journal* and his recently published biography of Clark Pinnock has broadened the reach of Barry's work. This work is a credit to the University. I believe that Barry has published at least three books since my last evaluation. He is an indefatigable researcher and writer. Barry remains a trusted colleague and an invaluable source of advice about University history and policy. His many years of experience as an AU administrator serve as important cautions and guides in departmental deliberations. He is a very loyal faculty member. He can be counted on to attend and participate in all department functions and gladly accepts assignments that he might be given from time to time. Despite a very heavy writing schedule, Barry also finds time to support student activities of all kinds.

Merle was kind, and certainly right about at least this. I was very busy and committed simultaneously to students, writing, and the well being of the Department of Religious Studies, the School of Theology, and Anderson University as a whole.

Ever since my April, 1989, election by the Anderson University board of trustees to the special rank of "University Professor," I had worked hard to be what that rank designated, "a senior and distinguished scholar/teacher-in-residence, honored for particular potential to combine publication and teaching in the service of the mission of the University." I treasure those words and the fact that the university chose to attach them to my name.

Journeying with High School Classmates

My many years of college and seminary teaching never distracted me from remembering, keeping in touch with, and serving the 1959 Jackson-Milton High School class of which I was a member. The class had elected me president in our junior year. Some thought I was smart and a natural leader. Some knew my care with detail and my rather shy nature. Maybe someone like me could get the job done (mostly symbolic) without much fuss or bother to the others—who certainly didn't want to do it themselves. Whatever the reason for my election, my own sense of leadership responsibility in this role did not end with our 1959 graduation. I am naturally nostalgic and committed to these people for life, even though I have lived quite a distance from all of them in miles and from most of them in life pursuit.

Beginning in the mid-1970s, I occasionally called a few class members just to stay in touch. Later, I visited the homes of many in Ohio, Florida, Vermont, and elsewhere. It was not until the eighteenth year after our graduation that we finally gathered for a first class reunion. After our second reunion at an irregular interval, we caught our stride by convening at our 35th, 40th, 45th, and 50th years beyond our graduation. We usually gathered in a restaurant in the area of the old high school where many people still lived. Our 50th was special. A new high school building was nearly finished in June, 2009. We were guided through it by the proud principal, then walked through the old school on our own, and finally came together at a lovely facility nearby associated with the church of one of our members. We touched the old in its last days, saw the new before its first days, and wondered how many days yet remained for each of us. Given our advancing ages, we abandoned the five-year intervals and began annual dinners.

I was the main organizer and master of ceremonies for all the reunions, my role as class president still persisting. I brought with me each time an updated and detailed class directory for everyone, having gathered the detail and done the printing myself. There was little alcohol and no loud band dominating our gatherings. The point was to get reacquainted and remember "the good old days." Well beyond half of the living class members were present at each reunion. At our 35th in 1994, we were at Wranglers in North Jackson where one of our members, Nancy (Yerke) Audino, was a cook. I did a taped interview with her before the big dinner event, research for my 1998 book *Seeking the Light.* This book includes a tracking of the lives of my classmates over the decades, intended as a barometer of the society at large. Once we were just kids together; now we were grandparents, at least those still alive. By 2006 the class had lost nine members, the earliest being Charles Creque in 1972 and the most recent Frank Balent in 2004. By our 50th in 2009, the number had grown to eleven of our original fifty-three with the loss of Bill Price and John Steffans—John having grown up in Craig Beach just three blocks from my home.

In April, 1987, I was invited to return to my high school in Ohio for a special banquet and all-school assembly. I and four other Jackson- Milton graduates had been selected as new inductees into the school's "Hall of

Fame." It was delightful to be back in the old gym. It still smelled the same as when I played basketball there in the 1950s. I was being honored along with a deputy sheriff from Los Angeles, a female captain in the U. S. Army, the president of an oil distribution company, and the owner of an environmental company that had completed a remarkable clean-up of nearby Lake Erie. I was celebrated before the student body as an accomplished author and the academic dean and vice-president of an American university. In my remarks, I noted that I once had been one of the Craig Beach kids bused to North Jackson. A group of ragged-looking characters stood and cheered at the mention of someone important having come from Craig Beach! I once had been one of them. I hope they were encouraged to open themselves to a possible future bigger than envisioned before.

Retiring, But Not Slowing Down

The new millennium found me beginning to think about retirement and pondering aspects of my life journey. It had taken an unexpected road. I was reared in a wonderful congregation in Newton Falls, Ohio, where the pastoral leadership was exceptional. One theme I heard stressed on occasion in that congregation was *the church as God intends it*. Sometimes this ideal was highlighted by using the failures from the long history of the Roman Catholic Church. This Church of God (Anderson) congregation featured a "radical," free-church, Wesleyan-informed mentality, but one with little awareness of the historic church beyond reacting to a long pattern of church apostasy that was perceived through "prophetic" eyes. Part of my ministry was to reassess that perspective (see my book *Faithful in the Meantime*). I have always chosen to remain rooted in my church heritage, but sometimes I have not mimicked some of its views,

From my home church I absorbed the love of good pastoral leadership, an appreciation for nurturing young leaders, and a vision of the church as much more than a flawed religious institution. After some years of my own ministry, my spiritual need had led me—of all places—to a Roman Catholic monastery! Beginning in the 1980s, I became an annual Protestant retreatant in a bastion of historic Catholicism. The location was the longtime home of Thomas Merton, one of the more widely published and read Roman Catholic spiritual writers of all time. The Abbey of Gethsemani has sat quietly in the hills of rural Kentucky since 1848 as a spiritual oasis. It carries on a ministry of hospitality, providing spiritual retreats characterized by solitude, silence, and Christian reflection. In one way, making this Abbey a spiritual home was quite a turn from my free-church Protestant upbringing; in another way, it was a growing up into the wider church without denying anything precious from my youth. My boyhood pastor and church heritage had called for an elimination of denominational walls and a unity of believers based on relationship to Jesus Christ and not organizational affiliations. I was practicing that radical call.

The monastery environment, contrary to common perception, is not intended to disdain the world. The point is an intentional holding still, being in touch with oneself and God, cherishing the long tradition of God in the world, actually practicing prayer and God's presence, relishing the sweet sounds of silence, and finally realizing that true value lies in *being* rather than in mere *doing*. My book *Authentic Spirituality* (2001, republished 2006) highlights the several historic streams of Christian spirituality, including the contemplative. Does this make me a Protestant or Catholic? The answer is that I now am a Christian who belongs to the whole church, protests on occasion, and chooses to be "catholic" in the best sense. I am reaching for the wider stream of Christian riches, benefiting from all and bound by none.

My journey of renewal has only begun, but at least the corner has been turned. I have been helped by intense involvement in a decade-long dialogue between the Church of God (Anderson) and the Independent Christian Churches/Churches of Christ, both bodies having much in common with the Believers Church tradition. The resulting 1997 book highlighting this ecumenical journey, co-authored by James North and myself, is titled *Coming Together in Christ: Pioneering a New Testament Way to Christian Unity*. At least for those of us involved, this was a wonderful journey of new acquaintance, cooperation, and insight. So has been my many years with the Wesleyan Theological Society and most recently the Wesleyan Holiness Connection.

This life journey of mine has been heavy with professional involvements and attempts at reaching for increased spiritual maturity. As the new millennium dawned, my journey came to include in 2003 a deep and dark valley that arrived unexpectedly, followed by the equally unexpected joys of a whole new day (losing a beloved spouse, Arlene, to cancer and receiving the gift of another spouse, Jan). This jolting experience of loss and gain was soon paralleled by my son's losing a spouse through divorce, not once but twice. Jan and I sought to stand supportively by him in these years of pain.

The 2005 year saw me choosing to end my teaching career at Anderson University, although I continued as Editor of Anderson University Press, taught part-time on occasion, and began a new role as Special Assistant to the General Director of Church of God Ministries. This meant moving my office across the street and focusing more directly on the life of the Church of God movement at large. I chose retirement because financially it was possible and I would have the time and freedom to pursue a range of other ministry tasks. When my first wife died, I gave my home on Falls Court to my son and bought a nearby condo. When I remarried, Jan and I sold our properties and began freshly together at our new location on Wilson Blvd. not far from the Anderson campus. My son Todd remarried, bringing into our lives the special gifts of Laura and her daughter Samantha.

Several gracious recognitions came with retirement, typical after a long tenure at Anderson University (1966-2005). I was honored with a party and gift from the Department of Religious Studies, voted the "Emeritus" status by the University board of trustees, honored along with three of my retiring colleagues (Donald Cruikshank, Barbara Douglas, and Jerry Sipe) at a wonderful campus dinner occasion, given a chair with the school's seal and my name inscribed, and asked to give the benediction at the 2006 University commencement. My wife Jan organized a display board in the reception area prior to the retirement dinner, featuring my books, old photos, etc. It made for good conversation as people arrived and visited.

I also was asked to deliver to the faculty an "Omega Lecture." My task was to highlight my many years on campus and then offer reflections and even recommendations. Here are a few of my retiring comments:

1. I owe a great debt to this campus. It has provided me with a vision of excellence, good academic tools, a large network of wonderful relationships, and a reasonable livelihood. I am truly thankful.

2. This campus was founded in 1917 to serve the ministry needs of sincere Christians. Time naturally has seen many expansionary changes in campus programming, facilities, and personnel appointments. None of these new directions or larger arenas in themselves are antithetical to the school's original purpose. Even so, mission can get lost easily in the flurry of intense activity and marketplace pressures. Today's School of Theology and Department of Religious Studies, for instance, may not always

be the cash cows of the institution; nevertheless, I hope that the day never comes when they are not respected and supported as being at the heart of what this place has always been about.

3. Campus growth continues. I was added to this faculty in 1966 because enrollment was growing and a new faculty position was justified. Now, as I retire thirty-nine years later, I am being replaced by two full-time persons during another time of institutional growth and faculty need. I rejoice in the growth and that my replacements are two women with exceptional qualifications and teaching potential. It is time to put our money where our mouths have been in actual support of women truly called of God to ministry.

4. The doors of tomorrow are wide open for me and for all of us. My companion of thirty-nine years, Arlene, died in 2003. Despite such a sad and unexpected omega, God truly specializes in alphas. I have received the divine gift of a wonderful new companion, Jan, and some fresh light for the path of life still ahead. So, I journey on in joy, full of gratitude, and directed by faith.

Upon my retirement from Anderson University in 2005 and the assuming of a part-time position as Special Assistant to the General Director of Church of God Ministries, I became technically unqualified to continue my service as a member and chair of the Committee on Bylaws and Organization of the General Assembly of the Church of God. One is not allowed to be an employee at the national church level and also serve on an Assembly committee. Therefore, my successor in the chair, P. Roger Brewer, called me to stand before the 2006 Assembly while he read the following resolution:

Whereas, Dr. Barry L. Callen has been a faithful member and servant of the Church of God and its General Assembly for many years; and

Whereas, Dr. Callen has served the Church of God as author, professor, and Dean of Anderson University and the School of Theology; and

Whereas, Dr. Callen served as Chair of the Bylaws Committee of the General Assembly of the Church of God from June 1, 1993, through June 30, 2005; and

Whereas, Dr. Callen has been sensitive to the needs and wishes of the General Assembly during his service; and

Whereas, Dr. Callen has been sensitive to the needs of the members of the Bylaws Committee in that he has pre-written the many changes and amendments needed for the General Assembly prior to the meetings of the Committee so as to make easier the work of the Committee; and

Whereas, Dr. Callen has guided the development and re-writing of the Bylaws for the General Assembly made necessary by the recent change of organizational structure;

Be It Therefore Resolved that the General Assembly of the Church of God recognize Dr. Callen's splendid leadership with a plaque that has been prepared by the office of the General Director; and

Be It Further Resolved that this Assembly recognize Dr. Callen's service with a demonstration of love through a standing ovation.

This resolution was "voted" by the suggested ovation. This public expression of appreciation and love comprised one of the special moments of my professional life. Ironically, because of a technical change in my relationship with Church of God Ministries, in 2011 I was elected by the General Assembly to renewed membership on its Bylaws Committee, rejoining as vice-chair. I concluded that role four years later as other duties crowded in.

A new millennium had begun, a major phase of my life was over with my campus retirement in 2005, and it was time to move on. In the Covenant Room at Park Place Church of God, my wife Jan and other family and friends staged a lovely retirement reception for me. Jan is gracious indeed! Of course, the grandchildren were there. They help a man start life again. I would dedicate books of mine to each of them.

For me, retirement was hardly intended as the end. This is how Dietrich Bonhoeffer took leave of his fellow prisoner, Payne Best, in the Flossenbürg concentration camp as Dietrich went to his execution on April 9, 1945: "This is the end—for me the beginning of life." Similarly, for me, Anderson University, rather than an occupational prison, had been a long and liberating experience. My retirement in 2005 from my faculty relationship (1966-2005) was an end and equally a beginning. By 2008 I was representing Church of God Ministries in select ecumenical circles and functioning as a member of the Executive Leadership Team envisioning the future of the Church of God movement. Retirement meant leaning forward with fresh eyes on fresh tasks.

I was not "burned out" like some of my colleagues whom I observed so anxious to leave their faculty positions as soon as possible. I still enjoyed the classroom interaction with students, although I was not longing for more of the meetings on perennial issues in Christian higher education and campus politics, occasionally fired in less than pleasant ways by a departmental personality or two. My friend Richard T. Hughes, then of Pepperdine University in California, delivered to the Anderson University faculty in 2004 an excellent lecture titled "What Makes Church-Related Higher Education 'Christian'?" I was pleased to edit and publish it as a booklet by that title through Anderson University Press. The administration gave copies to all faculty members, encouraging them to pursue the issues seriously.

Actually, I remained involved on campus in small ways. For instance, the first seven years of my retirement, my three successors in the dean's office at Anderson University, Drs. Patrick Allen, Carl Caldwell, and Marie Morris, asked annually that I support the orientation of new faculty members by providing background and answering questions about the sponsoring church body of the university and the relationship between Christian faith and quality academics. It was always a delight to do this. In addition, I remained the Editor of Anderson University Press.

I received many retirement cards. Later, I looked carefully through their printed messages and personal notes. Here is some of the retirement wisdom I gleaned from my family and friends. The retirement card from David and Shirley Coolidge defined true success in life as "giving your best in all you do, making a real difference with your knowledge and caring, appreciating each person's gifts and each day's opportunities—laughing, dreaming, learning, and growing all the days of your life." Attached to the card was this personal note: "You're a success in every sense of the word."

And what comes after true success? Floyd and Dorothy Saltzman's card said that retirement is "freedom to follow your heart and choose your own goals to pursue. . .a time to enjoy being you." I certainly intended to try, without being selfish about it. Personal comments included these from valued colleagues of many years:

- Ted and Carla Stoneberg: "It's time to relax and enjoy the things that make you happy."
- Becky Hull: "You have worn many hats at Anderson University—each one well, humbly, competently, with great care and sensitivity."
- James Lewis: "You exemplify for me the consummate scholar-teacher within a church-related context."
- Merle Strege: "You have never stopped pressing forward, and the results are there for all to see."
- Jan and Harold Linamen: "We have enjoyed and been blessed by your scholarship, humor, and friendship."
- Larry and Gini Green, parents of my physician Scott Green: "Friends

forever! Our love and appreciation for putting your footprints in our hearts and helping us to become who we are by your influence."

- James and Judy Bradley: "It will be different thinking of Anderson University without you. Are you sure there has not been a miscalculation of the number of years?"
- Norman and Marge Patton: "We've both had a great heritage, a great ride, and it is not over yet. Enjoy."

A new millennium had arrived. My full-time teaching career at Anderson University had ended. Doors to the future remained open. Friends were numerous. God was gracious and I was ready to move on.

As one grows older, it's a blessing to have continuing opportunities to be constructively active, to be wanted and needed. I called the original edition of this autobiography "an interim report," having no idea how many or full would be the years ahead. But full they have been! For instance, in just the month of January, 2012, I:

1. Sent to the publisher my book *Beneath the Surface*, something written during my months of taking chemotherapy for lymphoma;
2. Prepared to be an "expert witness" in a Colorado court involving a dispute over the ownership of church property;
3. Drafted resolutions for the 2012 General Assembly of the Church of God regarding issues of expected congregational giving, the roles of the Assembly's Chair-Elect, and the definition of the Assembly's quorum;
4. Accepted an invitation to be the founding Editor of Aldersgate Press recently formed by the Wesleyan Holiness Connection;
5. Worked with Donald Thorsen of Azusa Pacific University in California in compiling a major book on Christian holiness and the renewal of today's churches;
6. Continued in the choir of Park Place Church of God trying to learn to sing quality choral music; and

7. Prepared materials I would use for my Pentecost sermon to Park Place Church of God in May and my conferences at the Northeast Ohio Camp Meeting of the Church of God (Berlin Center) in July.

In the months prior to this busy January, I had participated as a member of the World Conference Planning Committee of the Church of God, attended and was secretary of the North American ministerial *Credentials Manual*), and functioned as a member and drafter of the report of the Study Committee on the future of the North American Convention of the Church of God.

In May, 2010, I led a "Theologue" for forty leaders of the Church of God in western Canada. We met for four days at Gardner College in Camrose, Alberta, a school that began in the early 1930s and sadly was closed in 2011. I had been there often over the years and grieved the loss. Bay Ridge Christian College in Texas also closed. Its daring and noble way of educating rural African-Americans in the deep South was pace-setting in the 1960s and antiquated in the new millennium. I have told the stories of these and all other colleges and universities of the Church of God in my 2007 book *Enriching Mind and Spirit*.

Times, leaders, and institutions were moving on. Many distinguished careers were ending around me in 2012 and just beyond. Retirements were coming for Dr. Ronald V. Duncan, General Director of Church of God Ministries in Anderson, and for Dr. James L. Edwards, president of Anderson University, both great friends and superb leaders. My own wife Jan retired in 2012 from a long and distinguished teaching career at Anderson High School. I had to believe that the God who had provided in the past would somehow do it again with fresh institutions and leaders prepared to carry on in faith as the tomorrows would come.

The summer 2010 issue of *Signatures*, the alumni magazine of Anderson University, featured as its cover story the first twenty years of the presidency of my long-time friend and colleague James L. Edwards.

Reading the story impressed me again with how time flies! As Edwards was beginning his presidency in 1990, I was ending my nearly two decades of administrative leadership at the university and returning to full-time teaching and writing. Since then, and by hard work and God's undeserved grace, both James and I have flourished in our parallel and complimentary roles in Christian higher education.

In the late summer of 2010, James and I were together at Kima International Theological Seminary in Kenya, East Africa, celebrating that school's graduation day. Two or three of my books were being used as textbooks there, causing the request from the graduating class that I address them briefly during the ceremony. I was pleased to do so, telling them that, just as I had used my writing gift over the years to assist them, they now had the challenge of using their various gifts of ministry for the benefit of God's people. Like time itself, generations of God's servants come and go. Like James Edwards, I am grateful that I have had my day on the servant stage and have had a role in preparing several generations of Christian leaders worldwide. Of course, I didn't know that many years and challenges still lay ahead.

A moment of fun with
Anderson College students in
2005. While I enjoyed my
administrative years, teaching
is at the heart of campus life.

With my good friend and
teaching colleague
Fredrick Shively.

With Gustav Jeeninga,
a lifelong colleague
and personal friend.

With my sister Bonnie and wife
Jan, at my retirement from
Anderson University in 2005.

Jodie and John Ackerman

Malcolm and Judy Hughes

Caroline Ackerman
Marschall

In 2010, I participated with other church world leaders in planning the 2013 Global Gathering of the Church of God. I am standing second from the right.

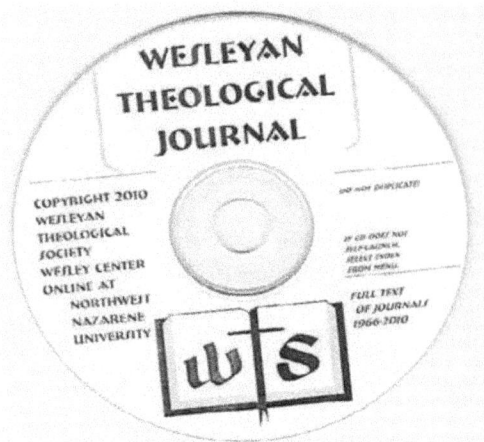

In 2011, I assumed the new role of Editor of Aldersgate Press.

Dr. George Lyons and I arranged for the complete history of the publishing of the *WTJ* to be placed on one, fully searchable electronic disk for the convenient use of scholars.

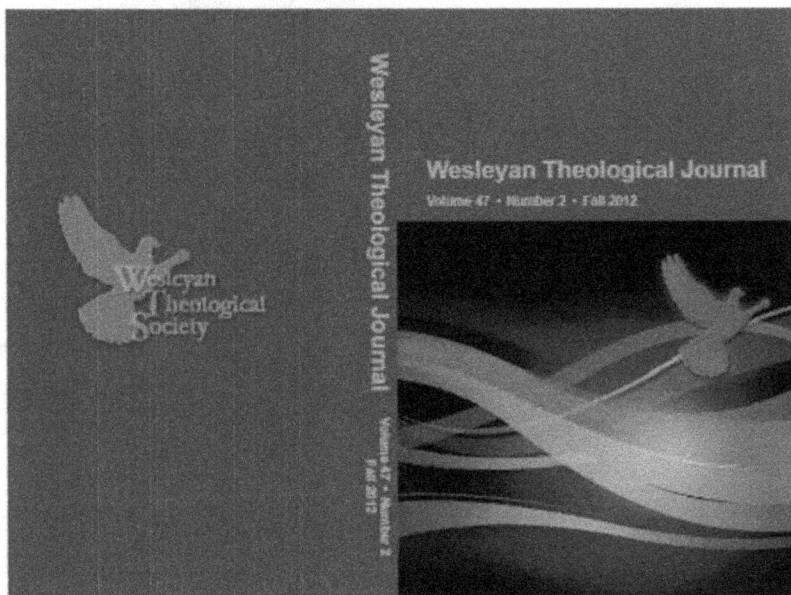

Beginning in 1993 I have served as Editor of the *Wesleyan Theological Journal*, with this entirely new format launched in the fall of 2012.

Chapter 10

Honoring and Being Honored

Worldly glory is a pleasurable but passing thing

The point of a faithful Christian life is hardly to be noticed widely for one's accomplishments. When honors come along, it is best to say a heartfelt "thank you" and then go gracefully about one's business. I will share a few honors that have come my way over the years, but also—and more importantly—I will recount the various efforts I have made to see that appropriate honor has come to others. Honors are fleeting things. Even so, they should be noted, especially those lavished on others. They represent significant milestones along the way.

An early honor of great meaning to me was my being the valedictorian of the Geneva College class of 1963. My humble beginnings hardly suggested the likelihood of such a status; even so, its achievement helped propel me along an academic path. Receiving my four graduate degrees in later years, all with the designation *summa cum laude*, was the result of much hard work and the assistance of numerous people, including the patience of my first wife, Arlene. Enjoying the good result is only natural; to take substantial credit myself would be misleading.

I view myself as a person clearly committed and intellectually strong, but not superior. I have been particularly productive because of special opportunities and hard work behind the scenes. In the process, some praise has come my way, as have some frustrations and a little criticism.

Such is the lot of any public person. I have chosen to accept it all as part of life. Some frustrations have brought fresh insight and better directions. Criticism can bring maturity. I hope that I have managed some needed growing up along the way. If so, I am in debt to my critics, and certainly to a series of my most treasured colleagues who have written kind endorsement statements for the cover and inside pages of this book.

Standing on Strong Shoulders

As the previous chapters make clear, I was privileged to come from sturdy family and church stock, and to have exceptional opportunities for a college and graduate education. I have stood on the strong shoulders of many outstanding men and women, a few of whom I highlighted in the previous chapter. Once turned toward an academic career as the main avenue of my Christian ministry, I soon was invited into high-profile seminary administration and national church life, and then lured across the campus from the graduate school deanship to being a college dean and vice-president for academic affairs for a university. Doors opened for publishing, editing, and traveling. As my friend Gus Jeeninga titled his autobiography that I edited for him, many of life's events have proven to be "doors to life" for me. They usually opened for me more because of the graciousness of others than because of my own achievements

I addressed the Anderson College faculty and student body on October 27, 1983, during the service of my installation to the college's deanship. Robed and standing in the pulpit of Park Place Church of God, I said:

My parents were not yet born when Anderson College was founded in 1917. I was five years old when the College was first accredited. The modest circumstances of my upbringing and the country school which I attended for eight years hardly propelled me into an academic career. The moving forces in my life that brought me to today included the inspired and encouraging leadership of an outstanding local church (Newton Falls, Ohio), four years spent as a student at a fine Christian liberal arts college (Geneva), and a host of individuals who took time to show me the way. Whatever gets built in my tomorrows will stand on the sturdy foundation of their yesterdays!... With a deep sense of gratitude and humility, I begin this adventure, challenge, and unique ministry as vice president for academic affairs and dean of this great institution.

I eventually found myself climbing humbly on the broad shoulders of William Russell, John Wesley, and Clark H. Pinnock, and following appreciatively the pioneering trails of Daniel S. Warner and Charles E. Brown. My book *Seeking the Light* (1998) in part was a tribute to Dr. Russell who taught me history at Geneva College. My many years as editor of the *Wesleyan Theological Journal* were one tribute to Mr. Wesley, as was my joining with William Kostlevy, then of Asbury Theological Seminary, in publishing in 2000 the anthology *Heart of the Heritage: Core Themes of the Wesleyan/Holiness Tradition*. My intellectual biography of Clark Pinnock, *Journey Toward Renewal* (2000), was received appreciatively by him and reviewed positively in places like *Pneuma*, the journal of the Society for Pentecostal Studies (spring 2002).

I wrote a biography of Daniel Warner (*It's God's Church!*, 1995). My book *Radical Christianity* (1999) honors the earlier work of Charles Brown (*When Souls Awaken*, 1954) on the "Radical Reformation" begun in the sixteenth century. I wrote two other biographies, *She Came Preaching* about Rev. Lillie S. McCutcheon (1992) and *Staying on Course* about Dr. Robert H. Reardon (2004). A central way I have sought to honor others is to be sure that they are not forgotten. Honoring James

Earl Massey came with my co-editing and publishing in 2018 the select writings of this dear friend (*Views from the Mountain*).

I recall the planning process for my ordination to Christian ministry in November, 1973. Under the auspices of the Indiana Assembly of the Church of God, there were four prominent leaders in the formal service, each of my own choosing. They were Boyce W. Blackwelder, Lillie S. McCutcheon, James Earl Massey, and Robert H. Reardon. By that early period in my ministry, each of these church leaders already was a giant along my path, and they honored me with their participation. In the years to come, I was able to be involved in a publishing effort to honor every one of them.

In my 1995 book *Contours of a Cause*, I sought to explore the theological vision and teaching tradition of the Church of God movement. The book's dedication was to six persons I identified as "visionary servants of Christ and His church, six leaders of this movement who have been especially influential on this writer." To those four leaders in my ordination service I added Gene W. Newberry and John W. V. Smith, my seminary teachers and then valued colleagues and friends. I had followed Gene in the deanship of the School of Theology and soon after had asked John to function with me as my associate dean. These six persons always were wise, consistent, and loyal to the mission of the church. In fact, they had done much to give the Church of God movement its contemporary contours. I hope that I have represented them and their work fairly.

Such publishing gestures have been modest attempts on my part to say "thank you" for the wisdom, experience, and kindness extended to me. One such kindness came from Gene W. Newberry. In his 86th year (2002), he read carefully my newest book and sent this to me for my sharing with others on his behalf: "Dr. Barry Callen's new book, *Authentic Spirituality*, is absolutely the best you can read on the subject. He handles crucial biblical texts, defines words like 'pneumatic,' clarifies classical and recent writings, and, best of all, shows that preaching the Christian Year would be a healthy diet toward sanctification." I also prize words that Lillie S. McCutcheon wrote with her own hand in my copy of her book *God's Magnificent Masterpiece* (1996): "To Barry, our star preacher! Our exceptional author—and a very wonderful brother in God's church. We are so grateful for all your written books and articles. In sincere love, Lillie." Gene had been my seminary teacher and dean, and Lillie my home pastor and spiritual guide. Their generous words are gems of joy for me.

Carl Erskine has been a friend of mine over the years. Famed pitcher of baseball's Brooklyn/Los Angeles Dodgers, he threw two no-hitters while his team was winning six pennants during his twelve-year career. Carl's hometown is Anderson, Indiana. When I participated actively as secretary of the board of trustees of Anderson University during most of the 1970s and 1980s, Carl was a prominent member of the board and a local banker. His son Jimmy is physically challenged and Beth, my son's first wife, once helped Jimmy get a restaurant job in Anderson, something for which he and his parents were deeply grateful. Carl finally published many of his beloved baseball stories in his book *Tales from the Dodger Dugout* (2000). I have found Carl and his book a delight.

I recall one of Carl's stories in particular. Its theme is standing on shoulders. More than fifty professional baseball players served in the armed forces and were killed in action during World War II. Carl later visited the high cliffs overlooking the Utah and Omaha beaches where so many Allied soldiers died on D-Day in 1944. He saw firsthand the rows of white crosses that now mark their graves. Keeping a diary of this trip, Carl wrote:

> Can we total the debt that we owe
> To so many whom we'll never know?
> Each life sacrificed,
> In a way was like Christ,
> We are free because they took the blow.

My father managed to survive the horrors of World War II. He came home to rebuild his life, the life that would be my childhood heritage. So did Jesus survive the cross to pave the way for my eternal life. What shoulders we stand on. Others took blows so that I (we) can be free!

Important role models for me have been my two grandfathers, especially Charles VanArsdale (1883-1967) with whom I spent much time when I was young. Here is how my mother, Charlotte (VanArsdale) Callen, put in verse form her tribute to her father on the occasion of his 78th birthday, March 25, 1961:

> If I were an artist I'd be able to paint
> A picture that would tell a story so true.
> It would show the sunrise of a brand new life;
> A small seed in good soil, and my how it grew!
>
> My picture would show more true warmth and humor
> Than any picture I'd painted would ever have had.
> Need I tell you the subject that centers the canvas?
> I knew you would guess it! The model's "My Dad."
>
> I would paint a sprinkle of stars to show how
> He lighted our way when things were so dreary.
> He would lift a burden much too heavy for us,
> Even though he himself would be a bit weary.
>
> As the black turned to silver, then silver to white,
> A symbol of purity I do behold;
> As I finish my picture, the colors are blending,
> Each added year brings just a little more gold.
>
> I would rather have my treasures in this old world
> To be memories of the life we have had,

Than the wealth of rich kings and castles so fair,
LOVE, LAUGHTER, AND FAITH—"MY LEGACY" from DAD.

My two grandfathers were godly men, a fact that helps me want so much to be a positive presence in the lives of my own grandchildren. In 1977, having been Dean of Anderson School of Theology for four years, I established and ever since have funded the annual *Distinguished Senior Award* given by the seminary. The official catalog description reads:

> In honor of his grandfathers, Rev. Charles B. Callen and Charles G. VanArsdale, dedicated servants of God, Dean Barry L. Callen annually presents a cash award to the graduating senior in the Master of Divinity program who has demonstrated excellence in both personal and professional preparation for Christian ministry. The recipient is chosen by nomination of the Financial Aid and Awards Committee and vote of the School of Theology faculty.

I have congratulated and sought to follow the many recipients of this award. I always was pleased to make the money available, and now I am pleased to have recorded their names—see the list in chapter twelve. What a delight that in July, 2001, as I turned sixty, and twenty years after his receiving this award, David E. Markle became my pastor at Park Place Church of God in Anderson. Things often circle back to meet one in unexpected ways. Whenever we have opportunity, we should give honor to whom honor is due.

Publishing Memories and Appreciations

When I began writing for publication in the early 1970s, it was in the midst of my hectic administrative schedule, first as a young professor, then department chair, and soon dean of a rapidly growing seminary. By the dawn of the twenty-first century I would be the most published author in the histories of Anderson University and the Church of God movement (see the list of publications in *Appendix F*). Gaining some record, however, was hardly the point. There was much to be done and said. For me, there were many issues, institutions, beliefs, movements, and outstanding leaders deserving the honor of being appropriately appreciated, put in helpful perspective, and made available for future generations.

In the epilogue written as the final pages of my biography of her (*She Came Preaching*, 1992), Lillie S. McCutcheon said: "Some time ago Dr. Callen and I shared a conversation concerning how people collect 'things.' He said, 'some people collect stamps, books, and pictures, but I collect people.' I am so honored to now be in his collection." Actually, the honor was mine. I was privileged to be one of the many young people in her Newton Falls, Ohio, congregation whom she mentored into Christian ministry.

My life had soon shifted from Ohio to Anderson, Indiana, where Robert H. Reardon was a prominent figure. Warner Press published *Educating for Service: Essays Presented to Robert H. Reardon* in 1984. With James Earl Massey the book's editor, I contributed a chapter titled "Faith and Freedom in Higher Education," material drawn largely from my doctoral dissertation at Indiana University. The gift copy of this book presented to me carries this handwritten message that I treasure: "For Barry, whom I love and trust, a dear brother of the years, with affection and admiration. Robert H. Reardon." Bob and Geraldine Hurst had been married in August, 1941, just weeks after I was born. When they celebrated their fiftieth wedding anniversary in 1991, they were retired and our immediate neighbors on Falls Court in Anderson. Arlene and I wrote the following to them on that special occasion:

Celebration is justified only when something has been genuinely good, especially if it has been really good for a long time. Much of your married life has been lived in the public eye. Thousands of people have witnessed in your relationship things needed so desperately in our day, things such as love, stability, mutual respect, and Christian grace. You have evidenced what it is like to have sturdy roots without being so anchored in one time and way of thinking that change becomes impossible. You have shown how to laugh with those who enjoy the goodness of life and how to cry tenderly and wisely with those overtaken by pain. Together you have "matured" and somehow stayed young, always encouraging the inexperienced to reach for the potential in life. So celebration is in order! Thank you for touching our lives. May joy and peace always be close by your sides.   .

I covet for myself someone being able to say that I had sturdy roots without being so anchored in one time and way of thinking that change for me became impossible. I trust that I have somehow stayed young in my maturing and always encouraged others along the way.

Also in 1991, I completed my book *Faith, Learning and Life*. This project allowed me to collect wisdom writings of the first three presidents of Anderson University and bring honor to these men by making their thoughts newly available in attractive form. I was able to further honor two of these men, one by writing a biography of Robert H. Reardon (*Staying on Course*, 2004) and then the other by publishing the autobiography of Robert A. Nicholson (*So I Said Yes!*, 2006). My 1992 book *Guide of Soul and Mind: The Story of Anderson University* was published on the seventy- fifth anniversary of the campus. This is the only one of my books that has been ceremoniously sealed with a few other items in a special metal box and placed in a brick wall of Decker Hall on the

the university campus, a time capsule to be opened as an historical treasure chest at some time in the future. When it happens, I hope that my book will be more than a clump of mildewed pulp! Things of earth do decay.

There were several other outstanding people who entered my life. I met Boyce W. Blackwelder as he and I were spending our first days at Anderson School of Theology in 1963. He had just joined the faculty in New Testament and I was an anxious new graduate student. As my academic advisor, he noticed that the class schedule I had prepared for him to sign did not include New Testament Greek (I was trying to avoid more language study). Surprisingly, he added Greek to an already full schedule, commenting only, "If I can teach it, you can take it!" I did, for two years, and actually did well. In the process, I came to admire this gifted man and become a close friend of my new classmate, Ronald J. Fowler, also reared in northeast Ohio and now tackling biblical Greek with me. He and I had no idea that years later I would be the vice-president for academic affairs of Anderson University when he was chair of its board of trustees!

Before graduating from Anderson School of Theology in 1966, I became aware of Gustav Jeeninga. He was a college faculty member scheduled to be on sabbatical leave in the Middle East for the next year. President Robert H. Reardon and the undergraduate dean, Robert A. Nicholson, wanted me to cover Jeeninga's office, classes, and little Bible museum until he got back. I agreed, walked daily up to the fourth floor of Old Main (out of breath!) where Gus's academic world was, and strained hard to stay ahead of the students as I met his classes for two semesters.

For me, this was a beginning that would be a forty-year career of teaching and administering on the Anderson campus. During those years to come, Gus and I would travel the world together. In 2002 I had the privilege of editing and publishing through Anderson University Press his autobiographical book *Doors to Life*. In these moving pages, he tells many stories, several involving me—especially a humorous one set in Athens,

Greece, that he often had told his classes. We enjoyed supporting, teasing, and honoring each other over the years.

My wife Jan and I cruised with Dr. Jeeninga in 2004 and 2005. The first venture was to Alaska as two young couples (he having married Barbara Pay after Aletta Jeeninga's death and I having married Jan Slattery after the deaths of Phil Slattery and my wife Arlene). The second venture was to the Baltic Sea countries and featured an arch in a Polish city that Gus's mother would have seen often as a young woman. It was a nostalgic time for Gus, with my wife Jan telling the story in David Liverett's book *Just Beyond the Passage* (2007, p. 42). Gus already was dying slowly of a blood disease. He wrote to me in February, 2006, from his retirement home in Penney Farms, Florida, asking if I would be the minister at his graveside service when death came, saying that I was "a life-long friend and co-worker involved with him to the end." He thanked me for helping him bring to reality his *Doors to Life* book, saying, "you were one of those doors that enriched my life's journey."

I gladly ministered as Dr. Jeeninga had requested, with the graveside service coming on June 12, 2006–much too soon. His ashes were placed next to those of Aletta who had died in 2000. I closed the service with these words of honor that end with subtle reference to the title of his autobiography: "As a young man, Gustav Jeeninga was an immigrant to a new world. Now he has lived his days and immigrated again, this time to a far better world. He is now at peace. May we who knew and loved him now go in peace, go to use our divine gifts–and may we go with the comfort and joy of the God who holds the keys of death and opens the doors to life"!

Living for so long in Anderson, Indiana, brought my way a parade of truly prominent people. None was more prominent than James Earl Massey. First the campus pastor beginning in 1969, he became dean of the School of Theology in 1990. I was privileged to function as acting dean for a year so that he could arrange to assume this high office. In his honor, I edited the book *Sharing Heaven's Music: The Heart of Christian Preaching* (1995). In 2002, as Editor of Anderson University Press, I was privileged to oversee the publishing of Dr. Massey's autobiography, *Aspects of My Journey*. Then, in 2005, I edited and Anderson University Press published his major history book, *African Americans and the Church of God*.

I traveled to the West Middlesex Camp Meeting in Pennsylvania to help Dr. Massey celebrate these major accomplishments and arrange for him to sign hundreds of copies of his books for admiring friends. I successfully nominated his 2005 book to receive the Smith/Wynkoop Book Award of the Wesleyan Theological Society. How wonderful it was to sit with him at an honor table and then stand with him as the ballroom crowd in Kansas City applauded him at length! I earlier had participated in his being honored by the WTS in Nampa, Idaho, with the Society's coveted "Lifetime Achievement Award" (an honor that also came to me in 2009).

Over the years, James Earl Massey became a precious brother to me, a close friend and highly honored colleague in Christian ministry. To be with him in any setting was always a personal privilege. When I developed cancer in 2011, he called me and announced that God had given him a Bible verse just for me—I carried it with me as I took my chemotherapy treatments. It was Deuteronomy 33:27 (KJV), "The eternal God is thy refuge, and underneath are the everlasting arms." Indeed! When he developed cancer in 2017, we talked by phone frequently until his death in 2018. At his request, I delivered a tribute at his funeral in Detroit and then released the volume of his writings that I co-edited.

Beyond the many outstanding individuals who have enhanced my life was a particular heritage that was the immediate context of much of my teaching and writing. Coming to love its high ideals, I began in the late 1960s to honor the reform tradition of the Church of God movement. My 1969 thesis at Asbury Theological Seminary was on this movement and its "ecumenical idealism." By 1978, with the movement's centennial approaching, I completed a series of six paperback books under the group title *A Time To Remember*, soon republished in two volumes as *The First Century*. In 1995 I added two books, a biography of Daniel S. Warner, the movement's primary pioneer, titled *It's God's Church!* and *Contours of a Cause* about the movement's teaching tradition. Then came my *Following the Light* (2000), *The Wisdom of the Saints* (2003), *Seeking Higher Ground*, the 2006 centennial history of Park Place Church of God in Anderson, *What We Teach* (booklet, 2005), and *Following Our Lord* (2008). The intent of all these publications was to honor a significant past and rethink that past for the sake of the future. Remembering appreciatively and critically is a high form of honoring.

My interests, however, soon moved well beyond this one reform movement. In 1997 I joined church historian James North in authoring *Coming Together in Christ*, a way of honoring parallel reform movements (the Church of God and the Independent Christian Churches/Churches of Christ) and the many church leaders who had carried on a serious dialogue between them for a decade. From my computer in 2000 came the intellectual biography of Clark H. Pinnock (*Journey Toward Renewal*), leading in 2006 to Clark and I writing and publishing together *The Scripture Principle*.

In 2001 I joined historian William Kostlevy in editing *Heart of the Heritage*, significant essays about the Wesleyan theological tradition. In 2004 Richard Thompson and I co-edited *Bible Reading in Wesleyan Ways*. In 2012 it was Don Thorsen and I co-editing *Heart & Life, rediscovering holy living for today's churches*. In 2015 Steve Hoskins and I co-authored the fiftieth anniversary celebration book of the Wesleyan Theological Society. My friends and I were teaming to honor the great Wesleyan tradition by retelling its past successes and seeking its contemporary applications.

In response to receiving in 2009 the "Lifetime Achievement Award" of the Wesleyan Theological Society, I said this to the crowded banquet hall at Anderson University: "Over the years I have watched at close range the Wesleyan, Holiness, and Pentecostal traditions of Christianity in action. They have given leadership to serious dialogues with scientists, philosophers, psychologists, historians, biblical scholars, educators, "open" and "process" theologians, Eastern Orthodox patriarchs, and more. The depth, range, and unifying power of the traditions rooted in the Wesleys keeps being evidenced. To have been with you in this process of dialoging, probing, and publishing has been a personal privilege."

In 2002 I ranged even more widely with my book *Authentic Spirituality*, using the dynamic of an experienced faith as a common point of contact among Christians from Eastern Orthodox and Roman Catholic to Holiness and Pentecostal traditions. My *Discerning the Divine* (2004), *Caught Between Truths* (2007), and then *Heart of the Matter* (2011) were joined in 2012 by *Beneath the Surface* in which I try to reclaim the Old Testament for today's Christian. These books were attempts to speak directly about the heart of Christian faith in ways more basic than any particular denominational concerns. What marvelous sets of shoulders to stand upon—giants of the whole Christian tradition, and the Jewish one before that! I hoped to honor the Bible and the deep wisdom of many Christian leaders of the past who now form a great cloud of witnesses.

While often returning home exhausted after long days on campus or extended trips on school or church business out of state and sometimes country, for the most part there was pleasure in the progress I was making and in the kind recognitions beginning to come for my efforts. For instance, in November, 1984, I received a surprising letter from Dr. Stewart Lee who was chairing the Search Committee for a new academic vice president at Geneva College, my undergraduate alma mater. The retiring dean was Dr. William Russell whom I appreciated greatly as my history teacher and mentor nearly twenty-five years earlier. My name, I was told, had been submitted to the committee as a viable candidate. The stated qualifications were an earned doctorate, demonstrated administrative ability in academic affairs, college teaching experience, and agreement with the published "Foundational Concepts of Christian Education" of Geneva. Although I probably could have made a good case for my qualifications in all these regards, my responding letter to Dr. Lee included this:

> I was warmed and challenged by your letter of November 30, informing me that my name had been submitted to the Search Committee which is seeking a new Academic Vice President. Dr. William Russell was a highly respected teacher of mine (I majored in Geneva's history department) and currently he is a trusted colleague and friend. I will always be deeply grateful for the fine education which both I and my wife Arlene received at Geneva. Presently, however, I am not inclined to encourage the consideration of my name for this important position. This hesitancy roots not in negatives about Geneva but in positives about my current family and professional circumstances at Anderson College. For the past two years, I have fulfilled the role of Vice President for Academic Affairs after having served for ten years as the Dean of the graduate-level School of Theology.

Other overtures came to me over the years in relation to presidencies or deanships in the world of Christian higher education. I always declined politely. I felt rooted in Anderson by tradition and family, and thought of myself as inadequate in the public relations and fundraising skills necessary to lead a large institution at the presidential level.

Transition to a Distinguished Professorship

A special honor came my way on the Anderson campus. My full-time teaching career at Anderson College (University) had begun in 1966 immediately after my graduation from seminary. I began with a temporary role at the Instructor rank to cover for the one-year sabbatical leave of Gustav Jeeninga. Transformed by the end of that year into a longterm appointment, I left for a two-year study leave and returned to the campus in 1969, having completed a second masters degree (Asbury Theological Seminary) and my first doctorate (Chicago Theological Seminary). I then was moved to the rank of Assistant Professor. By 1974 I had served briefly as the chair of the Department of Religious Studies and was the dean of the School of Theology. On February 15, 1974, I received a letter from President Robert H. Reardon informing me that, "taking cognizance of your professional development, your faithfulness to the College, and your dedication to its students," I was being elevated to the rank of Associate Professor.

My academic career was moving ahead rapidly. After the first eight of my years serving as Dean of the School of Theology, nearing completion of a second doctorate (Indiana University), and soon to be named the new Vice President for Academic Affairs and Dean of the College, the following letter came to me on June 22, 1982, from Robert A. Nicholson, then Vice President and college Dean:

> I note that you have been an Associate Professor since 1974. I think you ought to change your listing to full Professor as of your new [School of Theology] catalog. I mentioned this to the President several months ago, in advance of the publication of the new catalog, but perhaps he failed to mention it to you.... Let's simply get it done; you've passed all appropriate hurdles with flying colors.

At that time, I was handling all copy details for the graduate catalog, so I simply changed my listing to Full Professor. Editors really do have power!

In 1988 Robert A. Nicholson, then the president, and I began conversations about the best plan for my future role in the university. The organization of the campus had just changed, including the new "university" designation. I had been central in the study and design of this and several other changes. There now had evolved for my position, vice president for academic affairs and dean of the College, an arena for administrative supervision more complex and demanding than had ever existed previously. Reporting directly to me by 1987 were the three school deans (covering the entire undergraduate academic program), the Registrar, Director of Libraries, Director of Athletics, Dean for International Education, and four other major program directors. In addition, I was still functioning as corporate secretary of the university (involving attendance at and the writing of formal minutes for all meetings of the board of trustees and its executive committee). This load was too heavy and was making almost impossible my writing ministry. It was time for some change.

Robert Nicholson would soon retire from the presidency (1990) and Cleda Anderson already had retired in 1988 from her post as vice president for student affairs. A key decision was made. Jerry Grubbs, dean of the School of Theology since my leaving in 1983, would replace Anderson, thus leaving vacant the seminary deanship. Being far from retirement myself, and now functioning in an administrative complex that bore little resemblance to what existed when I came to it in 1983, it seemed a good time to reevaluate my circumstance. I did this reevaluation with President Nicholson in a series of conversations in early 1989. The president was someone I considered a wise personal friend, an excellent man with whom to explore new directions in new circumstances. He and I soon agreed on a plan of action, a professional transition for me that would be ideal for my particular set of gifts, and a transition that would take three years to fully complete.

A formal announcement of coming changes was released in a May 18, 1989, letter from the president to all Anderson University faculty and staff members following the spring meeting of the board of trustees. Dr. James Earl Massey had been elected the new dean of the School of Theology, although he would not be able to come from his position at Tuskegee University in Alabama until January of 1990. I had been serving as acting dean of the School of Theology during 1988-1989 and would continue until Massey could arrive. In addition, responding to the president's recommendation, the board of trustees established a new academic rank, "University Professor," and elected me as the first to hold it. The definition given to this rank was "a senior and distinguished scholar/teacher-in-residence honored for particular potential to combine research, publication, and teaching in the service of the mission of the University." This was an honor and fresh role that I welcomed gladly.

An immediate research-publication assignment for me would be the preparation of an institutional history to be published in 1992 on the occasion of the university's seventy-fifth anniversary. Beyond this academic distinction and initial responsibility, I would teach part-time, continue as corporate secretary of the university—at least into the tenure of a new administration, and function as special assistant to the president in primarily off-campus settings. James Earl Massey finally arrived in January of 1990 to relieve me of my interim responsibility in the School of Theology, Robert Nicholson retired in 1990, and James L. Edwards became the new president. In November, 1990, the new president and I met and discussed at length my special role as University Professor and my various administrative tasks left from the previous administration. The president then wrote the following to me on November 5, 1990:

> I want to affirm again the high regard with which you are held in this University . Your service to the church at large in leadership and as a prominent reflector of the church's history, theology, and

thought has won a place for you uniquely valued in the life of the church. You are a major contributor to the ongoing mission of this University as a prized, valued friend, colleague, and educator. Your place of service as University Professor gives us the opportunity to emphasize the primary mission of this University, which is to teach.

No longer would I be required to perform cumbersome administrative roles, but could expend primary energy in scholarship, teaching, and writing.

I had been given a gift, an open door, and the decade of the 1990s and beyond would be highly productive for me in academic ways out of the question had my previous responsibilities lingered. Having spent some time orienting both Patrick Allen and James Earl Massey to their new duties as Deans of the College and School of Theology respectively, I was now based in the Department of Religious Studies and free to pursue my academic life. It felt like a new beginning after a long sojourn in the demanding world of academic administration.

My son Todd was completing his student years on campus at the time. He graduated in June, 1991, with what I believe is the most outstanding academic record of any undergraduate in the history of Anderson University (combining volume and departmental spread of hours and quality of academic work). He had earned enough hours among his three majors to have completed both the B. A. and M. A. degrees—and all with a perfect 4.0 grade-point average. To put it mildly, Arlene and I were proud! On June 15, 1991, we sent him the following letter (more formal and lasting than personal words): "Congratulations, Todd. You did it!! You are now a college graduate—and with a 4.0! We are proud of you, son. As a graduation gift, we have decided that the Lancer [our second car] should become your personal property. In the months and years to come, may this vehicle take you to places of earning, learning, service, and personal happiness! Love, Mom and Dad."

I remember attending the Anderson School of Theology banquet in June of 1991 and listening to president James L. Edwards speak about three essential criteria for making any significant professional decision. They are, he said, the *ability* to do the job, the *opportunity* for a favorable doing of the job, and the *passion* for doing it with excited expectation. That caused me to reflect on decisions made about my own professional path in the years immediately past. It was becoming clear to me that God had shifted my focus through a complex of circumstances, renewing my passion and opening new doors. I was instructed by something that Parker J. Palmer wrote in 1996.

In his mid-thirties, Palmer had suffered from "terminal frustration" because he could not identify a vocation just right for him. He knew that giving himself to something not well suited to his nature and gifts was a poor way to live, no matter how hard he worked at succeeding. Valuable lessons can be learned about one's real nature and God-given gifts by experiencing fulfilled potential and running into personal limits. Said Palmer (in *Weavings*, May/June 1996, 19, 21-22):

> The truth is that my created nature, my God-given nature, makes me like an organism in an ecosystem: I thrive in some roles and relationships within that system, but in others I wither and die…. When I understand my limits not as defects to be repaired but as trade-offs for my strengths, something new and liberating happens within me…. The truth is that every time a door closes behind us, the rest of the world opens up in front of us.

I now see that this is something like what I went through in the late 1980s and early 1990s. I had shifted into a fresh "ecosystem" that was very healthy for my divine calling. I was thriving again, and without having to leave Anderson University to do it.

Beginning with my academic vice-presidency in 1983, I had worked very hard, accomplished a great deal, but increasingly had found myself struggling, frustrated too much of the time, not able to use my natural gifts to their best advantage. I had not died professionally, but there had been some withering of enthusiasm. My limits had been clarified, not as embarrassing defects, but as providential markers turning me toward more productive paths. I look back, remember, and rejoice. To be given opportunities that allow an organism to thrive in the right ecosystem is to be honored, liberated, and loved. That was my experience at Anderson University. How pleased I was to review in 2018 the directory of the Board of Trustees of Anderson University and realize that ten of them had been my former students.

A Few Honors Received

At no point have I been a public celebrity, something I have never wanted. Even so, occasionally my work has been recognized in public and with considerable appreciation. For instance, one publication widely circulated in Anderson, Indiana, and surrounding communities was the *Madison County Monthly* magazine. The editors took an active interest in my work. On three occasions in the 1990s I was honored as the *MCM* cover story.

In the May, 1993, issue, a photo of me filled the *MCM* cover, with many of the books I had authored stacked on the floor beside me. The occasion was the release of my 1992 history of Anderson University. The story was titled "Anderson University's Advocate: Barry Callen." It was accompanied inside by a photo of president James L. Edwards and myself presenting a copy of this book to Mark Lawler, mayor of Anderson, Indiana. The occasion for the cover story of the September, 1995, issue was the release of my volume *Sharing Heaven's Music*, done in honor of the distinguished dean of the School of Theology, James Earl Massey. At my insistence, his photo was placed on the cover, not mine. Given the racial prejudice that marks some of the history of Madison County, I was proud to be responsible for a distinguished African-American face appearing on the cover and in close relation to my own name.

The third cover story involving my work was the May, 1998, issue. Featured was a photo of my new book *Seeking the Light*. The inside story began with this: "It may be a prominent new publication on the national scene, but it was written right here in Madison County on the campus of Anderson University!" Most of the story about my new book was a reproduction of the address that I had delivered to an all-school assembly at Jackson-Milton High School in North Jackson, Ohio (my alma mater that was featured in the book).

An unusual honor came my way through the medium of public art. A "Portrait Unveiling Ceremony" was held in Frances Tallen Memorial Hall of Anderson University's School of Theology on Monday, June 14, 1993. Two original oil portraits executed by figurative realist Leo Neufeld were unveiled and celebrated by the crowd. One was of me and the other of my immediate successor as dean of the School of Theology, Jerry C. Grubbs. These now hang in the main hall of the seminary just outside the chapel entrance, along with those of earlier deans. Arlene and I had made several trips to Purdue University for me to sit quietly and pose for this portrait. After my many years of administration, someone finally had managed to "hang" me!

A form of professional recognition beyond publicity, plaques, and paintings comes when prominent individuals seek your assistance, translate your work, ask that you lend your work and name to their projects, appreciatively place their endorsing names and generous comments on the covers of your books, and quote your writing in their own publications. I have been privileged to receive a series of such recognitions. In 1981, for instance, I received a handsomely published two-volume set of books in leather binding and in the Japanese language.

They were a translation and republication of my two-volume set *The First Century*. This was a major project funded by a Christian dentist in Japan who had decided that my books must be available to the churches of his land in the local language.

Three requests came to me through Beacon Hill Press, the publishing house of the Church of the Nazarene. In 1997 I was requested to contribute a major article to the pastoral theological journal designed for Nazarene Hispanic leaders. I did so with pleasure, titling it "The Holy Life of the Church." In 1998, partly in light of the prominence I had gained from being Editor of the *Wesleyan Theological Journal*, there came two additional requests, both of which I accepted. Church historian Melvin Dieter was completing volume four of Beacon Hill's "Great Holiness Classics" series, to be titled *The 19th-Century Holiness Movement*. He asked that I provide guidance as "Volume Advisor." I did so and was pleased with the published result, a hardback book of 416 pages that reflects a series of changes I recommended after reviewing the original draft.

William M. Greathouse was a former college and seminary president, general superintendent, and respected scholar among the Nazarenes and in holiness circles generally. He asked that I share my name and endorsement on the cover of his coming 1998 book, *Wholeness in Christ: Toward a Biblical Theology of Holiness*. I was happy to do it, writing:

> With obvious expertise and appropriate humility—both marks of great maturity—Dr. Greathouse pursues this overture to biblical theology. The result is readable, relevant, carefully documented, and well worth the time of any believer who desires the fullness of what God intends and provides for a fallen creation. Although this work emerges from the Wesleyan theological tradition, its subject, biblical orientation, and clear treatment belong to the whole family of Christ's children.

Then in December, 1999, my friend Kenneth J. Collins of Asbury Theological Seminary in Kentucky (one of my alma maters) called to ask if I would contribute a chapter on the theology of Christian conversion for a major book on this subject that he was editing for Abingdon Press, the publishing house of the United Methodist Church. I agreed. My chapter in the resulting 2001 *Conversion in the Wesleyan Tradition* is titled "A Mutuality Model of Conversion."

I had worked earlier with Abingdon Press to publish my volume on homiletics in honor of James Earl Massey (*Sharing Heaven's Music*). It had been a good relationship for me, including Abingdon's Jack Keller traveling to Indianapolis for the 1995 annual meeting of the Church of God in Indiana–where I was privileged to introduce Jack and then present a leather-bound copy of the new book to Dr. Massey in front of several hundred of his admiring ministerial peers. It also was my privilege to become involved in a small way with the 2001 Abingdon Press publication of the book *Global Good News* edited by my friend Howard A. Snyder. The request this time was that I lend my name to the outside cover, along with an endorsing statement. I did and it reads:

> The gospel of Christ is good news, even in the current postmodern ethos. And if it is good news for *any*, it is good news for *all* (thus, global). The "scandal" of Christian particularity stands in the face of today's tolerant pluralism and is freshly explained in these pages by an impressive parade of competent Christian analysts and apologists. Here are the core issues for Christian mission today, and the gospel that remains at that mission's center in all times and places.

Later, I successfully nominated Howard Snyder's book *Populist Saints* (2006) for the 2007 Smith/Wynkoop book award of the Wesleyan Theological Society.

My friend William C. Kostlevy, then at Asbury Theological Seminary, joined me in compiling and editing *Heart of the Heritage,* a 2001 book identifying core themes of the Wesleyan/Holiness tradition as highlighted by the Wesleyan Theological Society from 1965 to 2000. Sometimes one thing leads to another. Dr. Kostlevy, an archivist, librarian, and professor of church history, played a key role in helping God's Bible School in Cincinnati, Ohio, to celebrate its centennial. Having learned about Martin Wells Knapp (1853-1901), the school's founder, in my work with *The 19th-Century Holiness Movement* project, and having become acquainted with Wallace Thornton, Jr., in 1998 when I published some of his work in the *Wesleyan Theological Journal,* I now was informed of two things. Thornton was authoring the interpretive history of God's Bible School and desired my name and endorsement to appear on the back of his volume. I was honored and pleased to do it. Especially was this the case when I realized that my great-grandfather, Christopher Rose (1849-1922), had been a charter member of the International Holiness Church and loved deeply the work of God's Bible School.

William Kostlevy has been a close friend and colleague of mine over the years. He became editor of the key reference work titled *Historical Dictionary of the Holiness Movement* (2001) and kindly included among the materials on truly outstanding people a substantive entry on me. He concludes it with this: "A truly 'catholic' theologian, Callen unites traditional Church of God (Anderson) ecclesiastical concerns and a Anabaptist emphasis on discipleship with a Wesleyan soteriology." I leave the details about these historical and theological references to interested scholars. It is enough to say that his generous evaluation of me is one that I would hope for myself, if only deserved in a modest way.

In addition to the word "catholic" to describe me, others have used the words "irenic" and "prodigious." According to Laurence Wood of Asbury Theological Seminary and Emeth Press, "Barry Callen has been a friend whom I have admired over the years as a model among Wesleyan theologians of one who possesses an irenic spirit and a creative mind. His (Anderson) Church of God tradition has been a dynamic and powerful influence within the Wesleyan/Holiness tradition. As he points out, the Church of God (Anderson) represents the essential spirit of the 'come-outers' who refuse to allow denominationalism to become a substitute for the meaning of the universal church of God" (in *The Continuing Relevance of Wesleyan Theology,* Nathan Crawford, ed., 2011, 267).

Other kind words about me came from Howard A. Snyder when he was serving at Tyndale Seminary in Toronto, Canada. In his 2011 book *Yes in Christ,* he makes extensive use of my 2000 book on Clark Pinnock (*Journey Toward Renewal*) and identifies me as a "Wesleyan theologian and historian" and the "prodigious" editor of the *Wesleyan Theological Journal* (143). I saw this latter designation and quickly checked the dictionary, being reassured that "prodigious" means "extraordinary" and not outlandish or unstable. I was privileged to nominate Snyder as the 2011 recipient of the Lifetime Achievement Award of the Wesleyan Theological Society. He was chosen and clearly himself is a "prodigious" scholar/leader. I have gladly stood on his and many other strong and wise shoulders.

I was pleased by the willingness of prominent individuals to spend time with my developing books and then support them by submitting their names and formal endorsement statements to appear on the covers. The earliest such endorsement came in 1976. By then I had taught Christian theology and ethics for several years and decided to write my own volume of theology. I worked hard on a manuscript that emphasized the essential paradoxes of Christian faith (Jesus as human *and* divine, the Bible as divinely inspired *and* humanly written, etc.). My first theology teacher, Gene W. Newberry, said that my manuscript was "a plea for liberated discipleship and consecrated scholarship, an honest book with perspective and balance."

For the Foreword, I was bold enough to turn to my beloved Quaker teacher, David Elton Trueblood. He reviewed my manuscript and in

March, 1976, wrote two pages in support of possible publication. However, it was not until 2007 that Emeth Press finally published this manuscript, titled *Caught Between Truths*, including Trueblood's old foreword, a cover endorsement written by Joseph D. Allison of Church of God Ministries, and another by Laurence W. Wood of Asbury Theological Seminary. Wood spoke kindly: "This book reflects the mature wisdom of a veteran scholar and highly respected theologian.... This work is both philosophical and pastoral, theological and personal, and is lucidly written."

In 1990 I edited the volume *Listening to the Word of God* as a tribute to my former Anderson seminary professor, Boyce W. Blackwelder. His wife Lela wrote this for the back cover: "My prayer is that this book will have far-reaching results in challenging men and women to follow the servanthood role of the Master and find fulfillment in a comprehensive study of the Word of God." Hollis S. Pistole, another of my seminary teachers in Anderson, brought me a gift copy of his 2004 autobiography titled *My Story*. He had written this inside for me: "Barry, probably the most gifted student I ever had in class—superb writer, communicator, teacher, gracious friend and colleague. Hollis." I treasure these words. Later his son John, my highly respected friend, would become President of Anderson University.

I released my *Faith, Learning and Life: Views from the President's Office of Anderson University* in 1991. This book was a way of making more widely available the substantial wisdom of presidents John A. Morrison, Robert H. Reardon, and Robert A. Nicholson (the latter two being so significant in my own life). The university's fourth president, James L. Edwards, had just taken office and agreed to write an endorsement of this book about his very special predecessors. In part, he said: "Great institutions have great stories.... Through this marvelous collection of wit and wisdom from the president's office of Anderson University, one can catch something of the heart of a university uniquely shaped by three remarkable tellers of its story.... You will love these stories and revere their tellers." I was pleased to be the man making these stories and their tellers freshly available to a new generation.

The university celebrated its seventy-fifth year in 1992, in part by publishing with Warner Press my extensive history of the university titled *Guide of Soul and Mind: The Story of Anderson University.* All three of the then-living presidents of the school wrote comments that are included in the book. Presidents Robert H. Reardon and Robert A. Nicholson wrote for the cover, and President, James L. Edwards, wrote a foreword. President Reardon said: "In a warm and thoughtful way, Dr. Barry Callen leads us on an instructive pilgrimage through the birth, development, and coming of age of Anderson University. It is a kaleidoscopic journey rich in the history of people and events, struggle, pain, excitement, and dreams denied and fulfilled." Wrote president Edwards (p. xiii):

> On the occasion of our diamond jubilee anniversary, it is the pleasure of Anderson University to offer this record of her life, the issues, persons, and events that have shaped her, and some glimpse of the ways in which she has shaped those whom she has served. Barry L. Callen is a dedicated and skilled reporter who has brought this collection to life in the pages to follow. His faithfulness and love for this dynamic, young place give evidence that he, too, has been touched by the "Anderson Experience." We are grateful to him for this offering, a true labor of love.

With my 1995 book *Contours of a Cause: The Theological Vision of the Church of God Movement,* there began a new pattern of publishers having prominent persons place endorsing statements on my book covers. In this case, there were five persons, including three from the Church of God and two scholars from related traditions. The two said in part that "this author has a keen understanding of the significant ideas being discussed among today's Christian thinkers" (J. Harvey Gossard, Winebrenner Seminary), and "here is a book that will be helpful to the Church of God movement, to Wesleyan and Anabaptist groups, and to the broader church" (Howard A. Snyder, United Theological Seminary). For those inside the Church of God, James Earl Massey, Dean of Anderson School of Theology at the time, said that "this writing will do for the present generation of the Church of God movement what Russell R. Byrum's *Christian Theology* (1925) did for an earlier one."

My 1996 *God As Loving Grace*, a systematic theology, was referred to by Dr. Massey as "biblical throughout" and "fresh material." Kenneth Kinghorn, then Dean of the School of Theology of Asbury Theological Seminary, called it an "impressively documented" book that "avoids fruitless speculation." This particular book would be in the list of eighteen published resources cited for best understanding the Wesleyan theological tradition (list prepared by Don Thorsen of Azusa Pacific University in *Resources for Ministry*, 1996).

The next year, my book on Christian eschatology, *Faithful in the Meantime*, was endorsed by two prominent Canadian theologians, both Baptists. Clark H. Pinnock of McMaster University saw it as "a responsible, informed, interesting, and up-to-date account of our blessed hope." Stanley J. Grenz of Carey Theological and Regent Colleges in Canada said it was a voice "calling us back to the fundamentals of biblical eschatology." Randy L. Maddox, then at Sioux Falls College, then Seattle Pacific University, and finally Duke University, kindly referred to me as "a church theologian in the finest sense." I treasure these outstanding Christian leaders and their kind words.

Also in 1997, I co-authored a book with my friend James B. North, dean of Cincinnati Bible College and Seminary in Ohio. Titled *Coming Together in Christ*, it grew out of ten years of dialogue among leaders of the Church of God movement and the Independent Christian Churches/Churches of Christ. Gilbert W. Stafford of Anderson School of

Theology said of North and myself, "we are in their debt for doing all of this in an interesting, engaging, and provocative manner." Henry E. Webb of Milligan College in Tennessee said that "all who read *Coming Together in Christ* will be challenged to reexamine their commitment to Christian unity and to expand their horizon for mission and service in the Kingdom of God."

I changed subjects entirely with my 1998 American history volume titled *Seeking the Light*. Retired United States Senator Mark O. Hatfield saw in it "a provocative analysis of the twentieth century in light of the values and ideals of America's founders." President George Brushaber of Bethel College and Seminary in Minnesota saw a "well-told story" executed with "insight and discernment," while dean Carl H. Caldwell of Anderson University, himself an accomplished historian, spoke of an "adept weaving of religious themes into a fabric which too often is limited by others to secular issues." Ian Worley of the University of Vermont (a high school classmate and special friend) saw me revealing "that rampant greed and avarice have a formidable adversary that lies in the good hearts, deep faith, and perseverance of those who would create a better world." These generous evaluations capture well the intent of my research and writing.

Such a better world has always been envisioned by the Believers Church tradition that I chronicled in my 1999 book *Radical Christianity*. Howard A. Snyder, then of Asbury Theological Seminary, said that, as Christendom ends and a new millennium begins, there is a growing consensus that the church needs a "Second Reformation," one that "reshapes the church and not just doctrine.... That is exactly what this new book by Dr. Barry Callen does." Clark H. Pinnock of McMaster University in Canada said that this book "inspires us all to treasure the gifts we have been given and to be faithful." Luke Keefer of Ashland Theological Seminary in Ohio observed this: "While commending the vision of these 'radical' Christians to the conscience of mainstream Christianity, the author also challenges those within the heritage to confront the erosion of their commitment to the Christ who ministered on the margins of society."

Two of my publications in 2000 carry formal endorsements from a range of well-known persons. The first, an intellectual biography of Clark H. Pinnock titled *Journey Toward Renewal*, attracted five scholars who had not previously addressed my work formally. Gary Dorrien of Kalamazoo College in Michigan called this book "detailed and sympathetic," a "vivid account" with "ample research." Philip R. Meadows then of Garrett-Evangelical Theological Seminary in Illinois judged it an "engaging" book that reminds believers that "theology is best done both on one's knees and walking in the Spirit." According to Henry H. Knight of St. Paul School of Theology in Kansas City, here is "a careful and accurate account" of a theological pilgrimage of perhaps "the most significant evangelical theologian of the last half of the twentieth century." John Sanders, then of Huntington College in Indiana, saw in these pages "the vision of an open and generous evangelical theology," a theology that Roger E. Olson of Truett Theological Seminary in Texas said was made available in "Callen's superbly critical and sympathetic portrayal of the man and his journey."

Steven J. Land of the Church of God Theological Seminary (Cleveland, Tenn.) called my book on Clark Pinnock "a distinctive integration of theology and spirituality." Since Pinnock "has been lauded as an inspiring theological pilgrim by his admirers and condemned as a dangerous renegade by his foes," Stanley J. Grenz of Carey and Regent Colleges in Canada said this book is "must reading" for "Clark's supporters and detractors alike. Why? According to Gregory A. Boyd of Bethel College and Seminary in Minnesota, "To understand the journey of this one brilliant thinker is to better understand the nature of contemporary evangelicalism, and Callen's masterful work succeeds at helping us to do both." From Ray C. W. Roennfeldt of Avondale College in Australia came this: "Barry Callen's work is essential reading for anyone who wants to know what the future of Evangelicalism might look like."

When Clark Pinnock's new book *Most Moved Mover* was released in 2001 by Baker Book House, its back cover carried this endorsement written by me at the publisher's request:

> The church and her mission cannot be more dynamic than her doctrine of God. Here is a theology for church renewal, a compelling call for an amicable conversation among evangelicals about the truly transcendent God who is said to choose significant involvement in the life of creation. Clark Pinnock offers the conversation a fresh divine-involvement focus, rejecting the concern of some that this path is theologically dangerous. To the contrary, it may be the best way to honor biblical revelation and highlight God's relational nature and creative love. These pages represent Pinnock's matured thought on relational theism. Let the conversation proceed!

Much of Pinnock's general view can also be seen in my writings after the year 2000. I am in debt to this good and wise man.

The second of my new books in the year 2000 was an extensive documentary history of the Church of God movement (Anderson) titled *Following the Light*. One would expect the two endorsements that came from key movement leaders, in this case the church historian, Merle D. Strege, and the General Director of Church of God Ministries in North America at the time, Robert W. Pearson. In addition was this from William C. Kostlevy, church historian and then bibliographer at Asbury Theological Seminary: "In this truly landmark study, Barry L. Callen allows the pivotal figures of the Church of God reformation movement (Anderson) center stage as they tell the story of the emergence, growth, and maturation of one of the great evangelical renewal movements in modern church history." That indeed was my goal.

Another published renewal effort in the year 2000 was aimed at "evangelicals" generally. It was by Stanley J. Grenz and titled *Renewing the Center*. Once a copy was in my hands, I was pleased to discover that this prominent writer had made ten references to my own work on Clark Pinnock (*Journey Toward Renewal*, 2000). What an honor it is to be thought of as having contributed something, however modest, to the renewal of contemporary Christianity!

My major work on Christian spirituality, *Authentic Spirituality: Moving Beyond Mere Religion*, came off the press of Baker Book House in 2001— my first time to work with this major evangelical publisher. Kenneth J. Collins of Asbury Theological Seminary observed that I had "written a work on Christian spirituality that is both ecumenical in scope and engaging in its conversation." Dwight L Grubbs and R. Eugene Sterner from the Church of God movement added that I had effectively "wed scholarship and sanctity" and "rescued spirituality from the common extremes and vagaries and rightly identified it with the whole Judeo-Christian tradition and experience." That certainly had been my hope. As the Nazarene scholar Wesley D. Tracy put it, I had presented in *Authentic Spirituality* "a safe home for believers lost in the postmodern swirl of anything-goes pluralistic spirituality."

I appreciate Clark H. Pinnock's additional judgment on my *Authentic Spirituality*. He said that I had produced "a comprehensive perspective on Christian existence and much encouragement to deepen our walk with God." After a series of presentations based on this book that I made at Park Place Church of God in Anderson, Indiana, my former seminary professor, Hollis S. Pistole, wrote this to me on April 12, 2002: "After nearly seventy years in the Church of God, I am most grateful for your gifted ministry in helping to define the maturing direction of the church we love so dearly." That had been my goal.

In 2006, Baker Book House allowed this book to go out of print. Emeth Press in Lexington, Kentucky, immediately republished it with an attractive new cover. This would be the beginning of my long and productive relationship with Emeth Press and its senior executive, Dr. Laurence Wood. This relationship would involve a series of my own books being published by Emeth and then the fact that in 2012 Emeth would become the initial operations partner of the new Aldersgate Press for which I have served as founding Editor since 2011.

The notoriety gained from my several publications came to the attention of my high school and college alma maters. I had enjoyed being inducted into Jackson-Milton High School's hall of fame in 1987. Then in 1999 my undergraduate alma mater, Geneva College, completed a year-long celebration of its 150th anniversary. Two of its celebration activities came to involve me personally. First, on April 24, 1998, there was a formal occasion convened in McCartney Library called "Geneva Authors Sesquicentennial Tea." This was a large gathering that included several of my "old" professors who had sent me to this library for class assignments nearly thirty years earlier. Now the estate of Helen Patterson Hill was funding a beautiful glassed set of built-in bookshelves just inside the main door of this stately old library. On these honor shelves were to go select publications of Geneva faculty and alumni. On this inaugural occasion, there were four persons honored and their books ceremoniously placed on the shelves. One was David Carson's new history of Geneva College titled *Pro Christo et Patria: A History of Geneva College* (1997). Another was my recently published social history of the final decades of the twentieth century in the United States (*Seeking the Light*, 1998).

Once the books were in place, I was asked to speak to the crowd about my book. I took the opportunity to call forward two of my former professors who had played key roles in my being able to do such research and writing. It was my pleasure to share my minutes of public honor with Dr. Geri Bass (English) and Dr. William Russell (history)—one had sensitized me to the art of language and the other to the significance of the past. Immediately following this occasion, I was ushered into the head librarian's office and informed that in a few minutes the phone would ring. When I answered, I would be on live Christian radio in Pittsburgh to be interviewed about my new book. It was quickly obvious that the skilled interviewer had read *Seeking the Light* in advance of our thirty minutes on the air. He hit me cold with a series of penetrating questions about my historical thesis, moral perspectives, and the unusual use I had made of the lives of my own high school class for illustrative material. I was told that some 500,000 people likely listened.

The second celebration event to involve me personally was Geneva's publishing of an alumni pride-book titled *Profiles in Servant Leadership*. The book features the photos and professional accomplishments of seventy-five Geneva alumni stretching over the school's 150 years (an average of one graduate selected for every two graduating classes). I was pleased to be among those featured for having "touched countless lives throughout the globe" by living out Geneva's mission of "serving Christ in all pursuits." To my delight, two of my friends in the class of 1963 also made the cut. They were Faith McBurney Martin, accomplished author and executive director of a Christian woman's association based in Pittsburgh, and Dr. James O. Jackson with whom I had played intercollegiate basketball during my Geneva years (he always was faster that I). I had had no contact with Jim since graduation in 1963, but learned when seeing this book that recently he had been named "Principal of the Year" by a New York education association.

James Jackson was the first African-American I ever knew up close. He got me off on the right foot in the area of race relations. I am deeply grateful. Immediately after my college years, Arlene and I were married and moved to Anderson, Indiana, for me to go to seminary. I soon met Ronald J. Fowler, another African-American who was to be our neighbor, my seminary classmate, and a lifelong friend and colleague in ministry. James Earl Massey soon entered my life. In the decades to follow, he and I would both be deans of the seminary in Anderson and very close friends. When God decided to create humans, the best of divine efforts brought into this world truly great souls like James O. Jackson, Ronald J. Fowler and James Earl Massey. I have been honored to walk by their sides. I trust that my walking alongside others has enhanced their life journeys at least a little.

A true highlight of my professional and church lives came in March, 2009, when Anderson University hosted the annual meeting of the Wesleyan Theological Society. Mainly because of my editorship of the Society's academic journal for nearly two decades, on this special occasion I was granted the "Lifetime Achievement Award." The tribute delivered by Dr. Richard Thompson of Northwest Nazarene University, and my formal response to it, are found in the *Wesleyan Theological Journal* (fall 2009 issue). My response came humbly in that packed banquet hall. I concluded with this:

> Over the years I have watched the Wesleyan, Holiness, and Pentecostal traditions give leadership to serious dialogues with scientists, philosophers, psychologists, historians, biblical scholars, educators, open theologians, process theologians, Eastern Orthodox patriarchs, and more. The depth, range, and unifying power of this tradition rooted in the Wesleys keep being evidenced in all of these dialogues, and with many of you in the lead. To have been with you in this process of dialoging, probing, and publishing about this great tradition has been a personal privilege. And, since you have not yet voted me out of the editorship, so far as I know, I look ahead with excitement to more of the process, and I certainly thank you for the kind and generous recognition evidenced by this Lifetime Achievement Award.

It is good for humans to honor each other when appropriate. We all need a little recognition and lots of encouragement. Even so, humans honoring each other must be kept in proper perspective.

I tried to identify the right perspective in my 2011 book *Heart of the Matter*. It is important to sort through the mass of ideas, theories, events, and people to locate what and who is worthy of being honored and followed most of all. In my judgment, the bottom line is Jesus Christ, exactly what is imaged on the cover of that book. I preached this perspective at Park Place Church of God in Anderson, Indiana, in July, 1990, in Sikeston, Missouri, in April, 2011 (my wife Jan's hometown), and often elsewhere.

In 2007 the Wesleyan Publishing House released my commentary on the New Testament book of Colossians. I began my narrative with this (243):

> The distinctive conviction of the whole New Testament is that Jesus is Lord! The executed peasant from Nazareth is said to be nothing short of God with us humans for our salvation. God in Jesus, through the Spirit, is set forth as the explanation of the past, the power required for the present, and the desired hope of the future for all humanity. Accordingly, the central message of the letter to the Colossians is the *all-sufficient Christ*. The Lord Jesus deserves *the* place, not *a* place, in our believing and living as Christian disciples.

Seeking to further illustrate this core conviction, I contributed a chapter to the 2011 book *The Continuing Relevance of Wesleyan Theology: Essays in Honor of Laurence W. Wood*, edited by Nathan Crawford. My chapter is titled "Heart of a Radical Reform: Christology and the Church of God Movement (Anderson)." I argue there that this church heritage of mine has centered its whole teaching heritage where it should, in the person and work of Jesus Christ. That is where the ultimate honor is due!

In 2018 my dear friend Dr. James Earl Massey died of cancer. He had asked me to edit and publish his life's writings. I was honored to do so. *Views from the Mountain* was noted by *Christianity Today* as one of the outstanding Christian publications of 2018.

One must make priority choices in life. It is vitally important to get beyond merely managing the constant flow of details. To avoid drifting through life, just responding to its conflicting forces, a decision is needed on what is really worthwhile. I once heard a successful leader say that three things are especially important to manage in a fruitful life—*attention, meaning, and trust.* To what will we give primary attention? What meaning will we allow to shape our journeys? Will we live in such a way that trust in us and our values is encouraged in others? These are the most important choices faced by all of us.

The world screams for our attention, and we each have only so much time to invest. Wisdom lies in focusing on what is important, and helping others to do the same. Making sense of this life is not easy. People naturally move toward stories that offer a framework of meaning for their life journeys. One who would lead and make a difference for others should tell the truly great stories and help others find themselves in those stories. They also should live in such a way that the guidance offered through practical modeling is credible. Integrity yields trust. For me, the story of *God in Jesus Christ* has gained my primary attention, shaped my life's meaning, drawn my faith, and even at times allowed me (I hope) to live as an attractive witness to this story before others.

God has been especially gracious to me and my family. Arlene and I had a wonderful beginning at Geneva College. The pilgrimage proceeded from there.

BARRY L. CALLEN

VALEDICTORIAN–SUMMA CUM LAUDE
GENEVA COLLEGE–1963 ANDERSON SCHOOL
OF THEOLOGY–1966 ASBURY THEOLOGICAL
SEMINARY–1968
MEMBER INTERNATION SOCIETY OF BETA PHI–1966
OUTSTANDING EDUCATORS IN AMERICA 1972
OUTSTANDING YOUNG MEN OF AMERICA 1975
CENTENNIAL DISTINGUISHED SERVICE AWARD 1980
DISTINGUISHED MINISTRIES AWARD 1983
ORDAINED MINISTER CHURCH OF GOD 1973

OF HONORS, PRIZES
OF DEGREES
Dr. Edwin C. Clarke, President
PRESENTATION OF BACCALAUREATE
DEGREE CANDIDATES
Director of Student Affairs . . . . Dr. Harold A. Bruce
PRESENTATION OF
HONORARY DEGREE CANDIDATES
Dean of the College . . . . . . Dr. John S. McIsaac

ALMA MATER
Directed by Professor Harold Gregg, Chairman Music Department
BENEDICTION . . . . Rev. Willard G. McMillan
Director of Spiritual Activities

☆   ☆   ☆

HONORS OF THE CLASS OF 1963

John Young Barr
Gale G. Croley . . . . Cum Laude
Nancy Harriet Elliott . . . . Cum Laude
Howard Terrance Manning . . . . Cum Laude
Susan Rae Murray . . . . Cum Laude
Robert Park Mullins . . . . Cum Laude
James M. White . . . . Cum Laude
Raymond Paul Culboth . . . . Cum Laude
Arlene Marie Conley . . . . Magna Cum Laude
Gerald J. Dritan . . . . Magna Cum Laude
Miss Fay Henchinson . . . . Magna Cum Laude
Jay M. Mann . . . . Magna Cum Laude
Edward J. Prout . . . . Magna Cum Laude
Donald Boyce Witham . . . . Magna Cum Laude
Barry Lee Callen . . . . Magna Cum Laude
Pena Fay Hutchinson . . . . Summa Cum Laude
Barry Lee Callen . . . . Salutatorian
Valedictorian

James O. Jackson

James Earl Massey

Ronald J. Fowler

Mendell Thompson

Jim Lyon

Laurence Wood

Hubert Harriman

David Bundy

David Han

Honor Table at the time of my retirement from Anderson University.

Back at Geneva College, April, 2002, I was being honored as an alumnus author.
With me are my former teachers (L. to R.) William Russell, Norman Carson, myself,
David Carson, and Willard McMillan.

A 2003 reunion of some members of my
Geneva College class of 1963. I am standing upper right.

A 2004 reunion of 1959 Jackson-Milton High School class. I am standing center back.

THE EARLY
MORNING LIGHT

A friendly reflection on some of the main
events in the life of the Church of God
reformation movement during
the first fifty years.

By

Robert H. Reardon

To Barry – a favorite friend and son
in the faith, with love and admiration.

Warner Press
Publication Board of the Church of God
Anderson, Indiana

To
Barry Lee Callen,
architect of the Press,
friend and brother
beloved.

James Earl Massey

A thousand thanks
for your sacrificial services
and generosity.

Bell tower of Park
Place Church of God,
Anderson, Indiana,
reaching skyward to
honor God. I have
been a member since
1963.

To Barry Callen
with the
affectionate regard
Elton Trueblood.
6-8-1965

Kind words from D. Elton Trueblood
and Robert A. Nicholson.

To Barry & Jan Callen —
What a pleasure
it is to work with
you. Again! Your
friendship and ministry
are wonderful!
Blessings! Nick

Reason to be proud
of my high-achieving
son, Todd.

Volume 122, Number 333
April 26, 1991

a.m. briefing

Local

Callen to graduate from AU with all A

Todd Callen was recognized recently at Anderson University graduating with a perfect 4.0 grade point average.

Callen
seated on stage
a   convocat
where   Presid
James L. Edwa
announced Calle
achievement.
An   Engl
education and p
chology   ma,
Callen will join
Callen   classmates June
at Warner Auditorium to receive
baccalaureate degrees.

The son of Dr. Barry and Arlene
Callen, 1703 Falls Court, he is a 19
Highland High School graduate.

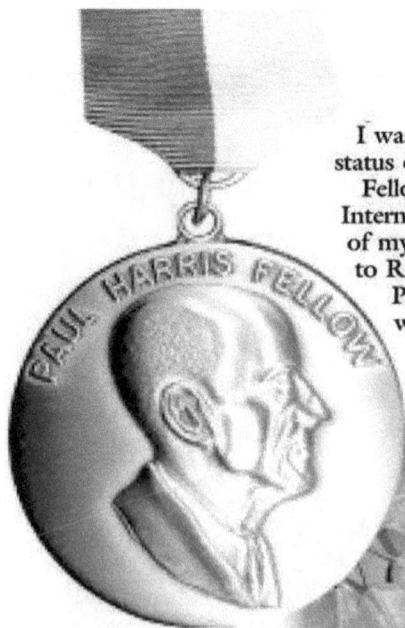

I was awarded the status of a Paul Harris Fellow of Rotary International because of my contributions to Rotary's "Polio Plus" effort worldwide.

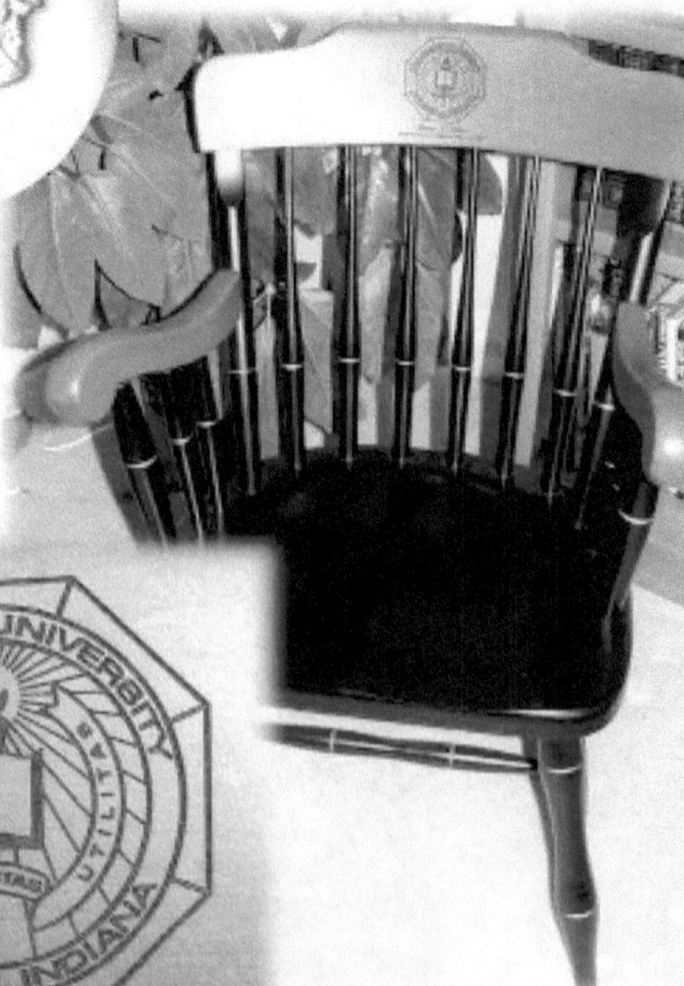

ROTARY
BARRY
Barry Callen
EDUCATION ADMINISTRATION
ANDERSON SUBURBAN INDIANA
INTERNATIONAL

ANDERSON UNIVERSITY
ANDERSON, INDIANA
VERITAS · FIDELITAS · UTILITAS

Barry L. Callen
September 1, 1966 to May 7, 2005

Anderson University gave me this chair of honor on the occasion of my retirement in 2005.

Dr. Richard Thompson of Northwest Nazarene University presenting me with the Lifetime Achievement Award of the Wesleyan Theological Society. The occasion was the 2009 annual meeting of the Society being hosted by Anderson University.

WTS

THE WESLEYAN
THEOLOGICAL SOCIETY

Honors

Barry L. Callen

Recipient of the Society's

Life-Time Achievement Award

2009

Chapter

A Fortunate Family Man

Being at home and surrounded by love

The earlier chapters of this book have revolved around my family history, education, published books, and numerous professional roles. It is so easy for a man to identify himself by places visited, tasks accomplished, and titles held. Time, however, brings greater clarity. Lasting importance lies in relationships built, people served, faith developed, and family loved—especially family (see *Appendix F* for my "family tree"). One's personal identity is especially influenced by the world of experiences and expectations that prevailed in the family of one's childhood. That is the beginning story from which one comes and with which one must deal as life goes on. For me, and for most males in contemporary America, the need to define "manhood" for oneself is a critical challenge. Potential distortion lies on every hand.

Alternate Visions of Manhood

The covered bridge in Newton Falls, Ohio, was built in 1831. It symbolizes how crucial the local rivers have been to that area's industrial might across much of the twentieth century. My father was a representative of that might. He was personally strong, self-made, and independent in spirit. He was a skilled carpenter who sometimes was a little insensitive to personal relationships within his family. As a veteran of World War II, he had sacrificed to help save the world. Afterward, he moved his family to the Newton Falls area of northeast Ohio from nearby western Pennsylvania to focus on building his own world in his own way. He was a good man, but clearly a man marked by his times—as we all tend to be. For Dad, manhood meant being your own strong and self-reliant person, marching to your own drummer. See my reflections on Dad and the old Newton Falls bridge in David Liverett's insightful book on bridges (*Love, Bridges of Reconciliation*, 2003).

Dad naturally wanted me to mimic his rugged style of manhood. I was his only son. We hunted, fished, and even built a house together in my early years, but the bridge to my future was over a river more intellectual than industrial. This was not exactly his ideal for me, and he had his way of showing a subtle impatience as I pursued my college and graduate educations. He and I were not at odds, arguing the matter, but we were in two somewhat different worlds—with Mom always trying to be a mediator. Dad and I connected our worlds satisfactorily over time, although rarely discussing the matter. Just before his too-early death in 1974, I had earned three graduate degrees, published my first book, been ordained to Christian ministry, moved into the deanship of Anderson School of Theology, and had a good wife and wonderful little son. By then, Dad was showing signs of genuinely appreciating my own brand of work and style of manhood. He really liked my choice of Arlene as a wife. He surely enjoyed Todd, although the contact was infrequent and all too brief.

Several times since Dad's death, I have visited his grave in the Palmyra cemetery, a quiet place not far from Craig Beach and Newton Falls, Ohio. There I have reflected on his life and learned increasingly to appreciate his values, limitations, accomplishments, and the kind of love he was able to express. I know he loved and finally respected who I am and what I do. I also learned that life's journey requires working intentionally toward bridging cultures and generations, attempting by God's grace to understand and appreciate the worlds of others. The future may not always mimic the past, but it's deeply rooted in it, and can be damaged or enriched by it. I was a son who would lose his parents too early. Dad died in 1974 at age fifty-five, and then Mom died in 1979 on the eve of her sixtieth birthday. In a sense, however, I have never lost either of them.

I will never forget a dramatic day in the fall of 1968. The scene was a classroom of doctoral candidates at Chicago Theological Seminary. There were fifteen men participating in a "T-Group" experience ("T" for "therapy"?) in which direct and very personal confrontations happened from week to week. Near the end of the quarter, the group and its two professors expressed their joint judgment to each class member on what in his life should be "flushed" in order to enable a more productive future. I was a member of this class and was most uncomfortable with this process, but there was no escaping my turn.

The advice given to me was to cleanse my life of the cramping impact of my father. My classmates had never met him, but had heard me describe his life journey and self-made style of functioning. Since the group found me protecting my inner fears and feelings with what they said were sophisticated verbal skills, they were calling for me to get in touch with my inner life and risk being more vulnerable to others. I had not learned to do that from my parents. My insecurity was great enough to block my inner feelings from public scrutiny. That had to change, so my colleagues judged. They had a point and made it very clearly.

My sister had her own challenges on the way to adulthood. I am "Barry Lee" and she "Bonnie Lou." Our parents thought we might be twins, but we came eighteen months apart and are quite different in some ways. The years would bring to her a rather different path of life from our parents and from mine, although both of our adulthoods would be spent mostly in Anderson, Indiana. Bonnie and I have sets of memories of our childhoods that vary a little, despite the same people and places having been around us. This is partly because we have different personalities and ways of perceiving and dealing with things. Who we are does affect what we see and later remember.

Bonnie attended Spring Arbor College in Michigan (1961-63) and then came to Anderson College, graduating in 1965 while I was a seminary student on the same campus. She had little money and some significant sickness. In 1968 she married a local man in Anderson, Rex Aley, whose family moved in different circles from Arlene and me. Although all of us were family oriented, circumstances kept us relatively apart for many years.

My sister and my wife Arlene were not able to relate to each other closely and warmly. Much of it was a clash of conflicting personal needs— Bonnie very much wanted close family contact and Arlene was more of a private person who needed her space and full ability to control her diet and schedule. This tension left me in the middle to keep peace and sort out my own version of family and manhood. I did not do the perfect job, to be sure. Arlene and I had our hands full rearing Todd. Bonnie's hands were especially full rearing her children Scott and Cassie, and having to do it alone after Rex died very young of cancer in 1982.

By the time Bonnie and I had reached our fifties, workplaces brought us closer together. While I was always on the Anderson University campus and in the public eye, she was not. She began working for the Missionary Board of the Church of God in 1987—located across the street from my campus office. She really cared about missionaries and national church leaders and sought to address their many needs, especially through effective communication. In 1999 she moved to my side of the street to become office manager for the admissions program of the campus. A very organized and social person, she soon knew well and was appreciated by many staff persons and students unknown to me. Naturally, she was sensitive when someone would say, "I didn't know he was your brother!" I had never tried to hide this fact; it just was not an obvious relationship that usually came to the attention of most people. Bonnie felt undervalued. She probably was, and for this I am sorry.

Charlotte, our mother, was intelligent, a dreamer, an encourager, a loving woman who came to feel isolated from the larger life that might have been out there for her had circumstances been different. She got stranded in little Craig Beach, Ohio. She was nostalgic and a bit poetic, as seen is this poem of hers that she wrote in November, 1965, and called "Just Hoping."

> Now I'm not one to be moody
> Temperamental or withdrawn;
> But there must be some small reason
> You can't make me move till dawn!
>
> Maybe it's 'cause there are no younguns
> Calling me to tasks galore.
> Could it be I'm really pining
> For tiny pit pats on the floor?
>
> I'd like to think I'm only waiting,
> Resting up for days ahead.
> Maybe I'll go buy a rocker;
> "Twould come in handy—well, nuff said!
>
> Someone just to coo and bill at,
> (Pa may soon be past that stage).
> Someday I may hear, "Hey, grandma,
> Really, why don't you act your age?"!!

Mom could be a little moody and withdrawn, despite her denial in the poem. She was lonely with us two kids gone from the home. She longed for grandchildren. Arlene and I would deliver her first in less than two years after she wrote the poem. Even so, Mom carried internal frustration with life in general, even some quiet depression. She felt threatened and jealous when her sister, my "Auntie," sometimes introduced me to her many friends like I was hers, and when Bonnie as a teenager would choose to spend her recreational time with another woman because she found her more fun to be with than Mom.

Mom had two siblings, neither particularly close to her in a wholesome way. Evangeline, "Auntie," lived in an apartment in the home of my Uncle Van in Beaver Falls, Pennsylvania, close to Geneva College where I attended. She had been hurt deeply by an aborted marriage—he had revealed his homosexuality soon after their marriage in the 1940s. Never really getting over this and never marrying again, she had a subtle way of trying to play the mother role with my sister and me, especially with me in the college setting during the four years that I lived with her. This would bring occasional friction between her and Mom. The brother, my Uncle Van, was a successful banker who lived in "higher" cultural circles and could convey some quiet cynicism about the lives of both of his sisters in their later years.

This tendency to make negative judgments could be seen as early as May, 1943. Uncle Van was married and in the Navy. Stationed away from immediate battle areas, he wrote to his mother who was still living in New Brighton, Pennsylvania—Grandpa VanArsdale was working across the state line in Newton Falls, Ohio, with the family soon to follow. Uncle Van was unhappy that my father had not taken his advice to stay home with his wife and two kids (I was born in July, 1941, and Bonnie in January, 1943). There were, he observed, "plenty of young fellows without any obligations to carry on, and the ones with the families should be doing their bit at home."

The way my father explained his decision to enter the war was different from Uncle Van's assumption. Dad assumed that he was going to be drafted. Not wanting to wind up in a foxhole in Europe, he and a few friends took things into their own hands. Dad's choice was the Merchant Marines, serving aboard transport ships as a carpenter, work he loved. Rather than irresponsibility, this decision to leave home was Dad's way of taking direct responsibility for his own life. It did come at a cost. I have a set of letters that he wrote to my mother from sea near the end of and just after World War II. Dad was bored, lonely, and very anxious to be back home to resume a more normal family life.

Contrasting views of adult responsibility moved through our family and impacted my generation. Over the years, my Uncle Van came to admire my successful professional life and, unfortunately, he tended to view my sister and her family in the suspect category into which he had placed his own sisters. When he died in February, 1993, portions of his estate came to Bonnie and me equally. However, he placed me in a supervisory role in relation to Bonnie's share, an inequity she naturally resented. Bonnie was a single mother with a homebound daughter. She was a woman of considerable responsibility who really needed the money immediately, and without restrictions. That was not to be, at least not at first.

My uncle cared about Bonnie's whole family unit and its special needs, but distrusted her independent judgment about money and wanted me to handle the distribution over a period of years. He had his own elevated view of manhood, judged others accordingly, and put me in a privileged position. I had no choice but to accept the role that his legal documents defined. My relation to my sister suffered for some years because of this. The dignity of womanhood suffered in the face of my uncle's particular model of manhood.

I was fortunate to have another male model in my young life. My fraternal grandparents were wonderful Christian people, but I had only infrequent contact with these Callens over the years. By contrast, my maternal grandparents lived just down Beach Lane from my home in

Craig Beach. Charles VanArsdale, was a particularly strong and constant presence. He was the one who first took my sister and me to the Church of God congregation in Newton Falls and was key to keeping us there.

A committed Christian man, he was known in that congregation as the "saint with the good singing voice," the one often called upon to pray in worship services. He owned the little cottage on the Free Methodist campgrounds in East Liverpool, Ohio, where I spent a week each summer and finally was converted to Christ.

Grandma VanArsdale died suddenly in 1954 and I, a new teenager, then spent many evenings and nights with the lonely and grieving man up the street whom I grew to know and love increasingly. In the mornings, I would catch the school bus on the corner between his home and mine on Beach Lane. He had a way of being constructively in the middle of various strained relationships, keeping his sweet and patient spirit. This model of manhood impacted me—and maybe my theology years later. Some scholar referred to my theological work as "on the progressive side of the middle." I like that characterization.

My College Sweetheart

Our romance almost never started. Arlene Marie Cooley and I had begun dating while we were both freshmen at Geneva College. We had met on our first day on campus in the fall of 1959 and quickly learned that we had much in common. Only financial necessity and family circumstances had gotten either of us to this campus—and Arlene's mother was not pleased when she heard that I was associated with the "Church of God." She envisioned emotional extremists who might babble in "tongues" and handle snakes in worship!

During our four college years in Beaver Falls, Pennsylvania, Arlene and I dated occasionally at first—and then as frequently as we could. There was no car and little money, so we walked in the College Hill residential community and went to various campus events together. She finally visited my home in Craig Beach, Ohio, during a school vacation and met my parents. They liked her, and she liked them. Dad asked her to pray at a meal in our crowded little kitchen eating area. She did in her quiet voice. He then said, "I could barely hear you." She responded, "I was not talking to you!" He was surprised, but liked that spunk coming out of what appeared to be a delicate young lady. Arlene sometimes said that she secretly wanted to be an auto mechanic—she could put a temporary fix on almost anything around the house. She respected my father's practical skills and worked around my general lack of them after we were married.

Arlene visited my home once during a summer when I was running the Ashland Marina on Lake Milton, and once she went on one of our family fishing trips to Canada. She and I rode all the way inside the "camper" that Dad had built to fit in the bed of his pick-up truck. It would sleep three and is where everything was packed for the week's vacation—including the two of us. We enjoyed the privacy. I recall crossing the international bridge in Toronto that included customs control for Canada. It was a hot summer day, traffic was heavy, the line moved slowly, and exhaust fumes made breathing labored inside the camper. It certainly was a cozy little place, but uncomfortable and even a little dangerous. Arlene and I survived and enjoyed the adventure.

The Flinners, Arlene's Aunt Bea and Uncle Lyle, were renting a home facing Old Main on the Geneva campus. She was a campus librarian and he a professor. Arlene lived with them while I lived with my Aunt Evangeline who was secretary to the college president and lived in the third-floor apartment of my Uncle Van's home just two blocks from the campus. One Christmas vacation, the Flinners went back to Uniontown, Pennsylvania, the hometown of Bea and Arlene. Arlene and I sat in the back and she drilled me with questions from my extensive class notes on the dynasties of ancient China—I had a final exam in Far East history right after the vacation. This study paid off, as did the relationship building that happened in that back seat and then at her home.

Once in Uniontown for the first time, I was taken to 100 Chaffee Street and met Arlene's mother, Evelyn. Her quaint little home was neatly kept, everything in place and every penny accounted for. Donald Cooley, Arlene's father, had been hospitalized with a severe mental condition ever since she was four years old. She soon would take me to meet him, feeling that I needed to see everything before I made any final decision about our possible future together. He was a sad sight indeed, in a wheelchair because both hips had been broken from shock treatments in the 1940s. He was very unkept by choice and denied that he even knew Arlene—heartbreaking for her. I was sobered but not discouraged about loving Arlene.

After the terrible trauma of Donald Cooley's initial hospitalization, Evelyn had managed well with very little over the decades. She lived alone, had a modest income from a job at Sears in Uniontown, and double tithed her finances to the local Free Methodist congregation—twenty percent of very little. Except for her sacrifice and the generosity of Bea and Lyle Flinner, Arlene likely would not have gone to college—as I might not have except for my aunt and uncle in Beaver Falls. Arlene and I each came from families with love, but not money. In addition to Evelyn, I came to know Arlene's extended family in Uniontown. Many visits to the city were to follow over the decades to come, with my growing especially close to Evelyn's youngest sister Juanita, her husband Richard Cramer, and their girls Cheri Truskey and Karyn Wayman.

These relationships were to last long beyond Arlene's death in 2003. When I then married Jan, she would quickly be "adopted" into the extended Cramer family, just as I had been decades before. I would have the honor of being a participant in the wedding of Cheri and later the officiating minister at the weddings of Karyn and Dale Wayman's sons, Richard and Kristofer.

Back at Geneva College in Beaver Falls, my memory is clear about a little song Arlene sang to me as we lounged one evening on the porch swing of the Flinner home. I feared that she meant literally the words that she playfully sang. They had to do with wanting a "pal" and not a "sweetheart." But my fear was groundless. Beginning with our junior year, the "pal" became "honey," and finally, on August 10, 1963, "hubby." Our wedding was in the New Brighton Free Methodist Church that my grandfather Callen had pastored many years before, and where Arlene and I had attended during much of our time in college. The Ackerman family from the Newton Falls Church of God congregation where I grew up made a beautiful wedding cake and delivered it from Ohio as their gift. Arlene's uncle, Lyle Flinner, my grandfather, Charles Callen, and my home pastor Lillie S. McCutcheon officiated in the marriage ceremony. Lacking any money except the few hundred dollars given to us at the wedding, our honeymoon was a drive to the mountain cabin near Uniontown, Pennsylvania, where Arlene's grandfather had been born. It was a quiet, quaint, free, and appropriately personal place for us.

Our marriage was a lifetime commitment that lasted nearly forty years, cut short only by Arlene's early death in 2003. My 1997 book *Faithful in the Meantime* is dedicated to her with these words: "To the Christian saints of all centuries, most of whom already rest in God, and many of whom yet remain in this life and are being called to live in hope and be faithful in the meantime. One who remains is Arlene, the wife who shares my life and desires above all to be about the Lord's business while time remains." A decade later, four years after her death, I dedicated to her memory my book *Caught Between Truths,* a manuscript long under development. I wrote, "To Arlene, now separated from me by death, who believed in the importance of this writing many years ago and always encouraged me to think deeply and write with courage."

What were Arlene's thoughts about me? A few months before my sixtieth birthday in July, 2001, Valentine's Day came. Arlene and I had been married nearly thirty-eight years. Being artistic and wanting to design her own card for me, she choose a "You are to me like. . ." theme that portrayed her feelings. It said that I was to her like an old shoe (comfortable), a security blanket (safety), a rock (dependable), and Santa Claus (generous provider). She was gracious and grateful, a loving and always loyal companion for whom—fortunately for me—I was particularly important. As she said on the card's inside, "If that isn't love, what is?!"

In 2006 I released my book *Seeking Higher Ground*, the centennial history of the Park Place Church of God congregation that Arlene and I attended for decades. On March 1, 2003, I lost Arlene to the scourge of cancer. I use the word "scourge," but note a comment Arlene made some weeks before her death: "Cancer is spelled with a small 'c' and Christ with a capital 'C'." By 2006 I had since married Jan (Slattery). That year's book dedication read: "To Arlene and Jan, two lovers of Park Place Church, both precious companions of my life, always seekers after the higher ground of God's grace, and always wonderful examples of self-less service to others." My book *The Wisdom of the Saints* had been released that May, carrying this on the dedication page: "My wife of forty years, Arlene, went home to be with the Lord just as I was completing work on this book. The Spirit of Christ radiated from her life and forever impacted mine. Thus, my rejoicing and appreciation are surrounded by a deep gratitude that goes beyond the ability of words to express."

What more need be said? I was a blessed man. And so was Arlene, so she said. I remember vividly a Sunday morning service at Park Place Church of God in the 1980s when Arlene gave a lay witness from the elevated lectern. She had worked hard on the wording of an essay that she delivered with feeling. A relatively private person, this was quite an event for her. She was very self-revealing, saying in part: "During all my young and not so young years, there were metabolic problems, mostly undiagnosed.... By the time I got on the far side of school teaching and family-making, this unnamed specter [hypoglycemia] was wreaking havoc on my physical, mental, emotional, and spiritual well-being. I was experiencing a dark night of the soul." The good news, she said, was that "instead of feeling defeated, I find affirmation and confirmation. There seems to be a centered peace and deep joy within."

Arlene was sensitive, self-critical, a disciplined seeker after holiness, and her own worst critic by far. Although I loved her so much, she had difficulty being sure of this, asking often for reaffirmation. This, I think, went back to her father's removal to a mental institution when she was only four years old. Abandonment was her lurking fear. She knew that neither I nor her Lord would ever limit our love for her. Even so, as she wrote in her private journal in December, 1987, "I find it distressingly difficult to walk in trust." But trust she did to the very day of her death in 2003.

Disoriented Delight: A Son

Arlene and I had one child, our son Todd, born July 29, 1967, at Community Hospital in Anderson, Indiana. We had moved to Anderson as newlyweds in August, 1963, and did not begin our family until I had finished seminary in 1966. Arlene's pregnancy stretched across much of the 1966-1967 school year. I was teaching at Anderson College (covering for Gus Jeeninga who was on sabbatical), she was completing her fourth and final year teaching fifth grade at the nearby Chesterfield Elementary School, and we were renting part of a house on Cottage Avenue just behind Park Place Church of God. She had considerable difficulty with sickness during the pregnancy, sometimes managing only carbonated beverages. The actual delivery was also hard. For her health's sake, we agreed that Todd would be our only child. Sometimes we teasingly added that, having done it right the first time, we did not want to risk a lesser child. At other times, we were sure that Todd was as time-consuming as two or three, and we could not handle more!

The "disoriented delight" phrase used above refers to my experience the day of the Todd's birth. During the many hours of labor, Arlene squeezed my arms until they were black and blue. When delivery neared, they put her to sleep and dismissed me (the practice of the day).

I was exhausted and had not eaten, so I wandered to the hospital cafeteria, now long after its open hours, and found a leftover piece of cake sealed in cellophane and left on a shelf, apparently free for the taking. I was very hungry, had no alternative, ate it, and became mildly nauseated. Since I was no longer needed or even welcome in the hospital for a couple of hours, I drove home to check on a few things at our rented home on Cottage Avenue. In a daze, I locked myself out of the car and house. Joy mixed with exhaustion can yield ecstasy and confusion! I somehow managed to be back at the hospital in plenty of time.

Life soon was to become even more hectic. When Todd was only weeks old, we moved to Wilmore, Kentucky, for me to continue my graduate education at Asbury Theological Seminary. I had been granted a permanent appointment to the Anderson College faculty and given a two- year leave in order to gain a second masters and then a doctoral degree. Our little Kentucky apartment, half of a duplex located on a concrete slab beside busy train tracks, was populated with mice and roaches! This was a nightmare for a week or so until we could get things clear. Arlene called life in Wilmore her time on the mission field. We survived the year, a very good academic one for me, and then were ready to move to the bustle of Chicago for my doctoral program. Little Todd was always on the move with us.

Before Chicago, however, I spent several amazing weeks in the Middle East with six Anderson College colleagues, with grant money paying the bills. Arlene and Todd stayed with her mother in Uniontown, Pennsylvania. I called from New York City as we were leaving the country. I was told that Todd had just taken his first steps—and I had missed them! Our first day in Chicago some weeks later was Todd's first birthday. I remember walking to a neighborhood store and buying one candle and a little cake. The three of us had a party with unpacked boxes stacked all around us. We did not know anyone we could invite to join us—and Arlene would have been embarrassed at the mess if we had.

Arlene and I took Todd to my home church in Newton Falls, Ohio, to be dedicated to God. Lillie S. McCutcheon was still the pastor. She had participated in our marriage ceremony in 1963 and now joined us in offering this special little boy back to the loving Father who had given him to us. It was the beginning of our sincere parental attempts to point Todd along paths that would be pleasing to God. The result has been an exceptional man with true Christian faith, dedicated to his wife and children, and with an admirable commitment to teaching junior and senior high school students, including some with special needs.

As is typical with parents, Arlene and I could take only partial credit, at best. There were times that we thought we might have failed as parents. More time has proven that we did not. After Arlene's death in 2003, my second wife, Jan, brought fresh wisdom to the parenting and especially the grandparenting process. I then had the challenge and joy of relating to her son Jordan, and soon to his wife Jenni and then their five wonderful children.

Once Arlene and I were back in Anderson, Indiana, from Chicago in 1969 with my doctorate in hand, Todd attended nursery school at the Children's Center of Park Place Church of God. His formal education would take him through the Anderson public school system, including Park Place Elementary, East Side Middle, and finally Highland High School. At East Side he first became involved in an organized music program, playing the saxophone. Arlene and I would never forget that moment of intense pride when, as part of the 1981 July 4th parade down the main street of Chesterfield, Indiana, standing in front of the school where she had taught years before, we watched and heard the wonderful Scottish marching band of Highland High School on full display, with Todd handsomely dressed in his kilts and playing the sax.

Todd's Scotch-Irish Callen ancestors would have been proud! His parents sure were. I often sat in the crowded bleachers at Highland's home basketball games watching Todd at the end of the court playing his sax as part of a lively pep band. Arlene usually did not go. She was not much of a sports fan, saying that it was just too loud for her—the hysteria of Indiana high school basketball. Todd learned to play the bagpipes. In later years, at his request, I brought home for him from Dublin, Ireland, an authentic Irish drum. Later marrying Laura Robbins, a fellow Highland piper, she and Todd were chosen one year as the two honored alumni to carry the school's banner in front of Highland's marching band that was being featured in the big Indianapolis parade before the "500" auto race.

Todd faced some challenges growing up, as do most teenagers. We were a conservative family, with Arlene especially restrictive about some activities he desired. She was concerned about protecting his health, as she very much was about her own. For some years, the three of us were at Wednesday evening prayer meeting each week at Park Place Church—with Todd usually the only person present even close to his age. We were anxious for him to hear the stories and testimonies of the older saints. At school, he showed obvious academic ability and did some dating that made us a little nervous. We all survived.

Some special things came along during Todd's growing up years, things that we participated in as a family. Arlene and I once crossed the continent by train, with Todd celebrating his fifth birthday on the rails heading west. He once went to a national church youth convention in Florida, riding on the Park Place Church bus, with Arlene and me trailing along in our car. Our family vacations were limited mostly to trips to our families in Ohio and Pennsylvania during Christmas and summer holidays. There were a few exceptions.

I once took Todd and some friends to a rock concert in Indianapolis—after his begging a little! I took him and a friend for a day of fishing in a chartered boat on Lake Michigan. It was quite an experience, one that I gladly would repeat on my 66th birthday with Todd and his two boys, Ian and Ethan—with Jan and I having just taken to a Michigan beach the two girls, Todd's daughter Emily and Hayley (whom he had adopted). Arlene and I once took Todd to a Billy Graham crusade—he went forward at the end. The three of us also took a wonderful trip to the British Isles. I remember taking Todd to a theater in Inverness, the capital of the Highlands (namesake of his high school), to see an early showing of "The Empire Strikes Back." He was so excited. I also took him with me as part of a campus travel group going to the 1987 World Conference of the Church of God convening in Seoul, South Korea. He and I visited Japan, Hong Kong, and China along the way. Arlene did not go, partly for financial and mostly for health and energy reasons.

Thirty-three years after our dedication of little Todd to God, Arlene and I had the privilege on August 27, 2000, of witnessing Todd's baptismal immersion as an adult Christian believer. It was a beautiful lakeshore event near Noblesville, Indiana. By then, he and his wife Beth had three small children of their own. They watched with a mixture of curiosity and anxiety as their "Papa" (Beth's father Al Hazen) baptized Todd before about one hundred applauding people. Emily, then almost four, was worried that her father might "sink." I assured her that he would rise, both out of the water and into new life in Christ. Also witnessing this sacred event was "GG," Arlene's mother Evelyn who was living with us and physically fragile by then, but had agreed to make the short trip from Anderson because Todd was so special to her. It was a time of rejoicing, the day when our dedicating a handsome infant boy was fulfilled by his self-chosen act of gratitude and dedication to his loving and saving Lord. Over the years he would grow into a strong Christian believer.

When high school graduation came for Todd in 1985, with his having a strong academic record, he received recruitment literature from many schools, but chose Anderson College. I had explained to him that we could not afford to fund his going to just any college, but we could afford Anderson because of the remitted tuition policy granted to the children of faculty members. Todd gladly stayed local, moving into Smith Hall just across the street from our 1703 Falls Court home. His rebellious tendencies at the time meant that his moving out was welcomed by him and us. Sometimes, love flourishes best with the help of a little distance.

College years would be great ones for our son. Todd was active socially, musically, and very much academically. He drained dry the remitted tuition policy, completing multiple majors (psychology, English, drama), all with a perfect gradepoint average. He nearly completed his teaching certification, which he would finish years later when he became a special education teacher back at Highland High School. The reason for not doing the certification earlier? He had not received the placement he wanted for student teaching [with his former teacher Ronald Clark], so he decided not to do it at all—a spurt of stubbornness based on what he thought would have been best for his professional preparation.

Todd's picture appeared on the front page of the *Herald Bulletin*, Anderson's city newspaper (April 26, 1991), with the headline: "Callen to Graduate from AU with All 'A's'." Arlene and I were proud. Anderson College had been a good choice for Todd. Although full of religious questions, he did not mind the religious dimension of the school, in part because the campus gave him room to question and explore. He was comfortable with the fence since there also was an open gate should he choose it. He did not. Rather, he came to admire campus leaders like president Robert H. Reardon and his teacher and campus pastor, Donald L. Collins—who much later would officiate at Todd's second marriage to Brooke. But first came Beth.

While still a student at Highland High School, Todd met a young woman whom he continued to know through her college years, also spent on the Anderson campus. Beth Hazen was a social work major, finally someone that Todd could no longer resist. I will never forget the day when they came into my campus office to announce some important news. They had decided to get married and wanted me to join her father, Al Hazen, a minister who had graduated from the Anderson seminary, in officiating at the wedding. It would be a new stage in all of our lives.

Todd and Beth had a "gusto" about life that spilled over on me. In July, 2000, they celebrated my birthday by renting three kayaks. Down the White River we went, dodging rocks and shallow spots in the river near Anderson, Indiana. It was a new challenge for me, but they thought that I would be brave and try. I was and did, having a great time. They were to have three wonderful children together, Ian, Emily, and Ethan.

What Arlene and I only glimpsed during these years was the deep tension in this marriage. Divorce lay over the horizon, one of the great sorrows of my life. Arlene would be spared the pain of going through Todd's divorce and the confusion and anger it brought to his children. She died in March, 2003, before Todd's divorce came. When it did come, I already was remarried to Jan Slattery—who was exceptionally helpful in comforting and guiding Todd in his grief and confusion. She had been prepared for this role by having suffered a difficult divorce earlier in her own life.

Soon Todd would transition professionally from the business world to being a special education teacher at his own high school, Highland in Anderson. Jan, a veteran teacher at Anderson High School, was there to provide important assistance again. When she retired from teaching in 2012 and Todd was transitioning back to the Anderson public school system after teaching a year in a local charter school, Jan again helped as she could. Both Todd and I were fortunate that she had come into our lives. Todd would go on to excel in the classroom. In 2018 he received the "High School Teacher of Excellence Award" from the National Council of Teachers of English—Anderson High School sent him to Houston, Texas, to receive this exceptional recognition.

I Became "Bappy": Grandchildren

For many years I had been called "Doctor" and "Dean" by numerous faculty members and students. After the first year or two back on the Anderson campus from Chicago in 1969, there was not much ego need left for such official designations. A new name soon would appear. Ian Patrick, my first grandchild, was born on May 16, 1995. Arlene, her mother Evelyn, and I were waiting anxiously in the hallway of Community Hospital in Anderson. We heard Ian's first cry through the door and, within minutes, we were able to hold him. This was an exciting new stage of our lives! In his second year, Ian decided on my new name. It would be "Bappy," possibly the adding of the "B" of Barry to the front of "Pappy." Whatever the derivation in his young mind, it now was my treasured grandfatherly identity—and he passed it on to his new sister Emily Elizabeth (born in September, 1996) and then to brother Ethan Alexander (born in July, 1998). Even Hayley, adopted by Todd in 2007, soon picked up the name.

A major part of the very young years of my grandchildren Ian and Emily was their regular attendance at the Children's Center at Park Place Church of God. I would come in the late afternoon and pick up these beautiful little children. In the September, 1998, issue of the congregation's INSPIRER publication, I wrote:

When I pick up Ian some afternoons to take him home for a short visit, he always greets me excitedly with: "Bappy!!— Let's go to the big sanctuary." He means, before we leave, let's do our private little pilgrimage tour of the places in the church so special to Bappy and Ian. So we go hand-in-hand to look again at the big organ, the balcony, the little microphones hanging over the heads of the choir, and especially the mysteries of the empty baptistry.

We go right down in and talk about the water stains that show how deep the water gets, and then look up at the glorious stained glass window that looms just above it. I hold him up in the pulpit and he pretends to read the Bible to all the empty pews. These are sacred minutes, just the two of us, about twice a week in a very special place. Then Ian says to me, "Now let's go to the little sanctuary." So we make our way down the long aisle to the narthex, on to the Welcome Center area, and through the beautiful new doors to another sacred place, one that seems designed just for little ones of about three. On earlier visits Ian had asked and heard the stories being told by the beautiful symbols on the walls and ceiling. Now he again asks to have read to him the words of Jesus written on the doors and over the Jesus window that overlooks the playground where he had been running just minutes before. He then goes to the little altar on the left, kneels, asks that his Bappy kneel on the one on the right. I do. He then says, "Pray." The last time we were there I looked at him and said, "Do you want to pray this time?" He said yes and, with eyes open and looking at the Jesus window, quietly announced, "God loves me!" That was it and we were done. But such brief moments tend to have meaning for a little boy that may never be done!

I loved these three children dearly and soon decided that coming books that I would write should to be dedicated to the grandchildren. In 1996 came my systematic theology titled *God As Loving Grace*, with this in the front: "Dedicated to Ian Patrick Callen, a fresh and wonderful gift from the God of loving grace." This book states the highest truth in the world, the God of love, and was dedicated to the first-born of a new generation of Callens, an exceptional little boy.

My social history of the recent decades of the United States, *Seeking the Light* (1998), includes much about the life journeys of the members of my high school class. It begins with: "To Emily Elizabeth Callen, beloved granddaughter, one of the many young persons now related to the Jackson-Milton High School class of 1959. Emily did not live through the final decades of the twentieth century, but she will face the challenges and opportunities of living in their wake. May she and they, recipients of the troubled world shaped by others, lead new generations into better paths of peace, justice, prosperity, and faith." Emily quickly proved herself to be an amazing little girl, a blue-eyed blonde full of presence and possibility.

Then came Ethan. He was handsome, gentle, and patient, sometimes stubborn, necessary traits to survive with his two intelligent and energetic siblings. Released in the year 2000 was my intellectual biography of the world-famous Christian theologian Clark H. Pinnock. As the book's subtitle says, Pinnock's was a "journey toward renewal" that provides wisdom for millions who seek the truth for themselves. This book's dedication reads: "To Ethan Alexander, my beloved grandson who has just begun the journey of life. Given this world of ours, there will come times when he will need renewal that can open a fresh path that leads him toward truth, peace, and joy. May something in these pages become light and encouragement along his way. Above all, may he never choose to walk alone, but always draw on past wisdom and follow faithfully the way of God's loving Spirit." What a special, clever, and funny young man Ethan already was turning out to be!

What of the parents of these three wonderful children? Arlene and I had only the one child, our son Todd. He married Beth Hazen in December, 1991, with her father Al and I co-officiating in Park Place Church of God in Anderson. We quickly came to love her as our own. Todd and Beth are independent types, well-educated free thinkers who respect their roots without being improperly cornered or stifled by them.

My book *Radical Christianity* (1999) seemed the appropriate one to dedicate to Todd and Beth. It highlights a tradition of Christianity that was their heritage, a tradition that resists institutional and creedal strictures on the divine freedom to inspire experience, thought, and life in the church. Reads the dedication:

> To Todd, my son, and to Beth, my daughter-in-law, young Christians reared in and now voluntarily participants in the Believers Church tradition. For them, the Christian heritage is a rich resource, not a restrictive prison of ideas, structures, and practices. Christian faith invites the believer to get at the root of things, to be "radical" for the sake of present meaning and integrity. May their personal quests for spiritual wholeness and relevance flower into all that they desire and all that they are meant to be. So may the quest of today's church which needs her apostolic roots, Spirit-life, and ability to be herself, free of domination from anything beyond the distinctiveness of her own divine nature and mission.

Arlene and I were relatively unaware of underlying tensions in Todd's marriage to Beth. Apparently they had existed from its beginning. They were significant enough that in 2005 (after Arlene's death, fortunately) Beth initiated divorce proceedings, with Todd still very much wanting the marriage to work. The pain of such a sad disruption of a sacred relationship was felt by all people involved in both families. Todd and Beth faced in their differing ways the new challenge of being "radical," now in the sense of reaching with both fear and resolve for very new futures that would be apart from each other. As always, the children suffered as much as the adults. I was determined to stand by Todd, and then with my wife Jan, to be a stable model of good marriage for the children to see.

Despite the problems, there certainly were good times. Sunday, July 22, 2001, had been a hot but very good day. It was only David Markle's third Sunday as the senior pastor of Park Place Church of God in Anderson. I was anxious to be present to support him, having played a role in his being called. But family called me elsewhere. The previous day had been the birthday party for our grandson Ethan, his third. Just ended was the Vacation Bible School of the new Faith Community Church in Noblesville, Indiana, where our son and his family attended. Beth's father Al was the pastor. All three of our grandchildren had attended the week-long summer school and July 22 was the Sunday morning for the VBS students to sing in the service.

I went to hear them while Arlene stayed home with her aging and fragile mother, Evelyn. The children were great, singing fun Christian songs with vigorous gestures. Ian was six, tall and handsome. Emily was nearly five, shy and beautiful. Ethan was three, the smallest in the children's choir, yet self-confident and relaxed in front of the crowd. Todd, their father, played his saxophone in support of congregational singing. It was so good to see him and his children sharing their gifts in God's service. Two weeks later, Todd and Beth played a duet to support their communion service, he the sax, she the flute. Arlene and I could not have been more pleased.

What a contrast it was on Sunday, December 11, 2005. It was the Christmas program being presented by the children of Faith Community Church in Noblesville. Ian was the narrator, and both Emily and Ethan had small parts. With Arlene now deceased and me remarried, Jan and I came this morning as proud grandparents—but it now was an awkward and sad setting. We sat with Todd, who was determined to be there as a supportive and proud father. But he was sullen, said little, and did not participate in the communion service. He and Beth were many months into their divorce process, which had soured his relationship with Al Hazen, Beth's dad, the congregation's pastor and my friend. Todd avoided encountering Al. I greeted Beth, Al, and Charla Hazen as I had opportunity during the morning, intending not to lose these relationships myself, despite all that was going on. Todd already had found a significant new relationship, Brooke Leever, and her daughter Hayley. In fact, after this service, Jan and I hosted Todd and all four of the kids at a downtown restaurant in Anderson where we met Brooke's parents for the first time.

Lives surely were in transition. Jan and I hoped to be steady and supportive anchors for others, especially for Todd, Ian, Emily, and Ethan. Whatever the future was to be, it surely would be different. Both Beth and Todd were in strained financial circumstances, to put it mildly, she moving back to the Corlett Way house in Anderson that they had been trying to sell, and Todd remaining in the Falls Court house that Arlene and I had bought in 1975 and in which Todd's family had lived since Arlene's death in 2003. He wanted to buy this house, but could not for financial reasons. So Jan and I, while celebrating our second wedding anniversary back in Fortville at the Ivy House Bed and Breakfast in December, 2005, worked out a plan that we presented to Todd soon after. We were prepared to sell him the home at a very modest cost and with no interest charged. We would be the lenders. He was pleased, grateful for the generosity, and now could see light on a viable housing future in the home in which he had grown up. However, because bankruptcy was a real possibility for Todd in the wake of the divorce, we dared not have this home as an asset in his name. So, actual ownership would be years away.

There is a pattern to be seen in my book dedications during these transitional years. They evolved one at a time, of course. However, now that I look back over them as a group, I see the constant of family. I sought to honor my loved ones through their recognition in my professional achievements. My wife Arlene, very self-giving, had cared for Ian, Emily, and Ethan in our home while I and their parents worked. She poured her life into them, making an investment for the future. They called her "Mamoo" and truly loved her. Her service to them and their parents tended to overshadow my mere book recognitions. She deserved more credit than most others recognized.

So prominent in my older adult life have been Ian, Emily, and Ethan. To them I have always been their "Bappy." When Todd married Brooke Leever in 2006, her daughter Hayley came into my life. She picked up the "Bappy" tradition, soon found a fresh place in my heart, and was formally adopted by Todd in January, 2007. Unfortunately, that would not be a long-term relationship.

Then, on April 8, Easter Sunday, 2007, still another grandchild came along. It was Bentley Allen Slattery, the first for Jordan (my step-son) and Jenni. My wife Jan had inherited grandchildren through me. Ben was her first "from scratch," as she said, and we loved this precious little boy from his first day of life. The same soon would be said about Emma, Max, Sam, and Zach.

The Love of My Later Life

My father died of cancer in the mid-1970s. Soon my mother sold the little home of my childhood in Craig Beach, Ohio. Arlene and I then bought a home at 1703 Falls Court on the edge of the Anderson University campus. Mom helped us with the downpayment by using some of the modest amount of money she got from her home. She then joined us in Indiana, moving into the apartment attached to our new home. Finally, she was in a stimulating environment that offered her numerous opportunities. She went to work for three years as office manager for the campus security station and found joy in the role and its social interaction. But her body wore out and she became limited physically and rather depressive. It came all too soon in 1979.

After Mom's death circumstances in the life of Arlene's mother, Evelyn, caused her to make the move from her lifetime home in Pennsylvania to Anderson—a second mother in our apartment. She was to live with us for over two decades. A strong-willed and meticulous Christian woman, she carved out a new and simple life in Anderson. She planted flowers, baked bread weekly, and played the organ at a local Free Methodist congregation to which she gave herself freely. She loved our grandchildren, with whom she had frequent contact in our home. Her highly disciplined standards sometimes made it hard for her to let them just be kids (Arlene had experienced the same problem in her own childhood). Evelyn adored her great-grandchildren but also worried about them and their parents. Eventually, Evelyn began to suffer the increasing effects of her older age, physically and mentally. It was sad to watch, and eventually it was not possible to maintain her in our home.

One day Evelyn wandered off in the freezing cold without a coat and was rescued by a neighbor. We knew what we had to do to protect her from herself. Arlene was then suffering from her advancing cancer. Together, we chose Monticello House, a lovely place in Anderson that specialized in serving elderly persons with Evelyn's limitations. It was a hard but necessary move for her. I am grateful that Arlene was still here to help me with this most difficult process. After her death several months later, I became the primary person to stay in touch with Evelyn and see that all of her medicines and personal needs were being cared for. She eventually relaxed and became quite affectionate toward me, overcoming her great reserve around men (going back to the difficult life with her husband Donald and his mental illness). When I would enter the home where she stayed, she would smile and clap her hands like an excited little child. This is a precious memory for me—in effect, I had become her son now that her daughter, her only child, had died.

Evelyn's own death came on November 15, 2004, at age eighty- eight. As I had prearranged, there was a visitation in Anderson and then she was taken back to her home in Uniontown, Pennsylvania, for burial with her husband Donald. The transport was her only time to fly—I had promised her that she would not have to leave the ground until she was dead! In her final months of life, I had introduced Evelyn to a special friend I then was dating. She approved of Jan, but admittedly with a muddled mind that couldn't keep straight whether or not her daughter Arlene was still alive.

Jan Slattery was an unexpected and wonderful blessing, soon to be the second companion in my life. She was from Sikeston, Missouri, and, after the premature death of her parents, had found her way to Anderson, Indiana, in 1970 to live with her brother Gene and wife Pat, finish high school, and attend college. Anderson and Park Place Church of God became her new home. I had known her casually over many years; now we became much better acquainted. My 2006 centennial history of our common congregation, titled *Seeking Higher Ground*, speaks occasionally of Jan's various contributions to the church, and includes a page and photo of the dramatic baptism of my wife Arlene just weeks before her death. The book's dedication, in honor of these two exceptional women, reads: "To Arlene and Jan, two lovers of Park Place Church, both precious companions of my life, always seekers after the higher ground of God's grace, and always wonderful examples of selfless service to others."

Jan came into my life quite unexpectedly. Given my personal journal, I can recount my courting of Jan on a daily basis. My grieving process had proceeded through the many hard months leading to Arlene's death on March 1, 2003. I had lost her slowly as cancer took her from me one pound at a time. I then sought personal counsel about my grieving from wise friends like James Earl Massey, Joe Womack, and Juanita Leonard. They told me what I already assumed. While treasuring the past, I was ready to move on, whatever that might turn out to mean. Arlene had released me to marry again, anxious that I find some good way to get on with my life. This was one of her final gifts to me. Neither she nor I ever thought of Jan Slattery as a potential part of my future. Jan's husband had died of a sudden heart attack in October, 2001. She and I were both teachers, me in college and she an English instructor at Anderson High

School. We both were active members of Park Place Church of God, sharing many good friends.

I had moved to the small condo at 1914 Summer Place near campus and thought I might live there alone for the rest of my life. But that was not to be. I first connected with Jan Slattery as we both participated in a musical presentation of the Park Place Church sanctuary choir in recognition of Good Friday in the late spring of 2003. She had recommended me for the role of narrator, something I learned only later. I was uncomfortable with the idea of working with the choir since I did not read music and had no choral experience, but I was determined to try new things. I said "yes" and found the resulting experience very satisfying.

In the process of the rehearsals, Jan—active in the choir—came to my attention and soon I chose to take a small initiative. I asked if she were willing to meet sometime to share our grief stories—maybe we each could learn something from the other. She was willing. On Thursday evening, May 8, Jan and I met for an evening of discussion about our experiences of losing spouses and coping with the resulting grief over time. We then began emailing and meeting regularly, talking much about many things. Our relationship was clearly and surprisingly intensifying.

Given this development, I sought some reality checks for myself. One was my calling a little meeting of Arlene's "sisters," Darlene Stafford and Sylvia Grubbs, women very close to my former wife. They rejoiced with me at the news of Jan and, in effect, gave me Arlene's blessing to proceed with my new relationship. I formally proposed marriage to Jan on June 28 before we left on July 3, journeying together to Scotland and Ireland with the faculty/staff TRI-S group of Anderson University. She felt as I did. We went immediately to the homes of our sons to tell them the news. Todd and Jordan were a little shocked and would need time to adjust to the new set of circumstances. Blending families is a delicate process.

Now proudly wearing the diamond I had given her, I took advantage of a series of beauty spots to propose marriage again and again to Jan—on the seashore at St. Andrews, in a cathedral in Edinburgh, in the garden of a very old castle, etc. Riding the bus through the Scottish Highlands, she and I planned our future, including when to schedule the wedding and where to live. I earlier had arranged a luncheon with Rev. David E. Markle of Park Place Church of God, asking for his counsel since, as I told our pastor, "two of your sheep are following each other around the pasture." I told him that, if he had any concerns, now was the time to speak. He only blushed, obviously pleased.

I soon would begin my work in retirement as Special Assistant to Ronald V. Duncan, General Director of Church of God Ministries. He also had become significant to me in a more personal way. Early in his career he had been an associate minister at Park Place Church of God in Anderson. Arlene and I had appreciated his evangelistic zeal. He also had officiated at the wedding of Jan's previous marriage to Philip Slattery. Jan and I now turned to him to do our marriage counseling during the fall of 2003, and then to officiate at the ceremony itself on December 21. He gladly did both and we were grateful.

Jan and I co-authored a small article that appeared in the September, 2004, *Inspirer*, the publication of Park Place Church of God, our mutual home congregation. Titled "God Had A Plan," we shared a little of our grief journeys and the surprising joy of having found each other. We concluded: "What we thought were dead-ends [death of two spouses] became a two-lane highway with many adventures along the way. God helped us with our roadmap, leading us to each other. We have found happiness and joy along the new path. We don't know where else this road will lead, but we have faith that it will be quite a journey." It surely would be that!

I had one son with Arlene. Now joining Todd was a step-son, Jordan. He and I were different in many ways and began the slow process of getting acquainted and learning to relate and even love. Jordan is a skilled electrician, a loyal family man, and a hard worker. While Todd was finding his way into the demanding world of special education at the secondary level, Jordan and his wife Jenni were building a business to supplement her teaching and his electrical work. They were buying and renting homes, something my father had done on a smaller scale decades earlier. In fact, one reason that I have found it easy to respect what Jordan is all about is that he embodies the best qualities that I remember in my father—practical skill, self-reliance, initiative, and hard work. In many ways, Jordan and Todd are so different, and also so very much alike. I am proud of them both!

Jan and I sold our homes, hers on Rangeline Road and mine the condo in College Park. We bought the 1209 Wilson Blvd. property together and prepared to begin a new life. There would be many changes and also much continuity. My son Todd already knew Jan well (they had done drama productions together), she and I were active members in the same congregation, and we had many friends in common. Our December 21, 2003, wedding was relaxed and beautiful. Park Place Church was fully decorated for Christmas. Our two families were there, as were members of Arlene's family who had driven in winter weather from northern Indiana and western Pennsylvania to celebrate with us—how special! Some 400 others came to rejoice with us. Afterwards, Jan and I went to the Ivy House bed and breakfast in nearby Fortville for a quick honeymoon and then remained in Anderson for Christmas (being with families for the holiday occasions). Then we left on a cruise in the Caribbean, a first for both of us. Arlene had said before her death that she hoped I could find someone who would love to travel with me. Jan was perfect in this and many other ways. God had opened a new future.

The joy did not stop. On September 8, 2005, Jan and I exchanged emails during the day, as we often did, I from the Anderson University campus and she from Anderson High School. I said, "We are both very busy today, so let's keep in mind (if not in sight) that love roots us together even when we are rushed and apart." Her quick reply, which I treasure, was: "There are no words for how I feel about you. I am the luckiest woman on the face of the earth." As we occasionally say to each other, "This is a God thing." As I write this many years later, our love has deepened even more.

Part of the goodness was the wonderful relationship that soon developed between Jan and my sister Bonnie. For instance, I pulled off a surprise to celebrate Jan's birthday in 2007. I had told Jan that on a Sunday evening I would take her "out of state" and be back by bedtime. Jan wondered if I had rented a plane for a wild outing. Bonnie joined us as my special guest as we went from central Indiana to "Oklahoma," the musical on stage in Indianapolis. It was a great evening together. My sister was a single mother with severe financial limitations. She found in Jan a new and supportive friend.

Interestingly, choral music provided a significant transition in 2003 from my life with Arlene to the one with Jan. Arlene never sang in the choir at Park Place Church of God in Anderson, our home church together, despite her exceptional and well-trained voice. She felt unneeded and lacked personal confidence for facing an "audition" with Pastor David Coolidge, choir director. Having had no musical training or choral experience, I had never considered choir membership for myself, even though I joined my wife in thoroughly enjoying the congregation's exceptional music ministry. Then came that critical Good Friday of 2003 and the Park Place choir's presentation of *Colors of Grace*, under the direction of Randy Bargerstock (Rev. Coolidge having retired). Surprisingly, I was asked to work with the choir and function as narrator. With considerable nervousness, I did so and enjoyed the outcome—if not all the process. Rev. Bargerstock then invited me to join the choir. I struggled with the decision and declined, saying to him that I would be more of a "project" than a contributing member.

I married Jan Slattery in late December, 2003. She was a veteran member of the choir and the one who, I learned only later, had recommended me for that narrator role in *Colors of Grace*. She continued to encourage me in my musical interest, but without ever pushing me in any direction. I came to rehearsals occasionally, even sang on Sunday morning, but would get discouraged and drop out—having trouble relating notes to their exact pitch. In March, 2007, after months of marginal participation, I wrote to the new director, Joani Brandon, and bowed out again. But soon I was back, joining my wife, contributing musically as I could, being less sensitive to not being "perfect" in what I did. Jan gave me a special Christmas gift in 2009, a set of music lessons with the organist Al Lucas. Since they were pre-paid, she had me cornered (lovingly so). I took them all, with some benefit, and have remained in the choir ever since as a modestly contributing baritone voice.

That *Oklahoma* musical production mentioned above had been staged at the wonderful dinner theater in Indianapolis called *Beef 'n Boards*. Jan, who has a theater background, for years had been attending productions at the Indiana Repertoire Theater. It is located in downtown Indianapolis and does first-class professional work. I joined a group of friends in attending for three seasons, seeing some exceptional productions. Then in 2007 dear friends Phil and Phyllis Kinley treated Jan and me to a production of *Smoke on the Mountain* at *Beef 'n Boards*. Appreciating the "lighter touch of the musicals there, and the practicality of easy parking with dinner included, Jan and I began doing for others what the Kinleys had done for us. We hosted for all the years since a wide range of family and friends for productions of nearly all the famous musicals that one could name. Meanwhile, we kept in touch with the community theater in Anderson, *Mainstage*. We would not soon forget the hilarious presentation in August, 2010, of the classic *Arsenic and Old Lace*. We sat with friends Robert and Marilyn Smith watching other good friends Rhonda Hamm and Rick Vale acting on stage.

On Sunday evening, October 22, 2006, Jan and I were guests in the condo home of Glenn and Berny Falls in University Village located near our home and the campus. With us were Joe and Jacquie Womack and Lee and Barbara Theodore. We four couples all had lost spouses and found new love later in life. We shared refreshments and told tales of how we found, courted, and married our new loves. We were very open, laughed at each other's similar experiences, and rejoiced at how good God had been to all of us. By then, Jan and I had been married almost three years. We were committed until death would intervene—hopefully many years down the road. As I now write, we already have had fifteen wonderful years together.

My family, now redefined because of Arlene's death, was very much alive! As I remember what God was doing, even in death, I surely do rejoice. On Easter day in 2007 the fourth of my grandchildren was born. Bentley Allen Slattery was a bundle of pure potential from day one. Ian Patrick Callen, the oldest (born in 1995), has become an exceptional teacher and musician. Emily and Ethan came next in 1996 and 1998. They are different and both wonderful in their special ways, Emily in nursing and Ethan in pre-law. I am the "Bappy" of these three, a pilgrim grandfather. My name is different with the Slattery children. Little Ben began calling me "Papa," as did his sister Emerson (Emma), born in April, 2009, and Maxwell (Max), born in September, 2011. There would be more—see *Appendix G.*

On March 27, 2010, my son Todd remarried, with me officiating at Park Place Church of God in Anderson. Laura Robbins had been a casual band friend of Todd's in high school and had suffered an unpleasant marriage and divorce years earlier. She and Todd now rediscovered each other after so many years and their injured lives began to blossom together with a fresh zest for life. Laura had a daughter, Samantha, then a college student. Emily sang a duet with Samantha as part of the ceremony, with Ethan also participating. We rejoiced with Todd as we learned to love Laura (not hard at all). She was a surgical technologist with a warm heart for people in crisis. Meanwhile, Todd was teaching English at the junior-high level in the Anderson Preparatory Academy. It was a new beginning for them.

Moments with the grandchildren are some of my best memories. While taking my chemotherapy in the summer and fall of 2011, the three youngest provided many moments. I teased little Max and a smile broke out all over his face. It was priceless. He would ask, almost with reverence, to touch the bump on my chest (my access port for the chemotherapy). Emma and I would gently bump foreheads just to be silly. I said, "Emma, you have a hard head." She responded, "I know, I eat ice!" Ben once responded to something I had said with, "Papa, you so silly!"

The others were much older. Ethan was at our home soon after my seventieth birthday (July 10, 2011, in the midst of my chemotherapy). I had two ten-dollar bills in my pocket and slipped them to him to wish him a happy birthday (also in July). Soon after, he came back to my chair and said, "Take one of these back. I didn't get you anything for your birthday." He was so sincere that I had to accept gratefully, even though he needed it more than I did. Emily had wanted to come and visit, but admitted that she was afraid I would die from the cancer and she did not want to face seeing me for the last time. I reassured her and she came with her guitar to play and sing a song she had written. Jan and I listened with curiosity and watched with pride this beautiful young woman.

Then, on October 18, 2011, came those breathtaking moments provided by Ian. I wrote this in my personal journal: "Then it happened, completely unexpected. After the Symphonic Band and Wind Ensemble [of Pendleton Heights High School] had played pieces by the famous John Williams and Percy Grainger, the finale was introduced. It would be a "World Premier" according to the program, and had been composed and would be conducted by a junior at the high school. I had not been alerted in advance. The junior composer-conductor was my grandson Ian! The next five minutes were amazing, Ian in a black tuxedo, tall, slender, fully in control, with his wand beating and flying. I was so proud. Ian has a gift of music, playing, composing, and conducting. Wow!

And the "wows" kept coming. As 2019 began, Ian was finishing his masters degree in music at Butler University and Emily her undergraduate degree in nursing at Anderson University. Ethan drafted a sample submission to the U.S. Supreme Court as council to a petitioner—part of his undergraduate program in pre-law at Purdue University. Ben appeared as a percussionist in his sixth-grade band. And a new level was reached. When my son Todd married Laura, her daughter Samantha joined the family. Soon Sam married Molly and in late 2018 they became the adoptive parents of two boys, Finn and Ezra. That made Jan and me great-grandparents!

This autobiography is dedicated in part to my family's coming generations and what they may become beyond my lifetime. Actually, I haven't even mentioned two young Africans who captured parts of our hearts. They are orphans Jan and I have sponsored through Horizon International. We met Liffy once at his tiny home and still hope for the opportunity to meet Tokologo in his, both of them living in Limpopo Province, South Africa. They represent millions of victimized children in desperate need of love and care. We have sought to do the little we could, "one child at a time" (a slogan of Horizon's ministry).

Loving my grandchildren, and now great-grandchildren, leads to a fervent hope. It's that, surrounding whatever lives lie before each of them, there always will be a stabilizing and enriching Christian faith to anchor, guide, and sustain. Highlights of my older adult life have been the occasions of Christian dedication and baptism. Jan and I were present and rejoicing at the dedications of Ben, Emma, and Max by their parents Jordan and Jenni Slattery. On August 17, 2008, the grandfathers Al Hazen and I baptized Ian and Emily in Morse Reservoir near Noblesville, Indiana. Then it was Ethan's turn on August 16, 2009. May what they confessed on those days never leave their hearts!

I celebrate with the first three of my nine grandchildren, Emily, Ethan, and Ian, on the day I married Jan Slattery, December 21, 2003.

Arlene and I were married on August 10, 1963, in New Brighton, Pennsylvania.

Arlene and I celebrating our 20th wedding anniversary in 1983.

With our infant son, Todd, and my parents Charlotte and Robert in 1968 at my boyhood home in Craig Beach, Lake Milton, Ohio.

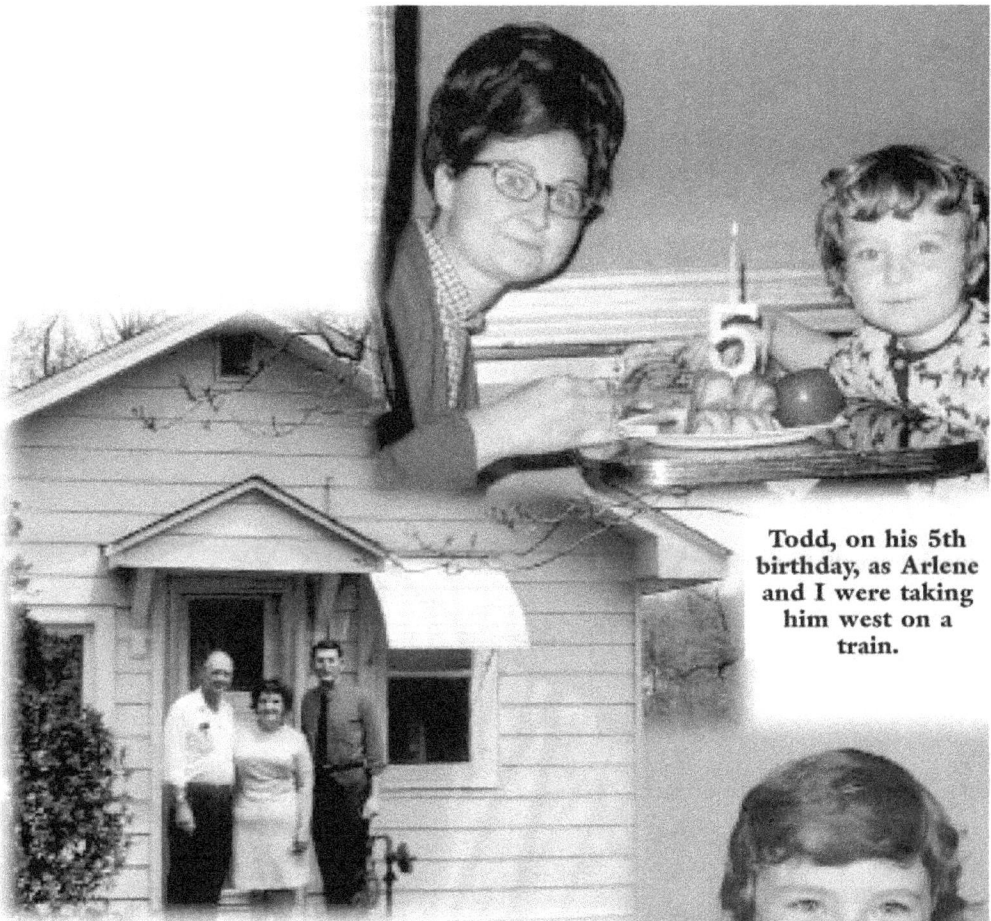

Todd, on his 5th birthday, as Arlene and I were taking him west on a train.

I returned in 1969 to visit my parents in the little home where I grew up in Ohio.

Young Todd, the pride of Arlene and me.

Todd with his beloved grandmother, Arlene's mother Evelyn, on her last birthday. My grandson Ethan is in the background.

Jan and I with a new generation of Callens.

Emily, Ian, Ethan and Hayley.

Leave (Liffy) Makgopa, the "son" supported by Jan and me in South Africa through Horizon International.

Wedding of Jan and me,
December 21, 2003.

Jan's son Jordan Slattery and his wife Jenni.

My son Todd's marriage to Laura. Jan and I celebrate with them.

In 2009, Jan and I pose with my son Todd and children, and with her son Jordan and wife Jennifer and children.

In 2012, my stepson Jordan and wife Jennifer, with their children Emma, Ben, and Max. Two more would soon arrive.

Grandma Jan with Max on
his first birthday, 2012.

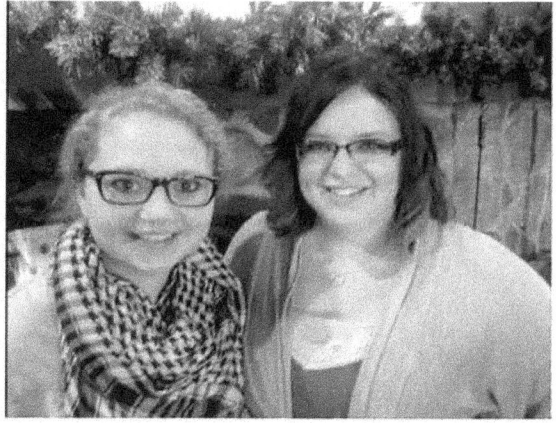

Granddaughters Emily and Samantha, 2012.

Grandpa Barry snuggling
with Emma.

Son Todd's kids at Halloween, 2000.

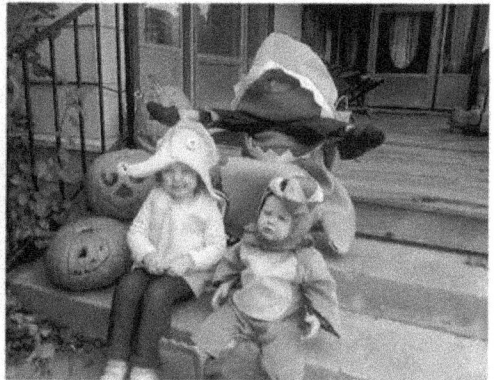

Son Jordan's kids at Halloween, 2012.

My sister, Bonnie Aley.

Bonnie Aley and her children
Scott and Cassie.

Jan and I with her brother Gene and wife Pat Hitt.

Ethan, Emily, Ian

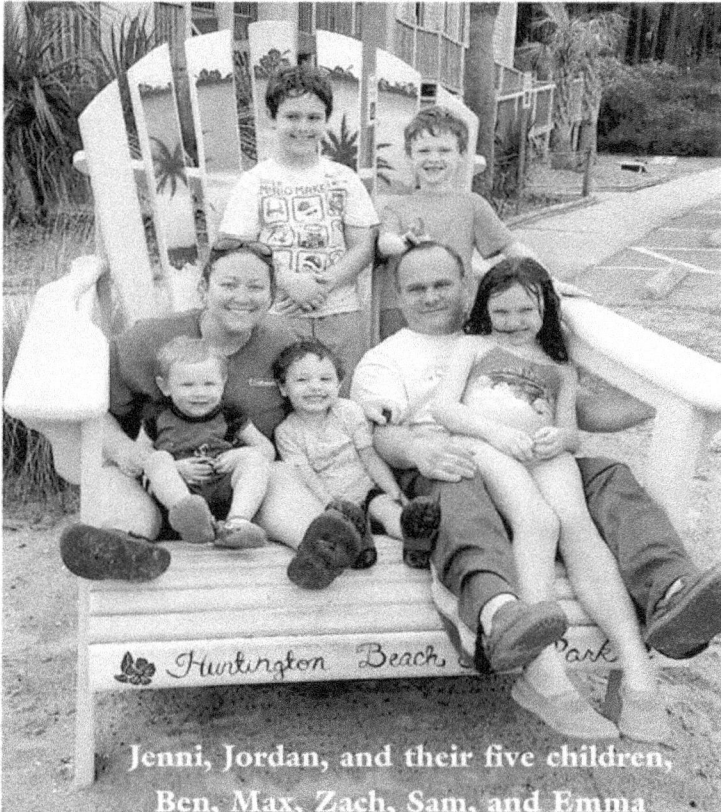

Jenni, Jordan, and their five children,
Ben, Max, Zach, Sam, and Emma

Samantha, Molly, and their sons Finn and Ezra,
our first great-grandchildren.

Chapter 12

Lessons and Legacy

A little wisdom gained through the years,
and maybe a little something to leave behind

The word "legacy" in the title of this chapter is used with hesitation. As a follower of Jesus, my goal has not been to be remembered fondly so much as to live faithfully, whatever the public perceptions. I certainly will not leave behind a material fortune, but true riches are hardly counted in dollars. In generations prior to mine, there was much good as well as much struggling. I hope to pass on mostly the good. Not all has been ideal in my years, but some has at least moved in the direction of the ideal. I reflect humbly, recognizing how fleeting one's life is and how brief and fickle are the perceptions and memories of others. A central question is, What is really worth remembering? See my reflections on this question in *Appendix A*.

The truth about life's legacy is portrayed well by Chris Browne in a "Hagar the Horrible" comic strip. It appeared in the Anderson, Indiana, newspaper on November 4, 2001. Hagar, the seemingly brutal but often hapless Viking warrior, waves his sword and announces to his family that he is off to England in search of immortality. The young son inquires of his mother about the meaning of "immortality." She explains that it is "an enduring fame that many people with big egos seek—but it never seems to last very long!" And so it is.

I do hope that something of worth from my life will endure beyond my short lifespan. The "fame" in view is limited to some opportunities made the best of, some seeds sown faithfully, some hope that the tomorrows of a few people will be enriched by where I have been and what I have tried to be and do. The 2007 birthday wishes to me from James L. Edwards, president of Anderson University, included: "All you do for so many is such a blessing!" I hope so.

I appreciate the wisdom of Timothy Johnson found in his 2004 book *Finding God in the Questions*: "In my experience, finding God in the questions does not mean finding complete answers. In fact, you may discover that along the path of faith you pick up more questions than you started with. But you might also discover that you need fewer answers, and those you *do* find are enough to live on" (183). The lessons I have learned may be relatively few, but they are enough, at least for me.

I write as an aging man who shares the feelings of Henry Clay Morrison. According to his biographer, Percival Wesche, Morrison said the following on his eighty-fourth birthday: "Looking backward, there is much to be thankful for, much to regret, and nothing to boast of. I think with gratitude of the countless mercies of God, his patience with an unworthy servant, and I go forward singing, 'Nothing in my hand I bring; simply to thy cross I cling'" (154). Only in this spirit do I use the word "legacy." It may consist mostly of my passing on a few of the lessons I have learned.

Scattered Fragments

Any long life is filled with countless aspects, memories, impressions, and reflections. Before I attempt to paint a picture of big lessons and a modest legacy, I acknowledge that usually life is dominated by a mass of little things, seemingly disconnected and yet sometimes so influential. Here is a sampling of the countless scattered fragments of my life. Each brings its own little lesson.

1. Major Social Changes. Change appears inevitable. In the final decades of my life I have watched a shifting culture in North America. The population has become much more pluralistic, with unparalleled racial and ethnic diversity and a protectionist backlash beginning in 2016 with the presidential election of Donald Trump. Hispanics overtook African Americans as the largest minority in the United States. "Gay" rights and acceptance of the gay lifestyle and same-sex marriage have gained considerable ground and legal status. Women achieved a higher status in the workplace. The traditional family unit was compromised by frequent divorces and the unconventional becoming almost standard. Electronic cash, entertainment on demand, and legalized gambling became the norm, and soon were accompanied by heavy debt loads, high anxiety, and pain pills to help the masses cope.

The dominance of Christianity in the North American culture melted away. Computers, smartphones, and social media altered nearly everything. So much in public life became bigger, louder, faster, and often more outrageous. In the middle of it all, there also emerged a personal emptiness that longs for filling, and an individualism that longs for real community. People were living longer and trying harder to look young. We had instant and constant communication. Our GPS units (global positioning systems) kept track of where we were and should be going–immediately, but not long-term! We now are always found and yet more frequently feel lost. We are more obese in the midst of an exercising and dieting boom. We are increasingly tolerant, and yet still so tribalized that war continues to devastate the earth. So much is new; sadly, most basic things are still the same.

The nation's economy has risen and fallen. In 1964 I was fresh out of college, married, and attending graduate school in Indiana. The big steel mills where I grew up in northeast Ohio were booming and General Motors broke ground near my boyhood home for a massive new auto assembly plant that would roll out new Chevrolet cars for decades and employ many of my high school classmates until their retirements. In Anderson, Indiana, where I was in school, General Motors also dominated the employment landscape. But in the 1980s the Ohio steel mills began closing, as did its big plants in Anderson, Indiana. In 2019 the GM plant closed its doors in northeast Ohio. I have lived in decades of major social change.

2. Getting Sealed in a Wall. In all the change, one wonders what will last. A major part of what I will leave behind will be in the form of paper, much paper that has been bound into tens of thousands of copies of my many books, booklets, articles, and edited academic journal issues (especially the *Wesleyan Theological Journal* that I have edited for many years). These materials now are resting on shelves in offices, homes, and libraries all over the world, and now some of them are among the numerous digital files crammed into computer memories. Maybe they are only collecting dust or draining power! A copy of one of them in paper form is sealed in an unusual place. Anderson University celebrated its 75th anniversary in 1992. That year I released my book *Guide of Soul and Mind: The Story of Anderson University* that had been commissioned by the university to be completed for this historic time of celebration.

On October 3, 1992, during the university's homecoming festivities, there was the "Old Main Cornerstone Ceremony." Placed into the external brick wall outside the north entrance of Decker Hall was the cornerstone of Old Main, the original 1906 building on the same site. The stone had been a discarded tombstone found in nearby Maplewood Cemetery very early in the twentieth century. The original epitaph on the stone was: "Remember, friends, as you pass by, As you are now, so once was I." Behind this old and now re-used stone, for secure and long-term keeping, was placed a sealed metal box containing a range of historic objects and materials, including my newly published history of Anderson University.

The university's plan is that, sometime in the middle of the twenty-first century, someone will ceremoniously remove this stone and open the sealed time capsule. I hope that the paper of my book is still readable and that the words on its many pages have meaning for a new generation. Those who forget are without roots and sadly withered, whether they realize it or not. I have sought over the decades to nourish and record some significant root systems, hoping that later they will support new people and important new ventures. Those few minutes of ceremony in the fall of 1992 were a small thing; may they one day be of fresh significance to people yet unborn.

3. Doors That Have Opened. In 2002 it was my privilege to edit and publish through Anderson University Press the autobiography of Dr. Gustav Jeeninga. He decided to title it *Doors to Life* since, in retrospect, so much revealed in his fascinating stories tell how he had been led by a higher hand into new avenues of faith and service. We walk through the doors that open for us. Some open by our own vision and diligence, while some of the biggest ones seem to open on their own. On one hand, time and perspective encourage us to believe that the matter of open doors is finally in the hands of God. On the other hand, God has chosen to work, at least in part, through our willing responses and initiatives. We help to open some of our own doors.

As I emphasized in my biography of Clark H. Pinnock (*Journey Toward Renewal*, 2000, 100-106), there is the crucial principle of "reciprocity" in our lives. God works, and we are given the privilege of working in partnership with the divine. I have been influenced by the little book *The Prayer of Jabez* by Bruce Wilkinson (2000). We are encouraged to pray that God will bless us, transforming us so that our wills are aligned with the divine will and the borders of our ministries will be enlarged by new doors opening to us. The goal is not a growing ego and legacy, but the expanding ability to be ever more effective in God's work.

While concerned about the kind of trail markers I leave behind, I am more impressed with the various life-trails of others that I have been privileged to walk in my lifetime. The beginnings of my memory lie in Craig Beach, Ohio, where commercial activity was limited to two family-owned grocery stores and a fire station that was locked most of the time. There were volunteer firemen only, my father being one, and occasional public elections, my mother usually helping. This quaint little village setting hardly suggested the likelihood of "world traveler" for any little boy being counted among its approximately 400 permanent residents. So, what came to be a globe-encircling and culturally rich life for me was unexpected, to say the least. Some of my life trails amaze me. As I remember them, I rejoice—and I recognize the hand of God.

Benjamin T. Roberts, founder of the Free Methodist Church in 1860, and Daniel S. Warner, primary pioneer of the Church of God movement in 1880, opened the revivalistic, holiness, and reformational Wesleyan doors for me. These men were leaders in differing wings of the holiness revivals of the nineteenth century. I explored part of this open door in my biography of Warner titled *It's God's Church!* (1995). Although Warner walked out of the organized life of the holiness movement in the late 1870s over a disagreement about the implications of a passion for both Christian holiness and Christian unity, a surprising door opened to me in 1992. Fortunately, I decided to walk through it. I was invited to assume the editorship of the *Wesleyan Theological Journal*, the academic publication of the Wesleyan Theological Society. This was a much bigger door than I imagined at the time.

In 2001, Thomas Phillips, then at Eastern Nazarene College, sent an email to a large body of Wesleyan scholars. He announced: "Let me be clear. I believe that the present Editor of the *Wesleyan Theological Journal*, Barry L. Callen, has saved the Wesleyan Theological Society by his diligence and commitment to the Journal. I honestly believe that the Society would have died in the mid-1990s if Barry had not taken over the editorship." However that may be, the big task I accepted opened many doors for me, and through them I have been able to open doors for many others.

I have had the opportunity of chairing and working closely with members of the *WTJ* editorial committee, including William Faupel, William Kostlevy, David Bundy, Stanley Ingersol, and Richard Thompson. Having first met theologian Clark H. Pinnock in 2000 at the annual meeting of the Wesleyan Theological Society where he was keynote speaker, I soon was privileged to write his biography (*Journey Toward Renewal*) and in 2006 co-author with him *The Scripture Principle*. In the introduction to his 2001 book *Most Moved Mover*, Pinnock comments: "It is not an accident that the memoir of my own work was written by a Wesleyan, Barry L. Callen, and published in cooperation with the Wesleyan Theological Society. The openness model [of Christian theism] has intellectual roots in Wesleyan-Arminian thinking...." I have been able to be a creative catalyst in the midst of a wonderful Christian tradition.

Beyond my biography of Daniel S. Warner (1995), I published in the *Wesleyan Theological Journal* (Spring 1999) Howard A. Snyder's study of Benjamin T. Roberts. Then in 2007 I was instrumental in his major biography of Roberts receiving the annual Smith/Wynkoop book award given by the Wesleyan Theological Society. The work of Snyder was helpful in opening the door to my better understanding the Free Methodist roots of my own family.

Then I learned through church historian Charles E. Brown's 1954 *When Souls Awaken* that the Church of God movement (Anderson) was a combination of the Wesleyan/Holiness and the more "radical" Believers Church traditions of Christianity. I walked through this door of insight, determined to probe the full extent of my church roots. Having participated for a decade in the dialogue between leaders of the Church of God movement and the Independent Christian Churches/Churches of Christ, I wrote about this "radical" tradition in my *Radical Christianity*

(1999) and, jointly with James North, in our 1997 *Coming Together in Christ.*

This "radical" open door took me down an interesting trail. In the fall of 2001 I led a seminar for Friends pastors that convened at the Quaker seminary, Earlham School of Religion, in Richmond, Indiana, where I had studied in the 1960s with the prominent Quaker philosopher and theologian David Elton Trueblood. These pastors had read in advance my book *Radical Christianity* (1999). We reflected together on the theme "Radical Christianity in a Postmodern World," especially in reference to the future life and witness of Quakerism. The tragic terrorist day of September 11, 2001, was fresh on all minds. Earlham was a special setting in which to explore the stance of Christian pacifism in the context of the United States already having begun its war in Afghanistan "to rid the world of evil." Then in March, 2007, I journeyed to Messiah College in Grantham, Pennsylvania, to deliver the Schrag Lectures on the theme of the radical Christian tradition and our postmodern times. The challenge was to share the heart of the "radical" tradition with college students seeking their religious identity in a rapidly changing world.

Individuals come to function as doors to the future. Gene W. Newberry was such an entrance for me. He was my first teacher of Christian theology and my seminary dean in Anderson School of Theology. He had a wholesome view of the church and tied academics closely to practical things. Following the wonderful local-church modeling of Rev. Lillie S. McCutcheon and Austin E. Sowers that had graced my early church life in Newton Falls, Ohio, Dr. Newberry came along to keep this door open in the midst of my pursuits of higher education at the graduate level. He pioneered the seminary deanship for me, with my assuming his office in 1973-1974. Having been my teacher and dean, he now was a faculty member under my deanship. This could have been awkward, but his graciousness kept it from being so.

In 2001 the seminary in Anderson was celebrating its fiftieth year of ministry. As part of the historic remembrance, it was my privilege to conduct a video-taped interview with Dr. Newberry—then retired for two decades—and to read at the annual commencement ceremony of Anderson University in Warner Auditorium the formal citation as the grateful campus bestowed on this good man an honorary Doctor of Divinity degree. Gene then chose to write an endorsement statement that appears in this present book. I am in debt to him and many others who shined warm and guiding light on my life's path.

Another door also opened at the beginning of the twenty-first century. At first it was just another assignment I was asked to fulfill. There was a "Wesley Study Project" convening in California and I was to go and represent the Church of God. I did and soon became a member and leader of the Wesleyan Holiness Connection that emerged. In 2011 Aldersgate Press developed within the Connection with me as Editor. The original small door, now many years later, opened more than I could have imagined. It's been a combination of God's calling, enabling, and my willingness to invest myself deeply in ministry faithfulness.

In life, some doors open. Things happen, people come along, and opportunities present themselves. In one way, this seems so erratic and unpredictable. In another way, looking back over time, there seem to be patterns in life's flow, even a subtle but significant and divinely-set direction. The final outcomes are determined in part by what opens and in part by what one chooses to go through, paying whatever price is required. I have sought to pay the necessary cost to get through many open doors. . I have become more sensitive to the reality of "providence" (see *Appendix A*). God graciously guides without being an all-controlling manipulator.

4. Storms That Have Raged. I was nine years old when a great storm hit northeast Ohio on the Thanksgiving weekend of 1950. A total of twenty-nine inches of snow buried the area, with high winds creating drifts as much as ten feet deep. The paralysis kept many people isolated in their homes for nearly a week. The National Guard was called to assist in road clearing. I remember Dad and me digging a trench from our house down the middle of Beach Lane to reach Baldwin's Market near the entrance to the amusement park, a distance of two blocks. It was both frightening and fascinating, clearly inconvenient and truly inspiring for a young boy.

I also remember Palm Sunday, 1965. Arlene and I sat huddled in our little Anderson apartment on East Fifth Street while a large tornado system passed over us and killed many people just to the north in Marion. Similarly, I remember being on an ice cream break during a 1985 meeting of the board of trustees of Anderson University. We were in the quaint little town of Nashville, Indiana. I observed a strange and threatening sky that also passed us by. Soon I learned that this storm worsened greatly as it crossed Ohio, sending a terrible tornado right through Newton Falls and seriously damaging my home church, nearly killing Lillie and Glenn McCutcheon in their parsonage next to the church. I wrote about this in my biography of Sister Lillie (*She Came Preaching*, 1992).

I remember well a snowy day in 1984 when the Baltimore Colts, a famous professional football team, suddenly left at night and moved their whole operation to Indianapolis in a secret parade of moving vans. The city of Baltimore was shocked and angry at the loss of its famed team. Indianapolis was rejoicing, as was Anderson College where the team began staging its summer training camps (practically across the street from our home on Falls Court). I was the vice-president for academic affairs and this was one of several public relations successes of the campus at the time. Another was Purdue University coming to the Anderson campus to do joint academic programming, a unique public-private partnership in higher education. These were busy and pioneering days for me.

To complete a cycle of irony with the Colts, in January, 2007, the team traveled east to participate in a big playoff game against the Baltimore Ravens, the new NFL team that finally had filled the vacuum left in Baltimore during the departure storm of 1984. Johnny Unitas (1933-2002), the legendary quarterback of the old Baltimore Colts, maybe the best of all time at his position, was now being replaced on the field by the quarterback of the Indianapolis Colts, Peyton Manning. He was the best in professional football in 2007, leading the Colts to that year's Super Bowl championship. Some storms eventually bring surprising results.

"Black Monday," August 28, 2000, seemed frightening indeed to me. Just as we were launching another successful school year on the Anderson campus, and I was working with the newly formed Editorial Committee to get Anderson University Press launched, disturbing rumors began flying. Six financial people had just resigned at the Board of Church Extension and Home Missions of the Church of God. Robert W. Pearson, General Director of the newly formed Church of God Ministries, had just done the same after only two years in the role.

Was the North American structure of the Church of God movement beginning to break apart? The years to follow would bring back some stability, but with the church's future still unclear. Ronald V. Duncan would serve as the new General Director, with me at his side as Special Assistant. His retirement in 2013 would be a time of more change and many questions. The Church of God was a reform movement lacking a clear vision of the reforming cause to which it was called in this new time. To compound the awkwardly transitional situation at a local level, in 2001 my own beloved home church in Newton Falls, Ohio, suffered a split, with many of the key lay leaders leaving and forming another congregation a few miles away in Lordstown.

How sad this church split was after the glory years for the church in Newton Falls during my youth. By the first years of the new millennium, Sister Lillie had died and Brother Austin, her brother and associate pastor in earlier years, was retired and in poor health—a precious man whom Jan and I would visit on occasion near Dayton, Ohio, prior to his death in

2018. Besides the Newton Falls problem, Brother Austin's missionary work in Australia in the 1970s had suffered a serious disruption that broke his heart. On the positive side, in the 1960s Austin had led in the establishment of the Berlin Center Camp Meeting grounds that continues to serve the Church of God in northeast Ohio. In July, 2012, I ministered there as a conference leader and then Jan and I stopped to visit Austin on our way back to Indiana. We were anxious to tell him of how his earlier ministry on behalf of this conference/retreat center was prospering.

Life is full of storms of various kinds. They threaten, blow, drench, and sometimes even cleanse. Winter winds blow, but periods of springtime renewal also come. On the North American church front, the Church of God movement was seeking a fresh way forward with its "Project Imagine" study. I functioned as its recording secretary, with the results of the study modest but meaningful. This reform movement needed to get beyond its founding reaction to the downsides of nineteenth-century denominationalism and face its own global reality in a very different time. I drafted a vision statement that spoke to this need and was widely discussed.

At the opening of the new century, more was happening than storms. In 2001, Arlene and I went to the reception at Park Place Church of God in Anderson celebrating the fiftieth wedding anniversary of Robert and Marilyn Smith, longtime friends and campus colleagues. I greeted Bob, offering congratulations. His response was, "Well, Barry, you now are the sole survivor of the class of 1969!" I had not had that sobering thought before. He meant that in the fall of 1969 about a dozen of us had joined the faculty of Anderson College (actually, while I was in that group, I had begun in 1966 and was coming back in 1969 after a two-year study leave). Included were Greta Domenic (music), Sid Guillén (Spanish), Duane Hoak (education), James Earl Massey (campus pastor and Bible), Larry Osnes (history), James Rouintree (music), and Robert Smith (drama). What a group of colleagues—and I now was the sole survivor!

The rest had retired or moved elsewhere after many years of outstanding service on the Anderson campus. I had fulfilled a wide range of roles over the years—teacher, department chair, program director, dean, vice-president, campus historian, press editor, corporate secretary, world tour leader, etc., but all on the same Anderson campus—and still with no retirement plans. It was a strange feeling to be the only one left!

My retirement came in 2005—if one can call what came after that "retirement!" In life, change and storms appear inevitable. So, by faith, I affirm the presence of God in the midst of it all. Nothing happens that is not at least allowed by God—although much that happens certainly is not God's choice. Believers have no exemption from pain in this world; what we do have is access to divine grace that guides and sustains in the middle of all storms.

5. Roads That I Have Walked. I always have found great meaning in Robert Frost's poem "The Road Not Taken." We all encounter forks in our roads of life. Frequently, choices taken are determined by subtle factors, with our not quite knowing how things would have turned out if we had taken the other way. What I do know is that "two roads diverged in a wood" and the ways I have gone "has made all the difference."

The road Philip took from Jerusalem down to Gaza (Acts 8:26) was a wilderness way, an uncertain path like the one we all must follow down the span of our years. Choices must be made. Forward sight has its limitations. As I explain in my book *The Jagged Journey* (2018), the life of faith will have its jerks and joys.

Our life roads are lined by glory and stained by evil. No one knows when the next bend will reveal something new and unexpected. As we travel life's uncertain road, we disciples of Jesus are called to live our days in faith that the guiding grace of God will be a constant companion. These words of Jon Mohr carry great meaning for me:

O may all who come behind us find us faithful,
May the fire of our devotion light their way.
May the footprints that we leave, lead them to believe,
And the lives we live inspire them to obey.
O may all who come behind us find us faithful.

My wife Arlene was less adventuresome than I and did not drive.
Sometimes I would steer our car down some country road just to see
unfamiliar territory—she would call it the "scenic route" that probably
should have been avoided since we might get lost and waste time. I have
always had a fascination with a fresh path. My second wife loves the word
"go," so later in life I've been able to test many new paths.

I remember with fondness a few occasions when I was a teenager out
for the day with my father. Sometimes we would have fishing lines out
each side of a boat, being pushed slowly across Lake Milton by a little
motor (allowing the mosquitoes to stay up with us!). At other times it was
the two of us walking in formation through a snowy cornfield or brushy
gully, following rabbit tracks and hoping to flush a furry animal into the
open. By the time I started attending college in 1959, these times with
Dad became rare (he died young, at age fifty-five in 1974). When they did
come, I only went hunting with him because I wanted exercise and the
time together. No longer did I carry a gun; I carried a camera and got
different kinds of "shots" of living creatures. I needed food for the soul
more than extra meat for the table.

We walk life's roads with special people who appear by our sides,
providentially at times. For instance, in my later years in Anderson,
Indiana, David Liverett and I were close friends and publishing colleagues.
Many years before and far away from Indiana and each other, our families
had acted similarly right after World War II. David was born in 1943. In
1945 his family bought a modest home on Cedar Street in Austinville,
Alabama. I was born in 1941 and in 1946 my family bought a modest

home on Beach Lane in Craig Beach, Ohio (the circumstance around which I built my 2011 novel *StarWalker*). David first came to Anderson, Indiana, as a college student in 1964. I arrived on the same Anderson campus in 1963 as a graduate student in the School of Theology. David and his wife Avis, and I and my wife Arlene, and then I and my wife Jan after Arlene's death, remained in Anderson and always were good friends. Such crossing paths would have seemed unlikely in the 1940s; in God's providence, the unlikely is not difficult at all.

I wrote "Let's Get On the Train!" for the national periodical of the Church of God, *Vital Christianity* (July 3, 1977). In this article I recalled being literally pushed by a moving traffic jam of hurrying humans into a commuter train in Tokyo, Japan. Our whole planet is now jammed with humans who have growing needs and shrinking resources. I wrote this in that 1977 article: "Our Lord keeps sending us to the despairing poor with words of love and deeds of sacrificial caring. God keeps urging us into the marketplace where the pains of life are inflicted and suffered. How much better if God would leave us in peace inside our air-conditioned churches where there is no rush for seats! But it just isn't that way. Apparently there is no other way to heaven except by responsible relatedness to our many brothers and sisters who are caught in the whirl of things. So let's get on the train!" I always have been getting on something.

As Christian disciples seeking to be faithful in this needy world, we each must identify our particular callings and then walk our own road. My personal gifts from God have not included an active engagement in evangelism, at least not as many would think of evangelism. On numerous occasions, however, I have preached evangelistic sermons in seminary chapels, local churches, and camp meetings in the United States, Australia, Canada, England, Germany, Jamaica, Japan, Kenya, Zambia, and Zimbabwe. I also have stood before scores of seminary and university classes over four decades and shared my Christian faith without reservation (or coercion, of course). As students routinely evaluated my teaching each semester, they sometimes observed that a gift of mine was teaching with clarity and conviction.

I have sought to witness to the credibility and meaningfulness of Christian faith in and beyond academic settings, including in seminars with ministers around the world. Whatever the setting and occasion, the message has been Jesus Christ. I have sought to be his servant. My 2007 commentary on the New Testament book of Colossians focuses on its central theme of "the all-sufficient Christ." My 2011 (rev. 2016) *Heart of the Matter* features a classic image of Jesus on the cover. Some roads are dead-ends. Jesus is the heart of things, the way, truth, and life, just as he said (John 14:6). His road may not always be smooth and safe, but it always takes one home.

I have been blessed to have had good role models to help show me the way down the uncertain roads of life. Beyond key family members and teachers, there have been special pastors. For instance, March 18, 2001, was a good day for me and Park Place Church of God in Anderson, Indiana. It ended fourteen months of search for a new senior pastor following the departure of Edward Nelson. After more than a year with Donald Collins and then Ann Smith functioning capably as interims—both superb Christians right from the congregation's pews, there now was a candidate. He was David E. Markle, then chair of the Religion Department at Warner Pacific College in Portland, Oregon.

In his sermon on the weekend with that congregation as a pastoral candidate, David announced his clear memory of attending a session of the General Assembly of the Church of God in June, 1981. It had convened in that very Park Place sanctuary, with me as David's seminary dean. I had introduced that year's School of Theology graduates by name, degree, and professional placement. Concerning David, he now recalled for the church that I had said he was a Church of God pastor "whose placement was still in process." Thirty years later, I stood before the congregation in the same location and, as the congregation's corporate secretary, helped with the process of voting on David's candidacy. I began the process teasingly by saying to the congregation that the Markle placement was *still* in process!

The vote that followed was a dramatic 354-0 in favor of his coming to Park Place, thanks in part to the excellent search process that had been guided by my valued colleagues Carl H. Caldwell and Gilbert W. Stafford. David chose to accept this call just as we were completing a major revision of the organizational life of the congregation, a process that my colleague Fredrick H. Shively and I had guided over many months. A new road would now be walked by David and the church. The spring and summer of 2001 seemed like a welcome new beginning for the Park Place congregation, and I was pleased to have played some part in the transition. As I write in 2019, David is still the pastor.

Arlene and I had been members of this church during the senior pastorates of Hillery Rice, Keith Huttenlocker, Donald Johnson, Edward Nelson, and now David Markle. Some key associate ministers during our years there included David Coolidge, Ronald Duncan, Donald Collins, Arlene Hall, James Martin, and Anita Womack. These special people formed a long and honorable trail of truly good and godly men and women who sought to lead an unusual congregation that has been an important part of my family's life since 1963. Marking its centennial year in 2006, I was privileged to write and publish the congregation's history (*Seeking Higher Ground*). Its magnificent structure was new when Arlene and I first moved to Anderson in 1963, living in a tiny apartment just opposite the church. On Sunday morning, May 16, 2010, Jan and I marched proudly with the congregation's choir "up the hill," what the congregation had done fifty years before in occupying the new from the old church building three blocks down the hill.

A colleague of mine at Anderson University was Kevin Radaker, chair of the English Department. We had common roots in northeast Ohio. He became important to my son Todd when he majored in Kevin's department. In 2000, he also joined in supporting my editorship of the new Anderson University Press by being a helpful member of the Editorial Committee. Kevin had emerged as a Henry David Thoreau (1817-1862) specialist, working in part through the National Chautauqua Tour in various parts of the United States to make dramatic presentations of Thoreau's provocative thoughts and life.

In November, 1999, I was pleased to be present as Dr. Radaker dramatized Thoreau in an Anderson University chapel session. He presented a monologue titled "I Wished To Live Deliberately." Part of the presentation came from Thoreau's essay called "Walking" that appeared in the *Atlantic Monthly* (June, 1862) after his death. It features the rural surroundings of Thoreau's nineteenth-century home in Concord, Massachusetts, and begins:

> I wish to speak a word for Nature, for absolute freedom and wildness, as contrasted with freedom and culture merely civil— to regard man as an inhabitant, or a part and parcel of Nature, rather than a member of society…. I think that I cannot preserve my health and spirits unless I spend four hours a day at least. . .sauntering through the woods and over the hills and fields, absolutely free from all worldly engagements.

Thoreau's vision of life is refreshing and tantalizing—even if impractical for most people, and maybe even somewhat irresponsible. Occasionally, however, I have heard him well and followed his lead.

I have spent considerable time walking the wooded trails around Aqua Gardens and through Mounds State Park in Anderson, Indiana, and in the hills surrounding the monastery in Trappist, Kentucky. In part, I also was trying to preserve my health and spirits. I walked once in the 1970s along the Apian Way into Rome, Italy, like the Apostle Paul had done long ago, and in 2009 joined my wife Jan in strolling down the main streets of the magnificent city of Ephesus where Paul once had lived and ministered. I took the dangerous walk with Gustav Jeeninga up the back and down the face of Massada along the Dead Sea in Israel (returning later with my wife Jan and making the trip in the comfort of a new cable car). I had the privilege in 1999 of walking along the Clyde River in Glasgow, Scotland, the place where many of the mighty ships and submarines of the world have been built. I also have strolled around the outer decks of large cruise ships in the Gulf of Mexico, the Caribbean Sea, the Inland Passage of Alaska, and the Adriatic, Arctic, Baltic, Mediterranean, and North Seas. I once sailed with Jan up the amazing Nile River through the desert of Egypt, and for a few minutes even got to pilot the Black Pearl, a modern pirate ship off the shore of Honduras. Often I found myself gazing across the waters and pondering my good fortune, and how insignificant I was, a mere speck in the great expanse of it all.

I recall my home pastor, Lillie S. McCutcheon, using the wilderness trail of Moses as a metaphor when she was concluding her long ministry in Newton Falls, Ohio (see my *She Came Preaching*, 310-311). We each have our unique journeys with God through the wilderness of this world. I remember mine well. As I do, I rejoice at the divine guidance all the way! Pastor McCutcheon's final instruction to her congregation was, "Go forward!" Like Moses, keep heading toward the promised land, traveling together as the people of God on mission.

Life is full of trails that lead in various directions and toward unknown destinations, some fading into the wilderness with no promised land in sight. Which ones are followed makes a significant difference. Judging the relative value of alternative roads is far from easy. I have been blessed with many good routes that have been pleasant to travel and have led to some wonderful destinations.

6. Prejudices I Have Overcome. I once heard this wisdom: "Love is the force that enables differences to become contributions and not irritations and divisions." I grew up with some prejudices deep in the American culture and church, differences that irritated and divided. The love of God and his people have enabled me to move beyond these prejudices, learning to love in a way that transforms them into contributions to my own life—and hopefully to the lives of others. Three prejudices follow, ones I have faced and, I hope, have moved beyond.

a. **National prejudice.** Being born just before the Japanese bombing of Pearl Harbor brought into my early life, mostly through my father, a view of Japanese persons as a plague on humanity. Politics, however, is an ever-changing thing. In my lifetime I have seen the bomb-ruined Japanese islands of the 1940s rise to be an economic and cultural leader in the world. I met Ann and Nathan Smith and Phil and Phyllis Kinley, Church of God missionaries to Japan, and felt their love for this ancient and complex land. I traveled to Japan in the early 1970s, leading an Anderson College TRI-S group and experiencing personally a cultural richness seldom paralleled. I have been forced to reflect on my own nation, a "super-power" in the world. Hearing so much hatred toward my country from various other peoples of earth, I have come to realize that patriotism is a wonderful and also, potentially, a very dangerous and divisive thing. Love builds bridges rather than walls. In my book *Heart of the Matter* (2011; rev. 2016) I have a chapter on patriotism and Christian faith. While always a loyal citizen of the United States, I soon became a citizen of a larger reality, the Kingdom of God.

b. **Racial prejudice.** The only African-Americans I ever saw as a boy were members of the rough labor crowd in the steel mills of Youngstown, Ohio, and the fun-seeking crowd that flooded the Craig Beach amusement park near my home on "colored day" each summer. These dark-skinned people appeared uncouth and even frightening to me as a boy. Then I played basketball with James Jackson at Geneva College, learned my biblical Greek with Ronald J. Fowler at Anderson School of Theology, and found my faculty colleague James Earl Massey to be a brother whose sophistication and wisdom are rarely equaled in this world. I learned to appreciate and love cross-culturally. What great contributions these "different" people have brought to my life! My most recent years with the ministry of Horizon International have found me in "black" Africa where my white skin put me in a very minority category. A little orphan girl once sat on my lap in Zimbabwe fingering my bare arm gently. She was testing to see if the white would rub off! My genetic origins point to my people group originating in Uganda. A long time "up north" has bleached my skin to pale white that no longer can tolerate the strong sun. I grew up with a prejudice against "my own people"! How wrong it is.

c. **Church arrogance and division.** The particular church heritage in which I have lived and ministered for most of my life is the Church of God movement (Anderson). This movement has cried out against the divisions among Christians that war against Christ's saving and healing mission in the world. Increasingly, I have sought to be a citizen of the whole people of God, not a member of some arrogant and isolated segment of it. This effort has brought many special contributions to my life. I want to be a small part of the answer to the prayer of Jesus "that they may all be one... so that the world may believe that you [Father] have sent me" (John 17:21).

Merle D. Strege, historian of the Church of God movement (Anderson), followed his mentor and my teacher, John W. V.

Smith, in chronicling the history of this reform movement of the Church of God. It is the story of the recent weakening of the core culture of the movement. Many factors have worked against the continuance of a cohesive and vibrant community of believers driven by the crusading vision of Daniel Warner in the late nineteenth century. Today is a very different time. I have lived through these years of the weakening of the movement's culture, experiencing and writing extensively about this body's proud past and now uncertain future. I have seen the confusion and felt the frustration and anxiety. I have tried to move in constructive directions that point toward a viable future.

I am confident that my deep involvement in the Wesleyan Holiness Connection, including being the Editor of its Aldersgate Press, has been an important frontier of contemporary church life that extends the original vision of the Church of God movement. This is seen in the Connection's web address that projects the heart of what the Church of God movement has envisioned for many decades. It is *HolinessAndUnity.org*. Transformed lives enable a unity among Christian believers that can enhance the church's mission in the world. I have intended to be part of inspiring a future for this vision, not lingering nostalgically in a particular form of its expression that seems to be weakening and even dying. As my dear friends James Earl Massey and Gilbert W. Stafford sometimes said, "I belong to the whole church, and the whole church belongs to me."

7. Names and Occasions. For me, legacy is not in places visited, lands owned, or fortunes possessed and passed on. It is in people. The pinnacle of God's creation is people. Investing in them is the only real future. So,

I share a few names and occasions—places where I have sought to make small investments in the lives of others.

Death brings its own special perspective on life. In the year 2001, Arlene and I turned sixty years old, she in May and I in July. Between June 14 and November 15 of that year, eight of our longtime friends and colleagues died—Nora Angus, William Dicus, Ruth Falls, Shirell Fox, Geraldine Reardon, Hillery Rice, Philip Slattery, and Peter Tjart. Of course, I had no idea that, a mere three years later, Arlene would become part of this growing list, and that after a time I would be married to Philip Slattery's widow! It was the rapid passing of the generation of my parents—and even some in my own generation. Geraldine Reardon, for instance, was born in 1919, the year when both of my parents were born. They had both died in the 1970s.

The list of the departed would keep lengthening, of course, one of the prices of growing older. In February, 2008, Rev. Oral Withrow died on the first day that his daughter Carma became an associate minister of Park Place Church of God in Anderson. In that great sanctuary in April, 2008, was the funeral of Dr. Gilbert W. Stafford. I had brought him to Anderson School of Theology in 1976 as a professor of theology and he had grown into a highly respected international churchman. His death was a great loss for the church and me personally. In 2010, Gil was followed in death by prominent theologian and my close friend Clark H. Pinnock, a Canadian Baptist. That same year Church of God educational leaders Drs. George Kufeldt (the last of my seminary teachers) and Leslie Ratzlaff died, both dear friends of mine. Dying also was James Meeker, father of my high school classmate Shirley Meeker Tomesko. Jim was the last of my father's friends from back in Craig Beach, Ohio. It was like the shifting of an era, with my time for joining the list of the deceased still unknown.

The reality of death comes especially close when it involves your own peers. By the year 2019, sixteen members of my 1959 Jackson-Milton High School class had died, sixteen of fifty-three. They were: Charles

Creque, 1972; Jeannette Grove, 1974; Irving Carnes, 1985; Dallas Cribley, 1994; Virginia Hetzel, 1994; James Davitt, 1999; Judy (Walton) Pipher, 2001; Richard Treharne, 2002; Frank Balent, 2004; John Steffans, 2008; William Price, 2010; Freda (Albert) Rininger, 2010; Judy (Rickenbrode) Ahart, 2015; William Bowers, 2015; Frank Stroney. 2017; and James Marshall, 2017. Their departures have been a sobering reality for me. They were my classmates, teammates, and childhood friends. For whatever reason, I am not yet on this growing list. Note my reflections on death in *Appendix J.*

There are other names, many others who are prominent in my memory for reasons other than death. For instance, it has been my privilege to accept calls to preach on the occasions when church leaders were being formally ordained to Christian ministry or were being installed as pastors of local congregations. For example, here are a few of the installations:

1. Michael Williams, November, 1980, Alabama
2. Larry Green, December, 1983, Detroit, Michigan
3. Dan Alexander, May, 1986, Alexandria, Indiana
4. Austin Sowers, February, 1990, Newton Falls, Ohio
5. Judy (Sowers) Hughes, October, 1994, Dayton, Ohio
6. G. Lee Wallace, April, 1995, Mt. Sterling, Kentucky
7. Timothy Kufeldt, July, 2001, Cincinnati, Ohio

In 1983 I preached at two state ordination services, each involving multiple persons (Kansas in April and Indiana in September). They were joyous occasions of God's calling and gifting for ministry.

Other church leaders come to mind because of their outstanding years as students in seminary and their obvious potential for unusual effectiveness in Christian ministry. In 1977, while I was Dean of Anderson School of Theology, and out of gratitude for my two grandfathers, I established and ever since have funded the annual *Distinguished Senior*

Award. Over the years, I have watched these called servants of God make a major difference in the church. I am humbled to have had a very small part in encouraging this Christian service.

DISTINGUISHED SENIOR AWARDS
Anderson School of Theology

In Honor of My Grandfathers,
Charles B. Callen and Charles G. VanArsdale
Awards have continued to the present

1977.	Timothy Foreman	1995.	Mary Ann Randolph
1978.	Larry Logue	1996.	David Pappas
1979.	David East	1997.	Christina Gangwer-Adams
1980.	Milan Dekich	1998.	R. Mark Eberly
1981.	David Markle	1999.	Susan Keown
1982.	Bernard Barton	2000.	Grant Horner
1983.	Donna Merrell	2001.	Timothy Vickey
1984.	Peggy Young	2002.	Julie Anna Kurrle
1985.	Robert Christensen	2003.	Kimberly Majeski
1986.	Gordon Steinke	2004.	Dan Turner
1987.	Dale Fontenot	2005.	David Ansley
1988.	Greggory Giles	2006.	Margaret Kirby
1989.	Donald Taylor	2007.	Martha Cramer
1990.	Sandra Hildebrand	2008.	Tamara Boggs
1991.	Michael Thompson	2009.	Julie Mullins
1992.	David Kardatzke	2010.	Kyle DeHaven
1993.	Gerald Cullison	2011.	Kirsten Streit-Harting
1994.	Nathan Steury	2012.	Zen Riggs

Although my ministry has been primarily educational rather than pastoral, there were several occasions when I functioned as the officiating or supporting minister at church weddings. Included are:

1. Bonnie Callen (my sister) and Rex Aley, 1968 (I assisted Lillie McCutcheon).
2. Bonnie Callison and Rick Newell in Springfield, Ohio, 1975, jointly with Arlo Newell.
3. A couple unknown to me, in London, England, in 1979, with Martin Goodridge as lead minister. I was a guest leader.
4. Treva Gressman and Patrick Donnelly, 1987, in Anderson, Indiana.
5. John Ackerman and Jodie Gross, 1976, in Anderson, Indiana.
6. Cheri Cramer and John Truskey, 1989, in Uniontown, Pennsylvania.
7. Todd Callen (my son) and Elizabeth Hazen, 1991, with Al Hazen, her father, in Anderson, Indiana.
8. Bryce and Rachel Shupe, 2000, on an outlook over the White River in downtown Anderson, Indiana. We returned to this lookout exactly one year later for me to officiate at a simple ceremony of their dedicating their new-born daughter, Lauren Elizabeth. In attendance were my wife Arlene, who sang beautifully to the baby, my son Todd, his wife Beth, and our three grandchildren at the time, Ian, Emily, and Ethan.
9. Richard Wayman (relative of my first wife, Arlene) and Jessica Pagano, in Findlay, Ohio, 2009.
10. Kristofer Wayman (relative of my first wife, Arlene) and Hannah Norby, near Indianapolis, Indiana, 2010.
11. Todd (my son) and Laura Robbins, in Anderson, Indiana, 2010, with me officiating in Park Place Church of God.

Also, I was privileged to dedicate to God my grandson Ian at the First Friends congregation in Anderson, Indiana, my granddaughter Emily at the Christian Church in Noblesville, Indiana (where her other grandfather, Al Hazen, was pastoring), and both Angela and Andrew Janutolo at Park Place Church of God in Anderson, Indiana.

Some real rewards follow these person-oriented ministries. For example, on their twenty-fifth wedding anniversary, John and Jodie Ackerman were serving as missionaries in Haiti. They wrote to me from the Dominican Republic where they were celebrating the occasion, saying: "When we look back on our lives together, we will always remember our wedding day. Barry, you kept us all in line. Thanks for being there then, prior, and ever since. When we reach our 50th, we'll again remind you of the important part in our lives that you have been. Our most sincere thanks and love, all because of Christ."

There also are very sad things that come along. A primary example for me was the ending in 2005-2006 of the marriage of my son, Todd, to Beth. They had brought our first three wonderful grandchildren into the world. However, after fourteen years of marriage, Beth chose a new direction for her life. I was filled with sadness, not anger. I sought to pray for her future well being, and especially to work for the well being of my son and the children in every way possible. When this divorce process occurred, Jan had been my wife for two years. Her wonderful spirit, plus her own divorce experience early in life, were sources of wisdom for Todd's struggle to rediscover himself and find a new future. By God's grace, he has succeeded spiritually and professionally.

When the future for Todd came to include Brooke Leever and her daughter Hayley, I chose not to provide counseling and leadership for Todd's second marriage—I was supportive, but just too close to do the best for them as a counselor. Donald Collins was available, was highly respected by Todd and me, and went on to counsel and officiate with sensitivity and dignity. It was a beautiful ceremony in Park Place Church of God on July 22, 2006. On January 19, 2007, Todd formally adopted Hayley, Brooke's daughter, as his own. Jan and I were present in the courtroom as the gavel fell, announcing that we had a new granddaughter in the full legal sense. A new life (so we all thought) was beginning for Todd, Brooke, and Hayley. The earlier children, Ian, Emily, and Ethan struggled to adapt to the challenge of a new family arrangement. Jan and I always tried to be there for them. As time would soon show, it was not enough. This marriage was ill-fated. Brooke and Hayley would leave Todd's life and ours.

Meanwhile, another grandchild was on the way. Jan's son Jordan and his wife Jenni were expecting—Jan, already a grandmother by marriage to me, teasingly said that this would be her first grandchild "from scratch." She and I were very excited when Bentley Allen Slattery arrived on Easter Sunday, April 8, 2007. Celebrating with us on that day was Robert A. Nicholson, the new mother's grandfather. "Nick" had been my colleague at Anderson University since 1966. I served under his presidency as vice-president for academic affairs. Now we were "family" in a new way. Life sometimes takes very sad and then very joyous turns. Following Ben in 2007 would come the births of one sister and three bothers. See *Appendix G.*

Part of my rejoicing involves precious words I will always carry with me. In 2008 I opened my copy of *Poor Richard's Almanac* and saw inside the cover these words in my mother's beautiful handwriting: "Christmas 1976. You've made me feel wanted, loved, and happy. Thank you. Your Mom." The card given to me by my son on Father's Day in June, 2011, had this in his handwriting: "Surely, God the Father must take special joy in the son/man/husband/father/grandfather/minister/scholar you are. You are the great patriarch for our family. I am proud to call you Dad and friend. I love you. Todd."

What more can a man hope for than that? Maybe this that Todd posted on his Facebook page in September, 2012:

I always knew that my parents loved me. Although I needed space to find myself, I knew they were my strong allies. I respected them then. Now I treasure what they gave me. More precious than gold, a home with a mother and a father who honored God and never let me play one against the other.... I urge others to just check out the one man [Jesus] who was so revolutionary to the human experience. Throw away what you thought you knew, and temporarily suspend your cynicism of what so many churches and church people have become. Go to the source material and really think about what Jesus actually said and did. Form your own conclusions, but while you are mulling it all over, I challenge you to ponder this question: Can you think of any other solution to the real problems of the world?

Changes, walls, doors, storms, roads, prejudices, people, occasions, life in turmoil, life ending, and life being born, these are fragments of human experience encountered by us all. When I remember mine, I cannot help but rejoice that God remains faithful and gracious.

Tributes at Times of Departing

There have been several occasions when I have been asked to offer the sermon, eulogy, or pastoral prayer on the occasion of the death of someone well-known and deeply loved by me and many others. Here are some of these persons and the roles I played at their times of departure. Their contributions to me and the nature of my faith show through.

1. Boyce W. Blackwelder. September, 1976, I delivered my tribute that later was published in my book in his honor, *Listening to the Word of God* (1990). He taught me New Testament Greek (1963-1965).

2. Vern Sowers. In Newton Falls, Ohio, June 3, 1982, I was preacher and eulogist. Vern was a brother of my childhood pastor, Rev. Lillie McCutheon.

3. John W. V. Smith. I was a pallbearer, November 23, 1984, Anderson, Indiana. John was my teacher of church history in seminary and then by Associate Dean.

4. Marie Strong. I read my tribute to her (later published in her book *A Common Sense Approach to the Book of Revelation* (1996). Marie was a beloved New Testament professor at Anderson College. I began my teaching career as her assistant while I was still a seminary student in 1965.

5. Lillie S. McCutcheon. On March 8, 1999, in Columbus, Ohio, I was eulogist, with my eulogy later published in *Reformation Witness* (fall, 1999), with another by Arlo F. Newell. Sister Lillie was my early spiritual mentor.

6. Ernest H. Gross. In January, 2000, I offered the graveside pastoral prayer, Anderson, Indiana, assisting James L. Edwards, president of Anderson University. See more detail below.

7. Frederick Shoot. On September 21, 2000, I read Scripture and offered the public tribute, Park Place Church of God, Anderson, Indiana. Fred was a New Testament professor at Anderson University. See detail below.

8. Robert H. Reardon. President Reardon of Anderson University died in February, 2007. In the General Assembly of the Church of God, convened in June, 2007, I released my history of higher education in the Church of God (*Enriching Mind and Spirit*). Standing with me on the platform was Connie Hippensteel, one of the Reardon children. The Assembly was informed that the book was being dedicated to Robert H. Reardon, my personal mentor and friend since 1966. I served under his presidency as

dean of Anderson School of Theology from 1973 to 1983. I authored his biography, *Staying on Course* (2004).

9. Paul C. Hutchins. On January 19, 2013, I delivered in Mooresville, Indiana, the funeral sermon for Rev. Paul Hutchins, a senior missionary of the Church of God in Africa and Asia. At the gravesite I prayed this: "Almighty God, by the death of Your Son Jesus Christ, You destroyed death. By His rest in the tomb You sanctified the graves of your saints, and by his glorious resurrection You brought life and immortality to light so that all who die in him abide in peace and hope."

10. Robert A. Nicholson. On November 29, 2017, I spoke at President Nicholson's funeral representing the faculty of Anderson University. I said he was "a man who could see the big picture and gently draw others into his line of sight. He was an Icon institutionally, a little bigger than life, a mentor personally, always encouraging life and growth, a model professionally, wisely guiding life, and a selfless servant, humbly giving life. He was a great gift from God to the people of God. What can we say except, 'Thanks be to God!' "

11. James Earl Massey. On July 7, 2018, the funeral of the beloved Dr. Massey was in Detroit's Metropolitan church that he founded in the 1950s. Many friends were present and participated, including at Massey's request Curtiss Paul DeYoung and myself (co-editors of the then-new book of Massey's writings, *Views from the Mountain*). This was the end of a great ministry! It was a privilege to be present and share warm personal reflections.

When Ernest Gross died in January, 2000, I was asked to participate with James L. Edwards, then president of Anderson University, who offered the sermon-eulogy. I prayed the final words at the gravesite in Maplewood Cemetery opposite the campus, near our home on Falls

Court, and very near the site where my beloved Arlene would be laid to rest in 2003. It was distressingly cold on that January day. These were some of the words of my prayer:

> O God, it is so cold! The air, the wind, they chill, stiffen, hurt. Death is so cold, so seemingly final and painful. But your divine presence and love are *so warm*, so needed right now. We repeat once more our warming faith. Christ has been raised from the dead, the first fruits of those who have fallen asleep! O death, where is your sting? Our dear brother, father, husband, grandfather, friend, sleeps, rests, has joined the Risen One. Ernie Gross, God's special son, is now *really well*, and has been welcomed home. But we are not so sure about ourselves. We hurt, even as we believe. Indeed, we are more than conquerors through the One who loves us. But, for now, we are also hurting humans. Comfort warmly, O God. Abide as undying hope with these many who loved Ernie so well and were so enriched by his exceptional life.

The funeral of Frederick Shoot was in Park Place Church in Anderson on September 21, 2000. I read Scripture and offered a tribute. Fred had been a faculty member at Anderson College from 1953 to 1980, and he had been a member of the translation team that first produced the *Revised Standard Version* of the Bible in the 1950s. We had been colleagues and friends. Following my remarks, I offered a tribute. Honoring the Bible scholar, I read John 14: 1-3, 27; Romans 8:18-28; and 2 Timothy 1:12b-14—from the New Revised Standard Version, of course. The Word spoke comfort in a sanctuary of grief. The servant that he was, Fred's body was donated to the Indiana School of Medicine for the benefit of science.

Many of my sermons and prayers at times of departing have been in honor of my own family members. For instance, the 1967 funeral for my beloved grandfather, Charles G. VanArsdale, was at the Newton Falls, Ohio, Church of God where he had been an active layperson for many years. My prayer included these words:

> We recognize, O God, your healing presence in our midst as we gather here—not so much to mourn the dead as to affirm his and our faith in the truth of life everlasting. Affirm in our hearts the truth that. . .
>
> > There is no death! The stars go down
> > To rise upon some other shore;
> > Heaven's jewels, They shine forevermore.
>
> We give thanks for the gift of this life now ceased, this star now momentarily gone from our sight, and for how much he meant to his family, church, and associates. May we follow the pattern of his life as he endeavored to follow Christ!

In May, 1970, Arlene, Todd, and I had spent one year back on the Anderson campus fresh from my doctoral work at Chicago Theological Seminary. Suddenly, my Aunt Elma VanArsdale died in Beaver Falls, Pennsylvania. She was the wife of my Uncle Van in whose home I had lived during my college years, 1959-1963 (in the third-floor apartment with my Aunt Evangeline VanArsdale). I offered this prayer at Aunt Elma's funeral on May 22:

> Our Father, we gather in moments of grief, but we gather in the context of the Christian faith—a faith which gives meaning to our loss and hope in the very midst of our deepest tragedy. We have come, therefore, not only to sorrow, but also to celebrate. We rejoice, knowing that the sting has been

removed from death, that another of Thy children has reached home safely, that after the darkest night there comes the bright horizon of a new day, and that You, in the voluntary giving of Your own Son, have walked this way before.

Death came to my wife Arlene's family in Pennsylvania in 1992. Donald Cooley, her father, finally came to the end of his mentally tormented life. Decades in an institution and then years isolated by choice in Arlene's original home in Uniontown were concluded by a losing bout with cancer. Arlene, I, and Evelyn (his wife then living with us in Anderson) journeyed back east to supervise a brief visitation and burial. There were many members of the extended Cooley family at the funeral home, most of whom had no church connections. Arlene and Evelyn asked if I would make some comments in the chapel if they called the visiting group together. I agreed, sharing an unprepared meditation on Psalm 23. Arlene was truly grateful, saying to me afterwards that this unusual group of the "Cooley clan" heard more of the Christian gospel that day than in their whole lives. I was glad to serve. Results are always left to God.

I don't know who will say what words of remembering and appreciation about my life when my final day comes. In one way, it matters very little. Time flees away, words evaporate, and memories quickly fade. In another way, it matters very much. As Christ's disciples, we each are to share a witness and leave a legacy of Christ-likeness truly sought and, we hope, well shared and truly appreciated. Finally, however we are known by others in this life, what counts is the One to whom we are responsible.

Saints and Icons

For most of my adult life I have been known as a minister, dean, and professor. The title "doctor" has been associated with my name since the late 1960s. Inside the family, I have been "Honey" and "Bappy." I have tried to be a faithful "friend" to many. Keenly aware of my own limitations and those of my fellow Christian believers, I have grown cautious about any casual use of the word "Christian." See *Appendix B* for my essay on this important subject.

The real issue of life is one of sainthood. Christians are called to be "saints." The true meaning of this is not centered in the formal process of being canonized by the political decision of a church; it is centered in a life lived humbly so that Jesus Christ can be seen in us by others. "Not I but Christ" is the disciple's true desire (Gal. 2:20). To live that desire is the definition of Christian sainthood. True saints are often the least publicized of believers—a circumstance quite acceptable to them. Holiness seeks not the bright lights of fame, but the quiet witness of the Spirit who ministers through frail but willing humans. The holy ones are to be "the light of the world" (Matt. 5:14) and the "children of light" (1 Thess. 5:5). The saint is not the one frozen in stunning stained glass in a great cathedral, but the one through whom the light of Christ shines. For more detail on "holiness," see the "manifesto" on the subject that I helped develop (*Appendix D*).

One contemporary saint is Billy Graham, the man who came to fame as a Christian evangelist when I was a boy and went on across my lifetime to preach the Christian gospel to more human beings than anyone else in history. In the twilight of his amazing life and ministry, Graham lived on a mountain in North Carolina. He was a humble man, full of faith and hope, less sure than some people about the answers to many difficult religious questions. I think he would appreciate my 2007 *Caught Between Truths* that argues for caution and humility in the face of the complexities of life and the paradoxes inherent in Christian faith (e.g., Jesus being the God-man and the Bible written by limited humans on whom the Spirit would breathe a wisdom beyond themselves). Humility is very appropriate, as the Christian poet Charles Wesley wrote in 1762:

> If perfect I myself profess,
> My own profession I disprove;
> The purest saint that lives below
> Doth his own sanctity disclaim.
> The wisest own, I nothing know,
> The holiest cries, I nothing am!

I have seen the divine light in Gene W. Newberry. In October, 2006, he sent me a handwritten note of encouragement, thanking me for my guest sermon the Sunday before at Park Place Church of God in Anderson. The sermon had been on suffering and he told me that, as an aging man, he was ready "to make that final move upward." He was ninety-one and still ministering as he could. I also saw the divine light in Robert H. Reardon who announced in August, 2006, that he had cancer and only months to live. He testified to being "very much at peace" and, as a Christian, "not living with a death sentence." His only wish was to be a useful servant during whatever time he had left. He succeeded and soon made his "move upward" in peace.

Drs. Newberry and Reardon had been important to me since the day I first arrived in Anderson, Indiana, in 1963. They were still showing the way in 2007. Reardon died that year. I had informed him beforehand that my coming new book, *Enriching Mind and Spirit* (2007, a history of higher education in the Church of God), would be dedicated in his honor. It was the last way that I could say "Thank You!" to this special brother, a true saint in the New Testament sense.

I tried to capture the rich meanings of sainthood in my book *Authentic Spirituality* (2001, 2006). In August, 2002, I was humbled when the "General Overseer" of the National Association of the Church of God,

Tyrone Cushman, introduced me to the great congregation of African-American Christians gathered at the West Middlesex, Pennsylvania, camp meeting. He said that I was a true "icon" of the Church of God. It was his way of extending a most generous compliment. But, quite apart from whether or not I am, what is an icon? It is a common instrument of devotion among Eastern Orthodox Christians. They use small depictions of Jesus and the saints as a means through which the living Christ can emerge freshly in their consciousness, much like Western Christians use the physical elements of the "sacrament" of the Lord's supper to get in touch with the historic sacrifice and current presence of Jesus, the crucified and still living Lord.

Me, an icon, someone who conveys the presence of God to others? I certainly have sought for decades to understand and live out the best of the vision of the church body through which I have functioned as an ordained minister. The Church of God movement has hoped to be an instrument letting the holy light of a truly united family of Christian believers shine again. During my lifetime, much has changed in the life of this Christian reform movement. I have been quite visible in the middle of this change as a teacher, administrator, historian, writer, editor, and theologian. I doubt that I managed to alter significantly the direction of the change—the forces of change were far bigger than me. What I may have managed to do, at least modestly, was help many people remember the past and think creatively about a new future that neither blindly repeats nor unwisely disconnects from the past.

Frederick G. Smith once said that he was a bridge between the first generation of Church of God people and those who were to follow. At a time when practically all other leaders and most of the constituency of the Church of God movement were "come-outers," having been previously associated with another church group before "seeing the light," Smith never knew any other affiliation. I see myself as having been something of a bridge between a self-confident, vigorous, and reasonably cohesive

Church of God movement and a movement now having to rediscover and even reinvent itself in very new times.

Appendix I contains the portion of my "Tract for Transitional Times" that identifies what I understand to be the five elements of this teaching tradition worthy of continuing consideration. Note also my 2002 booklet "Confessing and Celebrating: The Church of God (Anderson) in a New Millennium." Several of my books have been intended to keep core memories alive, recast key theological themes, rethink the place of the Church of God movement within world Christianity (partly by refocusing on its Wesleyan and Believers Church roots), and work with its changing organizational structures—particularly the General Assembly, Church of God Ministries, and the institutions of higher education.

Rev. Lillie S. McCutcheon once said that, at her service of ministerial ordination, she had felt the mantle of Frederick G. Smith pass to her (in *She Came Preaching*, 302). While I know of no specific mantle falling on me, I grew up under the exceptional ministry of Pastor McCutcheon, loved and respected her, but moved in some different directions. I am deeply in debt for the wisdom passed on to me by many church leaders, and I hope I have absorbed and used it well. I have sought to honor others, writing their biographies, publishing their autobiographies, preserving their best thoughts for new generations. This was my reason in compiling and publishing the books *Faith, Learning, and Life* (1991) and especially *The Wisdom of the Saints* (2003). I have wanted to note carefully those "icons" who deserve to be remembered.

More important than my role in relation to the life of a particular church body and one great academic institution, Anderson University, has been the call for me to be a Christian. I have sought to be a humble servant of Jesus, someone through whom the light of Christ could shine. When I have succeeded, I have been a simple "saint" who could join Paul in the great confession, "I have been crucified with Christ, and no longer live, but Christ lives in me" (Gal. 2:20). Note my cautionary essay on being called a "Christian" (*Appendix B*).

I remember times when I have been aware of Christ being alive and shining through me. Such was possible only by God's grace and gifting, of course. In this grace, gifting, and resultant shining I have found my true self, my ministry, and my destiny. In it all, as I remember, I cannot help but rejoice! A wise man once said that the difference between a "sinner" and a "saint" is the direction each is headed. The Church of God movement, never having achieved an ideal of perfection, to be sure, is yet a "saintly" movement in that it has held firmly and rightly to a vision of God's highest intention for believers and the church. In other words, this movement has been headed in the right direction. I hope that I have been too!

In June, 2010, my wife Jan and I were in Alabama with our friends David and Avis Liverett. We were privileged to visit the very modest birth places of Helen Keller and Jesse Owens. Both of them overcame tremendous odds to succeed. We watched an outdoor production of "The Miracle Worker" dramatizing a handicapped girl breaking through the language barrier, and we saw a film on the 1936 Olympics in Berlin, Germany, when a young African American captured four gold medals and embarrassed Adolf Hitler and his racial idolatry.

When compared with Keller and Owens, it seems that I have overcome relatively little, and what I have accomplished has been much less significant. The Callens and Liveretts also attended the outstanding congregation in Falkville, Alabama, pastored by Rev. Milan Dekich. He took the occasion to share in the sermon his appreciation for my impact on his life and ministry—I had been dean during his seminary years at Anderson School of Theology in the 1970s. As the song goes, little can be much when God is in it. I came away from Alabama grateful for Helen and Jesse, proud of Milan, and humbled by whatever God has permitted my life to mean for others.

I have been in second place in several professional settings, a position quite to my liking. At Anderson University, I rose from the bottom of the faculty ladder in 1966 to the second person in the institution, Vice President for Academic Affairs, beginning in 1983. Upon the retirement of Robert A. Nicholson as president in 1990, a few key leaders wanted to push my candidacy for the university presidency. I discouraged this, having no fundraising experience and being pleased to remain just out of the main spotlight. Soon after that, I became the international Editor of the *Wesleyan Theological Journal,* a prominent position in the Wesleyan Theological Society and the North American Wesleyan/Holiness world generally. Nearly two decades later, with a series of Society presidents having come into and out of office in the meantime, I happily remained the Editor, with no desire to move that final step "upward."

During the 2009 and 2010 years, with Horizon International (AIDS orphan ministry in Africa) and Church of God Ministries (North American organization of the Church of God) looking to protect themselves in case of a leadership a vacuum arising from some emergency, each developed a plan for interim executive leadership. In both cases, I was named as part or all of the crisis plan. I agreed, glad to serve in a time of sudden need, honored that I would be so trusted, but assuming and hoping that neither Robert Pearson (Horizon) nor Ronald Duncan (Church of God Ministries) would encounter any emergency that would necessitate my replacement services. Being second always has been more than enough for me, a little boy from the tiny village of Craig Beach in northeastern Ohio. I seem to fly best just "under the radar."

I echo what a famous Swiss theologian of the twentieth century said of his life's work. Referring to the donkey that carried Jesus to Jerusalem to begin the final events of his earthly life, Karl Barth wrote this (*Fragments Grave and Gay*, 1971, 116-117):

If I have done anything in this life of mine, I have done it as a relative of the donkey that went its way carrying an important burden. The disciples had said to its owner, "The Lord has need of it." And so it seems to have pleased God to have used me at this time, just as I was, in spite of all the things, the disagreeable things, that quite rightly are and will be said about me. Thus I was used.... I just happened to be on the right spot. A theology somewhat different from the current theology was apparently needed in our time, and I was permitted to be the donkey that carried this better theology for part of the way, or tried to carry it as best I could.

I also echo with enthusiasm the concluding words of my late friend and mentor Clark Pinnock's wonderful 1996 book *Flame of Love* (p. 248):

Theology does not depend on any single theologian. Truth will yield its secrets to the body of Christ if we will listen to God and to one another humbly, accepting correction. God bless you, my dear readers. May a gift be imparted to you. May the wind of God blow on you, may the Spirit draw you closer to God's loving heart. May Father, Son, and Spirit make their home in you.

Striking the Tent of Meeting

According to 1 Corinthians 15:26, the final enemy is death—and it already has been conquered in the resurrection of Jesus. A good way to think about the inevitable end of my own mortal existence is "striking the tent of meeting."

On October 27, 2006, about one hundred of us gathered on the big platform of Warner Auditorium in Anderson, Indiana. It would be the last time for anyone in that historic place. We were there to "strike the tent of meeting" just before the massive landmark was demolished. Above us was the vaulted ceiling, now stripped of the asbestos that had finally sealed the structure's doom. Before us was a blank concrete floor, now stripped of the seats that had held 7,500 worshippers per service each summer since the early 1960s. We sang "Great Is Thy Faithfulness," noted my essay in the printed program titled "Dying of the Dome," and joined in a litany of appreciation and parting led by Paul A. Tanner. Titled "We Strike the Tent of Meeting," the litany recalled the ancient Hebrews following their mobile God from place to place. This modern place, Warner Auditorium, was being struck in order to keep pace with the God who was and still is active in this world. God's people are to be ready and willing to move on to the next future being prepared by God.

Having shed a tear in 2006, we looked ahead in faith, leaving the great auditorium to its doom. A few years later we also would see the last of the big annual camp meetings convene in Anderson. Change seems inevitable. It's a Christian picture of the dying experience. We grieve loss of the known, even as we reach forward in search of a better tomorrow in a new time.

My dear ministerial friend Donald L. Collins published in 2010 his life's reflections in the book *There Were Angels Along My Way*. He speaks of his earliest years living during the Great Depression of the 1930s on Mable Avenue in Flint, Michigan. He remembered a red quarantine sign on a neighbor's front door because someone had scarlet fever or chickenpox or whooping cough. The public had to be warned of the dangerous infection. Not that far away in Craig Beach, Ohio, and only a few years later, it was the same story for me. Never mind the neighbors. I was the one who caught these infections, having significant cases of all three, my whooping cough turning into pneumonia and the only hospitalization of my life until now. It was a bumpy and then long and smooth road of health for me.

The first major health crisis was the cancer of my wife Arlene. It appeared in 2002, led to a major operation, and then to months of Hospice in our home in Anderson, Indiana. I continued to teach at Anderson University, often not sleeping much at night. Death came to her on March 1, 2003, as she lay on the couch in our back room and I was kneeling there thanking her for her love and letting her go. With me was our son Todd and dear family friend Darlene Stafford. At the funeral in Park Place Church, our beloved friend Donald Collins offered a moving prayer, including this: "Arlene's body became a battlefield on which cancer met its match. It didn't diminish her faith. It didn't destroy her friendships. It didn't cripple her love. It didn't shatter her hope in eternal life." How right he was! She now was gone from me, but more at home than ever before.

On the medical front, things quieted again. Except for a little arthritis in my knees, I remained well. Then came the nose and throat operation on my son Todd in 2010. An open blood vessel was missed in the closing process and Todd bled considerably before an emergency second surgery managed to find and stop the rupture. His wife Laura and I flanked his bed, me doing the blood-catching in a basin. Todd later posted this on the internet, some of the kindest words I've ever heard: "I am so grateful for those who worked to see me through. Laura was a champ, and I'll never forget my Dad holding the basin as the doctor forced me to vomit up all that blood all over everything and everyone. I can't imagine what it must have been like to see your only son doing that. He's got strong knees, probably from years of kneeling in prayer." Lives of faithfulness do tend to prepare us for crises.

Then in the spring of 2011 my turn finally came. I developed a small growth under my left eye. It was biopsied and diagnosed as a slow-growing type of lymphoma, probably not life-threatening but clearly needing immediate and major attention. Next it was an operation for another growth detected in my nasal cavity, same cancer. A needle biopsy in my back checked a "hot" lymph node, bringing the decision of my oncologist to launch me into five months of intensive chemotherapy. Hardly the summer expected, Jan and I cancelled various plans, including a big cruise to Spain, Portugal, and points east to celebrate my seventieth birthday in July. I would be on a very different journey.

The first of my six chemo treatments (infusions) happened on June 7, 2011, at the Erskine Center of Saint Johns Hospital in Anderson. Two of my nurses were Tracey Collins and Elizabeth Tobey, the same two Hospice nurses who had cared for my wife Arlene in our home eight years earlier. I was comforted with this surprising connection and the real concern of these wonderful women for my well being. Seeing them took me back to Arlene's situation in 2002 after her operation for colon cancer. Had she taken chemo treatments then, might she have survived? This question has no answer. She made her choice (being very afraid of the treatments) and the cancer spread with a vengeance. That was then. My decision now was to open myself to the treatments, whatever that would come to mean.

The treatments were taken for four months. They were unwelcome, tolerable even if troubling in various ways, and finally successful. My heart had been tested and declared healthy enough for a port to be inserted into my chest to receive the infusions, about six hours each three weeks and all going directly through my heart and into the blood stream. My hair fell out on June 25 and I was declared free of any detectable cancer on August 25, although treatments continued through September "for insurance." The chance of the cancer returning remains real, but it is not inevitable. An in- process testimony of mine was circulated widely in July, 2011. It included this:

Since the prognosis is that the cancer will be eliminated by the treatments, I may have another decade or more in this body now being filled with strange chemicals. So my prayer to God has become, "What shall I do to make these years worthwhile in Your mission among us fragile mortals?" We all die sometime; the important thing is finding out how best to use the years that we are alive!

Testing continues periodically but I remain "clean" as I write in 2019. This is a blessing and a responsibility that extra time be used well. The one additional health crisis came in February, 2018, when I suffered a major retinal detachment in one eye. Surgery repaired the damage with no loss of eyesight, another great blessing since I use my eyes so much.

I borrow some wisdom from my friend Gloria Gaither. In her 1997 book Because He Lives, she explains the challenging family circumstances that led Bill Gaither and her to write the beloved song the title of which was used for her book. We cannot live our lives, marry, have children, and face death with confidence because of anything rooted in this troubled world. We trust and risk and hope only because the resurrection of Jesus really happened, and because "it was not just a one-time event in history; it is a principle built into the very fabric of our beings.... The resurrection is the truth that brings victory and hope. Life wins! Life wins!" When all things have been considered and I think of myself, this pilgrim's progress has been possible only because of God's amazing and life-giving grace. Because of that divine and wholly unmerited grace, life wins!

A favorite writer of mine is William Barclay of Scotland. Clive Rawlins reports in his 1984 biography of Barclay (p. 694) that the aging biblical scholar said: "When I die, I should like to slip out of the room without fuss—for what matters is not what I am leaving, but where I am going." As we go, how do we find our way ahead? There is only one choice. We stay close to Jesus—who is the Way. When my final traveling time comes, may I remember with gratitude, yield quietly to the striking of my bodily tent, and journey on with Jesus, remembering with joy and rejoicing about what still lies ahead. My earthly remains will be buried alongside Arlene's in Maplewood Cemetery across from the Anderson University campus. But no matter—neither of us will be there. We both will have traveled to a better place.

This autobiography, then, is only an interim report. As I told my college students in my final year of full-time teaching in 2005, "I do not yet know what I want to be when I finally grow up!" Life in this world continues for me, for quite a while I hope. The shape and timing of my personal future here remains unknown. I proceed in faith and expectation knowing by faith that a better world lies ahead for me.

A longtime friend and teaching colleague on the Anderson campus was sociologist Val Clear. In reflecting on the history of the Church of God movement, intentionally a reformation movement within the larger church, he employed a sociological paradigm (*Where the Saints Have Trod*, 1977). The typical pattern of a reform movement's dynamic initial phase, Clear explained, moves over the years to an eventual institutionalization, which in turn leads to the possible need for another movement to reform the once- reforming movement. Just before a movement's birth there is a general milling around, an unsettledness and fresh vision that spawns the reformation. Much later, if the reform movement does not keep reforming itself, some of its own constituents will come to mill around again, threatening the continuing existence of the aging movement.

An individual's life is a little like that sociological scheme. I have sensed times of unsettledness that have emerged for me into times of major transition. I knew that something new was coming, but did not know for sure what that something was. I have sought to remain flexible and open to change, welcoming the new and happily moving on. I am seventy-seven years old as I write this. I report, with some excitement, that I am feeling a little unsettledness again. I am very happy with where I am, very grateful for my wonderful family and professional accomplishments, but I seem to be doing a little milling around nonetheless. I am still alive! Maybe God is not done with me. I hope not. Whatever might be next, my eyes are open, my interest is keen, and my wife Jan stands close by my side.

I am a pilgrim still in progress. My eventual destination is to be fully at home with the Lord by whose side I already walk. In the meantime, I wait to hear new guidance from that gentle voice from above. Wherever it points will be pleasing to me. How good it is to walk the pilgrim's pathway with the Lord, never being alone or lost, never going to die except for an eventual separation from this passing world. All praise belongs to God, in this world and the next!

I borrow some lines from a prayer once offered by a valued spiritual mentor of mine, James Earl Massey. He offered it at the rededication of a ministry facility in Michigan in 1980. I now adopt a few of his words as my personal prayer toward the end of my life.

For those who have gone before us, We thank Thee: They taught us, we learned, and believed;
They labored, and we entered into their labors.

For those who are now with us, We praise Thee: They trust and love us; We trust and love them;
They share themselves, and We are being blessed thereby.

For those who come after us, We intercede to Thee:
We ask that they will be wise, resourceful,
Appreciative, and responsible.

We rededicate ourselves now,
That the work they will inherit from us will be strong,
And the path we cut will be clear,
And the example we set will be holy.

To all of this I say AMEN!

UNDER THE WHEELS OF TIME

What's the big picture that only the spiritually mature can see? Just this. "The Lord God omnipotent reigneth!" (Rev. 19:6). Here was the central fact of life for Jesus. He could see that Caiaphas, Pilate, Herod, Caesar, and all the rest were little more than dust beneath the chariot wheels of time.

Barry L. Callen
The Jagged Journey (2018, p. 156)

EARTHRISE

I'm finishing this writing during the 2018 Christmas season. It's an historic time for me and the whole world. I've made at least modest progress as a faith pilgrim in my earthly life, recounting some of it in these pages. More is said in the booklet *My Final Will and Testimony*. I hope I can say as much for the Earth itself.

In 2018 the United States marked the 50th anniversary of the great sermon "I've Been to the Mountain" by Martin Luther King, Jr. That same year I keyed off this anniversary by co-editing and publishing through Aldersgate Press *Views from the Mountain*, the lifetime writings James Earl Massey. He was a friend of King, also my dear friend, and a wise prophet taken from us by death in 2018. This year saw all of this and was also the time of signal events.

The composition of the most beloved of all Christmas songs, *Silent Night*, marked its 200th anniversary in 2018. Some of its classic words are, "Silent night, holy night, All is calm, all is bright, Christ the Savior is born." I rejoice in that birth, surely a pivot point in human history. However, most people didn't receive the holy child in that little town of Bethlehem, and most humans still are not following the way of life he graciously brought. All is hardly calm or especially bright. We needed a jolt in our complacency, another trip to the mountaintop, a fresh distant view to give perspective to life on Earth.

The year 2018 marked yet another grand event. Fifty years earlier three humans flew into orbit for the first time, circled the Moon ten times, and returned safely to the clutches of Earth's gravity. Humans finally had escaped the Earth! The crew of Apollo 8, with the lunarscape as foreground, snapped an amazing photo on Christmas Eve, 1968. Now called *Earthrise*, it dramatically shows the Earth in all of its marbled beauty. How round, lovely, and fragile it seemed as it floated out there in the vastness of space. This was humanity's first sight of itself in a mirror.

Millions in all nations were captured by the sight of a slightly misshapen bowling ball rolling around in deep darkness with all of its inhabitants somehow hanging on.

This distant image of the Earth taken from the Moon should have accomplished more than it did. It should have put an end to our petty human conceits and launched a fresh determination to care for this pale blue treasure, our little home amidst the unknown vastness of space. The reality is now obvious. Earth is cosmically insignificant, and yet all we have as a species. No national boundaries are visible in the photo. No hostilities between people groups seem to make any sense. We are together on this tiny celestial ship. The humbling sight made those Apollo 8 astronauts want to come home and break down all barriers. They read to the world from the book of Genesis. How very contemporary seemed those lines of the ancient creation story.

Those astronauts might have gone on to sing the haunting lines of *Silent Night.* Looking from so far away, this planet, the home of us humans, is bright, calm, and yet so in need of a Savior. Jesus came long ago from the heart of the Father, the comprehensive reality distant beyond imagination and also as close as a baby lying in a feeding trough. That baby brought to a passing speck in the sky the hope of life which is eternal. In my days, I have tasted that life and am forever grateful! My prayer is that the whole of humanity will finally come to realize and sing, "Joy to the world, the Lord *has come.*"

Generations come and go. The VanArsdales pictured above include my beloved grandfather Charles (right), grandmother (3rd from left), Grandpa's mother (standing center), and the three children, Evangeline (my Auntie, left), Laverne (my Uncle Van standing center), and my mother Charlotte next to Grandpa. Below are Mom and Grandpa in later years, and Grandpa at the gravesite of his wife—and soon to be his own, outside New Brighton, Pennsylvania (my birthplace).

The passing years have
brought ever-increasing
evidence of the goodness
and guidance of God. My
clothes and hairstyles
have changed, but the
grace of God has
remained the same.

With my Christian friend messianic rabbi Jeff Adler in the Garden Tomb area of Jerusalem. As Jan and I took communion together under Jeff's leadership, we rejoiced that the tomb of Jesus is still empty! According to the title of one of my books, and until our Lord returns, we are to be "faithful in the meantime."

FAITHFUL IN THE MEANTIME

A BIBLICAL VIEW OF FINAL THINGS AND PRESENT RESPONSIBILITIES

Barry L. Callen

My wife Arlene tearfully shared her Christian witness as she was baptized at Park Place Church of God just weeks before her death. Ministering to her were her dear friends Judy (Sowers) Hughes (left) and Sylvia Grubbs.

Ian, Emily, and Ethan. Arlene was their "Mamoo" and loved them dearly.

Beth (Hazen) Callen provided loving assistance near the end of Arlene's life.

Resting place of my mother and father, near
my boyhood home in Lake Milton, Ohio.

Since my death date is not yet carved into this book of life that sits just north
of the Anderson University campus, I gladly continue my pilgrim's progress.

WHAT'S COMING AT THE END

Here's what I expect when my final moments of life arrive. By God's sheer grace and in light of my faith, I anticipate the dark gloom of this life being penetrated, heaven's morning bursting forth in full light, with all troubling shadows fleeing away forever!

Barry L. Callen
God in the Shadows (2018, p. 137)

APPENDIX A

Providence or Politics?

Psalm 114, a contemporary and prayerful paraphrase

by Barry L. Callen

D ear Lord, since confession is good for the soul, I'm prepared right now to do my soul a big favor! I confess that I and humans generally seem to see only what is on the surface of things and remember only what we choose to remember. I recognize and readily admit how easily this subtle process of seeing so little and selecting our memories can serve selfish ends. I probably have done just this somewhere in this autobiography. Please forgive my own inability to perceive the depths of what is really real and my inclination to selective memory.

Here is the big question. What is really worth perceiving and then remembering? What escapes mere self-service and lies beyond the prejudice of my private bias and personal circumstances? What pinpoints actual reality rather than being infected by how we are fond of naming and recalling it? What has happened on the human scene that is so important, so intentional on Your part that it should *shape us* rather than we *shaping it*? If you, O God of Abraham, Father of Jesus, and Lord of nations and all creation were to show us the real truth and focus our blurred memories on the really important, what would we be seeing and remembering most of all? This question is my most profound prayer.

I know something that would be emphasized. You, the gracious and revealing God, would teach that our human history, all those events, generations, battles and sufferings, joys and questions, have not been a random and empty process. What has happened, ultimately, has or still can have meaning because You, the ruler of nature and nations, has put *a God-shaped plot* into the drama of history, making it truly *His*-story, Your story of a good creation, a costly involvement, and a glorious redemption. We are obligated, therefore, to do more than just sing about this being "our Father's world." We must remember that it *actually is!*

Let's get specific. When those ancient Israelites escaped their Egyptian bondage, it just wasn't one of those numerous and annoying slave revolts. It wasn't even an escape. It was a *deliverance*. The Egyptians were baffled, the mountains trembled, and the sea had to get out of the way as You, Oh God, made for Yourself a people. Moses may have been up front, but You were the leader. The Egyptians may have seen nothing divine about it at all, but that doesn't alter reality. Surface observations may have concentrated on human determination and opportune events of nature. An adequate understanding, however, brings one back to You.

What really has happened? Where is the wisdom in all the data of my life and of our "modern" days, the right perspective in the pluralistic maze that prevails in the twenty-first century? It always has been You, my God, hasn't it? Now I am remembering *rightly*. There is You and there is Your plan. Behind the sound and fury of my days and world events, somewhere in the shadows of time, there stands the One who created the world and remains Lord over its peoples and events. Even though You, dear God, are anything but a cold, calculating manipulator, You nonetheless are the chief architect of time and eternity. In the final analysis, your *providence* is more potent than our *politics*. Your sovereign will superintends our fragile and often foolish human ways.

Oh, that Your people could comprehend their divine birthright and the potential always latent in Your creating and leading. Let the mountains dance again! May the rivers that still obstruct and the captors who still enslave bow before the design that is deepest in things. And when it happens, may I and all others recognize Your hand and gladly join the trail of destiny. You, my God, are still making history, not only by establishing a special people, but by ministering through this people. To see and know and be transformed by this ultimate reality is hope and life itself. What a realization! What a memory! What a responsibility!

> Let all things their creator bless,
>> And worship him in humbleness;
>>> O praise him, Alleluia![1]

> Lead on, O King eternal,
>> the day of march has come,
>>> Henceforth in fields of conquest,
>>>> Thy tents shall be our home.[2]

Steven B. Sherman, in his 2008 book *Revitalizing Theological Epistemology* (Pickwick Publications) has chronicled a significant shift in the theological landscape of contemporary Christian "evangelicals." He includes the name "Barry L. Callen" among a select group of prominent Christian thinkers championing a new "post-conservative" theology (p. 14). Appreciative references are made to my 2000 book *Clark H. Pinnock: Journey Toward Renewal.* In the face of such recognition of my work, I must ask: "How did a little boy from Craig Beach in northeastern Ohio ever become identified with a sophisticated company of scholars affecting the nature of Christian thought in the twenty-first century?" The only adequate answer must feature the grace and providence of God. I have sought to be faithful with what gifts I have; the rest lies in God's gracious hands.

---

[1] Excerpt from "All Creatures of Our God and King" by Francis of Assisi.

[2] Excerpt from the hymn "Lead On, O King Eternal" by Ernest Shurtleff.

How fortunate I have been to be surrounded by gifted servant leaders of the Church of God (Anderson), Anderson University, and Park Place Church of God. Pictured are only a few of them.

James L. Edwards

Ronald V. Duncan

Robert A. Nicholson

Carl H. Caldwell

Barry L. Callen

Jeannette Flynn

Marie Morris

David E. Markle

Robert L. Moss

APPENDIX B

Please Don't Call Me "Christian"!

by Barry L. Callen

T he title of this essay may seem surprising, even a little shocking, but it should not be. No, I have not abandoned my faith or converted to something entirely new. To the contrary, the living of life, coupled with my long experience in the fields of Christian theology and church history, have both deepened my faith and brought me some cautionary lessons. One result is this. I request that people avoid calling me "Christian." This desired favor was freshly inspired by my reading of Timothy Johnson's book *Finding God in the Questions* (2004). Johnson prefers being called a "follower of Jesus" rather than a "Christian." This preference rests on a range of what I consider good reasons.

One reason for Johnson's preference, and also for my present request, is the observation that "Christianity" as a formal religion is not something found in the New Testament. Nor was it a term commonly used until the second century when a Roman historian finally did so. In other words, the designation of the faith as *Christianity* was not original with the rise of the Jesus people, but something that appeared later in a given set of political circumstances. As a matter of fact, when a Roman emperor decided around 315 A.D. that it was to his political advantage to adopt the Jesus movement of Judaism as his very own, many religious historians and theologians see the faith having "fallen" into serious compromise. Jesus people had become virtual wards of the empire.

Another reason for my current preference is that much that is part of the "Christian" world today is not worth supporting or being associated with by a serious believer in Jesus. Indeed, it may be better to be known simply as a follower or dedicated disciple of Jesus than to be painted with a broader "religious" brush. To take the general name Christian usually requires explaining what is not being meant. Then one must go on to clarify what is meant by adding strategic adjectives to the word Christian—liberal, fundamentalist, ecumenical, pentecostal, Eastern, Western, etc. All of these adjectives have volatile histories of their own and a series of associated meanings, any one of which might be assumed by the one hearing them used.

Therefore, there is merit in going back to the New Testament accounts of Jesus and focusing one's identity more directly on his actual person and recorded teachings. Such a going back seeks (1) to relax the need to explain the "kind" of Christian one now is, (2) to distance oneself at least a little from the terrible misdeeds of some past representatives of Christianity (the crusades, the support for slavery, the persecution of Jews, etc.), and (3) to find relative relief from being restricted by a given creedal tradition of the faith that has both its strengths and inevitable frailties.

My concern is hardly new. In fact, I have traced the long trail of this reforming impulse among Christians in my book *Radical Christianity* (1999). The Church of God movement (Anderson) has been saying much of what I am trying to say. Denominations tend to be tribal and artificially narrowing of Christian fellowship and cooperation in mission. Formal creeds, especially when required for group membership, tend to stifle searching after the fuller truth and encourage a destructive division among believers. Religious labels tend to stereotype unfairly and then isolate us unnecessarily from our brothers and sisters in the faith. So, leaders of this Church of God movement have hoped to somehow step outside all of this "sectism," return to the freshness of the "apostolic" foundations of the faith, and be sincere followers of Jesus by the wisdom and power of Christ's Spirit.

It may be that this attempt to "come out" and "go back" is too idealistic. To be sure, the Church of God movement has experienced only partial success in its own implementation of the larger vision. But, even after this necessary admission, I still find this visionary idealism a good way to go. Here one finds a glimpse of what God intends for the church. The church is the fellowship of all blood-washed people who are deeply committed to Jesus Christ, who have been changed by the power of Christ's Spirit, who are hungering daily for a further maturing of their spiritual experience and understanding, who have been seized by a vision of all God's people as one united and living family, and who are humble and tolerant enough to keep growing and learning without restricting the freedom of others to do the same.

I do not want to be known as an adherent of some section of Christians who sit smugly over in a corner and look critically at all others who understand differently a point or two of doctrine or practice. I want to be identified with Jesus, with all of his people, and with a reaching for the fullness of the truth that is in him—but not with all that has been called "Christian" over the centuries. I want to keep trying to reach beyond the common compromises of the highly institutionalized churches and the tragically divided Christian world.

Effective evangelism today requires moving from fine talk about the church to a *real being of the church in its intended holiness and unity*. No group of believers has a corner on truth. Authority lies in the biblical revelation of God in Jesus Christ, not in the interpretations and traditions of any one body of believers, including the Church of God movement. The call is still "back to the blessed old Bible." So, please just call me a follower of Jesus. As the beloved Dale Oldham has put it in a song title, "Let Me See Jesus Only!" was none other than God with us.

The center of the Christian faith is Jesus Christ, not a full identifying with all of the history, structures, and creeds that have carried the name "Christian." This stained glass window is in the Adam W. Miller chapel of Anderson School of Theology. I created the conceptual design while dean of the seminary. The faith derives its life and meaning from this man who was none other than God with us.

My commentary on the book of Colossians (see *Appendix E*) elaborates on the biblical view of the person and meaning of Jesus Christ for all humanity and all time. Most of all, I wish to be a citizen of the "kingdom" of God rather than of any human "empire," religious or not.

APPENDIX C

A Fresh Vision of the Holy

Lecture One (abbreviated) of the three Robertson Lectures, delivered by
Dr. Barry L. Callen
at Azusa Pacific University, Azusa, California, September, 2005

How one conceives of the nature of God is basic to all that Christians understand that they are to be and do. Therefore, the first of my three lectures focuses on a particular Christian understanding of God, while the other two trace implications of this understanding for the Christian practices of prayer and biblical interpretation. My primary authority base is biblical; my primary Christian heritage context is Wesleyan; and the special theological focus I will stress is sometimes called "openness theology."

There is considerable controversy among Christians today about how the sovereign God interacts with this world. In my book *Discerning the Divine* (2004), I trace the roots of this controversy across the centuries of Christian thought. Beginning biblically, God has said, "You shall be holy, for I am holy" (1 Peter 1:16). Thus, holiness is clearly the divine nature and the divine intention for us; but how is divine holiness to be understood and then received and lived out on our human scene? Who really is God and how does God relate to a fallen creation, seeking to foster a recovery of holiness at the human level?

The amazing openness to us fallen humans of the sovereign God is knowable only because of God's activity in human history. William Willimon says it well: "Scripture thinks that our greatest need is be with the God who, in Jesus Christ, has shown such remarkable determination to be with us. A vision of God, rather than helpful hints for everyday living, is what Scripture seeks" (*Proclamation and Theology*, 46). To understand such a beautiful vision of God, we must draw primarily on the Hebrew (biblical) rather than the Greek philosophic tradition.

Marvin Wilson wisely insists that, for the biblical authors, "God is not understood philosophically, but functionally. God acts, and thus is known. The Hebrews primarily thought of God pictorially, in terms of personality and activity, not in terms of pure being or in any static sense" (*Our Father Abraham*, 146). Moses, Isaiah, Amos, Jeremiah, and the others saw God create a people, save a people, implement justice, and offer hope for the future. Who is God, then? God is the source and measure of human salvation, justice, and hope.

The common "evangelical" philosophic reference today differs in some significant ways from this Hebrew perspective. It tends to go back to Aristotle whose ultimate deity was his unmoved-mover, God as pure consciousness, timeless, self-sufficient, immutable, impassible, and simple (no differentiation). To have relationships with others would constitute divine dependence on others, and thus violate God's fixed perfection. God by definition has no friends. Any speaking of God by use of human terms necessarily reduces God to the "finite," therefore, committing idolatry.

Following this philosophic line of thought, the Hebrew Scriptures, so opposed to idolatry, appear to be the chief of idolators. God is understood in the Bible to be voluntarily present, relational, vulnerable. See my book *The Jagged Journey* where I explain that suffering reveals the heart of God and also our calling to be God's obedient and sometimes suffering children. Love reaches, relates, risks, and redeems.

Clark H. Pinnock, central pioneer of the openness-theology movement, has been leading a theological crusade since the 1970s. See his whole story in my book *Journey Toward Renewal* (2000). For Pinnock, today's faulty Christian theism is fixable by renewed biblical understanding. He is convinced that the current problem has been caused largely by the Hellenistic-oriented (Aristotle) and thus in some ways misguided Christian theology ever since Augustine. Pinnock calls this aberration "classical theism" and admits that "it has been a burden of mine for decades to overcome the tilt toward hyper-transcendence and to overcome the soul-destroying abstract categories just like John Wesley began to do. . .[by] following a personalistic (biblical) rather than an absolutistic (philosophical) conception of God." Observes Pinnock, for Wesley "it was not so much God as creator, judge, and king, with the emphasis on divine control and unchangeability, as it was on God as saviour, lover, and friend, with the emphasis on relationality and [human] response-ability. Wesley viewed God not as a unilateral power that takes no risks, but as a bilateral power which gives creatures room" [*Wesleyan Theological Journal*, fall, 2003, 58].

Reviewing the Hebrew Scriptures, we see that God had become known within the ancient Jewish community as the One who is living, holy, jealous, righteous, gracious, and purposeful (see my book *God As Loving Grace*, reprinted 2018). Granted, all of these descriptions are limited human understandings of the Divine, analogies employed to describe what is finally indescribable. Nonetheless, they are meaningful metaphors that speak of the One who had become known as really being active is in these particular ways. Taken together, these six adjectives were believed by the biblical writers to constitute a basic and balanced understanding of the divine being. God's nature surely is congruent with the nature of God's consistent actions. Especially when Jesus is added to the revelational mix, God becomes pictured biblically as *gracious and holy love*. Therefore, concludes Pinnock, the Christian concept of Trinity "depicts God as beautiful and supremely lovable. God is not a featureless monad, isolated and motionless, but a dynamic event of loving actions and personal relationality. What loveliness and sheer liveliness God is!" (*Flame of Love*, 42).

Gregory Boyd refers to the "beautiful sovereignty" of the God who has determined "not to always unilaterally decide matters. God enlists our input, not because he needs it, but because he desires to have an authentic, dynamic relationship with us as real, empowered persons. Like a loving parent or spouse, God wants not only to influence us but to be influenced by us" (*God of the Possible,* 96). The dominating motivation of divine sovereignty is more the motive of love than the maintenance of full control. As Donald Bloesch puts the apparent paradox of divine sovereignty: "Suffering is not inherent in God, but God freely wills to enter into our suffering so that it can be overcome. God cannot be changed by either heavenly or earthly powers, but God can change himself. He remains unchanging in his will for the world, but he alters his ways with his people in conjunction with their response to his gracious initiative. God enters into a reciprocal relationship with his people so that we can have a role in the realization of his plan and purpose" (*God the Almighty*, 95).

"Openness" theologians like myself affirm both the loving vulnerability of God and the absolute sovereignty of God. God's loving ways are generally persuasive and not coercive, but coercion for cause is always a possibility for the God who remains sovereignly transcendent in the midst of loving immanence. Openness thought is not a diminishment of God, as many evangelicals fear. God is so sovereign that, because of an overwhelming and compassionate love, God freely chooses to save the world through weakness and risk (the Incarnation). Jesus arrived among us, not as conqueror on a mighty white horse, but as a helpless baby in a smelly animal stable. The key fact of Christian faith is that the Word became flesh, a dramatic statement of God's relational engagement and changing unchangeability! In the paradox of this changing and unchanging lies the pulsating heart of biblical revelation, which includes both the sovereign God who stands above creation and the compassionate God who stoops to significant involvement with the creation.

How to balance the apparent opposites related to human understanding of God is an ongoing challenge—as are all dimensions of Christian belief (see my book *Caught Between Truths*, 2007). The challenge we face appears to be maintaining a biblically-informed equilibrium between apparent opposites—the classic transcendence-immanence paradox. Openness thought seeks to balance the excessive transcendence focus of classic Calvinism without reverting so far as to join the "process" theologians who tend to abandon vital aspects of divine sovereignty.

John Wesley, of course, did not participate in this theistic debate, at least not as the issues are now framed. However, Clark Pinnock sees a "transforming vision of God. . .at the heart of Wesley's reform" [*WTJ*, fall, 2003, 58]. Wesley's focus is on divine love, the program of salvation, and the transforming work of the Spirit.... His distinctive concern was that God's power not be defined in any way that undercuts human responsibility in the salvation process. According to Wesley, "one basic error the Calvinists had committed was to consider the sovereignty of God in an un-nuanced fashion, that is, not in concert with the other salient attributes of the Most High.... Justifying and regenerating graces are neither irresistible nor coerced" (Kenneth Collins, *John Wesley*, 170-171).

A vision of the holy and loving God, the engaging and interacting, the reaching and risking God, is basic for all aspects of Christian life. The New Testament says that God has created another race, a chosen race (1 Pet. 2:9-10). Christ is the head of a new creation, the church, that is called to accept the Spirit's ministry and thus become first-fruits of the coming new order (Rom. 8:23; 2 Cor. 1:22, 5:5; Eph. 1:13-14). The church is to live in the power of Christ's resurrection (Col. 3:3-4), which is the dynamic of the coming new day. The future reign of God now works in the world by the power of the divine Spirit, who already is introducing that reign and one day will bring it to fullness. The church is to know God as present and active, a loving sovereignty who calls for the real partnership of response-able and thus responsible disciples.

Fresh visions of the holy come in the playful side of love, the tender thoughts of a loving wife, and when extending the ministries of others.

You are to me like . . .

an old shoe.
I feel comfortable with you.

a security blanket.
I feel safe with you.

a rock.
I feel I can depend on you.

my very own Santa Claus.
I feel grateful for all you do.

Near the end of her life, Arlene designed and drew a personal Valentine's Day card for me in 2001.

My first wife Arlene and I enjoyed pretending we were our own great grandparents.

My acting career has been limited to playing Daniel S. Warner, primary pioneer of the Church of God movement. Some of the "historic singers" with me at the North American Convention of the Church of God, Anderson, Indiana, June, 1996, were (l. to r.) Robert A. Nicholson, David L. Coolidge, and Vivian Nieman.

RADICAL

Christianity

The Believers Church Tradition in Christianity's History and Future

BARRY L. CALLEN

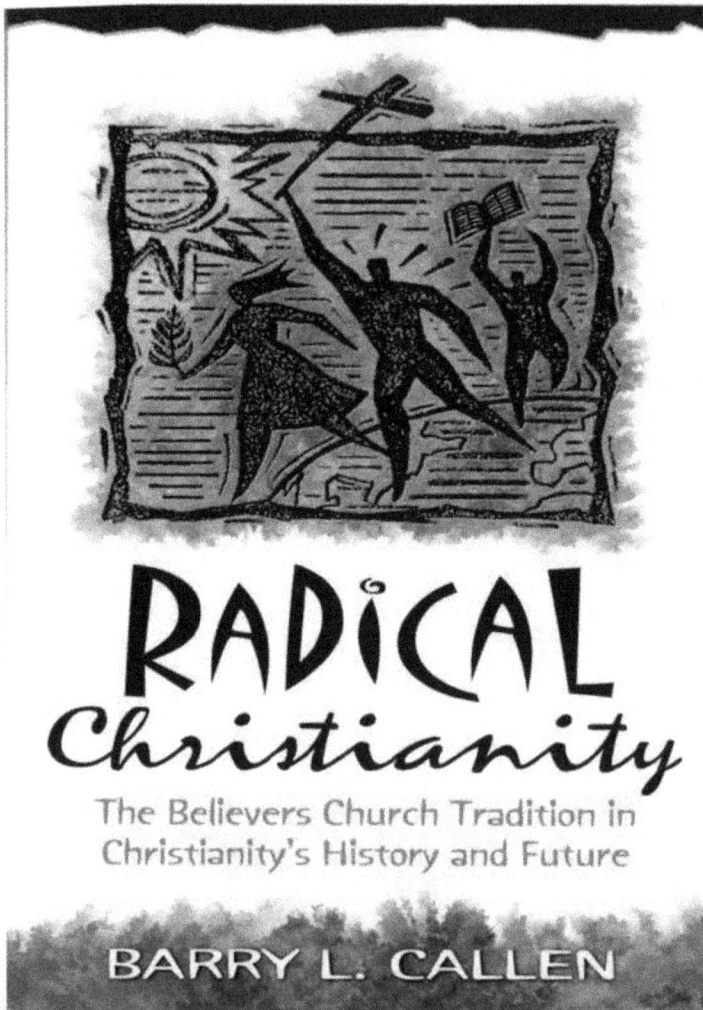

Howard A. Snyder:

> As a growing consensus emerges that the church today needs a "Second Reformation," one that reshapes the church and not just doctrine, we need to take a closer look at the Believers' Church tradition. That is exactly what this book by Barry L. Callen does, and in a very helpful way.

Clark H. Pinnock:

> There is great value in the way Barry Callen lifts up for us in a clear and informed manner the thrilling history of the Believers Church tradition. It can only have the effect of inspiring us all to treasure the gifts we have been given and be faithful.

APPENDIX D

The Holiness Manifesto

by Barry L. Callen and Others

The "Holiness Manifesto" is a 2006 document written by fifteen church leaders and scholars, myself included, all from the interrelated Wesleyan, Holiness, and Pentecostal traditions of Christianity. The manifesto summarizes the heart of Christian holiness beliefs, values, and practices that are relevant to the twenty-first century. It also shares my own heart. Holiness is not a new topic; it is as old as the Bible and lies at the heart of the Church of God movement. Yet, holiness is not always a theme to which Christians are drawn. A lull in its perceived relevance in the opening years of the twenty-first century was the occasion for writing and issuing widely the following "manifesto." It also was the occasion for Hubert Harriman and I to write *Color Me Holy* (Aldersgate Press, 2013).

The text of the manifesto reads as follows, with a broader history of the process that brought it into being available in an essay by my friend Don Thorsen that I published in the fall 2007 issue of the *Wesleyan Theological Journal*. For related documents, see web site *www.holinessand unity.org*. This process led to the formation of the Wesleyan Holiness Connection, and through it the formation in 2011-2012 of Aldersgate Press which I have served as founding Editor and also Chair of the Publications Team until 2018. Now for the actual text of the 2006 Manifesto.

The Crisis We Face. There has never been a time in greater need of a compelling articulation of the message of holiness. Pastors and church leaders at every level of the church have come to new heights of frustration in seeking ways to revitalize their congregations and denominations. What we are doing is not working. Membership in churches of all traditions has flat-lined. In many cases, churches are declining. We are not even keeping pace with the biological growth rate in North America. The power and health of churches have also been drained by the incessant search for a better method, a more effective fad, a newer and bigger program to yield growth. In the process of trying to lead growing, vibrant churches, our people have become largely ineffective and fallen prey to a generic Christianity that results in congregations that are indistinguishable from the culture around them. Churches need a clear, compelling message that will replace the "holy grail" of methods as the focus of our mission.

Many church leaders have become hostages to the success mentality of numeric and programmatic influence. They have become so concerned about "how" they do church that they have neglected the weightier matter of "what" the church declares. We have inundated the "market" with methodological efforts to grow the church. In the process, many of our leaders have lost the ability to lead. They cannot lead because they have no compelling message to give, no compelling vision of God, no transformational understanding of God's otherness. They know it and long to find the centering power of a message that makes a difference. Now more than ever, they long to soak up a deep understanding of God's call to holiness—transformed living. They want a mission. They want a message!

People all around are looking for a future without possessing a spiritual memory. They beg for a generous and integrative word from Christians that makes sense and makes a difference. If God is going to be relevant to people, we have a responsibility to make it clear to them. We have to shed our obsession with cumbersome language, awkward expectations, and intransigent patterns. What is the core, the center, the essence of God's call? That is our message, and that is our mission!

People in churches are tired of our petty lines of demarcation that artificially create compartments, denominations, and divisions. They are tired of building institutions. They long for a clear, articulate message that transcends institutionalism and in-fighting among followers of Jesus Christ. They are embarrassed by the corporate mentality of churches that defend parts of the gospel as if it were their own. They want to know the unifying power of God that transforms. They want to see the awesomeness of God's holiness that compels us to oneness in which there is a testimony of power. They accept the fact that not all of us will look alike; there will be diversity. But they want to know that churches and leaders believe that we are one—bound by the holy character of God who gives us all life and love. They want a message that is unifying. The only message that can do that comes from the nature of God, who is unity in diversity.

Therefore, in this critical time, we set forth for the church's well being a fresh focus on holiness. In our view, this focus is the heart of Scripture concerning Christian existence for all times—and clearly for our time.

The Message We Have. God is holy and calls us to be a holy people. God, who is holy, has abundant and steadfast love for us. God's holy love is revealed to us in the life and teachings, death and resurrection of Jesus Christ, our Savior and Lord. God continues to work, giving life, hope and salvation through the indwelling of the Holy Spirit, drawing us into God's own holy, loving life. God transforms us, delivering us from sin, idolatry, bondage, and self-centeredness to love and serve God, others, and to be stewards of creation. Thus, we are renewed in the image of God as revealed in Jesus Christ.

Apart from God, no one is holy. Holy people are set apart for God's purpose in the world. Empowered by the Holy Spirit, holy people live and love like Jesus Christ. Holiness is both gift and response, renewing and transforming, personal and communal, ethical and missional. The holy people of God follow Jesus Christ in engaging all the cultures of the world and drawing all peoples to God. Holy people are not legalistic or judgmental. They do not pursue an exclusive, private state of being better than others. Holiness is not flawlessness, but the fulfillment of God's intention for us. The pursuit of holiness can never cease because love can never be exhausted.

God wants us to be, think, speak, and act in the world in a Christ-like manner. We invite all to embrace God's call to:

- Be filled with all the fullness of God in Jesus Christ—Holy Spirit-endowed co-workers for the reign of God;
- Live lives that are devout, pure, and reconciled, thereby being Jesus Christ's agents of transformation in the world;
- Live as a faithful covenant people, building accountable community, growing up into Jesus Christ, embodying the spirit of God's law in holy love;
- Exercise for the common good an effective array of ministries and callings, according to the diversity of the gifts of the Holy Spirit;
- Practice compassionate ministries, solidarity with the poor, advocacy for equality, justice, reconciliation, and peace; and
- Care for the earth, God's gift in trust to us, working in faith, hope, and confidence for the healing and care of all creation.

The Action We Take. May this call impel us to rise to this biblical vision of Christian mission:

- Preach the transforming message of holiness;
- Teach the principles of Christ-like love and forgiveness;
- Embody lives that reflect Jesus Christ;
- Lead in engaging with the cultures of the world; and

- Lead in engaging with the cultures of the world; and
- Partner with others to multiply its effect for the reconciliation of all things.

For this we live and labor to the glory of God.

There is a river whose
streams make glad the
city of God, the holy
place where the Most High dwells.

God is within her, she will
not fall; God will help her
at break of day.

(Psalm 46:4-5)

THE SCRIPTURE PRINCIPLE

Reclaiming the Full Authority of the Bible

Third Edition

Clark H. Pinnock
Barry L. Callen

Joel B. Green:

In the ongoing struggle to articulate the role of Scripture in Christian faith and life, this is a landmark study.

David R. Bauer:

This is one of the most balanced and judicious treatments on biblical authority I have read. Callen and Pinnock write with passion but without polemic.

APPENDIX E

Heaven's Eventual Population

by Barry L. Callen

Jesus only? He said, "I am the way and the truth and the life. *No one* comes to the Father except through me" (Jn. 14:6). This claim of exclusivity views the revelation of God in Israel and then finally in Jesus Christ as the singular and fully adequate one that must be embraced if there is hope of eternal salvation. This is the "scandal" of Christianity's *particularity*. Knowledge of and a saving relationship with Jesus is required to join heaven's eventual population.

A natural question is fundamental. Doesn't this particularity drastically and unfairly limit heaven's population? The majority of humanity has existed without ever hearing the Christian gospel. Are all non-Christian religious communities excluded from heaven? What are the proper Christian attitudes toward non-Jesus people who nonetheless are serious about what they believe and how they live? Does God's redeeming love transcend the walls of our churches and the frailty of even Christian theological thinking?

Basic Theological Assumptions

The Bible takes sin seriously and hardly encourages us to think that everyone will accept God's love, although offered to all, or believe that God will use superior power to overcome love's rejections. Nonetheless, Scripture also emphasizes the universality of Christ's atonement and "the ever-present Spirit who can foster transforming relationships with God anywhere and everywhere and inspires hope in us, not only for our future but also for the future of the world and the ungodly whom God would justify (Rom. 15:13)."[1]

Christ is the only Mediator between God and humans, but the Spirit, who pre-dates and post-dates the Christ atonement in our human history, offers hope for salvation beyond engagement with this historical event. Surely it's possible "to cast oneself on the mercy of God even when one's theology is conceptually incomplete. God is a Person and people can receive the gift of his love without knowing exactly who the giver is or how much it cost."[2] "Prevenient grace" refers to such a gracious and universal ministry of the Spirit.[3] We should acknowledge that the Spirit of God is working wherever we see traces of people opening themselves to the loving ideals of Jesus.

A basic knowledge of God is universally available, although always to be thought of as an expression of God's gracious activity in Jesus Christ. The Cross was in the heart of God before it was planted in a hill outside Jerusalem. Otherwise, it never would have appeared on our historical scene.[4] One can benefit from Christ without direct awareness of his name, historical life, and saving work.[5] All human response to God in Christ is possible only because of the universal and previous presence of God's grace. That grace is always rooted in the atoning work of Christ—and always active in the universal ministry of Christ's Spirit.

---

1. Clark H. Pinnock, *Flame of Love* (InterVarsity Press, 1996), 187.

2. Pinnock, *Flame of Love*, 198.

3. On the possibility of the salvation of non-Christians in the teachings of John Wesley, see Randy Maddox, *Responsible Grace* (Abingdon Press, Kingswood Books, 1994), 32-34, and in the *Wesleyan Theological Journal*, 27 (1992), 7-29.

4. See Barry L. Callen, *The Jagged Journey* (Aldersgate Press, 2018) that explores the cross in God's heart that leads to Jesus saying that his true children will take up their own crosses and live in the loving way of their gracious God.

5. See John Sanders, "Evangelical Responses to Salvation Outside the Church,"

Final Population Projection

The Wesleyan Holiness tradition of Christianity, of which I have been an active part, stresses the importance of human response to divine grace. This tradition is open to but hesitates to embrace universalism (all finally will be saved).[6] Instead, the belief is that all *can* be saved but likely all *will not be*. Confidence in Christ is always warranted, but a claim to knowing precisely heaven's eventual numbers, ethnicities, denominations, faith communities, and theological understandings is not.

There are two errors to be avoided. One is to say dogmatically that all will be saved. The other is to say dogmatically that only a select few will be saved. Rather than stepping into the arrogant hole of either dogmatism, we should focus on a humble acceptance of the amazing grace of God, spread the good news of Christ as we are able, and leave to God a determination of the eventual population of heaven.

in *Christian Scholar's Review* 24:1 (Sept. 1994), 52.

6. Clark Pinnock helpfully explores the "hermeneutic of hopefulness" in his insightful *A Wideness in God's Mercy* (1992).

Grandchildren Ethan, Ian, and Emily find
their way into the future, as we all must.

Appendix F

Bibliography

Works Authored, Edited, and/or Published by Barry L. Callen

Publications in Academic Journals: Articles and Book Reviews

The following are the articles and book reviews by Barry L. Callen that have appeared in the most recent years. For the several in the *Wesleyan Theological Journal*, I use the abbreviation *WTJ* and include the journal volume and issue number for each. The others are identified similarly with the journal names identified separately. All appear in chronological order.

Book Reviews Published (in the *Wesleyan Theological Journal*):

(29:1, 2, 1994). *Sacraments and the Salvation Army: Pneumatological Foundations*

(32:1, 1997). *Flame of Love: A Theology of the Holy Spirit*

(33:2, 1998). *The 19th-Century Holiness Movement*

(35:2, 2000). *Future for Truth: Evangelical Theology in a Postmodern World*

(42:2, 2007). *Charles Wesley's Hymns: "Prints" and Practices of Love Divine*

Lead Articles Published (*WTJ* is *Wesleyan Theological Journal*):

Vital Christianity, national periodical of the Church of God, many articles across the 1970s and 1980s

Faculty Dialogue (Winter, 1985-1986), article titled "Faith and Freedom in Higher Education, " and (Spring, 1991), article titled "The 'Higher' in Higher Education"

WTJ (30:1,1995). "Daniel Warner: Joining Holiness and All Truth"

WTJ (36:1, 2001). "Tulip to Rose: Clark H. Pinnock on the Open and Risking God"

WTJ (37:1, 2002). "Reconciling Clashing Ecumenical Visions: The Church of God (Anderson) and the Free Methodist Church"

The Holiness Manifesto (2006). First appeared in various publications simultaneously in 2006, then republished in the 2008 book *The Holiness Manifesto* (Kevin Mannoia and Don Thorsen, eds.), with Barry Callen writing the lead chapter titled "The Context: Past and Present"

Brethren in Christ: History & Life (30:2, 2007), article titled "Postmodern Openings for 'Radical' Christianity"

Church of God Peace Fellowship Newsletter (Winter, 2007), article titled "The Powerful Weakness of God"

Journal of Research on Christian Education (17:1, January-June, 2008), article titled "Issues That Have Made a Difference"

WTJ (44:2, 2009), article titled "Heart of a Radical Reform: Christology and the Church of God Movement (Anderson)"

WTJ (46:2, 2011), article titled "Soteriological Synergism and Its Surrounding Seductions"

WTJ (53:1, 2018), article titled "The Precarious Church Paradox and the National Association of the Church of God"

Books Authored or Edited

1. *Where Life Begins*, Warner Press, 1973.

2. *A Time To Remember* (six-paperback book series, Warner Press, 1977-1978), republished as a two-volume hardbound set under the title *The First Century* (Warner Press, 1979).

3. *The First Century* (two-volumes, hardback), a republishing of the series *A Time To Remember* (Warner Press, 1979).

4. *Preparation for Service: A History of Higher Education in the Church of God*, Warner Press, 1988.

5. *Listening to the Word of God*, ed., essays in honor of Boyce W. Blackwelder, Warner Press, 1990.

6. *Faith, Learning, and Life*, ed., collected writings of Anderson University presidents John Morrison, Robert Reardon, and Robert Nicholson, Warner Press, 1991.

7. *She Came Preaching: Life and Ministry of Lillie S. McCutcheon*, Warner Press, 1992, now available by reprint, Reformation Publishers.

8. *Guide of Soul and Mind: The Story of Anderson University*, Anderson University and Warner Press, 1992. Available through Anderson University

9. *Thinking and Acting Together, General Assembly of the Church of God*, Warner Press, 1992.

10. *Contours of a Cause: The Theological Vision of the Church of God*, Anderson University School of Theology, 1995. Available through Anderson University or Reformation Publishers.

11. *It's God's Church: Life and Legacy of Daniel S. Warner*, Warner Press, 1995.

12. *Sharing Heaven's Music*, ed., essays on preaching in honor of James Earl Massey, Nashville: Abingdon Press, 1995.

13. *God As Loving Grace: The Biblically Revealed Nature and Work of*

God (a systematic theology), Evangel Publishing House, 1996, reprint 2018 by Wipf & Stock.

14. *Journeying Together: A Documentary History of the Church of God*, ed., Leadership Council of the Church of God and Warner Press, 1996.

15. *Faithful in the Meantime: A Biblical View of Final Things and Present Responsibilities*, Evangel Publishing House, 1997, reprint 2018 by Wipf & Stock.

16. *Coming Together in Christ*, with James North, College Press Publishing Co., 1997.

17. *Great Holiness Classics*, vol. 4, *The Nineteenth-Century Holiness Movement,* by Melvin Dieter, "Volume Advisor" (Callen), Beacon Hill Press of Kansas City, 1998.

18. *Seeking the Light: America's Modern Quest for Peace, Justice, Prosperity, and Faith,* Evangel Publishing House, 1998.

19. *Radical Christianity: The Believers Church Tradition in Christianity's History and Future*, Evangel Publishing House, 1999.

20. *Journey Toward Renewal: An Intellectual Biography of Clark H. Pinnock*, Evangel Publishing House, 2000.

21. *Following the Light: Teachings, Testimonies, Trials, and Triumphs of the Church of God* (Anderson), Warner Press, 2000.

22. *Heart of the Heritage: Core Themes of the Wesleyan/Holiness Tradition*, with William Kostlevy, Schmul Publishers, 2001.

23. *Authentic Spirituality: Moving Beyond Mere Religion*, Baker Book House (North America) and Paternoster Press (Europe), 2002. New edition, Emeth Press, 2006.

24. *Aspects of My Pilgrimage*, ed., the autobiography of James Earl Massey, Anderson University Press, 2002.

25. *The Wisdom of the Saints*, ed., Anderson University Press and Warner Press, 2003.

26. *Staying on Course: The Biography of Robert H. Reardon*, Anderson University Press, 2004.

27. *Bible Reading in Wesleyan Ways*, eds. Barry Callen and Richard Thompson, Beacon Hill Press of Kansas City, 2004.

28. *Discerning the Divine: God Through Christian Eyes*, Westminster/John Knox, 2004.

29. *Seeking Higher Ground: The Centennial History of Park Place Church of God, Anderson, Indiana, Park Place Church of God*, 2006.

39. *Coming Home, a novel of search for personal and religious identity, set in rural Kentucky* (Emeth Press, 2010).

40. *StarWalker, a novel of hope trying to emerge in one boy's life*, Emeth Press, 2011.

41. *The Prayer of Holiness-Hungry People: A Disciple's Guide to the Lord's Prayer*, Francis Asbury Press, 2011, audio edition, 2019.

42. *Heart of the Matter: Frank Conversations among Great Christian Thinkers on the Major Subjects of Christian Theology*, Emeth Press, 2011, rev. ed., 2016.

43. *Beneath the Surface: Reclaiming the Old Testament for Today's Christians*, Emeth Press, 2012.

44. *Heart & Life: Rediscovering Holy Living*, co-edited with DonThorsen, Aldersgate Press, 2012.

45. *Color Me Holy: Holy God, Holy People*, Aldersgate Press, 2013, 2015.

46. *Catch Your Breath!: Exhaling Death and Inhaling Life*, Aldersgate Press, 2014.

47. *The Wesleyan Theological Society*, with Steve Hoskins, Fiftieth Anniversary Celebration Volume, 2015, Emeth Press.

48. *Approaching Theology: Asking the Right Questions Enables the Right Answers*, Emeth Press, 2015.

49. *The Holy River of God: Currents and Contributions of the Wesleyan*

Holiness Stream of Christianity, 2016.

50. *Bible Stories for Strong Stomachs: The Bible is Full of Shocking Stories*, Cascade Books, Wipf & Stock, 2017.

51. *The Jagged Journey: Suffering—God's Heart and Our Calling*, Cascade Books, Wipf & Stock, 2018.

52. *God in the Shadows: Finding God in the Back Alleys of Our Scary Lives*, Emeth Press, 2018.

53. *Views from the Mountain: Select Writings of James Earl Massey*, co-ed. with Curtiss Paul DeYoung, Aldersgate Press, 2018.

54. Projected: *General Assembly of the Church of God in the United States and Canada*, Warner Press, 2019.

Chapters Contributed to Books Edited by Others

1. "The Church: Tomorrow's People for Today's World," chapter 9 of Lane Scott and Leon Hynson,

   eds., Christian Ethics (Wesleyan Theological Perspectives, Warner Press, 1983).

2. "Faith and Freedom in Higher Education," chapter 8 of James Earl Massey, ed., *Educating for Service* (Warner Press, 1984).

3. "A Mutuality Model of Conversion," chapter 8 of Kenneth J. Collins and John H. Tyson, eds., *Conversion in the Wesleyan Tradition* (Abingdon Press, 2001).

4. "Blazing Radiance," in David Liverett, ed., *When Hope Shines Through* (Chinaberry House, 2001).

5. "Into the Wider Stream," in David Liverett, ed., *Faith for the Journey* (Chinaberry House, 2002).

6. "Clark H. Pinnock: His Life and Work," chapter 1 of Stanley E. Porter and Anthony R. Cross, eds., *Semper Reformandum* (England: Paternoster Press, 2003).

7. "Father and Son," in David Liverett, *Love, Bridges of Reconciliation*

(Chinaberry House, 2003).

8. "Wisdom in a Round Barn," in David Liverett, ed., *Light from the Barn* (Chinaberry House, 2006).

9. "The Context: Past and Present," chapter 1 of Kevin W. Mannoia and Don Thorsen, eds., *The Holiness Manifesto* (Eerdmans Publishing, 2008).

10. Contributed support materials that appear in the Wesley Study Bible (NRSV) (Abingdon Press, 2009).

11. "Dare We Ask God Anything?" in David Liverett, Questions for God (Chinaberry House, 2009).

12. "Daniel Sydney Warner: Joining Holiness and All Truth," in Henry Knight III, ed., *From Aldersgate to Azusa Street: Wesleyan, Holiness, and Pentecostal Visions of the New Creation* (Pickwick Publications, 2010).

13. "Heart of a Radical Reform: Christology and the Church of God Movement (Anderson)," chapter 3 in Nathan Crawford, ed., *The Continuing Relevance of Wesleyan Theology*, a book in honor of my friend Laurence W. Wood (Pickwick Publications, 2012).

14. Four entries on various subjects, in Al Truesdale, gen. ed., *Global Wesleyan Dictionary of Theology* (Beacon Hill Press of Kansas City, 2012).

15. "John Wesley and Relational Theology," in Brint Montgomery, Thomas Oord, Karen Winslow, eds., *Relational Theology: A Contemporary Introduction* (Beacon Hill Press, 2012).

Booklets Authored

1. "We Believe: A Statement of Conviction on the Occasion of the Centennial of the Church of God Reformation Movement" (editor, with members of the Anderson School of Theology faculty), Warner Press, 1979.

2. "Confessing and Celebrating: Church of God (Anderson) in a New Millennium," Anderson University Press, 2000. See *Appendix I.*

3. "What We Teach" [the Church of God movement], Anderson University Press, 2005.

4. "The Top Ten." Why Daniel Warner is Still Relevant. Anderson University Press, 2014.

5. "My Last Will and Testimony," 2019.

Documents authored/edited for Anderson University and the Church of God (Anderson)

1. 1978, edited the institutional *Self-Study of Anderson University* (college and seminary) required for reaccreditation by the North Central Association and the Association of Theological Schools.

2. 1997, edited for the Church of God its new *Credentials Manual* for all ministers in the United States and Canada.

3. 1998, rewrote the *Constitution and Bylaws of the General Assembly of he Church of God* to accommodate the major restructuring of the church's North American ministries.

4. 1999, edited the institutional *Self-Study of Anderson University* (college and seminary) required for reaccreditation by the North Central Association and the Association of Theological Schools.

5. 2006, edited a *Policies Manual for Church of God Ministries.*

6. 2007, re-edited for the Church of God its revised *Credentials Manual* for all ministers in the United States and Canada. I did so for earlier and later editions, including the 2017 edition when I also was named Chair of the new "Standing Committee on Credentials

of the General Assembly."

7. 2007 and 2013, edited with Vernon Maddox, A New *Operations Manual for the Regional Pastors of the Church of God.*

8. 2008, edited the institutional *Self-Study of Anderson University* (college and seminary) required for reaccreditation by the North Central Association and the Association of Theological Schools.

9. 2018 authored the final report of "Project Imagine" as the Church of God was exploring a better future for itself.

Books I Edited and/or Published for Others

Primarily in my role as Editor of Anderson University Press beginning in 2000, here are a few of the books by others that I edited and published:

2001. Douglas E. Welch, *Ahead of His Times: A Life of George P. Tasker*

2002. Gustav Jeeninga, *Doors to Life: The Stories of Gustav Jeeninga*

2002. James Earl Massey, *Aspects of My Pilgrimage: An Autobiography.*

2005. James Earl Massey, *African Americans and the Church of God.*

2006. Robert A. Nicholson, *So I Said Yes!: Memoirs.*

2009. Mary Ann Hawkins and Juanita Evans Leonard, *A Thread of Hope: Church of God Women in Mission.*

2010. Willi Krenz, *Always Looking Forward: Memories of My Adventurous Life with God.*

2012. *Voices from Riley* (Riley Hospital for Children, Indiana University Health, Indianapolis).

Books that I published through Aldersgate Press (2011-2018)

1. *A Long Walk Home*, by Larry Walkemeyer.

2. *Biblical Heights for Today's Valleys*, by H. Ray Dunning.

3. *Higher Higher Education*, by Jonathan S. Raymond.

4. *Honorable Influence*, by David Hagenbuch.

5. *Masterful Living*, by Kevin Mannoia.

6. *Social Holiness*, by Jonathan S. Raymond.

7. *Work That Matters*, by Kevin Brown and Michael Wiese.

8. *Views from the Mountain*, the writings of James Earl Massey.

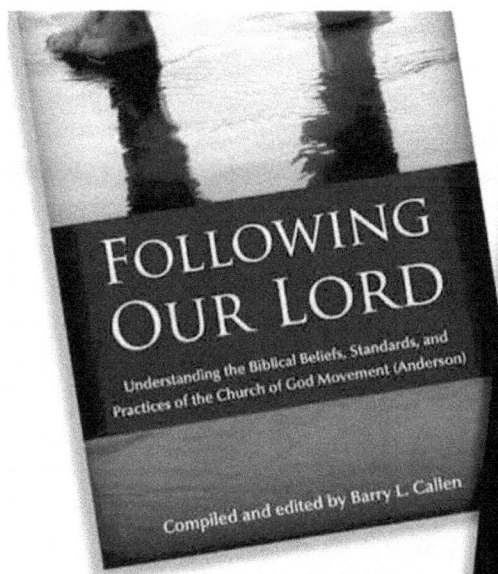

FOLLOWING OUR LORD

Understanding the Biblical Beliefs, Standards, and
Practices of the Church of God Movement (Anderson)

Compiled and edited by Barry L. Callen

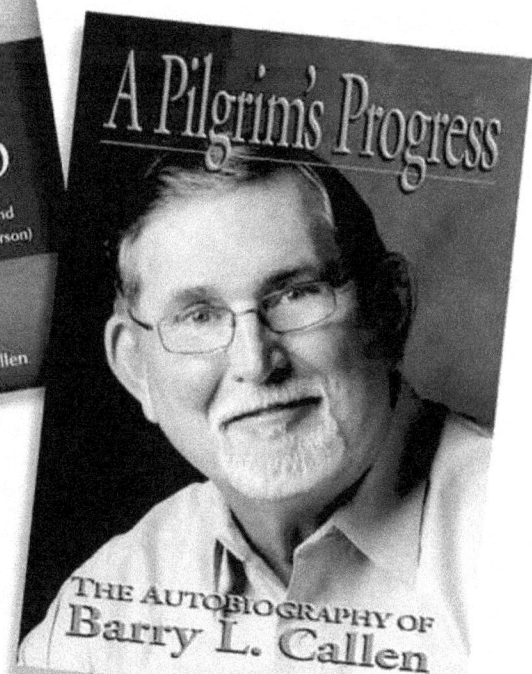

A Pilgrim's Progress

THE AUTOBIOGRAPHY OF
Barry L. Callen

APPENDIX G

FAMILY TREE OF BARRY L. CALLEN

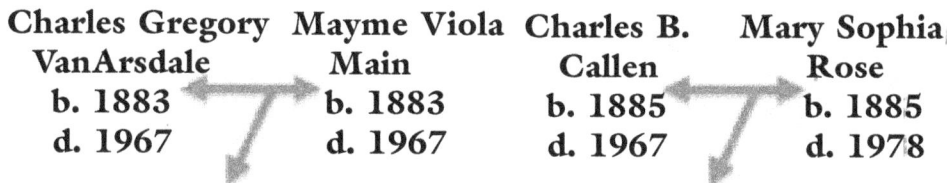

Charles Gregory VanArsdale
b. 1883
d. 1967

Mayme Viola Main
b. 1883
d. 1967

Charles B. Callen
b. 1885
d. 1967

Mary Sophia Rose
b. 1885
d. 1978

These grandparents had three children, with Charlotte Marie VanArsdale being the mother of Bonnie and myself.
b. 1919
d. 1979

These grandparents had six children, with Robert Christopher Callen being the father of Bonnie and myself.
b. 1919
d. 1974

BARRY LEE CALLEN
b. 1941
d.—

Barry's first wife
Arlene Marie Cooley
b. 1941
d. 2003
Married to Barry
1963 to 2003

Children and Grandchildren of Barry

Barry's second wife
Jan Ruth Hitt
b. 1952
d. —
Married to Barry
2003 to the present

Son of Barry and Arlene
Todd
b. 1967
d.—

Son of Jan, step-son of Barry
Jordan
b. 1978
d. —

Children of Todd:		Children of Jordan:	
Ian Patrick	b. 1995	Bentley Allen	b. 2007
Emily Elizabeth	b. 1996	Emerson Joy	b. 2009
Ethan Alexander	b. 1998	Maxwell Philip	b. 2011
Samantha Brianne	b. 1990	Samson Robert	b. 2013
		Zachariah Anthony	b. 2015

Voices
from Riley

A collection of prayers from the patients, families and caregivers of one of the nation's top children's hospitals.

Through Anderson University Press in 2012,
I published this book of child-healing testimonies for
Riley Hospital for Children in Indianapolis.

The Christian's Journey to Joy

I Rejoice in the Pilgrimage of Faith Found in the Psalms

We are all on a journey, with its ups and downs, but always gaining upward ground by God's grace.

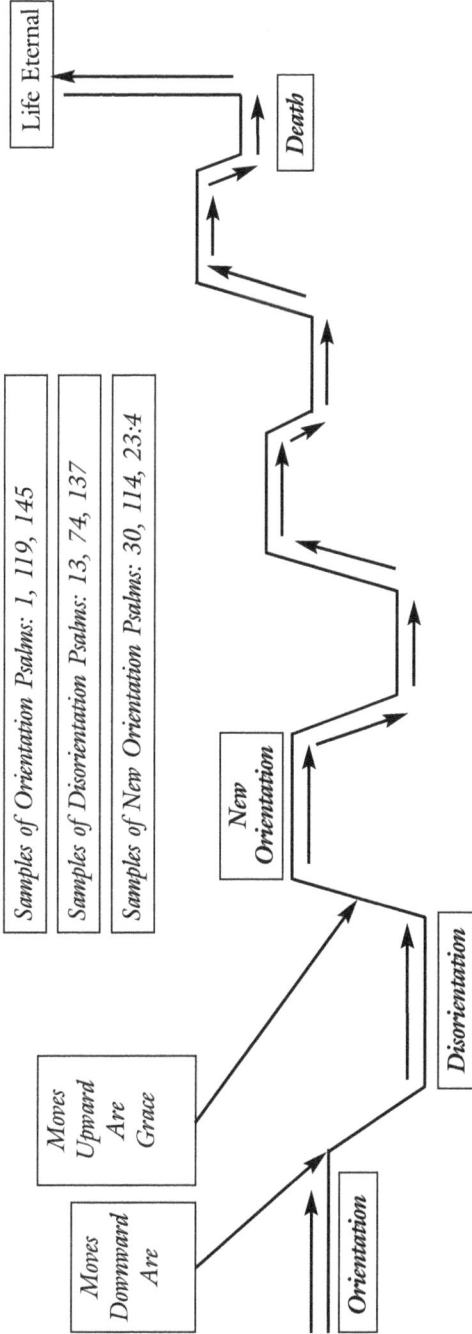

Life Eternal

Death

Samples of Orientation Psalms: 1, 119, 145

Samples of Disorientation Psalms: 13, 74, 137

Samples of New Orientation Psalms: 30, 114, 23:4

New Orientation

Moves Upward Are Grace

Moves Downward Are

Disorientation

Orientation

My Personal Testimony: A Pilgrim's Progress

Some Times of Orientation: New Birth in Christ; Marriage to Arlene; Call to Christian Ministry; Wonderful Education; Open Doors at Anderson University, A.U. Press, Wesleyan Theological Society, Aldersgate Press, and More!

Some Times of Disorientation: Death of Arlene; Divorce of Todd and Beth; my cancer journey and eye surgery

Some Times of New Orientation: Having a Son; Marriage to Jan; Having a Stepson; Marriage of Todd and Laura; Nine Wonderful Grandchildren; Two Great-Grandchildren, Retirement and New Servant Roles with Church of God Ministries and Horizon International.

Source: Walter Brueggemann, The Message of the Psalms (1984)   See more in my The Jagged Journey.

THE PRESENT AND THE FUTURE

Barry Callen, church theologian in the finest sense, brings commitments of the Pietist, Anabaptist, and Wesleyan streams into conversation with the issues and debates in contemporary church life. The result, his book *Faithful in the Meantime*, is a convincing reminder that Christian teachings about "ultimate things" are much more concerned with providing hope and direction for living faithfully in our present settings than providing timetables for the future.

Randy L. Maddox
Professor of Wesleyan and Methodist Studies
Duke University Divinity School

APPENDIX I

Guidelines for the Church's Future

From my booklet "Confessing and Celebrating: A Tract for Transitional Times" published in two forms in 2001 and then by me through Anderson University Press in 2002. The timing was crucial. It was just as the new millennium began and the Church of God movement (Anderson) was searching for its own future in a new time.

Whatever its limitations, and all church bodies have them, a few aspects of the teaching tradition of the Church of God movement (Anderson) are worthy of careful consideration in this new time. Supplementing the book I edited titled *The Church that God Intends* (Emeth Press, 2009), I note in brief the following from my 2002 booklet. They are worthy guidelines for the church's future.

1.   **God's Time.** Daniel Warner (1842-1895) was the primary pioneer of the Church of God (Anderson) movement in the late nineteenth century. He and his colleagues were "flying messengers" with an urgent word of judgment and good news for the church and world of their time. They were sure that it was a period of God's special working. Yes, they were wrong about the soon-coming of Christ and the mass coming-out of people from the denominations; but they were right that God then was active in the life of the church on behalf of the church's holiness, unity, and mission before Christ's return. Still today, that divine initiative continues, maybe even at an accelerated pace. Experienced holiness and Christian unity are closely related. Flying messengers of our new time are needed to show the way again. God's time still is always now!

[Note: My book *Faithful in the Meantime* highlights the constant importance of the present time, de-emphasizing speculation about detailed knowledge of "end times." I certainly have witnessed and participated in the recent ministries of the Wesleyan Holiness Conference as evidence that today is God's time! See the "Holiness Manifesto" in *Appendix D*.]

2. A New World. What is "post-modernism"? Its meaning is still emerging, but it is defining our times and is at least a repudiation of some of the unfortunate preoccupations of church people that have been resisted for generations by the Church of God movement. They include the temptation to focus on mandatory theological systems, to feature the power of human reason to know and "prove" the truth, and to insist on rigid doctrinal propositions and revered religious institutions to preserve and project the faith to others. Such things now are being "deconstructed." As Church of God leaders have insisted since the 1880s, authentic Christianity requires faith, grace, and inner transformation, a holy church community, with room left for necessary mystery, diversity, and spiritual growth. Even if not implementing this vision adequately, the Church of God movement saw beyond "modernism" long before it had a popular name. The movement has sought to reach beyond the common compromises of the hurtfully institutionalized and tragically divided Christian world. Dynamic new life in God's Spirit is to be the *central reality always*!

3. On "Seeing" the Church. There has been an unfortunate Protestant emphasis on the "invisible" church ever since the Protestant Reformation of the sixteenth century. This emphasis has lowered the vision of God's intention for the church in the world. It has justified a rampant denominationalism and encouraged an abortive individualism among believers. Now it is the time to restore the ancient Christian emphasis on the "visible" church. God intends the appearance in this world of a very real and united family of new creatures in Christ. The sectarian spirit among contemporary Christians is to be repudiated. Church of God people have been saying this for generations—if not always doing it well. Now is a wonderful time to start "seeing" the church again! Effective evangelism requires moving from good talking about the church to *being the church in its intended holiness and unity.* Effectiveness will come less from argumentation and more from *visible demonstration!*

> [Note the book I edited and titled *The Church that God Intends* (Emeth Press, 2009). It reconsiders the reformation heritage of the Church of God in multiple ways. Note also the book by my dear friend Gilbert W. Stafford, *Signals at the Crossroads,* 2011.]

4. Biblical and Apostolic. Postmodern thought is certainly right about one thing. There is no such thing as a detached observer or an unbiased interpreter. Creedal and denominational (movement) arrogance is unwarranted. All believers should be humble and journey together in their growing understanding and sharing of the faith. No group has a corner on truth. Authority lies in biblical revelation and apostolic teachings as ministered to our understanding by God's Holy Spirit. The call is still "back to the blessed old Bible." Going back to the right past, and doing it in community with each other and the whole Christian tradition, is a necessary way to get to the right future!

> [Note the classic book by Charles E. Brown titled *The Apostolic Church* (1947). It may not be the last word on the subject, but it is a good word in the right direction. Note my 1999 book *Radical Christianity* that builds on the work of Brown.]

5. Spirit and Form. The Church of God movement overacted at first to abuses in organized Christianity. Pioneer leaders cried out against virtually all organization in church life. The movement was right about starting with God's Spirit. Jesus said (Acts 1:4-5) that disciples should wait and receive the Spirit's baptism, the Father's promise, before proceeding with their world mission. Again, see my 1999 book *Radical Christianity*, chapter two. Gilbert Stafford has written helpfully of the two essential dimensions of church life, the *dynamic* (charismatic) and the *stabilizing* (continuity with the tradition of the whole church in the whole of its history). He says that both are essential for the church to be fully herself and in full health for her mission (*Theology for Disciples*, 1996, 263-64). Believers in Christ are to be both *free* in the Spirit and *mutually accountable*. *Form* is necessary, although it is fragile and only to be a temporary vehicle for the life and work of the God's Spirit. Our real life is not in church institutions, but in the life of the *eternal Spirit*!

> [Note my book *Authentic Spirituality* (2001, revised 2006) that explores the Christian spiritual life in detail. Note also chapters six and seven of my book *God As Loving Grace* (1996, reprint 2018).]

Death and Beyond

This Aisle

Referring to the long center aisle of Park Place Church of God, Anderson, Indiana, this was written for the occasion of the wedding of Barry L. Callen and Jan R. Slattery, December 21, 2003. It was written by Jan and Barry and appeared in the wedding bulletin for all to share

How many times have we walked this aisle?
This aisle has seen our happiest dreams,
Jordan's baby dedication, Todd and Beth's wedding,
Countless Christmas Eves and Easters,
Inspiring services graced by beautiful music.

It has also seen our saddest times.
Arlene's and Phil's funerals,
Where hundreds of you cried with us,
Sharing our pain to lessen it—
Pouring your love into our wounds,
Keeping our hearts from bursting by loving us through it.

God's ways are mysterious ways.
We prayed for God's will,
But never dreamed of finding it in each other.
So, here we are again walking this aisle—
This time joyously, gratefully,
This time, for the first time, we walk it together.

> We cherish your presence in our lives,
> Our dear family and trusted friends,
> Through all these times—good and bad,
> Joyous and heart wrenching.
> We know every time we walk this aisle,
> you walk with us.

So it is with life in general. How we need the church and each other. How blessed we are by the grace of a loving God. How mysterious and yet wonderful are the ways of God. We all are pilgrims still in progress, walking by faith, and with each other. For all that has been and yet will be, to God be the glory!

Death and Beyond

Excerpts from my personal journal at the time of the death of first my wife, Arlene, in 2003.

February 27, Thursday, 2003

Tuesday night found me alone with Arlene, staying on the couch next to her and helping her nausea when it came, and handling the ice pack changes on a two-hour basis. It appears that the end surely will come for her in only ten days or so. She and I pray together often now, mostly giving thanks for God's goodness and his many gracious helpers (Hospice nurses and others) and asking for mercy with the pain and nausea.... Arlene said to me, "I want anything between us that needs to be forgiven to be so." We assured each other that all was well. She insisted that she wants me to feel no guilt about anything when she is gone. I will try.

March 1, Saturday, 2003

Arlene just breathed her last. Minutes before the end I had leaned over and said in her ear, "Thanks for everything, Honey. We are all here and love you very much.

If God is calling you home now, feel free to go to your better place." Shortly after, she breathed very slowly, then quietly she stopped, was calm and gone. It was over…. It had been a long and hard journey since the first cancer diagnosis last April, nearly a year, but finally Arlene had left the dark valley and journeyed into the great light of God's love beyond.

September 21, Sunday, 2003

During the morning service at Park Place Church of God, I thought much about Arlene. Last March she had gotten what she wanted! She used to say to me, when frustrated about her health or spiritual struggles, that she wished it were all over for her. Then she would be free of her limitations and I would be free to marry again, this time to someone who would be freely and comfortably social and love to travel with me. So it has turned out! Arlene is fully free and I will be marrying Jan Slattery exactly three months from today. God is surprising and amazing!

My Final Words

In 2019 I prepared a little booklet to be distributed by the family at the time of my death—which I hope is still years away. I titled it "*MY LAST WILL AND TESTIMONY.*"

My Last Will and Testimony

Barry L. Callen

A Humble Servant of the Church
with a Few Last Things to Say

APPENDIX K

LIVING A HOLY "YES!"

by Barry L. Callen

New Testament writers often conclude prayers with an "Amen." This word meant more than "I'm done now" or "Now we can start eating." It carried a burst of rich meaning, like when Paul ended his second letter to Timothy (4:18): "The Lord will rescue me from every evil attack and will save me for his heavenly kingdom. To him be the glory forever and ever. Amen!" The reader can sense in that last word a "Wonderful!" and a grateful "YES!"

The "Amen" at the *end* of the Lord's Prayer is intended as the keynote for our *beginning*. Having laid our lives before God throughout the prayer, we are to end with a great word of faith and commitment. God has done all for us, so now we are to lead new lives in Christ and by God's power. "Amen"—"YES!" We now can and will do just that. We've placed our faith in the One who sits above time and is in charge of eternity. We now belong to God and are to reflect the divine character in this world and enjoy divine fellowship even beyond this world.[1]

I witness to having found that precious place where the enabling and healing waters of Jesus Christ run quiet and deep and always. My adequacy to be a child of God lies only in the constant availability of those grace-full waters of Christ's prevailing presence. I gladly join the great holiness evangelist E. Stanley Jones in witnessing, "With the Holy Spirit, I am not a *mess* but a *message*."

---

1. See Barry L. Callen, *The Prayer of Holiness-Hungry People* (Francis Asbury Press, 2011), chapter 9, "Living a Holy Yes!"

So, please look beyond my *limitations* and see my *Lord.* Hear my departing testimony.[2] I echo the words of Jones, hoping to *live* the message and thus *be* the message of the Lord's Prayer:

> So I live in a state of "Yes-ness." Yes to the Lord Jesus; Yes to life and its responsibilities; Yes to approaching death; and Yes to the future, through and beyond death; Yes to God's everything![3]

---

2. See my 2019 booklet *My Last Will and Testimony.*
3. E. Stanley Jones, *Song of Ascents* (Abingdon Press, 1968), 26, 316.

EPILOGUE

NEW CONTENT FOR THE

FOURTH EDITION

2024

Brief additions to each of the chapters
as presented in previous editions.

DEDICATION

My DEDICATION in the Third Edition (2019) stands, except for the following areas of change, inevitable over time. The previous prominence of America's Christian Credit Union was in response to circumstances of the time of the earlier edition. My admiration for it is unchanged, but my current wish is to broaden the range of particular institutions and individuals named.

I must add Emeth Press and Anderson University that have graciously published all four editions of my autobiography. Anderson University has been the site of my first graduate education and the scene of much of my professional ministry for the decades that have followed. Its presidential leaders have been exceptional indeed.

Recently I have written biographies of the current president of Anderson University and the founder of the Wesleyan Holiness Connection. Commendations of this volume by them follow. They are exceptional Christian brothers to whom I am in debt.

COMMENDATIONS

Much flows through my memory as I glance at the earlier kind comments about my life found in previous editions. Time has seen all of these gracious people move on, with a few now in the Lord's eternal care. I have been so blessed to have known well these amazing people. Just noting their names brings a flood of memories: Donald Dayton, William Kostlevy, James Earl Massey, Eugene Newberry, Steven O'Malley, Randy Maddox, Robert Pearson, Clark Pinnock, Handel Smith, David Elton Trueblood, and Laurence Wood. What richness they have brought into my life!

Since the last edition of this autobiography, I have been privileged to author the biographies of two more outstanding Christian leaders, Drs. Kevin W. Mannoia and John S. Pistole. Each now has his say about my life story.

Kevin W. Mannoia:

The opportunity to look into the life of Barry Callen is a wonderful chance to see how God mightily uses a willing heart and a competent mind. His thoughtful work as theologian, professor, and writer is an exemplary model of servant leadership. The impact of his life will benefit church leaders and students for generations to come. It is difficult to imagine any serious engagement with the study of church history, holiness, or church unity without his influence. His impact on the establishment of the Wesleyan Holiness Connection and Aldersgate Press has been considerable.

John S. Pistole:

Barry Callen has influenced the church's theological life for decades, impacting countless lives for Christ and God's kingdom. The academic rigor and thoughtfulness of Barry's research and writing continue to be a blessing to all of us at Anderson University where he served as a Professor, Dean, and Vice-President before "retiring" to full-time writing, speaking, and mentoring others. His is a life well lived and very well worth examining closely.

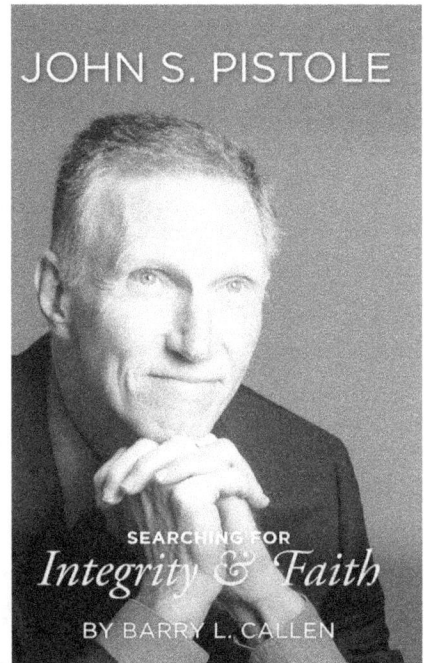

ON WRITING AN AUTOBIOGRAPHY

I say in "On Writing an Autobiography" (third edition in 2019, 17ff) that I was "approaching eighty years old." Now I have arrived and gone three years past that pivotal milestone. My motivation for the writing, however, remains unchanged and my gratitude for the continuing opportunity only magnified. Let me explain my motivation for now updating my life story.

In 2021 I was completing the biography of John S. Pistole, current president of Anderson University. His life story surely deserved being told. What caused me to respond to his request to be the biographer was his expressed motivation. His concern was Christian witness, not personal ego. This troubled world would be much better off if there were many more giants like John who have crossed my path. I'm honored to have played a small role in being sure that his story isn't forgotten.

Then came Kevin W. Mannoia, another giant who has crossed my path. The motivation for his story being told was much like John's, Christin witness and not personal ego. The purpose of all my life's recording likewise is not to draw attention to myself—which wouldn't be worth your time—but showing how God graciously works in the course of our living, believing, and serving. If that's been true for me in my circumstances, and it surely has, it also could be true for you in yours!

The grace of God has followed me along life's long path. Theologically speaking, who have I been while traveling this path? I resonate with a characterization of me once announced to a crowd by a scholar friend. "Dr. Callen is a creative catalyst on the progressive side of the middle of the theological spectrum." That seems about right to me. I have cherished deep roots that make possible fresh fruit. I am an historian by instinct and training, as can be seen in many of my books.

I want future generations to be aware of the wisdom of yesterday that has helped make possible their todays and still-coming tomorrows. I have been privileged to stand on many strong shoulders. I hope that the modest footprints I have left in the sand will guide someone in the future to some good place.

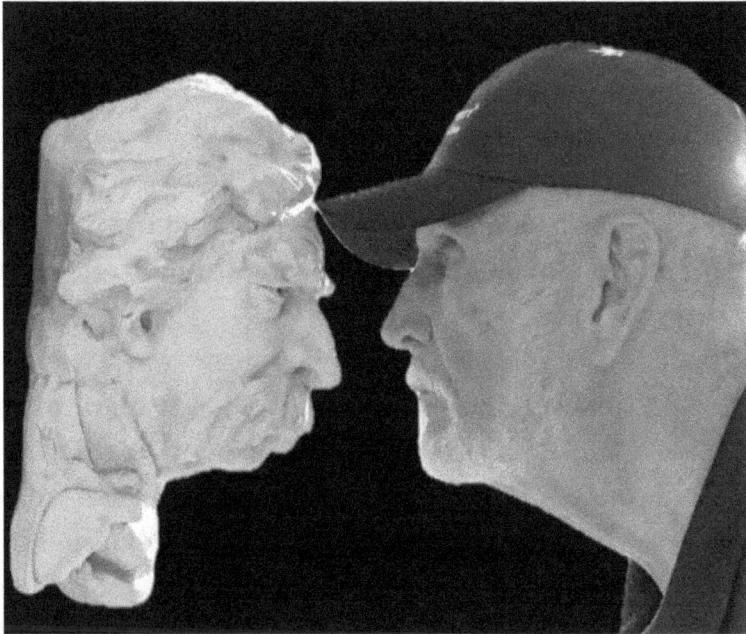

"My works are like water. The works of the great masters are like wine. But everyone drinks water." --Mark Twain's Notebook, 1885. I came face-to-face with Samuel Clemens (Twain) in 2019. Have I written water or wine? Only in a time beyond mine will that become clear.

CHAPTER ONE

OLD WORLD, NEW WORLD

Always Hoping for Better

I've already spoken of my family's distant heritage as best I know it, German, Dutch, Scotch-Irish, and even Ugandan in Africa long before anything European. Our history involves much pride and a little shame, with the full truth now forgotten. While genealogy is interesting and enlightening, it tends to perpetuate old nationalisms and prejudices that have troubled all recorded human history. I want none of that.

In December, 2022, my wife Jan and I sailed among the islands of the eastern Caribbean. We often heard guides mention Christopher Columbus, never flatteringly. He "discovered" this island and that one, say the misinformed books, when in fact he probably was lost and grateful he landed on anything solid. Other Europeans soon appeared and nationalistic struggles began, always at the expense of the locals present long before anyone from Spain, England, France, or Holland by accident or deliberately landed and fought to take over. History gets written by the conquerors. I've written plenty of history. I hope I've not twisted it excessively in my preferred directions.

Here's one Caribbean story we heard that has a better ending than most. One island only 34 square miles in size is the smallest landmass in the world to be owned by two different nations, France and the Netherlands. Thanks to a treaty signed 350 years ago and still in force, citizens from either side of the island function commercially on the opposite side with no red tape or boundary checks. This peaceful coexistence of Saint Martin and Saint Maarten may be the oldest active and undisputed such treaty on the planet. Somewhat differing lifestyles function side-by-side in both contrast and harmony.

My father was in the line of Callen generations on the move to find a newer and better world. Fortunately, they were more builders than conquerors. After World War II my father, Robert, made an effort at modest migration. He hoped to transplant our family to Wisconsin, newly locating on some lovely fishing lake far from the ugliness of war. He found no practical way to get this done.

The lesson is that we limited humans always find ourselves in circumstances less than ideal. Rather than having to move on to be satisfied, we must be open to the arriving of God's new creation right where we are. I grew up in tiny Craig Beach, Ohio, with my parents and sister Bonnie. After high school I moved to the world of higher education in several states, more fortunate than my father had managed. Then I settled down in central Indiana for the balance of my adult life. Anderson isn't the perfect place, but God's best for me was found there over the decades.

When I now think of Scotland and Germany and my family heritage in each, I'm proud and only a bit ashamed. I readily brag on some things and avoid addressing others. The Bible speaks of God who is merciful and gracious through all times and places (Ex. 34:6-7). I've been blessed greatly by some marvelous people of yesterday, including my parents, even though they necessarily were persons limited by their time and place. Aren't we all? I pray that I will leave behind something that will nourish and not haunt coming generations.

I was born in 1941 just when Spring Arbor University was finishing its new dorm for women, Muffitt Hall. In a few years my younger sister Bonnie would be a college student on this small Michigan campus and living in this dorm. Torn down in 2019, I visited the campus in 2023 doing research for my biography of Kevin Mannoia. I managed to secure for Bonnie a brick from the building—she was so pleased! History moves quickly and sometimes leaves little behind.

The tiny town of Cordova Mines, Ontario, Canada, dates back to the 1860s when gold was discovered in the area. Never a big success, all mining ended in 1940 just before my birth. The small dam at one end of the beautiful lake, now called Cordova Lake, was used for years by the Deer Lake Fish Hatchery. During my few visits for family fishing in the summers of my boyhood, Cordova was merely a backwater village, even smaller than my Craig Beach village childhood home in Ohio. Even so, it was a memorable diversion.

Craig Beach is situated on the western shore of Lake Milton, created early in the twentieth century to supply a water reserve for the industries of nearby Youngstown. During my childhood years there, I had no awareness of the industrial backgrounds of either of these lovely lakes in neighboring countries. I simply enjoyed the beauty each left behind. One day my father saw a speedboat on the Canadian waters and decided that such recreational development spoiled the reason for our going there again—too much like the lake by which we lived in the United States. Development is inevitable and not always for the best. I have resisted returning to those Canadian shores in late adulthood for fear that my lovely memories would be shattered.

The present is a quickly passing reality. It's caught between the elsewheres of yesterday and the somewheres of the coming tomorrows. Living well involves drawing the best from yesterday and preparing well for what is soon to come.

CHAPTER TWO

THE LAKE AND THE VALLEY

Still a Blue Jay

Here I am, now eighty-three years old and still a Jackson-Milton Blue Jay! In some ways I've come to reflect the bird that Mark Twain wrote about in "What Stumped the Blue Jays?" The poor bird got confused about a knothole in the roof. It kept making deposits but the hole never filled up. No matter. It kept talking. Says Twain:

> There's more to a bluejay than any other creature. He has got more moods and more different kinds of feelings than other creatures; and mind you, whatever a bluejay feels, he can put into language. And no mere commonplace language, either, but rattling, out-and-out book talk—and bristling with metaphors too—just bristling! And as for command of language, why you never see a bluejay get stuck for a word. They just boil out of him!

My wife says my "sickness" is that I am unable to stop writing. When in high school, I hardly expected to put countless words into more than sixty books. But here I am, writing an Epilogue to the fourth edition of my autobiography, with other books still in the pipeline. My publishers are amazingly patient. Why doesn't that hole ever fill up? No matter. I'll keep writing and depositing.

Graduating from high school in 1959, I carried the title "Class President" and have sought ever since to dignify this role the best way possible. I've organized and convened all our class reunions over the decades, including our big 50th in 2009. Since then we've had informal annual dinners, getting too old to risk waiting every five years to get together. Our high school building was about to be demolished in 2009, so we walked its old halls for a final time and then were hosted by the principal for a tour of the new high school being built down the road and almost complete. Time does move on.

Ian Worley, a dear friend of mine in the 1959 class and now a retiree from his academic position in the University of Vermont, was at that fiftieth-year celebration. We went out to Lake Milton near my boyhood home and spent hours watching today's life on the water and talking about our experiences and views of world events. Then, at the reunion occasion itself, I read a congratulations letter from the governor of Ohio and shared class updates, including the growing list of our deceased members.

That list of lost friends now has lengthened to twenty-two, more than one-third of the original class. The most recent to go was Shirley (Meeker) Tomesko who grew up with me in the little village of Craig Beach. She fell victim to a recent hurricane in Florida, cleaning up debris, breaking a hip, and never leaving the hospital. How fragile we all have become, with most of our lives now behind us.

Some of my classmates can't (or shouldn't) drive anymore, and a few are using walkers to stay upright. Fortunately, I still can make the drive from Indiana to the Ohio reunions with no difficulty. Once together, our much smaller group talks mostly about our beloved yesterdays and current pains and recent operations. Still Blue Jays, we now are perching more than flying, and we do keep talking. Wonderful memories surround uncertain futures. Amazingly, Jan and I still are traveling around the world—a fortunate couple indeed.

My primary emotion now is not fear of tomorrow but sadness mixed with joy coming from treasured memories of increasingly distant yesterdays. Most of my adult life has been spent far away from lovely

Lake Milton in northeastern Ohio. A few of the class of '59 have never left. Soon all of us will be gone, hopefully to a better place.

I've done what I could to keep present and vibrant the treasured memories of yesterday, always knowing that life moves on and I must be prepared to go with it, taking with me what little I can. Some of my longtime friends are pictured in the 50th photo, three very special friends highlighted with myself. Two life-long friends, Chuck and Carole, are also pictured. Five pictured in the larger group are no longer with us. God speed, good friends!

Fifty-Year Reunion 2009
Jackson-Milton High School
Class of 1959
North Jackson, Ohio
Special Friends:
Barry Callen, Ian Worley,
Delores (Ward) Stroup,
and Richard Stroup

JACKSON-MILTON
Class of 1959
55 YEAR
CLASS REUNION

Charles and Carole Williams

CHAPTER THREE

BESIDE THE BEAVER VALE
A Proud Tradition Stands

My undergraduate college experience at Geneva College in Beaver Falls, Pennsylvania, was valuable to me beyond measure. It was going home since I lived with relatives and my birthplace was the next town up the river, New Brighton. My Free Methodist and Church of God Christian backgrounds clashed in some minor ways and was enriched in others by this conservative "Reformed" Calvinistic campus setting. The years since my 1963 graduation have seen this campus stay true to its Christian role in higher education. It's managed to "modernize" nicely without sacrificing its special heritage, still symbolized by Old Main standing centrally on campus and the Bible and Jesus Christ openly honored in all that's done.

My family is deeply rooted in Western Pennsylvania where I returned from "out west" (Ohio). I went to Geneva because I had no practical alternative. Even so, I couldn't have done better and clearly am in debt to Aunt Evangeline and Uncle Lavern (Auntie and Uncle Van) who lived just off the campus and helped make it possible. My studies went deep into the humanities (world literature and history), an excellent base for later ministerial studies at other institutions. Nothing can replace coming to know where we've been as humans (history) and what we've analyzed and envisioned (literature).

The Geneva faculty who served me well are all gone now, the last being Dr. William Russell, chair of the history department in which I majored. He was a great model, a serious Christian scholar, superb professor, and kind gentleman. I'm amused these days to see Joe Namath, famous NFL quarterback, now on TV doing Medicare commercials. He was a high school student of mine briefly when I was a student teacher at Beaver Falls High School. Hardly a serious student, Joe at least had a great football throwing arm. I featured him as a crazy character in my submarine novel *In Deep Water*. I sent a copy but don't know if he ever read it.

One event is never to be forgotten, the Cuban Missile Crisis of 1962. I was teaching government to high school students as part of Geneva's educational requirements. Suddenly, decisions were being made in Washington and Moscow of momentous import to us all. The USSR was refusing to call back its freighters loaded with military equipment for Cuba, just off the American coast, and the USA was refusing to call off its blockade. The world was going to sleep at night wondering anxiously if there would be a world to wake up to in the morning.

We did survive that awful tension so far. Now, decades later, the very survival of the human race seems more endangered than ever. Russia is at war with its neighbors in Europe, Israel is at war with its neighbors in the Middle East, and the United States is shipping vast quantities of military equipment to both arenas of conflict. Innocents are dying by the tens of thousands, and for what? It's for greed, nationalism, revenge, lust for power, even just glory.

While a Geneva student, assuming the country would survive, I had no idea that my life's ministry would be mostly on such a campus. Being inaugurated as Vice President for Academic Affairs at Anderson University in 1983, I responded by offering my thanks to the college back in Pennsylvania that had set the stage for me. Geneva was the birthplace of my great appreciation for Christian higher education, and where I first met fellow student Arlene Cooley who later became my beloved companion for nearly four decades and mother of my son Todd.

My second wife, Jan, has no personal history with Geneva and and so fails to appreciate the giant "G" on the hillside across the river overlooking the football field. At homecoming each year it's set ablaze in the night sky before kickoff. The "G"eneva somehow suddenly defines reality itself and fires the spirits of the faithful "Golden Tornadoes" on the field and in the stands. Granted, when seen in the daylight by a non-Genevan, it looks small and insignificant. To appreciate the excitement it once inspired for me, one had to be there. I was, and I'm grateful indeed.

The year 2023 saw the Geneva campus celebrating its 175th anniversary of preparing young persons for Christian service in the church and world. I'm privileged to be one of them. Jan and I visited the campus in October, 2023, to enjoy the historic homecoming and participate in the 60th-year reunion of my graduating class (1963). The only sadness was that Arlene (Cooley), my beloved first wife also part of that class, didn't live to see this historic celebration. The football field was painted with pride. I shared the feeling of pride and appreciation.

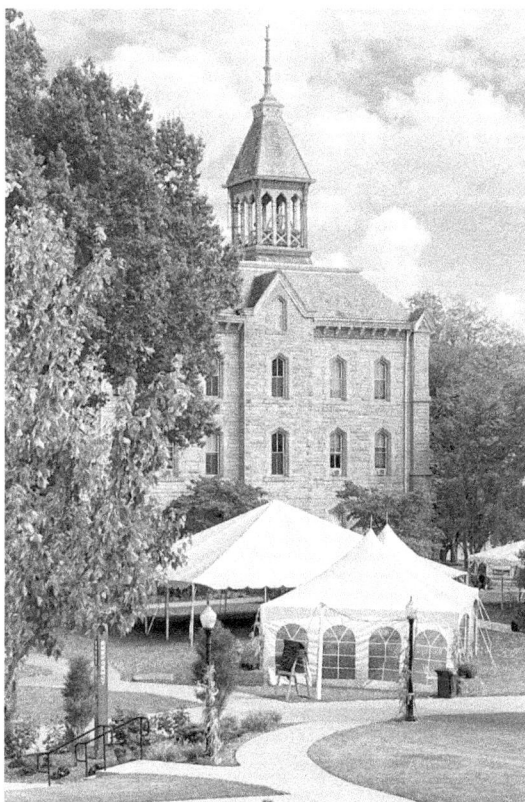

CHAPTER FOUR

ON THE WAY TO VOCATION

Still Moving and Enriched by Diversity

Being different is difficult. Being threatened by and resisting differences seems instinctual for people. At Geneva College I faced some difference but grew greatly by managing to embrace it for the most part. My vocational path shifted after Geneva from public school teaching, for which I had become certified in Pennsylvania, to Christian ministry. I married and immediately moved to Indiana to begin my initial seminary education. Arlene and I had just married and knew no one in Indiana, but we were following a divine call to church vocation.

The faculty at Anderson School of Theology represented much of my growing-up religious roots in Newton Falls, Ohio. Even so, they introduced me to much more newness. I found a home in Anderson and eventually this campus would be where I would serve in various capacities over the decades to follow. First, however, my little family (wife Arlene, newborn Todd, and me) would be off to little Wilmore, Kentucky, where I had nearly attended seminary right out of college. I was anxious to know what differences I had missed by not going to the bigger and better-known Asbury Theological Seminary. Although there only one year for a second masters degree, I was not disappointed. I have kept my Asbury ties alive and active to this very day, a great enrichment to me.

Then came an even more dramatic difference, Chicago Theological Seminary. It was a tense and very stretching time for both Arlene and me. Our son Todd was one year old when we arrived in Chicago to live in debt in a big city in social turmoil, so very different from the tiny little

Wilmore, Kentucky. It was time to really grow up in almost every way. I had been a bit of a theological "liberal" in Wilmore; now in Chicago I was seen as a real "conservative" not always appreciated for my apparent "backwardness" for the supposed new day for church and world.

I was to begin my path to the doctorate in a dramatic way designed to dramatize the urban life at its worst. A "plunge" was required of incoming doctoral students, only $5 in the pocket and the challenge of finding a way to survive on the Chicago streets for a week! The thought terrified me and was successfully avoided because of the 1967 war that had left so much new misery in Lebanon, Israel, and Jordan.

I got my relief by gaining permission to replace the plunge with a major tour of the ravaged Middle East with five of my Anderson University colleagues, funded by a grant intended to bring enhanced quality into seminary education in Indiana. This was every bit as stretching as any big-city plunge, although considerably less threatening personally. Both the ancient Bible and the most recent human misery came alive for me and my Anderson colleagues. What a blessing this was personally and professionally.

The Doctor of Religion program in Chicago featured the careful combination of theory and practice, with the social scene being the chaotic city always in view for the practical application of Christian faith. That was critical learning for me. In all the years to come, such a theory-practice combination would be standard. My later second doctorate, the Doctor of Education degree from Indiana University, was an attempt to adapt Christian faith to the needs and challenges of the young searching for identity and vocation for themselves. I recall facing one professor at IU who openly ridiculed Christian liberal arts colleges like mine in Anderson as "parochial." My doctoral dissertation, in response, struggled with the tension of faculty academic freedom in institutions with clear theological commitments. I made the case for the legitimacy of institutions like Geneva College and Anderson University, that dissenting professor notwithstanding.

Beginning with the new millennium, I experienced three more significant integration stretchings. Two were my long editorship of the *Wesleyan Theological Journal* and considerable involvement in the launching of the Wesleyan Holiness Connection. I represented the Church of God (Anderson) in both and then became a leader of the WHC and its publishing arm, Aldersgate Press, editing the volume identifying constituent bodies (*The Holy River of God*) and then n 2024 authoring the biography of the WHC's visionary founder, Kevin W. Mannoia. The question always was, how can belief in Christian holiness be taught and applied by the church in ways relevant to the secular culture of today?

The other big stretching for me was the launching in 2001 of Horizon International for which I always have served as Corporate Secretary. The big question was, how can relatively rich North Americans address meaningfully the terrible AIDS pandemic ravishing many African nations, leaving behind millions of orphaned children? I would "plunge" again, now into these challenging African fronts of Christian ministry, making what small contributions I could, with Robert Pearson taking the lead as president.

Ever since heading for Chicago in 1968 by way of the Middle East, I have tried to grow and serve without fear of difference and with whatever gifts I have been given. Included, beginning in the early 1970s and still in full motion, has been stretching into the world of Christian publishing. As I thought and acted and taught, I began to write more and more. I trust that the result has made a positive difference for thousands of people whom I have never met but who have read my books and expressed their thanks in many settings.

One subject about which I have written early and often has been the clash of church traditions in my family history and personal experience, particularly that awkward era of strong polemics between two "holiness" bodies (1880s-1950s, the Free Methodist Church and the Church of God, Anderson). It's a study of clashing ecumenical visions, differing approaches to how authority should be configured in church life. I have highlighted the positive shift in this relationship in more recent decades and the lessons hopefully learned that appear important for the future.[1] This set of issues and church relationships was important on my way to vocation and beyond. So was some theological "surgery."

I sometimes have thought of myself as a "recovering fundamentalist."[2] Reading the Bible in literal ways that supposedly yield fixed doctrine on nearly every page is to do the Bible and our faith a disservice. We become ultra-conservative Pharisees again needing much correction from Jesus. We become all head and with little heart, brittle thinkers about mysterious and majestic matters always beyond whatever we claim we know for sure. I said this to the Wesleyan Theological Society meeting in Wilmore, KY, 2023:

> Regarding religious truth, it's human to know and not know for sure. Although the biblical message is fixed, how best to conceive and apply it is fluid. Balance is critical between the fixed and fluid. Christian "experience" can be a common centering for the global Christian community with all its diversity. Such spiritual experience, to be truly Christian, requires a limited and carefully chosen *fixed*, what is absolutely core Christian doctrine, while it allows for a considerable range of *fluidity*. The experience of new life in

the Spirit is a unifying reality that forms and enables the church everywhere.

The challenge is not to be washed away in a flood of the fluid. In my writings I have sought to manage this delicate balance. In *Beneath the Surface* I sought the consistent theological themes common to the Old and New Testaments. In *God As Loving Grace* I highlighted a core characteristic of God's very being, the eternal fixed that necessarily frames all the fluids. In *The Heart of the Matter* I regularly brought discussion of all theological issues back to the person of Jesus. In the booklet *The Heart of the Church of God Teaching Tradition*, a colleague and I attempted to name nine "core commitments" of this teaching tradition, the essential fixed, allowing much of the rest to travel fluidly as the Spirit may direct.

In all these cases, I have understood myself to be something of a contemporary Isaac, the man in the middle, the link between the greats of father Abraham and son Jacob. While not particularly remarkable himself, Isaac did carry the heritage of the faith from the past to the future. That's been my role, to remember well the greats of yesterday and pass on their visions and flame to the greats who will come after my time. The middle-man, while not necessarily great, nonetheless is essential to the whole ongoing of the enterprise. To this I was called, my vocation.

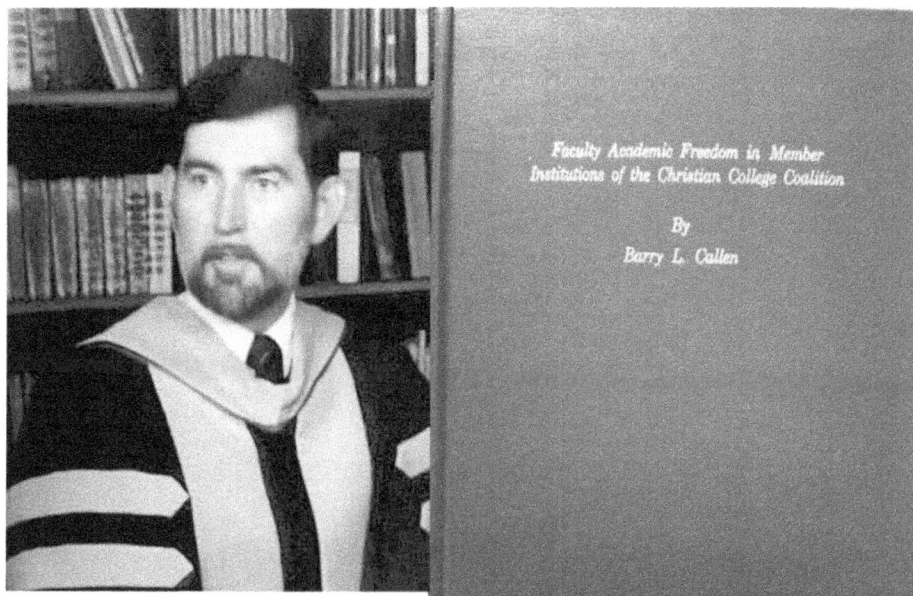

Faculty Academic Freedom in Member
Institutions of the Christian College Coalition

By
Barry L. Callen

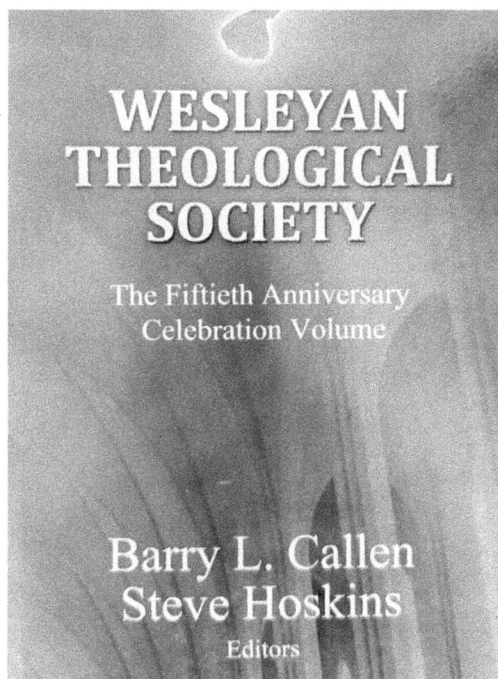

WESLEYAN THEOLOGICAL SOCIETY

The Fiftieth Anniversary
Celebration Volume

Barry L. Callen
Steve Hoskins
Editors

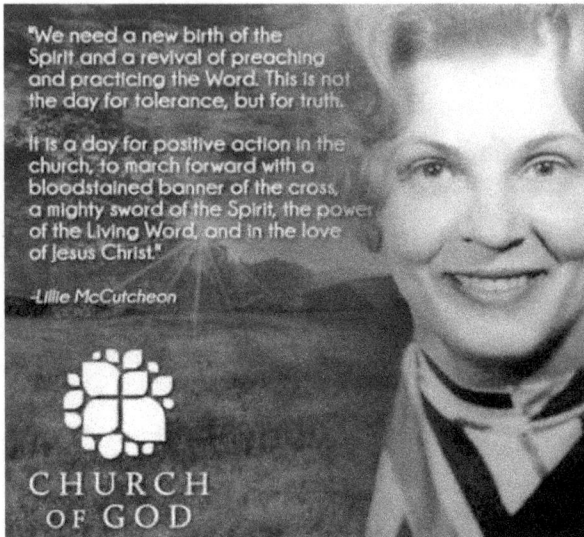

"We need a new birth of the Spirit and a revival of preaching and practicing the Word. This is not the day for tolerance, but for truth.

It is a day for positive action in the church, to march forward with a bloodstained banner of the cross, a mighty sword of the Spirit, the power of the Living Word, and in the love of Jesus Christ."

-Lillie McCutcheon

CHURCH OF GOD

"Sister Lillie," home pastor

This room named in honor of Gene and Agnes Newberry

Dr. Gene Newberry, first theology professor

CHAPTER FIVE

LEADING THE CHURCH'S SEMINARY

Still Educating Ministers for Excellence

The Anderson seminary was joined in 2016 by the Department of Religious Studies to form Anderson University's School of Theology and Christian Ministries, with Dr. Nathan Willowby its Dean. Significant enrollment problems again had emerged, forcing this merger on campus, much like we had done briefly in the early 1970s under the Center for Pastoral Studies umbrella. I saw Willowby in a position similar to mine in 1973, young, good academic credentials, strong church relationship, and being perceived as a breath of fresh hope in a time of institutional stress involving the seminary. Now in the early years of the twenty-first century, undergraduate and graduate enrollments both were down significantly and the new campus president, John S. Pistole, was aggressively making needed changes, much as Robert H. Reardon had done in my earlier time of seminary leadership.

The passing of time and changing circumstances beyond our control have more influence than we would like. President Reardon in 1974 told Anderson's Board of Trustees that "traditional separatist concepts" (campus undergraduate and seminary religion faculties and programs) are "cowardly" and must not be allowed to block the future. These walls were dropped as I began my deanship, but soon were reestablished for practical reasons as the seminary enrollment grew dramatically. These new walls again defined separate campus units for many years, only to collapse again in 2016, again for practical reasons. Vision, resolve, and practicality struggle with each other over the years.

Do we shape our times or are we shaped by them? Yes. A new positive is that in 2022 the Hispanic community was the fastest growth group in the United States, in the church and North American society generally. The new School of Theology and Christian Ministries in Anderson has recognized this, conceived fresh programming to support Hispanic ministerial education, and received a large grant to enable such initiative. The future of the seminary will be different necessarily, but possibly freshly relevant and viable again

In my decade as seminary Dean (1973-1983) there was dramatic enrollment growth (tripled). The 1976 General Assembly of the Church of God, now much more aware of the seminary's presence and significance, declared seminary education the "normal" and "ideal" level of formal ministerial education, a dramatic stance for a "free-church" and revivalist holiness tradition. This was, however, aspirational only, in no sense obligatory or even lasting as an aspiration. Three North American campuses of the Church of God today (other than Anderson) no longer form a feeder system for the Anderson seminary, maintaining their own ministerial education programs.

The path toward ordination for ministry now is "Leadership Focus," a fine program but one without formal educational requirements. Many who complete it have never nor likely will ever attend college. I was the primary author of the 2022 booklet *The Teaching Tradition of the Church of God Movement* that now is included in the church's *Credentials Manual* as a recognized reference point for candidate examination. Ordination candidates at least are expected to know the key teaching perspectives of their own church body. I have been the Editor of this Manual since its inception in the 1980s.

I am privileged to still be somewhat involved on the Anderson campus, authoring president Pistole's biography at his request (2021), using a nice office in the School of Theology building made available to me on an honorary basis, and authoring various books and booklets carrying the name "Anderson University Press" (which I founded). A few faculty members who served under my deanship are still around, including retirees Fred Burnett, Walter Froese, Jerry Grubbs, Fred Shively, Ted Stoneberg, Merle Strege, and Douglas Welch. Gone by death are the first two presidents under whom I served, Robert H. Reardon and Robert A. Nicholson, who both put so much faith in me during my leadership years. I authored the biographies of R.eardon and Pistole and edited and published the autobiography of Nicholson.

The seminary building on the Anderson campus now has been repurposed to a facility named after the other recent president, James L. Edwards. A greatly reduced student body now functions largely online. It's difficult to maintain a viable graduate-level seminary with no endowment and a sponsoring church body not requiring any specific educational attainment for ministerial ordination. How privileged I was to have my leadership years at the peak of the seminary's existence in the 1970s and early 1980s!

The Heart of the Church of God Teaching Tradition

Barry L. Callen
Cliff D. Sanders

GOD'S ON THE MOVE!

THE CHURCH OF GOD MOVEMENT

BARRY L. CALLEN

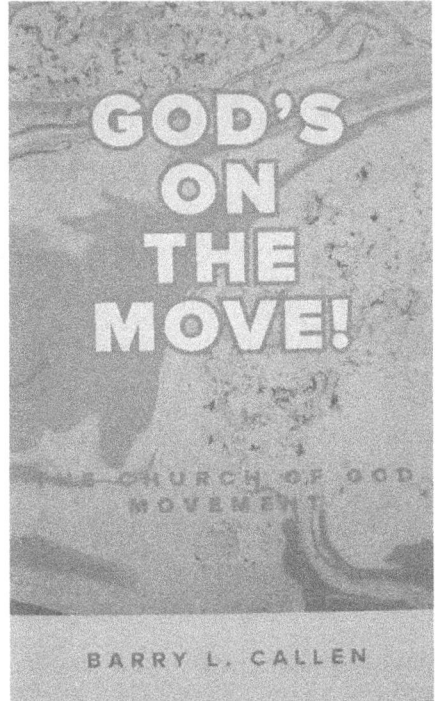

Two of my efforts to explain and excite a new generation about the church movement that has been so central to my life.

In 2024 I was called on to function as a prominent "traditionalist" resisting two dear ministerial colleagues pushing online a full affirmation of "queer" people in all levels of church life. While I was successful, it was a most unpleasant task

CHAPTER SIX

MOVING TO THE
LARGER ACADEMIC SCENE

Personal Discipline and Health

There is no way to know what would have happened over the years if in 1983 I had refused President Nicholson's urging to become a university vice-president in his new administration. It was the best of times in the seminary's history and I fit well as Dean. Still, I was open to a new call, had just completed a doctoral degree at Indiana University that positioned me for the proposed VP role, and I was a "company man" willing to serve as the campus needed me.

I've already told the story of my years spent functioning as the academic leader of Anderson University as its Vice-President for Academic Affairs. They were highly productive and quite stressful years for me and my family. In part it was the role itself (five exceptional persons have filled this office since my departure, two for quite short periods). What needs elaboration was my need, then and since, to keep my spirit and body in balance when under considerable pressure.

My vice-presidential years forced attention to this need. One issue was body weight and high blood pressure, along with lack of a well-disciplined spiritual life. Arlene worried much, Todd was actively trying to find his own way in life, sometimes pulling away from us, and often I was too busy to give personal things adequate attention. I lacked a developed prayer life or any of the classic quieting spiritual practices.

How to Retreat Forward?

My occasional efforts forward, limited by family and work circumstances, were retreats alone to a state park or Roman Catholic retreat center. I needed and relished these changes of pace, the beautiful outdoors and ancient disciplines of the monks, particularly at Gethsemani in Kentucky. I also managed to discover that writing was my preferred means of being quiet and thinking deeply, meditatively, prayerfully. It even became a growing vehicle for public ministry. Eventually I would author or edit many more books than any previous leader of Anderson University or the Church of God or any scholar friend I knew. I hope that some quality went along with the quantity.

I wrote one of my more substantial books, *Authentic Spirituality*, and more recently the two-volume set *A Year with Rabbi Jesus*. These publications were designed for use as a means of reflecting biblically and prayerfully on Christian life and ministry. I was trying to assist ministers and laypersons engage the Bible, using the Christian Year as the format, highlighting current themes, and concluding with personal prayers. Such was the case with my latest two publications, *All of God's Word for All of My Needs* and *Christian Holiness: Biblical Foundations and Spiritual Resources for Today*.

We Christians aren't the same in many ways, including what plan of spiritual discipline best nourishes our souls. I'm glad I finally found mine. Coming from a home without such disciplines, and beginning professional life with a series of strenuous academic paths to advanced degrees, I wasn't quite prepared to be a balanced, healthy, and richly spiritual person. I presume the Lord understands and forgives.

My bodily health was stressed, especially during those frantic years of the 1980s. I have been relatively fortunate once the blood pressure was under control. I've had only four serious health crises in the decades since, a bout with cancer that was eliminated with rounds of chemotherapy, major eye surgery for a seriously detached retina, emergency surgery to remove my gallbladder close to rupturing, and prostate surgery to relieve frustrating issues that come with the aging of many men—not a new cancer.

Now, after eighty-three years of rather hard use, my body still is serving me rather well. There is much for which to give thanks. While my lifespan is nearly over, it's been a great run.

ALL OF GOD'S WORD FOR ALL OF MY NEEDS

The Entire Bible in One Year, Designed for Personal Spiritual Formation and Sermon Planning

Barry L. Callen

A Year with Rabbi Jesus

Biblical and Wesleyan-Holiness Lessons for Maturing Disciples of Jesus

Barry L. Callen
Steven Hoskins

CHAPTER SEVEN

GOING ON THE ROAD

I've Travelled Far on Many Roads and Seas

One of the more widely read, quoted, and translated theologians of recent times told his dramatic life story in 2009 under the title *A Broad Place*. Jürgen Moltmann knew the horrors of World War II very personally and yet was blessed afterwards with a broad place in which to evolve the Christian "theology of hope" movement. I have shared his blessing of a gracious setting in life despite some inevitable negatives. I've applauded his life's positive trajectory theologically, while certainly not sharing his worldwide influence. I've been on the road, sometimes difficult, mostly wonderful. Moltmann died in 2024. My time will come.

The Ever-Widening Road

The widening road of blessing across my lifetime has featured Christian individuals and church bodies that have enriched my life greatly. A few most recently have included Kevin Mannoia, James Earl Massey, Clark Pinnock, David Bundy, Donald Dayton, Howard Snyder, Don Thorsen, Dan Schafer, John Mark Richardson, Cheryl Johns, John Pistole, Steve Hoskins, Roger Green, Carla Sunberg, Joshua Brandt, Cliff Sanders, and various African church leaders from Uganda, Ethiopia, South Africa, Zimbabwe, Zambia, and Kenya. A dozen others have been featured already in the original chapter nine above. They have been very visible Christian leaders, all graciously relating to me and humbly agreeing that "visible" and "significant" aren't necessarily synonyms.

Geneva College, the Wesleyan Holiness Connection, Horizon International, Anderson University, and Asbury Theological Seminary have been particularly productive of wonderful relationships for me. I am so much better for having known and served with such individuals and institutions. The formation in 2022 of the Global Wesleyan Church was unexpected, especially my involvement as a consultant on that year's new hymnal, *Our Great Redeemer's Praise*. Division isn't pleasant, but forks in the road do come and good can come from the pain of separations. I managed to get included in this fine new hymnal fourteen classic Church of God songs. It was a pleasant "ecumenical" effort.

I had not expected to become active with Indiana Ministries of the Church of God, the body that holds my ordination credentials. Active on the national scene of this church body since the 1970s, finally I began serving closer to home. By February, 2023, I was a member of a state credentials committee interviewing new ordination candidates and of a team implementing the five-year review process of ministers long active in ministry. This fresh activity seemed right since it drew on my years of experience in ministerial education and credentialing.

I hope to make some difference that will impact the future beyond my brief lifetime. I've enjoyed particularly being interviewed by some twenty ordination candidates, each at their initiative, about my ministry motivations and experiences over many years. Encouraging young leaders for the church is a joy indeed.

The Ever-Lengthening Routes and Destinations

Despite the two-year virtual closure of the travel industry worldwide because of the COVID pandemic, Jan and I managed to stay on the move. Many of my standard meetings went online via Zoom, which I had never used prior to this time. It was a most welcome lifesaver, keeping me in active visual touch with many colleagues and ministries. For instance, developing the biography of John Pistole during COVID lockdown in 2021, I did about forty research interviews via Zoom, including fourteen with John himself, and many others who were leaders of the nation's federal government. Technology, sometimes distracting and troublesome, was a welcome gift. I used Zoom even after the COVID lockdown to research the biography of Kevin Mannoia, reaching people beyond the time and expense of physical travel.

International travel has been a major feature of the married life of Jan and myself, now more than twenty years after my first wife's death. It began months before our marriage with a land tour of Scotland and Ireland in conjunction with a program for the faculty and staff of Anderson University. Following our marriage in December, 2003, Jan and I took a honeymoon cruise in the Caribbean. Neither of us had been near a cruise ship before because of limited funds and time. Since then, combining land and cruise travel, Jan and I have been in over 50 countries together, sailing on many of the seas of the world. The scenes and experiencing have been amazing.

Given the Covid pandemic, we did nothing in 2020 or 2021, although we had managed marvelous trips in 2019, one a cruise involving the coastal cities of Brazil, Argentina, and Chile with a group of friends and participation in the 50th anniversary annual meeting of the Wesleyan Holiness Connection hosted by the Salvation Army in its London, England, headquarters. Jan and I thoroughly enjoyed the opportunity to be guided by these wonderful Christian brothers and sisters around the many London area sites featuring the lives and ministries of the founders of the Salvation Army, William and Catherine Booth, and the Wesleyan tradition launched by John and Charles Wesley.

We repeated in 2022 our honeymoon cruise before traveling in the spring of 2023 on the Viking cruise line for the third time, a wonderful experience around the amazing island of Iceland, and then on to Greenland, Newfoundland, and finally New York City. This was followed by a trip up the dramatic coastline of Norway across the Artic Circle into the "world of the midnight sun."

All this international travel did not ignore the amazing country in which we have been privileged to live. Jan and I have hit the rails from Chicago to south Texas, took two extensive bus tours to the national parks in the upper and lower western sections of the United States, sailed the Mississippi from New Orleans in the south to Minneapolis in the north, and in 2024 sailed the dramatic rivers of the Pacific Northwest, tracing the pioneering ventures of Lewis and Clark, and then a cruise down the eastern coast of the United States.

Looking back on the tens of thousands of miles and the amazing tours, sites, sounds, and smells, I admit to reading and writing during many of the leisure times aboard cruise ships. My wife is very patient, reporting that I'm incapable of not writing. We are not "party people." During our many trips, no money was ever spent on liquor or in a casino. We buy very little, and some trips were focused on active Christian ministry, such as in Jamaica, Haiti, and our trips to the amazing continent of Africa, including South Africa, Uganda, Zambia, Kenya, and Zimbabwe with Horizon International assisting the orphaned children in these lands as our primary goal.

What a privilege Jan and I have enjoyed circling the Earth. We have sampled its beauty and sought to assist in modest ways with its extreme poverty and corruption. The creative hand of God has been our resource and guide, wonderful beyond description. God's people need to step forward in partnership with the divine hand to stop the pollution of the land, seas, and air on which we all depend. Jan and I pray that our travels have not been exceedingly selfish in nature. We have experienced enrichment and relaxation, and certainly a broadening of cultural perspectives—and I've managed writing a book or two (or five or six) along the way.

It's said that life is a book. The one who doesn't travel reads only one page. I've been enriched by several chapters filled with people, places, and stretching experiences. This diversity has challenged my narrowness and enhanced my understanding of God's great creation. I'm so grateful!

The "Cruise Crew" (2024)

London, England

Honored with the WTS "Lifetime Award"
D. Bundy, D. Dayton, B. Callen, H. Snyder

My Love, Jan

My friend, John Pistole, President of
Anderson University

CHAPTER EIGHT

THOUSANDS OF PUBLISHED PAGES
More books and expressed Hopes

I'm surprised to see the sheer volume of books I've authored or edited over the years. I identify somewhat with William Barclay, biblical scholar, who reports this about himself. "I have essentially a second-class mind." He means that mostly he has emphasized and expounded on the ideas of others, being less an originating scholar himself. He was "a theological middle-man." We all stand on the work of others before us. I apply to myself this sentiment of John Wesley: "I design plain truth for plain people." It's important to make some old truths shine with new life.

The years 2015 to 2024 saw me very active in attempting to reinvigorate the life of the Church of God Movement and reinforce appreciation for the Wesleyan-Holiness Christian tradition in general. This latter effort included five major books, my 2016 *The Holy River of God*, the 2021 and 2022 volumes of *A Year with Rabbi Jesus*, the 2023 *Christian Holiness*, and the 2024 *Golden Nuggets*. I also edited and published *Views from the Mountain*, the collected writings of James Earl Massey, a major Black figure in this tradition and my dear friend whose excellent writing legacy must not be forgotten.

I presented a formal academic paper to the 2023 annual meeting of the Wesleyan Theological Society titled "Balancing Mind and Spirit in Service of the Global Church." There also were the two biographies I researched and wrote in this period telling the dramatic stories of two outstanding Christian leaders from the Wesleyan tradition who were making a major impact in government, Christian higher education, and engagement of the Christian faith with the secular culture—John S. Pistole and Kevin W. Mannoia.

Regarding the Church of God Movement, my contributions in these most recent years have included three publications and one national administrative role. I tried in the 2021 book *Forward, Ever Forward!* to look at the whole history of the Movement and then project it ahead on solid ground. I also tried to restate the core vision of the Movement for a new generation, putting it in simple language supported with colorful graphics in the booklet *God's On the Move!* Then I was joined by Dr. Cliff Sanders in jointly producing the booklet *The Heart of the Teaching Tradition of the Church of God Movement.* Once circulated nationally, these booklets bought much appreciation. The first then appeared in a Spanish translation and the second was incorporated in the Movement's *Credentials Manual* as a recommended reference when ordination candidates are being examined theologically.

A major administrative role of mine followed a vigorous two years of churchwide activity culminating in the 2017 General Assembly of the Movement in the United States and Canada. Multiple "Congress" gatherings around the U.S.A. eventuated in a major new edition of the ministerial *Credentials Manual* and determination that it would be required for use by all assemblies and ordination candidates. I participated in these gatherings as the Editor of all the previous and now the emerged new edition of the Manual.

When the 2017 General Assembly convened, it approved the proposed new Manual, celebrated it as a significant step forward in standardizing ministerial credentialing, and established a standing Committee on Credentials. This COC was empowered to interpret, revise as necessary, and supervise the formal adoption and use of the Manual by all assemblies. I was named the COC Chair and worked during the following four years to carry out this major assignment. While there was some resistance to such "centralized power" in the church, not surprising for a reform movement championing freedom of the Spirit over human domination in church life, all assemblies finally approved the new Manual.

This Manual, along with the excellent *Leadership Focus* program of the Movement, now combine to standardize and strengthen greatly ministerial ordination preparation. How surprising—and delightful—that the three key leaders involved, Jeannette Flynn, Robert Moss, and myself, three "kids" from the same home church, Newton Falls, Ohio. Leadership in our growing-up years was excellent! Today all three of us have moved on from this particular responsibility but have left our marks. The 2024 credentials manual of Indiana Ministries carries the entire text of the booklet *The Heart of the Teaching Tradition of the Church of God Movement* (Callen/Sanders).

Here is a continuation of the previous list of my publications.

53. *Leaning Forward,* History and Actions of the General Assembly of the Church of God, Emeth Press, 2019).

54. *Forward, Ever Forward!* The Church of God Movement, Yesterday and Tomorrow, Anderson University Press and Emeth Press, 2021.

55. *John S. Pistole*: Searching for Integrity and Faith, A. U. Press and Emeth Press, 2021.

56. *A Year with Rabbi Jesus,* with Steve Hoskins, Emeth Press, A. U. Press, Trevecca Nazarene University Press, 2021; and volume 2, with Steve Hoskins and Jonathan Powers, 2022.

57. *God's on the Move!* (booklet), 2021.

58. *The Heart of the Church of God Teaching Tradition* (booklet), with Cliff Sanders, 2022.

59. *The Living Dead,* Cascade Books, Wipf & Stock, 2023.

60. *Christian Holiness*, Emeth Press and Aldersgate Press, 2023.

61. *All of God's Word for All of My Needs*, Emeth Press and Aldersgate Press, 2023.

62. *Golden Nuggets*, with Kevin Mannoia and Don Thorsen, Aldersgate Press, 2024.

63. *Anchored and Reaching*, biography of Kevin W. Mannoia, Aldersgate Press, 2024.

64. *A Pilgrim's Progress*, my autobiography, fourth ed. (Anderson University Press and Emeth Press, 2024).

I have continued to assist others with their publications. For instance:

The Brightest Star by Andrea Morehead and James Morehead (about James).

Our Great Redeemer's Praise, major new hymnal in the Wesleyan tradition (my role limited to being a content consultant).

Expressing Life by Kevin W. Mannoia, I was copy editor for Aldersgate Press.

Other books carry endorsement statements requested of me or were brought to publication through my role as Editorial Director of Aldersgate Press.

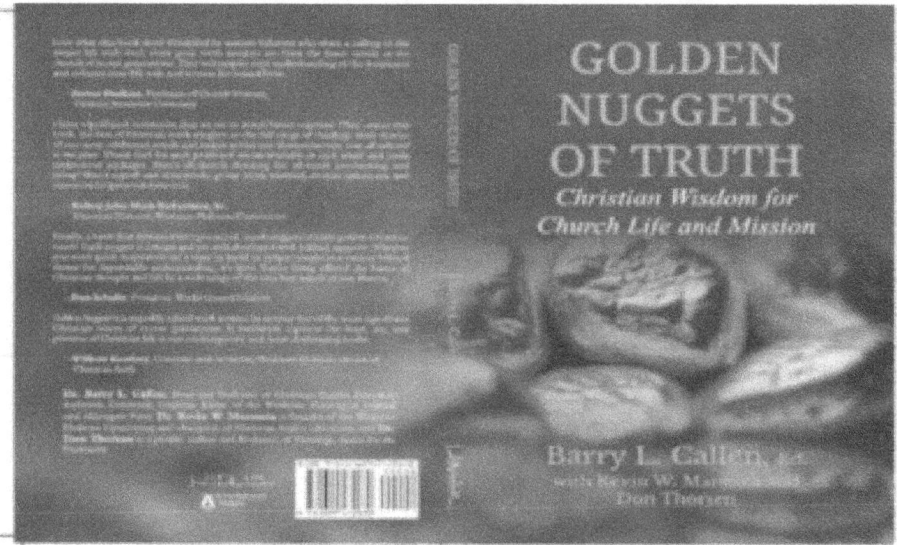

CHAPTER NINE

MILLENNIUM NUMBER THREE
The Troubled World Moves On

Seventy-two years after being torpedoed and becoming the greatest naval loss in the history of the United States, the USS Indianapolis was found in 2017. She lies 18,000 feet down in the Philippine Sea and presumably will stay there. Queen Elizabeth of England died in late 2022 after 70 years on the throne. She now lies peacefully while her son Charles reigns as King. Ships and people go down, but the world moves on, troubles and all.

Political unity in the United States seems nowhere to be found. Making "America Great Again!" may be a commonly repeated goal, but the nation is sharply divided on what that means and how to achieve it. Recent presidential elections have swung sharply back and forth. There was the historic Barack Obama elections, his serving from 2009-2017 as the first African-American, followed by the sharp political opposite, Donald Trump, 2017-2021, and then another sharp swing to Joe Biden, with another election battle looming in 2024.

Who can predict what's next? Issues are felt deeply and the very soul of the nation seems at stake. Beyond our borders, one hotly-debated issue has been global warming, worsened if not primarily caused by human greed being practiced worldwide. One serious side-effect has been waves of desperate immigrants trying to get into the rich nations, with some countries building walls to keep them out—including the United States on sections of its border with Mexico.

The future of humanity itself, at least as we have known it, has come into question. The seas and atmosphere are being polluted, temperatures are rising, storms worsening, glaciers melting, and humans still going to war. Russia brutally attacked Ukraine in 2022 to restore a portion of the "Fatherland" lost in the earlier breakup of the Soviet Union. Weapons for defense flowed in from Europe and the United States to assist Ukraine that fought bravely to protect its homeland. There was the danger of Russia using its huge nuclear arsenal to achieve a selfish goal.

Meanwhile, Israel attacked Gaza brutally attempting to eliminate Hamas and protect itself, with much of the world accusing it of genocide against the Palestinian people. Said one commentator, "We humans seem fully prepared and are all too willing to light the fuse that will incinerate the world!"

Humanity Struggles On

My Pennsylvania birth in 1941 happened as the world was plunging into a terrible global war. Would raw power, greed for dominance, and racial arrogance prevail? The results have proved mixed at best. The German/Japanese Axis finally fell, but racial prejudice and the use of military power for national agendas have hardly disappeared. I walked through new refugee camps in the Middle East in 1968 when a recent war was still smoldering. I asked this question in my 2009 submarine novel *In Deep Water* set in World War II: "Will there ever be an end to human madness, war?" My sad answer was: "Seemingly not, at least not in this world. After the fire always comes more fire. Yesterday's warriors and weapons pass on; tomorrow's people forget and stoke the flames again." Oh, for the return of the Prince of Peace!

There was the shocking terrorist attack on the United States in 2001 and the responding declaration of war on terrorism by President

George Bush. I was unaware at the time that John S. Pistole, prominent leader in the FBI and known to me since his childhood, was working behind the scenes to stop any further attacks. In 2021, at his request, I was privileged to write John's biography, allowing me a glimpse into the world of international spying and cyber-security. John, now president of Anderson University, is a Christian gentleman of superb skill and integrity.

This struggling world of ours desperately needs many more Johns. While he is not a celebrated teacher or writer in the world of Christian spirituality, he deserves to be a celebrated model of what it means to be a humble man living in the image of Jesus Christ and making a difference in this world. I hope for renewed sanity among world leaders and the eventual arrival of the God who will make all things right.

Continued our long service to African orphans through Horizon International.

CHAPTER TEN

RECOGNIZING AND BEING RECOGNIZED

More Shoulders on Which to Stand

I'm pleased to report that things have gone mostly as they should—my being busy honoring others more than they have needed to spend time recognizing me. One recent exception was in May, 2019, when I was privileged to walk in front of a long line of graduates of Asbury Theological Seminary. I was wearing a gold robe and attractive medallion, being one of several "Golden Grads" being honored by the seminary. I qualified, of course, because I had lived for half a century as an Asbury degree holder without embarrassing this fine school in the process!

It certainly has been an honor to be sought out over the years to add my endorsing name to books of others, and occasionally march in celebrations of presidential inaugurations at various institutions, me robed and representing Anderson University. I especially recall such an celebration at my own undergraduate alma mater, Geneva College, in 1984. What an honor to be chosen to represent one campus on another, my original own.

Recently I have been interviewed as a "legacy minister" by a dozen ordination candidates of the Church of God, and in 2023 I was invited to join an ordination team in my home state of Indiana and also the state team interviewing active pastors after each five years of ministry. I have served over the years as chair or recording secretary of several major church bodies, like the 2018 Roundtable of "Project Imagine" of the Church of God (recording secretary) and the North American Committee on Credentials of the General Assembly of the Church of God (chair, 2017-2021).

It certainly was an honor to be asked by John Pistole, former Deputy Director of the FBI and current President of Anderson University, to write his biography. Then Kevin Mannoia did the same in 2023, he the former President of the National Association of Evangelicals and founder of the Wesleyan Holiness Connection. I consider these invitations and roles personal privileges more than bragging rights—they were also a lot of hard work!

I must not overlook the fact that Anderson University Press and Emeth Press have been most gracious in partnering to publish all editions of this autobiography, seeing public and future worth in the telling of my life story. I'm in their debt and hope their judgment is correct. Also, noted in the front of this volume is its inclusion in the Asbury Theological Seminary Series in Wesleyan/Holiness Studies, an honor not granted many books. The series editor, Dr. J. Steven O'Malley, says:

> Professor Callen here offers a candid and thoughtful disclosure of his personal, spiritual, and academic development over the past seven decades, drawing from the ecumenical perspective of his church tradition, and interfaced with a robust commitment to a Wesleyan/Holiness soteriology, grounded in his formative studies at Asbury Seminary. His life and work offer a personal embodiment of salient features of the developing revitalization of world Christianity.

Such words are a treasured honor, especially the last sentence which I would not dare write about myself. Having been given much, I've hoped to return at least a little.

Benjamin T. Roberts (1823-1893) was a sophisticated and political-ly active religious leader in the American holiness movement of the nineteenth century. He was founder of Roberts Wesleyan University and the Free Methodist Church, so central to the lives of both sets of my grandparents, and which sponsored the camp meeting in Ohio where I was converted in the 1950s. I was privileged to nominate Howard A. Snyder's 2006 biography, *Populist Saints: B. T. and Ellen Roberts,* which received the 2007 Smith/Wynkoop Book Award of the Wesleyan Theological Society. In 2023, the 200th anniversary of the birth of Roberts, I began the process of authoring the biography of Kevin W. Mannoia.

Kevin is continuing in new settings the rich heritage of Roberts and I am honored to present his life story. Like Roberts, he is featuring "the Bible standard of Christianity," the free and abundant life in the Spirit of Jesus, the equality of all people, the freedom of women to preach and lead in the church, and the end of the evils of slavery and other forms of human oppression. I have been blessed by and have hoped to be a small blessing to this wonderful holiness heritage. My grandfathers were Free Methodist leaders in the Pittsburgh Conference, Charles Callen a pastor and Charles VanArsdale a lay leader.

Now eighty-three years old, it's natural that a 50-year ministry pin would come my way in 2023. I'm still anticipating the biggest honor of all. One day, by God's grace, I'll reach the other side and be assured that my name actually is in the big Book of Life. While hardly deserved, what an honor that will be!

November 30, 2023, was the funeral of Dwight Grubbs. I delivered a tribute and then conducted the graveside service. His dear wife Sylvia was close to my first wife, Arlene, and their son Jonathan currently serves as my pastor at Park Place Church in Anderson, Indiana. Dwight was a superb servant of the Master. I trust that someday soon someone will be able to say something like that about me.

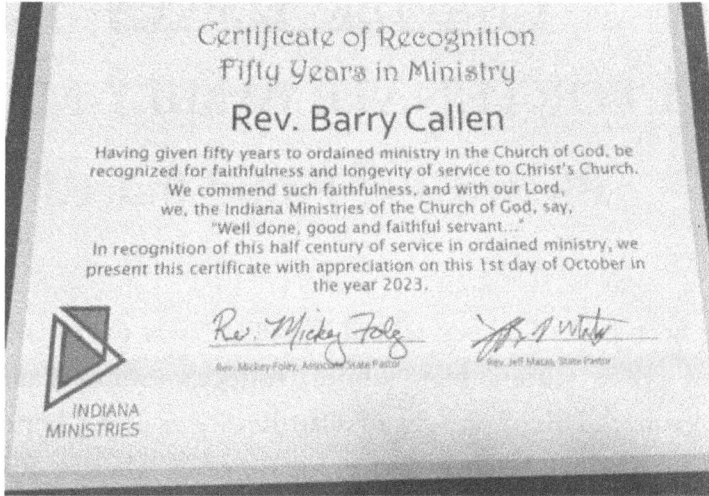

Honored as a "Golden Grad" by Asbury Theological Seminary for "fifty years of exceptional ministry" after graduation.

CHAPTER ELEVEN

A FORTUNATE FAMILY MAN

Blessed and Proud Indeed

I've been part of several school "families" over the decades that have included grade school, high school, college, seminary, and graduate school groups. I think fondly of Carole (Soos) and Charles Williams, known to me since being in first grade together. There is Roger Carrier and Ian Worley from the high school years, and Ronald Fowler and Dan Mulhauser from my seminary years—one an outstanding Protestant Black preacher and the other a loyal Jesuit priest.

Long and rich relationships developed at Anderson University over the decades, functioning much like family. I'll note just one. In the Spring of 2022 Jan and I attended the 77th anniversary concert of the A. U. Chorale. I had worked closely with Robert Nicholson who founded this marvelous singing body in the 1940s, and with its living leaders since, including Dale Bengston, Paul Smith, David Coolidge, and Richard Sowers, each present and directing one or two pieces of this reunion choir made up of the present Chorale and some 100 former members. As is traditional, the concert concluded with a rousing rendition of "When I Survey the Wondrous Cross!" supported by the great organ of Park Place Church. What a family and what a faith!

More precious still are the two women who have been my companions in life, Arlene for thirty-nine years, ended by her death in 2003, and Jan who now has been a precious life partner for twenty years and counting. One son came from the first marriage, Todd, and Jordan from the second. They and now their spouses have brought into my life a host of grandchildren, and now even great-grandchildren. What growth, diversity, and joy they are. As the new generations have come, Jan and I have faced the death of her only sibling, brother Eugene Hitt who was a retired Christian minister living in Texas. His wife Pat very much remains a loved member of our family.

My one sister, Bonnie, has weathered the early death of her husband and the challenges of the special needs of a child, Cassie, and then a grandchild, Chantel, and now the death of her daughter, all somehow handled alone and on very limited income. It would seem that justice should have shared a few of my blessings with her. Jan and I have sought in recent years to help at least in modest ways. Fortunately, Bonnie has many friends and a good church base.

Son Todd has gained a quality education, survived two divorces, had three very special kids, has married well, gaining an exceptionally new daughter with Samantha, and has matured into an outstanding publi school teacher. Son Jordan has married well with Laura, had six amazing kids, and is a skilled and hardworking electrician. As typical in this world, there have been explosions of joy and a few heartaches for each son. In sum, however, they comprise a great family that has blessed me beyond measure. Bonnie is a strong and loving person who lives close to our home in Anderson, Indiana.

A brief family tree appears as *Appendix G*. Comment must be made of further family expansion since the 2019 edition. *Appendix G* is now missing an additional grandson, Wilson Davis, and even a new "great" generation of Anna Belle, Brooks Michael Allan, Etta Lou, Ezra Gideon, Finn Hayes, and Theo Maly. There also are wonderful new spouses, Molly of Samantha, Carly of Ian, and Ricky of Emily. While generations come and go, my hope for them all is highlighted in Colossians 2:6-7. I trust that one day soon they all will fit into this world in their individual ways and help make the positive difference needed so badly by this hurting globe.

Arlene, my first wife, did all she could to represent Jesus to others, although her health and other restraints limited her ability to do so internationally. Regardless, she had a missionary heart. She hosted a group Bible study, worked with a local school in remedial reading, cared for three of our grandchildren for years while parents worked, taught nutrition classes in the Life Enrichment program of our local church, advised the seminary group of women whose husbands were preparing for ministry, and cooked wonderful meals for numerous groups that would meet in our home. Cancer took her when she was sixty-one. She went to a much better place.

I recall fondly a little item Arlene included in our January, 2000, newsletter to family and friends. "Although Barry's travels have taken him hither and yon, his most unusual recent foray took him as a group leader to our church's World Conference in Birmingham, England, in July, 1999, and then on to Scotland and Wales. He called me from Edinburgh so that I could hear a bagpiper playing outside a telephone booth. Neat!" Arlene was a skilled vocal musician, studying voice on and off for much of her adulthood.

I recently reviewed the newspaper obituary of my father Robert who died in 1974 at the young age of 55. After service in World War II, in 1946 he brought our little family to Craig Beach in Ohio to carve out a new life, beginning with almost nothing and never having much except the will to build and manage with what little we had. Dad was a good and hardworking man who loved and provided for his family—and regained his Christian faith shortly before death. I cherish his memory. We each do what we can in the limitations of our time.

As a family man myself, I've hardly been perfect, although I've never lost my faith and always have tried my best in the midst of all that was happening in and around me. I naturally treasure something my son Todd wrote to me on Father's Day, 2022:

You have always been there for me. I have learned so much about so many things from you that it would be hard to imagine a better father. You are precious to me, so keep taking care of yourself old man. I love you! T—

On pages 461-463 of this autobiography I mention eleven persons close to me who died and for whom I gave public tribute in their services of memory. I add here four more names and hope there aren't any more. The new ones are Austin Sowers (2018), his daughter Judy and her husband Malcolm Hughes (2019), Sadie Evans (2022), and Dwight Grubbs (2023). The actual tributes are now placed with my papers housed in the Archives at Anderson University. Generations come and go. Our Lord remains forever!

Jan's brother Gene Hitt and wife Pat.

Jan, Laura, and Todd with me on my surprise 80th celebration.

Wedding of Ricky and Emily (Callen) Bodily, Sept. 2023. They are holding my great-grandson Brooks. I'm standing behind.

Jan and I love each other and the
Anderson Symphony Orchestra

The Slattery Family

Samantha and Molly, with Etta, Anna, Theo, Finn, and Ezra,
on Theo's adoption day, March 1, 2024

CHAPTER TWELVE

LESSONS AND LEGACY

Final Words and Hopes

From childhood with my mother and little sister to the seminary deanship and oil painting.

It's a dual task and therefore especially difficult. We believers in the biblical God are to do two things, both very important and yet seemingly headed in opposite directions. We are to remember and then forget. Psalm 126, for instance, begins by looking to the past and ends by looking to the future. Both directions are critically important, each to be enriched but not paralyzed by the other. While people always need to live by both memory and hope, the psalmist does not look to the past and hope for a mere restoration of some old way of life. The intent is to find in yesterday how to live into God's new way of being and doing, a newness relevant for the changing circumstances of today and tomorrow. The best remembering is anticipating and claiming God's fresh tomorrow. Such constructive remembering hardly comes naturally.

Change in the Wind

My wife Jan and I attended a camp meeting service in 2022 led by a group of singing youth dressed in shorts and ripped jeans and singing songs we didn't know and weren't inclined to try to learn. They were loud and endlessly repetitive, designed apparently for a new generation. Were we just old? Apparently we were being called to adapt to a "style" our parents would have judged distasteful and wholly inappropriate in a worship service. And yet, maybe our grandchildren would hear the gospel of Christ only through such a medium, very familiar to them even if strange and almost offensive to us.

That year 2022 was my personal eighty-first. Dizzying change was in the wind on virtually every front. How could I be a Psalm 126 believer, a man looking back gratefully and forward hopefully, without insisting that tomorrow necessarily become a repeat of yesterday? After that camp meeting service, my wife and I sat with dear friends and watched a documentary about the lives and careers of our common personal friends Bill and Gloria Gaither. They lived close to our home and had been named "Songwriters of the Century" in the field of Christian music, being composers of "He Touched Me," "Because He Lives," "The King Is Coming," and many more. The documentary showed how they took the "old" and made it work in fresh ways for new times.

Here's the lesson, the biblical challenge, the best way to go about life. I can choose to look back and lament the wonderful things I once knew that now are gone or changed almost beyond recognition. Or I can look back and rejoice in past privileges that have been mine and draw from them the strength and wisdom necessary for engaging the present, joining God who is moving on. A few current examples of major change flow into my mind and I trust have some meaning for you.

- ✓ I grew up in the 1950s, post-war years when people were anxious to buy, consume, and play hard however they could. My little Craig Beach village home in Ohio had music playing in the amusement park two blocks from my modest home. Speedboats were roaring about Lake Milton, allowing me to work for two summers fueling those boats to afford going back to college each fall. Of course, civil rights were still largely an unaddressed problem and the Cold War was very much on. Still, these were my "good old days." Whatever the wrong, can I look back and see God at work in ways not unlike today?

- ✓ Church life doesn't always look or work the same. Institutions, even "religious" ones, have life cycles. In the 1950s I was privileged to be part of the Church of God congregation in Newton Falls, Ohio. That and the next decade were its glory time, big numbers in a little town, marvelous ministerial leaders who really cared about my future and made a huge difference. In the 1960s, 70s, and 80s, I then was an active part of the Park Place Church of God congregation in Anderson, Indiana, its glory years. By 2022 both of these congregations were way down in numbers and looking for a new way into the future. The choice? Lament the loss or remember yesterday with joy and use the experience and energy to help find a new way into a new future.

- ✓ Recalling that awkward 2022 camp meeting experience noted above, I can remember in Anderson, Indiana, the final decades of the 20th century when the national Church of God Camp Meeting convened annually, bringing thousands to town with gatherings in the giant Warner Auditorium. By 2024 that impressive auditorium had been long gone and those gatherings replaced by much smaller regional gatherings attempting to accomplish much the same thing in new places and new ways. Sad, yes; hopeful, yes, if we will let it be so.

✓ I was privileged to be Dean of Anderson University's graduate School of Theology from 1973 to 1983. That was the decade of the glory years of the seminary when the new Miller Chapel was added and the student body tripled. A range of things have changed in the church's life since and the seminary has struggled. Now in 2024 it's being kept going partly by merging it with the undergraduate Department of Religion, and the new leadership and faculty reaching out for new constituents and forms of educational service. It won't ever look the same again, and yet God surely has fresh ways into a meaningful future.

I'm called to look back and see God at work. I then am called not to be consumed by grief at the loss but to know that, in the inevitable experimentations and discomforts of the new, God is there still at work, calling me and the church forward. Will we weep over lost yesterdays or determine to work for the flourishing of new tomorrows? I've tried to do the latter as best I could.

My *All of God's Word for All of My Needs* reviews the book of Numbers. The Israelites finally are on the threshold of their promised land. Their leader, Moses, is dead. Sometimes a faith leader sees the vision but isn't able personally to enter into its fulfillment. The leader pays the price of trail-blazing while only others are privileged to travel their pioneering trail and actually enter in. I hope I have done a little blazing and am satisfied to leave the results, the future victories, to others. I need to *be* whether or not in this world I ever *see*.

Just Listen!

Is it possible today to have honest conversations about controversial topics? People have been so politicized and made argumentative. How can we prepare our ministers for this challenge if we cannot talk patiently and constructively about what they will face? Institutions of any sort, including churches, have an instinct for survival. Their leaders seek above all a stable environment, peace in the ranks, steady progress. Any new development of whatever sort is typically greeted with suspicion and a longing for the golden days of yesterday's equilibrium (which, in fact, was also in flux as days always are).

In the present situation, with its dizzying pace of social change and intellectual fluidity, is it possible for the church to do anything other than dig in its change-resisting heels? Can the church survive as a viable community if it admits to itself that some certainties of yesterday are now up for serious discussion? Maybe we're living with the haunting question of Dostoesvsky's *Grand Inquisitor*. Don't people just want certainty? And don't many people stick with the church because it provides or at least promises certainty?

Part of my approach to Christian education has been to raise questions since young students haven't yet thought seriously about much of anything and the older teachers know that none of us has yet gotten things just right. I heard a cynic once say that getting educated is just getting confused at a higher level. At least, gaining much knowledge should bring the humbling wisdom of realizing that we know so very little!

Now eighty-three years old, I'm increasingly aware that bodies indeed are mortal, mine included. I've been so fortunate, notwithstanding a bout with cancer, emergency gallbladder and prostate surgeries, and a major eye retina tear. Whatever the paths taken and bumps along the way, finally it's "dust to dust" for us all. Meanwhile, I cherish the image projected by my honored colleague and friend David McKenna. In his memoir he writes:

> Through threads of grace and truth, the experiences of my life are being woven into the whole cloth of God's perfect will. I do not fix my gaze on the knots that make up the underside of my life's tapestry, but on the beauty of the design on the topside. With all joy, I give thanks to God for letting me get a glimpse of the whole cloth.

Likewise, my life has its many little underside knots, not always welcome but somehow maybe necessary for what by God's grace was evolving on top. I also have at least glimpsed the lovely design woven by God from whatever I was able and enabled to do in life. Any related glory hardly belongs to me.

When my remains are deposited in Anderson's Maplewood Cemetery, I'll be elsewhere! What do we humans leave behind? On his 78th birthday, my mother Charlotte wrote a poem honoring her father, my Grandpa VanArsdale. Lines toward the end read:

> Oh Yes, my Dad is leaving me a legacy
> of goodwill and trust and a character true;
> A sermon he has preached with his life, not his lips.
> May I prove this gift worthy 'ere *my* life is thro'.

I hope that this present record of my life's journey will gratefully witness to the goodness and mercy of God that have followed me all my days.

lay the task aside with deep thanksgiving to my Lord. As I do, allow one related thought. William Barclay, renowned biblical scholar from Scotland where I have family heritage, said this when elderly: "When I die, I should like to slip out of the room without fuss—for what matters is not that I am leaving but where I am going."[1] May it be so for me.

The scenes of the past, and now the hopes of the future, rely on these three profound facts. God *is, has come* in Christ, and always *will be* the reaching and saving Spirit of love who creates, re-creates, and assures a gracious eternity. Knowing these profound facts and having attempted to witness to them over the decades of my life, I want my ending moments of life to reflect the final words of Charles Wesley. He was on his death bed. Feeble as his fingers then were, he managed to write these final lines:

> Jesus, my only hope Thou art,
> Strength of my failing flesh and heart;
> O could I catch a smile from Thee,
> And drop into eternity!

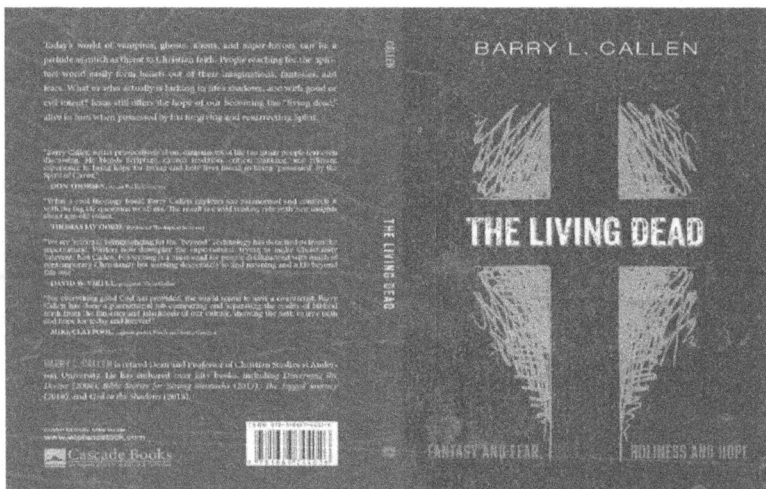

1. Clive Rawlins, *William Barclay*, 1984.

God goes unseen into the future where we cannot go. Thousands of students have passed through my classrooms and then left Anderson University graduations to take their places in the world. May they be blessed and bless more people than I will ever know!

Index of Names

So many wonderful people have graced the pathways of my life

in many different ways. They all have been influential

in the places I have walked and on the progress

I have made. I gratefully stand on

their shoulders!

www.ingramcontent.com/pod-product-compliance
Lightning Source LLC
Chambersburg PA
CBHW020409100426
42812CB00001B/256